THE
AFRICAN
CULTURAL
HERITAGE
TOPICAL
BIBLE

New International Version

PUBLISHING

Published by Pneuma Life Publishing

THE AFRICAN
CULTURAL HERITAGE
TOPICAL BIBLE

Copyright © 1995 by Pneuma Life Publishing
Printed in the United States of America

African Cultural Heritage Topical Bible – New International Version
ISBN 1-56229-437-7: $22.95

PNEUMA LIFE PUBLISHING
Post Office Box 10612
Bakersfield, CA 93389 U.S.A.
(805) 324-1741 (805) 324-1775 FAX

Grateful acknowledgment is hereby expressed to the following Publishers who have granted permission to include copyrighted materials in this book. Any inadvertent omission of credit will be gladly corrected in future editions.

Christian Publications: Born after Midnight, The Dwelling Place of God, Of God and Men, Roots of the Righteous, and That Incredible Christian by A. W. Tozer, published by Christian Publications of Camp Hill, PA; used by permission.

Baker Book House: The Vance Havner Quote Book by Dennis J. Hester. Copyright 1986 by Baker Book House. 3000 Quotations on Christian Themes by Carroll E. Simcox. Copyright © 1975. 12,000 Religious Quotations by Frank S. Mead. Copyright © 1965.

CONTRIBUTORS

to the *African Cultural Heritage Topical Bible*

David Daniels, Ph.D
Contributor, Christian Witness of African Peoples Through the Ages in Africa, Europe and the Americas

B.A., Religion, Bowdoin College
Masters of Divinity, Yale University
Ph.D., Church History, Union Theological Seminary
Associate Professor of Church History, McCormick Theological Seminary, Chicago, IL

Wayne Perryman
Contributor, The 1993 Trial on the Curse of Ham, Understanding the Power of Culture

Author, Thought Provoking Bible Studies
Author, The Black Church the Foundation of the Black Culture

Leonard Lovett, B.A., M.A., Ph.D
Contributor, Racism: Death of the Gods

B.A., History, Morehouse
M.Div., Crozer Theological Seminary
Doctor of Philosophy in Ethics, Emery University
Author, Opening the Front Door of Your Church

Mensa Otabil
Contributor, God's Visitation, Get Ready to Run, Understanding

Author, Four Laws of Productivity
Author, Beyond the Rivers of Ethiopia
Pastor, International Central Gospel, Accra–Ghana, Africa

Myles Munroe, B.A., M.A.
Contributor, Learning to be Leaders

B.A., Education, Fine Arts, and Theology from Oral Roberts University
M.A., Administration, University of Tulsa
President of Bahamas Faith Ministries
Author, Single-Married-Seperated-Divorce, Understanding Your Potential, Releasing Your Potential, and Becoming A Leader

Trevor Grizzle, B.A., M.Div., Ph.D
Contributor, Introduction

B.A., Religion, Lee College
M.Div. and Ph.D., Philosophy, Southwestern Baptist Theological Seminary
Associate Professor of New Testament Oral Roberts University
Associate Pastor of Care Fellowship Church of God

James Giles
Contributor, Embracing the Call to Greatness, Principles of Greatness

Pastor, New Vision Christian Center
Author, The Essence of Greatness
Author, And Ye Shall Know the Truth
Author, The God Factor

Derwin Stewart
Contributor, The Topical Bible

Publisher and Chief Executive Officer of Pneuma Life Publishing and Rising Magazine
Author, The Believer's Topical Bible
Author, The Minister's Topical Bible
Author, Inevitable Success

CONTENTS

to the *African Cultural Heritage Topical Bible*

THE TOPICAL BIBLE

DEVELOPING YOUR RELATIONSHIP WITH GOD

SALVATION

HOLY SPIRIT

DEVELOPING THE WHOLE MAN

1. THE SPIRIT

2. THE MIND

3. THE BODY

PREPARING THE MIND AND HEART TO RECEIVE GOD'S BLESSINGS

THE PURPOSE FOR FINANCES

GOD'S FINANCIAL BUSINESS PLAN FOR YOU

OVERCOMING SIN

INTRODUCTION

The meandering stream of Black history began its long journey at the cradle of creation. Inexorably snaking its way through the untrammeled frontier of time and growing larger as it advances, it has produced myriads of tributaries that have richly contributed to the continents of the world. In the wake, it has left a trail of kings, queens, poets, philosophers, architects, artisans and others that date back to the dawn of human history.

Indeed, Africa has bequeathed a rich and noble legacy to all humankind, a legacy whose imprint is indelibly stamped upon nearly every field of human endeavor.

Unfortunately, not all Blacks are cognizant of their illustrious history. Such ignorance has been devastating in its consequence.

God's Word, through his prophet Hosea to Israel, echoes with striking relevance in its application to today's Africans everywhere: "My people are destroyed from lack of knowledge" (4:6 NIV). And with mature wisdom the silver-haired Socrates exhorts: "Know thyself."

Helping people of color know themselves is what *The African Cultural Heritage Topical Bible* is all about. It is an anthology of essays on Black history, Biblical and cultural heritage written by persons of color with a passionate commitment to debunking and destroying popular myths about Blacks. It is a treasure chest of eye-opening and liberating facts. As such, this unique reference tool provides knowledge that will empower Blacks everywhere to rip from their minds the veil that conceals their true identity. This Bible will help loose the psychological bondage thralldom that has circumscribed their world and potential for many years.

A native of Jamaica, I have been privileged to live on three continents. On each, I have observed a common tread in the lives of many people of color, whether in Jamaica, England, Africa or America: visible scars from deep psychological wounds inflicted by a cruel taskmaster who for centuries has held them firm with an iron hand. I have seen the glazed eyes of a people who, as though hypnotized by the magic wand of some distant invisible enchanter or bewitched by some malevolent deity, see but do not perceive.

I have seen their indecisiveness in direction and action. I have seen a people who stagger and stumble as though burdened by a backbreaking load or inebriated by some potent intoxicant. I have seen a people adrift on the sea of life; a people on the move but without rubber, chart or compass. And, I have seen spirits broken by dashed hopes and unrealized dreams evident in faces that mirror mobile billboards that advertise a pain too deep for words.

I have also seen something else: Knowledge enlightens. Knowledge empowers. Knowledge liberates. Authentic liberation, however, is more than the divesting of physical chains. Authentic freedom is the unrestrained and un-coerced ability to think, act, soar, be and become — to realize all our potential in God. This kind of liberation is the unfettering of the spirit and the mind whereby our thoughts become wings.

In the history and culture of a people lies the genetic code to their identity and mission. African-Americans are no exception. Regrettably, for more than two centuries the rich history of African-Americans has been either discarded or distorted in its transmission. The latter has been the worse of the two evils, because what has passed off as authentic history is not. Its effects upon people of color today is like that of nuclear fallout on the environment.

The *African Cultural Heritage Topical Bible* traces Black history to the dawn of creation. It showcases the many rulers, kings, queens, statesmen, and a host of other Black personages who have helped shape biblical history and world civilization. Its contribution to reference tools is its rich variety of styles comprising a symphony designed to people of color to sing praises of their Creator.

God made no mistake when he made the Black race. Blackness is an expression of his creative genius. We should celebrate what God has created and called "very good."

Interwoven into the very tapestry of biblical history are Blacks, many singularly empowered and equipped by God to play significant roles in the unfolding drama of redemption both in the Old and New Testaments. At no time has God left out the Black race. We matter to Him!

One of the sterling contributions of *The African Cultural Heritage Topical Bible* is to affirm the diversity and unity of all humankind — a diversity and unity grounded in God Himself. From Genesis through the New Testament, it shows, in systematic fashion, the involvement of Blacks in the history of redemption.

Christianity is the only major world religion whose canon acknowledges the presence and contribution of Blacks in its history and formulation. *The African Cultural Heritage Topical Bible* unveils a God who has demonstrated, throughout the Bible and history that indeed "from one man he made every nation of men" (Acts 17:26, NIV) and that "God does not show favoritism."

Trevor L. Grizzle, Ph.D
Associate Professor of New Testament
Graduate School of Theology & Missions
Oral Roberts University

PART I

Black Presence in the Bible and History

Articles

The Black Race and the Bible
The 1993 Trial on the Curse of Ham
Christian Witness of African Peoples Through the Ages in
Africa, Europe and the Americas

THE BLACK RACE
& THE BIBLE

by Wayne Perryman

The Black Race and the Bible

In mixed marriages involving blacks, who decides which race the child should belong to and what criteria are used to make this determination?

In America, race determination falls under the jurisdiction of the Department of Commerce's Bureau of the Census. In mixed marriages involving blacks, this agency (which first began in 1790), maintained that if a child's father is black and the mother is of a different race, the child (regardless of its physical features) will be considered the race of its father. And if the child's mother is black and the father is of another race, the child (regardless of its physical features) will be considered the race of its mother, this criterion was used until 1970. Since the time of recorded mixed marriages (Abraham), more Blacks have warmly accepted children born from mixed relationships than any other race.

The Census Bureau apparently had some biblical basis for its classification process. Looking at four examples in the bible, it is clear that the Egyptians, Canaanites and Ethiopians are all original members of the black race.

1. The children by Abraham's black wives, Hagar (black Egyptian) and Keturah (black Canaanite), are still considered as non-Jews today. This is true even though their father (Abraham) is one of the most powerful figures in Jewish history. The sons of Hagar and Keturah were classified with the race of their black mothers not with their Jewish dad.

2. Joseph's children, Manasseh and Ephraim, by his black Egyptian wife, Asenath, weren't classified as Jews until their grandfather, Jacob, being led of God in his old age, did something that his grandfather, Abraham, failed to do with his own boys. He adopted his two half-Jewish and Black grandsons as his own children (Gen 48:1-22). Without their grandfather's adoption, through God's leading, the two probably would have had a difficult time being accepted by their Jewish relatives. Even though they were adopted by this

9

renowned patriarch, Jewish history has very little to say about the sons of the (black) Egyptian woman, Asenath.

3. Moses' sons, Gershom and Eliezer, by Zipporah (his Ethiopian wife) are two others that are hardly mentioned in Jewish history (only in Exodus 18:4 & I Chronicles 23:15-17). God showed his acceptance of them when he demanded that they be circumcised. Although Moses was considered to be among the most powerful leaders in Jewish history, Christians today know very little about his black children.

4. Ham was the darkest of Noah's three sons. Because he was so dark, and bore a name (hamm) which meant "a man with a dark complexion, "he is credited with producing (through his descendants) our world's black nations. Today these nations are called ancient Egypt, Ethiopia, Canaan, and Libya. This again shows that in race determination, if the father is black then the children will be considered black as well.

Based on these Biblical accounts, it appears that the precedent for determining the race of a child from a mixed marriage was set long before the U.S. Census Bureau was established. Apparently, like today, it was done to preserve racial purity. Remember, the Bureau's criteria had nothing to do with the child's physical appearance, only with the race of the mother or the father, if they were black.

For years the Christian church has either dodged or ignored the issue of race, particularly as it pertained to characters in the Bible. Most Christians unconsciously assumed that all Biblical characters were persons with Caucasian features. These unconscious attitudes are evident, and reflected, in the illustrations of most Sunday School and Christian Education materials. Virtually none of the illustrations remotely resemble blacks and very few resemble Jews. The characters usually have European features. Only recently have slightly darker skin tones been used.

Since the beginning of modern times, Bible historians have failed to recognize the role that the dark race played in making Bible history. History, when viewed appropriately, will clearly show that

God has used blacks and other nonwhites to rescue, build, protect, teach, and glorify His name. This special study is designed to highlight the truth about God and the people whom He chose to be members of the black race.

Adam: The First Man

Scripture References: Gen. 2:10-14; Acts 17:26

According to Acts 17:26, "by the blood of one man, God has made all nations." But many ask," What color were the first people?" The name "Adam" is often translated as "Red Man." Others believe he was the color of the fertile soil God made him from: black. In a compromise, many believe he probably resembled the dark east Indians whose skin tones ranged from a dark reddish-brown to black.

Because of the Garden of Eden's location, climate, and the people's diet, the evidence overwhelmingly suggests that the people who occupied the Garden were from a dark race. Adam did not resemble today's traditional white man. He and his family lived in a hot tropical environment unlike any other known today; therefore, it would have been impossible for him to be pale-skinned under such conditions.

The Garden of Eden is described as a tropical paradise. Its primary source of water was a river that flowed through the Garden and from underground springs (Gen. 2:14; Gen. 7:11). The King James version mentions two countries near the Garden, Havilah (which is near Egypt) and Ethiopia (two countries where the oldest fossils of man were found, according to the 1985 November issue of *National Geographic* magazine). Both Ethiopia and Egypt are considered to be black nations. They often are referred to as the land of Ham or the land of Cush, the father and grandfather of all black nations (Gen. 2:10-13).

According to the Bible, the first rain on earth was recorded after the fall in the Garden of Eden. According to the story of Noah, it took 120 years, after Noah began building the ark, for rain to fall (in the year of 1656 A.M. or 2348 B.C.). Can you imagine what the people would look like after decades of warm weather? What other color complexion could the people be other than dark skinned?

11

Science has proven that the dark race is the only race capable of producing people in a variety of colors as indicated in Acts 17:26. In other words, whites have never by themselves produced dark people. Therefore, the Scripture "from one blood came all the nations," could not be referring to the white race.

Science has proven that the climate, diet, and environment do affect skin color and other physical characteristics. The "*Encyclopedia Americana*" Anthropology section states, "The physical anthropologist thus looks at gross climate factors to which human populations adjusted, variations in heat and cold, high and low humidity, altitude. . ., associated with particular environments as screening devices that have contributed to human diversity through natural selection. . . Racial differences thus reflect current environments . . . Each such environment would have its own selective advantage and disadvantage for the physical types (genetically based) living with it."

"Were the race-characters constant in degree or even in kind, the classification of races would be easy; but this is not so. Every division of mankind presents in every characteristic wide deviations from a standard. Thus the black race well marked as it may seem at first glance, proves on closer examination to include several shades of complexion and features in some districts, varying far from the accepted Negro type . . . Innumerable varieties of mankind run into one another by insensible degrees. This state of things, due partly to mixture and crossing of races, and partly to independent variations of types makes the attempt to arrange the whole human species within exactly bounded divisions an apparently hopeless task. . ." (*Encyclopedia Britannica*, Anthropology: Race).

Scientists also know that people who have always lived in these warm lands have medium-to dark-colored skins, eyes and hair. For that matter, most human beings are medium to dark-colored. These facts led scientists to believe that the first men were probably dark-skinned too. They were probably not as dark as the blue-black Central Africans, but were most likely a medium or dark brown.

Robert Cohen, a noted author and social psychologist, writes in *The Color of Man*, "The earliest known traces of human life have generally been found in tropical and subtropical lands. So, it seems safe to say that man first appeared in warm regions. Certainly it would have been easier to survive in a warm place, because man had no thick coat of fur to protect him from the cold."

As long as the descendants of the first man lived close to one another, they remained alike in color and in other inherited traits. But as the number of men grew, so did the distance between groups. They spread out to look for food. Some migrated for long distances (Gen. 11:8).

Recent articles in *National Geographic, Time, Newsweek and U.S. News and World Report* magazines also indicate that the first human was of African origin and that the roots of all languages originated in Africa. Both science and the Bible now agree on the following: the approximate location of the first man, the color of the first man, what his climate and diet consisted of, and the fact that from one language all languages were developed (Gen 11:1-9).

Ham: The Father & Grandfather of All Black Nations.

Scripture References: Gen. 5:32, 6:10, 7:13, 9:18; 1 Chron. 1:4&8, 4:40; Psalms 78:51, 105:23 & 27, 106:22

Most historians consider Ham (whose name means swarthy, dark complexion or sun burnt) to be the father of the (Hamitics) black race and the people with Negroid features. Some, however, argue that all of Ham's sons were black except Canaan.

Unfortunately, many who believe this to be true also believe *all* blacks have the same basic physical characteristics consisting of dark skin, kinky hair, wide noses and thick lips. To the contrary, not all members of the black race have Negroid features. Many Ethiopians have small keen noses and thin lips and millions of American blacks (with two black parents) also have features that do not resemble what we would call the typical black Negro. Also, the Filipinos and the Arabs, who are also considered by some anthropologists to be members of the black race, have different physical characteristics than those of blacks.

Ishmael is an example of the different physical features found among the black race. Ishmael, the son of Abraham and Hagar, is considered to be the father of the Arab nations. By the looks of modern day Arabs, Ishmael probably didn't have Negroid features. However, this is not true with all Arabs. Prince Bandar, Saudi Arabia's Minister of Defense, and nephew of the King of Saudi Arabia, has typical Negroid features that include dark skin and "kinky" hair. President Sadat, former leader of Egypt, also resembled today's Negro and looked much like my own father.

This is not surprising since the mother of the Arab nations (Hagar) was a black Egyptian woman and a descendant of Ham. Ishmael himself married an Egyptian woman who was a descendant of Ham (Gen. 21:21). Based on these facts, we must conclude that these descendants of Ham (the father of the Black race), must themselves (regardless of their physical features) be members of the black race also. Again, according to the United States government, a child whose father is black, will be considered black as well.

The following are sons and grandsons of Ham and the countries they founded. The sons are Cush, Mizraim, Canaan, & Phut. Ham's grandsons are Nimrod, Raamah, Seba, Havilah, Sabtah, and Sabtecha (all sons of Cush), and Sidon, Heth Jebusite, Amorite, Girgashite, Hivite, Arkite, Sinite, Arvadite, Zemarite, and Hamathite (all sons of Canaan).

Countries and cities founded by the descendants of Ham represent some of the greatest civilizations of ancient times. These include Babel (also known as Babylon), Erech, Akkad, Calneh, Egypt, Ethiopia and Canaan. According to the *Encyclopedia Americana* (Ham, pp. 661 & 662) and the *Aid To Bible Understanding* (Ham, pp. 705), Ham's descendants include the people of Phoenicia, Palestine and African and Arab nations (Gen. 17:20, 27; 21:14-18; and 25:1-5).

Cush: A Father of Black Nations

Scripture References: Gen 10:6-8; I Chron 1:8-10

Cush, the son of Ham, is primarily credited with producing the Negro race and the following countries: Egypt, Ethiopia, and Libya. He is also the father of one of the greatest warriors of all times, Nimrod. Since Cush is the father of these countries, this again is proof that the Black race consists of more than just people with Negroid features. Although many of the Egyptians were dark and many were black, all did not have Negroid features much like the physically diverse black race today.

Nimrod: A Mighty Hunter, Blessed by God

Scripture Reference: Gen. 10

Nimrod was the son of Cush, the grandson of Ham and the great grandson of Noah. He ". . . became the first of the kings. He was a mighty hunter, blessed of God, and his name became proverbial. People would speak of someone as being `like Nimrod' -- mighty hunter, blessed by God" (Gen. 10:8-10, Living Bible.) His kingdom included the area that produced one of the greatest empires of ancient times, Babylon. Nimrod was also the father and founder of many great cities, including Nineveh and Calah in Assyria. The latter is the home of the Queen of Sheba. Not only was Nimrod a great warrior and hunter who captured nations and their wealth, his rule was referred to as the era of the Golden Age. He is best known for his unsuccessful attempt to build an enduring tower to heaven, the tower of Babel.

Nineveh was founded and established by blacks. In Nineveh, Nimrod's administration and descendants were credited with building dams, administrative buildings, parks, and beautiful palaces. Nineveh was a walled city that had impressive libraries, cemeteries, and the space to house as many as 175,000 people. According to historians, Nineveh's histories, grammatical and scientific texts, and letters, made the Assyrian literature much better-known than that of any other ancient people, except the Hebrews, who like many other people borrowed and learned many things from the descendants of Ham.

The city of Babel was originally founded by Nimrod, the son of Cush, the grandson of Ham, and the great grandson of Noah (Gen. 10:10, 11:1-9). After the flood, Nimrod and his staff developed the world's first architectural building made of brick. The city's name was derived from the "confusion" that took place at the site of a huge building project. This was the "Tower of Babel" or the "tower of confusion."

The Lord monitored this black man's project and saw the people's progress, their unique architectural ability, their tremendous building skills and their lack of reverence for Him. God stopped the project by changing the language of the workers. This is the first Biblical reference where people were separated because of their "differences." However, the difference was in their languages, not their physical features! One could conclude that our different languages today are indications or reminders of man's disrespect for God and his efforts to be equal to God. Nimrod is indirectly responsible for both the different languages we have today as well as the migration of man into other parts of the world. People separated from each other due to their inability to communicate with one another.

Later, this same site became what is known as Babylon, one of the greatest empires in ancient history. Some historians suggest that many of the newer buildings in Babylonia were constructed from Nimrod's architectural designs. Especially the temples which were called "Ziggurats." In 2250 B.C., King Sharkalisharri of Agrade, who claimed he actually restored the Tower of Babel, built a tower quite similar to Nimrod's.

Canaan: Builder of Cities

Scripture References: Gen. 6-8, 10:6, 15:8

Canaan is the fourth son of Ham. His sons include Heth, Jebusite, Amorite, Girgashite, Hivite, Arkite, Sinite, Arvadite, Zemarite, and Hamathite.

His descendants occupied the cities of Canaan and ancient Palestine. Although historians agree that Canaan's father, Ham, was black, certain historians argue that Canaan himself was not black. Perhaps what they are trying to say is that Canaan may not have had Negro physical features or did not speak the Hamitic language. Although he and the Canaanites are direct descendants of Ham, they would not have had to speak the same language to be kin. Many black African and Arab nations do not speak the same language, but they are still kindred to the black race. Several different groups make up the white race, and many do not look the same nor do they speak the same language. The same is true within Asian groups. Although their features and languages vary, Japanese and Chinese individuals, for example, are Asian.

In 1745 B.C., a woman by the name of Bilhah (who is believed to be a Canaanite), was given to Rachel as a handmaiden by her father, Laban (Gen. 29:29). When Rachel discovered that she could not have children, she gave this Canaanite woman to her husband, Jacob, as a concubine wife to bear children (much like the situation with Sarah). When Bilhah conceived and delivered a son, Rachel named the child Dan (Gen. 30:6). Before Jacob died, he named his son from this Canaanite woman (Dan) as one of the twelve tribes of Israel (Gen. 49:16-17). Approximately 3,725 years later, during the 1980's, the remnants of this tribe made international headlines when they travelled 1,000 miles from Ethiopia to Israel. Authorities believe this group is actually a part of the lost tribe of Dan. They called them the Falashas or Ethiopian Jews.

According to Howard Sharron, a syndicated columnist for Jewish magazines, "The Falasha's form of Judaism is pre-rabbinical, based on religious practices and customs prevalent at the time of the destruction of the first temple in Jerusalem in 586 BC, a long time before the rise of power of the Rabbis . . . Judaism has traditionally maintained a unity between religion and race, and the color of the Falashas has provoked incredulity that they could be true Jews. The Falashas are insulted at any questioning of their provenance; since Biblical times they have rigidly observed the Mosaic Law. . ." In response the Falashas said, "Many Israelis still do not believe we can be Jews because we are Black, but we have kept the Old Testament more strictly than the Israelis and we have suffered because we are Jews. It is not possible to convert to Judaism someone who is already a Jew." The Jews raised millions of dollars and risked their lives to help their Black Ethiopian brothers.

In an exclusive interview with Howard Sharron, Rabbi Zhodi, the leader of these Ethiopian Jews, pointed out that he was convinced that this moment and time (1980's) was the partial fulfillment of Isaiah 11:11 (Living Bible). It states: "At that time the Lord will bring back a remnant of his people for the second time, returning them to the land of Israel from Assyria, Upper and Lower Egypt, Ethiopia, Elam, Babylonia, Hamath and all the distant coastal lands."

All of these countries are descendants of Ham. The King James replaces the names of Egypt and Ethiopia with Cush.

Zipporah: Moses' Egyptian Wife and Life-Saver

Scripture References: Gen. 17:23-27; Ex. 2:16-21,22, 18:3-4, 4:24

Zipporah was Moses' Egyptian wife. Her name means "little bird" or "swallow." She not only bore him two sons, (Gershom and Eliezer), but she is also credited with saving her husband's life. According to Scripture, God, in Exodus 4:24, would have killed Moses if not for Zipporah's swift action. She quickly grabbed a sharp stone and circumcised her son, thus saving her husband's life. Circumcision was a sign of covenant that God had instituted with Abraham (Gen 17:23-27). Moses' life was spared because of his wife's act of obedience to God. History and the nation of Israel, however, have never given this black woman the credit due for her heroic act on behalf of her husband.

Zipporah's homeland, Egypt, one of the most talked about ancient civilizations, is often referred to as the Land of Ham. Egyptians commonly refer to their country as "Kemyt," which means "Black." The Hebrew word for "Kemyt" corresponds with the Hebrew name Ham (hamm) which means "swarthy" or "sunburnt" skin color.

Evidence suggests that the original inhabitants and leaders of Egypt were indeed black. The evidence also suggests that blacks were still in control up to the time of the Jews' exodus. Egypt's black rule is perhaps one of the reasons why Moses' sister, Miriam, was upset when she learned that her brother, Moses, had married Zipporah, a black woman (Numbers 12:1-15), for Moses' black wife reminded Miriam of the people (the black Egyptians) that had oppressed the Jews for so many years. The Lord became angry with Miriam when she referred to Zipporah as "that black woman." In today's context, the tone of Miriam's reference to her sister-in-law's color would be similar to calling her a nigger. God immediately cursed Miriam with leprosy and turned her white as snow. Note: the color of Zipporah was the only thing that seem to have angered Miriam. This act by God shows and proves His distaste for racial prejudice (Deut. 1:17, 16:1; Acts 10:34).

Hagar & Keturah: Abraham's Two Black Wives

Scripture References: Gen 16:15-16, 17:18-27, 21:9-21, 25:1-5

Abraham married two black women, Hagar and Keturah. He divorced them both and paid them what we would call today child support and alimony. "But to the sons of the concubines, which Abraham had, Abraham gave gifts and sent them away from Isaac his son" (Gen. 25:6).

Genesis 21:9 tells us that Abram married a black Egyptian woman named Hagar. He had a son by her at the age of 86 (Gen 16:15). When her son reached the age 16, Sarah forced Hagar to leave their home because she felt Hagar was arrogant. Hagar returned only to be forced out years later because Sarah was upset with Ishmael and didn't want him around to try to inherit Abraham's fortune (Gen. 21:8-21, Gal.4:30). In the wilderness, Hagar cried out to the Lord and He heard her. The Lord told her that young Ishmael, would receive a promise from God and become a great nation (Gen. 21:18; Gal. 4:24).

It is interesting and ironic that God chose to change Abraham's name from Abram (meaning Exalted Father) to Abraham (meaning Father of many Nations), only after he married this black woman and had a child by her (Gen 17:1-8). When the child reached age 13, God added "ham" to Abram's name. He then told Abraham that his descendants will become Kings and form many nations. The name change includes the descendants of Ham, who are included in the covenant God made with Abraham (Isaiah 11:11). Including all of Abraham's children in the covenant is proof that God recognized, accepted and loved the children of Hagar and Keturah.

Also keep in mind, the descendants of Ham had kings long before the nation of Israel (1 Samuel 8:5). And while the Jews are known for forming only one nation, Israel, the descendants of Ham are recognized for forming many nations. These include the nations from Ishmael's 12 sons, called "twelve princes and their nations" in Gen. 25:12-16.

Dennis Prager and Joseph Telushkin writes in the book, *Bar Mitzvah*, "... In the ancient world, of which the Jews are one surviving intact culture, it was common for a nation to have a religion that was unique to it. Jews are and always have been both a nation and a religion combined. A completely irreligious Jew   is as much a Jew as a religious one, because Jews are also a nation. To this day, the Jews remain a nation defined by its religion."

In addition to the descendants of Ham, the references to "Father of many nations" also refers to those (who as Paul put it) have been grafted into the family of Abraham through salvation in Christ Jesus (Romans 11:17-24).

Shortly after Sarah died, Abraham married a young black Canaanite woman named Keturah (which means a pleasant fragrance). She became the mother of six sons, including Midian. Keturah was asked to leave the household of Abraham in 1853 B.C. to protect Isaac's inheritance. She and her six boys settled in the land of Midian. Midian and the Midianites became the home and relatives of Jethro, Moses' father-in-law and Zipporah, his black wife.

The descendants of the sons of Keturah and Hagar (Ishmael & Midian) apparently knew each other as half brothers and spent time with one another (Gen. 37:25, 27-28). Some Bible experts consider both groups, (the Midianites and the Ishmaelites) to be one and the same, while others consider them as two separate groups. Nevertheless, most experts have concluded that the Midianites and the Ishmaelites were very successful black businessmen.

Asenath: Joseph's Egyptian Wife
Scripture References: Gen. 37:25-28, 41:45, 41:50-52, 46:20

Joseph was sold to a group of Midianites, Ishmaelites who were black businessmen and descendants from Abraham's household, Ishmael, Hagar's son, and Midian, Keturah's son. Little did he know that not only would the Lord bless him with a high ranking position in Egypt, but he would also be blessed with a beautiful black wife, Asenath. This woman is the mother of his two sons Manasseh and Ephraim. Both were eventually adopted by their grandfather, Jacob, to help make up the twelve tribes of Israel.

According to *Nelson's Illustrated Bible Dictionary*, the tribe of Manasseh was known for its valor, and for its two famous judges,

Gideon and Jephthah (Judges 6:11-8:35, 11:1, 12-7). Manasseh's group was very supportive of David and rallied behind him to make him king (I Chron. 12:19-20, 31, 37).

In the early days, the tribe of Ephraim was an influential force in Israel. They were highly commended by Gideon (Judges 8:2) and occupied such key religious and political centers as Bethel and Shechem. After Solomon's rule, Ephraim also became the leader in the northern kingdom of Israel after the revolt of the ten tribes (I Kings 12:25-33).

The Shulammite Bride: An Unforgettable Woman and Wife

Scripture References: Song of Solomon, I Kings 11:1-8

Although Solomon had 700 wives and 300 concubines, his favorite wife was a black Shulammite woman. The entire book of the Song of Solomon is dedicated to the relationship between Solomon and this beautiful black woman. At the time this book was written, Solomon had 60 wives and 80 concubines.

There is no other book in the Bible like the Song of Solomon. Not only is God not mentioned in the entire book, in these eight chapters there are 23 references to this black woman's beauty and 28 references to parts of her gorgeous body including her breasts and thighs. In chapter 6, verses 8-9, Solomon says that none of his other wives can compare to this black woman's beauty. Even the women of Jerusalem acknowledged her beauty.

Some have said this book is not about a love relationship between Solomon and a black woman, but rather, it symbolically represents the love relationship between God and Solomon (or God and Israel). If this is true, and Israel represents the girl, and Solomon represents God, then God's chosen people would have to be black according to Song of Solomon 1:5-6, "I am black, but comely... Look not upon me because I am black. . ."

After realizing that such symbolism would possibly mean that God's chosen people are black, many immediately divorced the idea. They felt that it was much easier to accept Solomon with a beautiful black woman than to accept a God that gave black people a special place in his heart above all others. Besides, they had a difficult time fitting in or trying to explain the references to woman's beautiful breasts, thighs and lips.

Abishag: Black Woman Used to Save David's Life

Scripture References: I King 1:1-4; 2:17-22

"In his old age King David was confined to his bed; but no matter how many blankets were heaped on him, he was always cold. `The cure for this,' his aides told him, `is to find a young virgin to be your concubine and nurse. She will lie in your arms and keep you warm.' So they searched from one end to the other to find the most beautiful girl in all the land. Abishag, from Shunam, was finally selected. They brought her to the king and she lay in his arms to warm him (but he had no sexual relations with her)" (I Kings 1:1-4, Living Bible). As beautiful as she was, David was too sick to be aroused by her and he eventually died.

Many experts believe Abishag and the black Shulammite woman mentioned in the Song of Solomon (both from the town of Shunam) are one and the same and that later she became Solomon's wife. This black lady was so beautiful that Solomon's half brother, Adonijah, wanted her himself. Solomon refused and was so angry at his brother's inappropriate, ridiculous request, that he had his half brother killed immediately (I King 2:25).

Jethro: The Wise Priest

Scripture References: Ex. 2:15-22, 3:1, 4:18, 18:13-27; Num. 10:29; Judges 1:16; Acts 7:29-30

Jethro was an ancestor of Abraham through Abraham's wife, Keturah, and her son, Midian. He wore several hats in the land named after his distant relative, Midian. He was a priest, an Arabian chief, a rancher, an educator, and the father of at least seven daughters and one son. His black daughter, Zipporah, married Moses.

According to Exodus 2:1-10 and Acts 7:20-22, Moses' mother, Jochebed, was hired by Pharaoh's daughter to nurse her child (Exodus 2:9). Jochebed and Moses' father were cousins (Exodus 6:18, 20). Their marriage to their own kin was much like Abraham's, who married Sarah, his half sister (Gen. 11:31) and Isaac's, who married his uncle's daughter, Rebekah (Gen. 24).

After Moses was weaned (Acts 7:20-22), he was turned over to the Egyptians to be educated. Many believe Moses graduated with a law degree and a degree in political science. According to historian, Abul Farajius, Moses had two of the wisest men in the country as teachers, Janess and Jimbrees. Although Moses knew much about the Egyptian cultures and laws, he knew very little about his past as a Jew. Because of his upbringing and education he related more to the black Egyptians than he did with his own people.

This soon changed at the age of 40, when he killed a fellow Egyptian for beating a Hebrew slave. When the word spread of his act of aggression (Ex. 2:15), he fled to Midian where he fell in love with and married Zipporah.

Because Moses was not permitted as a child to live with his father, Amram, Jethro was Moses' only true father figure and role model. For forty years Jethro taught Moses about his past, much like Abraham and his predecessors did with members of their household (Gen 17:9-14). The story-telling cycle, which connected all Jews with their history back to the Garden of Eden, was broken when Moses was separated from his family as a child.

Jethro, a direct descendant from the household of Abraham, was able to connect Moses with 2,473 years of history, back to the beginning of Creation. It took approximately 40 years of intense schooling to thus connect Moses with his Hebrew past. No one knows whether this brilliant black man, Jethro, actually helped Moses write the first books of the Bible. However, the facts reveal that Jethro's family and their Abrahamic connection was the only known link to Moses' past after he was separated from his people as a child.

Only God knows exactly what happened during Moses' 40 year stay with Jethro. But one thing is certain, under the guidance of this black, godly priest– only one of two godly people to carry the title of priest in Old Testament before the crossing of the Red Sea– Moses, a murderer and fugitive was transformed into a humble, meek man and eventually the most effective Jewish leader of all time (Numbers 12:3).

History also documents the tremendous amount of respect Moses had for his black father-in-law. For example, after God met Moses at the burning bush and told him to go free his people, Moses instead went back to his father-in-law and asked him for permission to go to Egypt (Ex 4:18). Jethro gave Moses his blessing. In Exodus 18:1-12 (approximately 1490 B.C.), when Jethro brought his daughter Zipporah and her sons to join Moses in the wilderness, Jethro, the priest, conducted Israel's first burnt offering sacrifice to God (much as his ancestor Abraham did). Moses invited his brother Aaron (who later became Israel's first priest) and all of Israel's elders to join him and his father-in-law in the sacrifice to God. It was the first official sacrifice and religious ceremony after the crossing of the Red Sea, and both were conducted by a black man.

In Exodus 18:14-27, when Jethro observed how his son-in-law was handling legal affairs, he instructed Moses to set up a multi-court judicial system. Moses immediately followed his father-in-law's advice. No other individual had such a profound impact on Moses and the development of the Bible as we know it today and no other individual in history has affected the nation of Israel like Jethro, and yet he is not recognized in any Jewish ceremony; he is virtually unknown by most Bible scholars, and he is overlooked by most Christian leaders.

Hobab: Leader in the Wilderness

Scripture References: Num 10:29; Judges 1:16, 4:11

Hobab, Jethro's son, Zipporah's brother, and Moses' brother-in-law, played a key role in Israel's survival in the wilderness. He served as a scout to lead them through the wilderness. He understood and knew the desert well, after having lived in the area for several years. History records that he knew more about the area than any other person. The land was so barren that God had to provide miracles of water and food to sustain the nation of Israel during its travel.

Rahab: Courageous Canaanite Woman

Scripture References: Josh 2, 6:17-23, Ruth 4:20-22, Matthew 1:5-6

Rahab was a Canaanite (black) prostitute who risked her life in hiding the spies from Israel. When Israel invaded Canaan, her life was spared. She was later converted from her religion to the Jewish faith. This former prostitute then became the wife of Salmon, and the mother of Boaz. Boaz married Ruth and had a son named Obed. Obed had a son named Jesse. Jesse was King David's father, thus making Rahab David's great great grandmother. Rahab is one of four women mentioned in Matthew's genealogy of Jesus, making her a distant relative of Jesus.

Shelomith: Married A Black Man

Scripture References: Lev. 24:10-14, 23; Num. 25

Shelomith, a daughter of Dibri from the tribe of Dan, married a black Egyptian man. Their son was killed in the wilderness when he abused the name of the Lord. According to the story regarding the Falashas (the Ethiopian Jews), Shelomith wasn't the only Jew from the tribe of Dan who married blacks. As we learned before, Jacob's concubine, Bilhah, a Canaanite, is the mother of the tribe of Dan. All of the known remaining members of the tribe of Dan today are black.

Cozbi: Irresistible Midianite Woman

Scripture Reference: Num. 25

There are many Scriptures that discuss the sexual encounters between the Israelites and the descendants of Ham. The Jews found Ham's descendants to be very attractive and were constantly selecting them over their own people to be their wives and husbands. Even though God spoke against having sex and marrying the Midianite women because they turned their backs on God, Zimri, the son of Salu, a leader of the tribe of Simeon, couldn't resist Cozbi, a daughter of Zur, a Midianite prince. While God was killing as many as 24,000 Jews for having relationships with these women, Zimri, boldly took this black woman into his tent to make love to her. In the process, Aaron's grandson Phinehas became so angry that he took a spear and thrust it through their bodies while they were having sexual intercourse.

Other individuals in the Bible also married or had sex with the descendants of Ham. These include Esau who married Hittite women (Gen 26:34), Canaanite women, as well as Ishmael's daughter (Gen 28:8-9). Jacob had sex with Bilhah, who was his concubine that served as a maid servant of Rachel (Gen. 30:1-6). Reuben, Jacob's oldest son, also had sex with Bilhah (Gen. 35:21-22). All of these women are the descendants of Ham and are members of the black race.

Simon of Cyrene: Carries the Cross for Jesus

Scripture References: Matt. 27:32, Mark 15:21, Luke 23:26

Simon, a Hellenistic black Jew, lived in Cyrene on the North Coast of Africa near Libya. He was chosen by God, to help Jesus carry out a special mission that was planned before the foundation of the world. Mark hints at the reliability, punctuality and stamina of this black man, when he recorded in Mark 15:21, that Simon arrived at the exact spot, at the precise time, to help Christ carry the cross. That is, after travelling several hundred miles (some estimate as much as 750 miles) from his home in Cyrene to get to Jerusalem for the Passover.

Ebed-Melech: Saves a Prophet from Death

Scripture Reference: Jer. 38

Ebed-Melech, a black Eunuch in the house of King Zedekiah, is credited with risking his life to save Jeremiah, one of Israel's greatest prophets. When the princes of Judah falsely charged Jeremiah with sedition, he was sentenced to die in the bottom of the courtyard dungeon. Ebed-Melech went against public opinion and spoke on behalf of Jeremiah and asked that his life be spared. King Zedekiah had so much respect for this black palace official that he granted his request. Ebed-Melech took thirty men and some rope and pulled Jeremiah from the dungeon.

The Ethiopian Eunuch: Egyptian Official Who Worshipped God

Scripture Reference: Acts 8:27-39

This eunuch was the Treasurer of Ethiopia under Queen Candace. He, therefore, was considered to be a very influential man. He apparently was bilingual, and well educated for he could speak and read Hebrew.

When the angel of the Lord God instructed Philip to go to the desert of Gaza, he ran into this distinguished black man who had just come from worshipping in Jerusalem. Philip noticed he was reading from the book of Isaiah and offered assistance.

The meeting between these two resulted in the Eunuch accepting Christ, followed by a baptismal ceremony conducted by Philip. After the baptism, Philip disappeared and the Eunuch went on his way rejoicing. God loved this black man so much that He sent Philip on a special mission just to meet him. When white missionaries from Europe and the United States arrived in Ethiopia centuries later, they discovered many of the blacks were already practicing Christianity. This proved that the American white man was not the first to introduce the black man to Christianity.

Jesus: A Man of Color? You Decide!

Scripture References: Matt. 1:5-6; Rev. 1:14-15, 2:18

The descendants of Ham are mentioned in Jesus' family tree. Although no one today really knows what Jesus looked like when he was on earth, John the Revelator gives the only physical description ever recorded. It resembles an aging black man with woolly hair. "His head and his hairs were white like wool, as white as snow and His eyes were as flames of fire. And his feet like unto fine brass as if they burned in a furnace" (Revelation 1:14).

Great Contributions

In God's Word, the black race is credited with several achievements. Nimrod and his staff were the first (Nimrod) to design and construct buildings made of brick. The greatest empires of ancient times were built, including Egypt and Babylonia, designed and ruled by blacks. Some of the most beautiful cities, complete with libraries and garden plazas, were designed by blacks and their descendants (Nineveh). The first worship service conducted by a Priest after the crossing of the Red Sea was conducted by a black man (Jethro).

The first known multilevel court system was also Jethro's idea. In addition to developing systems and communities, God has used blacks on numerous occasions to save the lives of many. Moses' life was saved by his black wife when God sought to kill him. Egypt was available to feed the nation of Israel when there was a worldwide famine. The lives of the spies who entered Canaan were saved by a black prostitute. Jeremiah's life was saved by a black eunuch when he was sentenced to death. And a black man arrived just in time to help Jesus when He could go no further.

The scripture tells us in Genesis 17:18-27 and Genesis 25:1-5 that God blessed Abraham's black wives, Hagar and Keturah, and their descendants. Those descendants, in turn, blessed the rest of the world with their gifts and unique talents.

History has revealed some very insightful and positive information about the black race, but none as important as the following:

1. When the black race walked with God, they were blessed by God. But when they walked away from God they have always walked into destructive life-styles and away from His divine blessings and protection.

2. The members of the black race can never reach their fullest potential if they deny and fail to embrace their spiritual roots in the Lord. God has been very good to the black race and for that they should be forever most grateful, and continue to use their God-given gifts and talents to help themselves as well as the world around them, for His Glory.

3. Finally, it is easier to remove the blackness from the black man's skin, than it is to remove God from his historical past. If you can separate the black man from God, and destroy his spiritual roots, you will also destroy his identity, his pride, his family, and eventually destroy his race. To be truly black means to be truly spiritual. Black people who are not spiritually in tune with God, will never know what it really means to be black. The two are meant to be part of one, and should never be separated. It was God who meticulously made the unique black man what he is, and without God, he will be like a ship drifting, without a sail.

THE 1993 TRIAL ON THE CURSE OF HAM

Is the Black Race Cursed?

by Wayne Perryman

The 1993 Trial on the Curse of Ham

For the past 300 years men have debated as to what really happened in the tent of Noah, and who was actually cursed as a result of their actions. Many scholars in Western Christianity have taken the view that it was Ham and his black descendants who were cursed. The ridiculous reasons given went from one extreme to another.

Some claimed that Ham took advantage of his drunken father, Noah, and had a homosexual relationship with him. Others said that Ham enjoyed observing his father's nudity and made jokes about it to his brothers. Whatever the reason given, their wrong conclusions have had a devastating affect on the Black race over the years.

Many Christians used the alleged curse as legal grounds to outlaw marriages between Blacks and Whites. Others used it to deny Blacks the position of priesthood within their denomination, and still others used the curse theory to justify using Blacks as slaves.

Yes, the so called "Curse on Ham" was the inspiration and justification for the mistreatment of Blacks in America. The "Curse Theory" inspired new laws limiting a variety of opportunities to Blacks and justified city, state, and federal governments to permit separate restrooms, restaurants, schools and drinking fountains. There was one set of facilities for Black people and another for all others. It inspired new studies and research to see why Blacks were inferior. It justified insensitive joke telling and other inhumane treatment directed toward blacks. Blacks felt there was no end to their nightmare.

The sad commentary to all of this was the fact that the "Curse Theory" was started by White Bible-believing Christians, who in turn introduced this theory to the rest of society. Even though they had no evidence to support the so-called curse, their story (based on circumstantial evidence), was persuasive enough to convince Blacks themselves that they were indeed the descendants of a cursed people.

How did they convince Blacks and others? They spent millions of dollars and used scholars from the major Christian publishers to interpret, twist, and stretch the meaning of Scripture. The theory of the curse became so mainstream that many of the top encyclopedias adopted the "Curse Theory." No blacks were ready to challenge the encyclopedia. The general feeling was, if it's in the encyclopedia, it must be true.

A question was asked: "If these scholars were required to submit solid evidence in a court of law to prove that Ham, the father of the Black race, had indeed committed an act so horrible that it resulted in a curse on him and his descendants, could they do it? We decided to hold a trial to see.

On July 26, 1993, a mock trial was held in the State of California, in the County of Orange, at the Friendship Baptist Church. Several hundred people, representing various racial groups, attended the trial and the lectures each day. The jury was stunned after hearing some of the most powerful evidence ever presented in a trial of this nature. The evidence presented by the defense included shocking facts from over 442 Scriptures.

This publication contains the modified transcripts of that mock trial as well as other supportive evidence which was offered in the week-long lecture series that followed the trial. This marks the first time in history that someone has stepped forward to defend Ham; it is also the first time in history that Ham has had an opportunity to tell his side of the story and to offer an explanation of what actually happened in his father's tent. Because of this historical document, like those attending the actual trial, you too will be able to determine for the first time, the guilt or innocence of Ham. We are confident you will thoroughly enjoy every element of this exciting trial.

The Defense's Case

Opening Remarks:

Your Honor, ladies and gentlemen of the jury, my name is Wayne Perryman, defense attorney for Mr. Ham, the third son of Noah.

As you know, my client has been accused and charged with the following:

1. He sexually abused his father, Mr. Noah.
2. He dishonored his father.
3. He was cursed, and is therefore responsible for his descendants' perpetual enslavement.
4. He was cursed with black skin.

My job as defense attorney is to prove to you, beyond a reasonable doubt, that my client is innocent of all charges. Many say this will not be an easy task because of the impressive credentials of those testifying for the prosecution.

The prosecutor feels he has a solid case. For the past 300 years he has called a variety of witnesses and you have heard their testimonies. But what you haven't heard is my client's story, the only eye witness to what took place in Noah's tent. What you haven't heard is the truth, the whole truth, and nothing but the truth. But you will hear it today.

For the past 300 plus years you have heard testimonies from some of the most brilliant scholars in the world whose publications and books are used in the best seminaries in the world. They all claimed that my client is guilty of sexually abusing and or dishonoring his father. In addition to these charges, they claimed that God himself honored a curse pronounced on Mr. Ham and his descendants by his father, Noah.

The witnesses for the prosecution have all documented their testimonies in a variety of impressive publications. Their opinions regarding the curse were proudly published by the world's top Christian publishers, including:

1. Zondervan
2. Word Book Publishers
3. Moody Press
4. Thomas Nelson

As we review their testimonies, as well as the evidence that has been suppressed for centuries, I'm confident that we, the defense, will prove beyond a reasonable doubt that my client is innocent of all charges - and that these so-called experts on the Scripture, with all due respect, were perhaps blinded by their own prejudice on this particular matter.

In my defense, I will sort fact from fiction and prove the following:

1. Ham is the third son of Noah.

2. On the day in question, my client did indeed enter his father's tent, but he did no wrong.

3. My client did not dishonor his father.

4. My client and his descendants, (with the exception of Canaan) were not cursed and no one was turned black.

Before I begin my defense, I would like to review for the record, a few of the testimonies of those key witnesses who testified for the prosecution.

Mathew Henry testified from his **Mathew Henry Commentary** produced by Zondervan's Publishers in 1961, pp. 23 that: "Ham saw the nakedness of his father, and told his two brethren. He pleased himself with the sight. Perhaps Ham had sometimes been himself drunk. It is common for those who walk in false ways themselves to rejoice at the false steps which they sometimes see others make.... He [Noah] pronounces a curse on Canaan the son of Ham, in whom Ham is himself cursed. The particular curse is, A servant of servants (that is, the meanest and most despicable servant) shall he be, even to his brethren. God often visits the iniquity of the fathers upon the children, when the children inherit the fathers' wicked dispositions and imitate the fathers' wicked practices, and do nothing to cut off the entail of the curse...."

Next you heard the testimony of the scholars from the **Layman's Bible Encyclopedia**, published by R.R. Donelley & Sons in 1964, pp. 298. They gave the following testimony: *"As a result of Ham's disrespect for his father, his descendants were cursed by Noah to the effect that they would be slaves and servants of the descendants of Shem and Japheth, Ham's two brothers."*

The prosecution then called the scholars from the **Broadman Bible Commentary**, published in 1969, pp. 147, 148. They gave the following testimony: "There is hardly an Old Testament passage more difficult to interpret. This scripture was the favorite text of Southern preachers during the Civil War as they asserted the right of White men to enslave the Negro. Often used in recent times to defend segregation, the passage is the unrecognized source of the common saying, "A Negro is all right in his place," by which is meant that his proper position is secondary to that of the White man..... What was the sin of Ham? Some would suggest that verse 24 implies that he had committed a homosexual act with his father (Lev. 18:7). This interpretation is quite unfounded.... What did Ham do to his father? He disgraced him by exposing his shame to the world.... What his brothers did he should have done: he should have covered his father and said nothing about it.... The most perplexing task confronting the traditional interpretation of the passage is to give an adequate explanation for the curse's having fallen upon Canaan rather than upon Ham.... Noah, given insight into the future of the nations, sees the consequences of Ham's sin issuing in the fate of his son. With a father like Ham, the son is doomed."

The scholars from the **Self-Interpreting Bible** were prosecution's next group of witnesses. Their publication was first published in 1896, pp. 226. They gave the following testimony: "The mind of the writer [Moses] being specially directed to that incident, he naturally connects Canaan with Ham. It would seem, too, from the tenor of the whole narrative, that Canaan must have been in some way implicated. Probably he was the first who discovered Noah, and then told his father...The descendants of Ham, by his sons Cush, Mizraim, Phut, and Canaan, peopled Africa and Western Asia. For about four thousand years past the bulk of the Africans have been abandoned of Heaven to the most gross ignorance, rigid slavery, stupid idolatry, and savage barbarity...." pp. 226

The prosecution then called the experts from the **Wesleyan Bible Commentary**. Their publication was published in 1975 by William B. Eerdman's Publishing Company, pp. 53. The following is the testimony they gave: "In his drunken state he immodestly exposed himself. Ham, his son saw him thus exposed and reported the incident to his brothers. They, with greater respect for their father's dignity, took a garment, walked backwards into the tent, and covered him without gazing upon him. When Noah awakened, he cursed Ham's son, Canaan, and blessed Shem and Japheth. Why he cursed Canaan instead of Ham is not clear. One suggestion is that Ham had a natural tendency to the unclean, a tendency which lead him to enjoy thus gazing upon his father and to delight in telling his brothers about what he saw - a tendency which Noah had already observed in an enlarged sense in Ham's son, Canaan, in whose descendants the tendency led to their extreme depravity, their enslavement to immorality, and eventual destruction....."

The scholars from the **Wycliffe Bible Encyclopedia** gave the shortest testimony. The following is their testimony as recorded by their publisher Moody Press in 1975, pp. 746: "The history of the Canaanites is foreshadowed in the dishonoring of Noah by Ham when his father lay in a drunken stupor...."

The scholars of Thomas Nelson's Publishers were called next. They produced the **1986 edition of the Nelson's Illustrated Bible Dictionary**, pp. 454 They, too, were very brief. The following is their testimony: "Ham found his father naked and drunk, asleep in his tent. Ham told his brothers, Shem and Japheth, who covered their father without looking on his nakedness. Noah was furious because Ham had seen him naked, and he placed a curse on Ham and his descendants."

The surprise witness for the prosecution was the scholarship from the **Encyclopedia Britannica**. They quoted from their 1992 edition, Vol. 8 pp. 737, and gave the following testimony: "Noah's drunkenness and the disrespect it provokes in his son Ham, (or Canaan) resulted in Noah's laying of a curse on Ham and his descendants."

The last witness for the prosecution was, Gordon J. Wenham, author of the **Word Biblical Commentary**. His publication which was published by *Word Publishers in 1987*, pp. 198-201, gave the following testimony: "....Ham's actions show clear disrespect for his father and this merited his father's wrath. Uncovering oneself was dishonorable, and Noah's son should have quietly covered him up, not gossiped about it to his brothers. Others have felt that Noah's reaction indicates that Ham must have done something worse than is actually described. Seeing his father's nakedness must be a euphemism for a more serious offense.... Westermann is right to see the chief thrust of the story as blaming Ham for his improper, quite unfilial behavior...By looking on his naked father, Ham had acquired Noah's potency; That was why he had to tell his brothers about it.... Why should Noah have cursed Canaan, Ham's son, and not Ham himself? The question has baffled commentators for centuries, and there is no obvious answer."

Defense attorney: Your Honor, before we call our first witness, the defense would like to admit as evidence, two exhibits. Exhibit A, are 442 Scripture references that we will refer to throughout this case, and Exhibit B, is the 1985 New Strong's Concordance of The Bible.

The Defense Presents Their Case

Defense attorney: Mr. Wenham's last statement is what this case is all about - "the question that has baffled commentators for centuries." Why was Canaan cursed and not Ham? The testimony of my first witness, my key witness and my only witness will provide that answer for us. Your honor, I would like to call Mr. Ham to the witness stand.

The Testimony of Ham

Court Clerk: Will Mr. Ham please take the witness stand?

Court Clerk: Do you promise to tell the truth, the whole truth, and nothing but the truth, in the presence of God?

Ham: I do.

Court Clerk: Please be seated.

Defense attorney: State your name please?

Ham: My name is Ham, I'm the third son of my father, Noah (Gen. 5:32).

Defense attorney: Ham, you heard the testimony from some of the most brilliant scholars of our times and they all have testified that you did something to your father that dishonored him, so he cursed you and your descendants. Is this true?

Ham: No sir, it is not true. I did nothing to my father. It was my youngest son, Canaan, that was cursed by my father [Noah], not me (Gen. 9:25).

Defense attorney: In addition to their testimony, a number of other people have testified that God turned you and some of your descendants black for what you did. Is this true?

Ham: Well, sort of.

Defense attorney: What do you mean "sort of?" Did he or didn't he?

Ham: It is true that God was responsible for my color, but I didn't do anything wrong to become black, I was born black, not cursed black. The definition of my name is "Black," "sun-hot," and or "man with dark skin." My father and mother always told me they thought I looked very unique as a baby. You see, my dad was 500 years old when he started having children (Gen. 5:32). When I was born, I was so dark, that is, darker than my other two brothers, that my parents felt that Ham (meaning dark skin) was the most appropriate name for me.

Defense attorney: What do you mean darker than your other two brothers? What color were they?

Ham: They were brown. You see, we lived in a warm climate and it didn't rain for 120 years while my father preached his sermons on repentance (Gen. 6:3). So you might say everyone was a little darker than normal with our diet and 120 years of constant sunlight.

Defense attorney: So if I understand you correctly, are you trying to say you were not turned Black as a result of what you did?

Ham: Right. Sir, let me say it again for the record. I did no wrong, neither was I turned black. I was born black and had been black for over 100 years when the incident took place in my father's tent. May I add something while we are on this subject so we can have a better understanding of the times I lived in?

Defense attorney: Yes, you may proceed.

Ham: When my brothers and I were just little boys, my father's father, Lamech [our grandfather] (Gen. 5:28-29), told us stories about how the world was started many years before we were born. He told us that his distant father, Adam, lived in a beautiful area called, the Garden of Eden. It was a place where the sun was always shining and it never rained (Gen. 2:5). It, too, was a very warm climate. The sun, along with the deep dark rich soil, made it possible to grow every type of plant on earth (Gen. 1:29). Grandfather said, it was from this dark soil that God made Adam (Gen. 1:27 & Gen. 3:19). Grandfather also said that the garden included the entire country of Ethiopia (Gen. 2:13), a country known as "**the land of black people**". So I guess everyone of that time had dark skin, including our distant grandfather, Adam. Grandfather Lamech himself said he talked to Adam. This was possible because my Grandfather was about 47 years old when Adam died. Adam lived to be 930 years old (Gen. 5:5 & Gen. 5:1-28).

Defense attorney: They say you and your sons are the fathers of the Black race or the people of Africa, is that true?

Ham: I guess so.

Defense attorney: What do you mean, you guess so?

Judge: Counselor, where is this line of questioning going?

Defense attorney: Your honor, there has been much testimony over the years that the Black race are the descendants of Ham, and as a result of the curse on Ham they were placed into slavery in America. I'm trying to identify his descendants to determine whether or not this charge is true.

Judge: You may proceed.

Defense attorney: You stated, "you guess so" when I asked, whether you were the father of the Black race. What is your response?

Ham: In your country (America), the Department of Commerce through its Bureau of Census, has maintained that if the father is Black, the children, regardless of their physical features, will be considered Black as well. I'm Black, my name means Black, so I guess my children are Black, according to your government.

Defense attorney: Then the members of the Black race are your children, is that what you're saying?

Ham: I guess. It depends on whether your definition of the Black race is a broad one or narrow one.

Defense attorney: What's the difference?

Ham: A narrow definition would be that the Black race consists only of those people who have Negroid features. A broad definition would include all of the children who came from my seed, and that would include people whose skin tones range from very light to very dark and whose hair textures range from coarse to very straight. Your so-called American Black represent the broad definition because they possess this wide diversity of physical characteristics. Black men like myself have always been able to produce children of diversity. If you take a close look at my children and the countries they founded, you can see that what I'm saying is true.

Defense attorney: Perhaps you can tell the court the names of your children and grandchildren and the countries and cities they founded.

Ham: There are quite a few. Are you sure that you want me to name all of them?

Defense attorney: For the sake of time, why don't you name your children and a few of the well known countries that they and their descendants are credited with finding.

Ham: My sons are Cush, Mizraim, Phut, and Canaan (Gen. 10:6) and I'm proud to say, they have produced some of the greatest countries and civilizations of all times. Among them include, Egypt, Ethiopia, Babylon, and cities like Nineveh (Gen. 10:6-20).

Defense attorney: Would you say these countries are Black nations?

Ham: Let me say again for the record, it is your government who has maintained that if the father is Black his children would also be classified as Black. I am Black, my name means Black, and these are my children. What else can I say?

Defense attorney: So your children produced Babylon, Egypt and Ethiopia.

Ham: Yes, and may I add that the names Cush, Ethiopia and Egypt all mean Black and none of these countries or individuals to my knowledge, have ever been cursed because of what took place in my father's tent.

Defense attorney: Let's deal with what actually happened that day in the tent. But before we do, let me ask you this question. What took place in the tent has been debated and has been a focus of controversy for several hundred years. In all of these years, has anyone ever asked to hear your side of the story?

Ham: No sir. This is the first time I have ever had the privilege of telling my side of the story; outside of my immediate family who knows I was the only eye witness to what actually took place (Gen. 9:22).

Defense attorney: Did you ever discuss the incident with your family?

Ham: Yes.

Defense attorney: When?

Ham: The same day it happened.

Defense attorney: Why do you think no one has asked to hear your side of the story?

Ham: I guess no one really cared to hear the truth.

Defense attorney: How do you feel about what they have said about you over the years?

Ham: It hurts. People are very cruel. Some have called me a homosexual and others thought that God turned against me and cursed me with black skin. If they wanted to know what happened, all they had to do was read the Bible. My distant nephew, Moses, through the teaching of his Black father-in-law, Jethro, gave these scholars enough information to figure out what happened. It's simple.

Defense attorney: You said Moses and his Black father-in-law recorded what happened. Is that correct?

Ham: Well, Moses was the one who wrote about it in Genesis around 1490 BC, 858 years after it happened [2348 BC], but he learned all the details from his father-in-law.

Defense attorney: Explain what you mean.

Ham: Moses learned about this incident while living with his father-in-law, Jethro. Everyone knows that Moses was separated from his family as a child. Your modern New Testament even records this truth in Acts 7:21-23 when it said, ..."And when he [Moses] was cast out, Pharaoh's daughter took him up and nourished him for her own son. And Moses was learned in all the wisdom of the Egyptians," but knew nothing about his Jewish ancestry until he became a member of his fathers-in-law's household. His father-in-law, Jethro, was a relative of Midian who was the son of Keturah, Abraham's Black Canaanite wife (Gen. 25:1-4 Exodus 2:21).

Defense attorney: Are you trying to tell the court that Moses heard about the incident involving your father, Noah, through his father-in-law, Jethro?

Ham: Yes sir. Jethro was a descendant of mine. He was also a descendant of Abraham through Keturah. Keturah was Abraham's third wife which makes her Jethro's distant grandmother through her son Midian. Jethro was a very intelligent Black man who spent a lot of time teaching Moses about his Jewish ancestry. He not only taught Moses for 40 years while living in his [Jethro's] home, he also taught Moses a thing or two after the crossing of the Red Sea. Moses had a lot of respect for his father-in-law and did everything his father-in-law said. Jethro always told him if he [Moses] would listen to him and follow his Godly advice, God would be with him (Exodus 18:19 & 24). Jethro was a true man of God. Moses and his father-in-law were very close, a perfect father and son combination. Having been raised by Pharaoh's daughter, Jethro was the only father figure Moses has ever had (Acts 7:20 Exodus 4:18 & Exodus 18:7). Yes sir, it was Jethro who first told Moses about our family's problems. Jethro's story was later confirmed by Moses' brother and sister, as well as by other Jews, as they wandered through the wilderness.

Defense attorney: You say Moses' brother and sister confirmed Jethro's story? Exactly what did they tell him regarding the incident in your father's tent?

Ham: The truth.

Defense attorney: Explain that to the court. In your opinion, what is that truth?

Ham: Sir, it is not an opinion. What I'm about to say is fact. I was an eye witness. Even your Bible states that I was the one who SAW something (Gen. 9:22). Note it didn't say that I did anything to my father or my mother. It only states; that I was an eye witness to what actually happened.

Defense attorney: If you didn't do anything, who did? And what exactly did they do?

Ham: It's very difficult to talk about it. [Ham paused for a while then said], it was my youngest son, Canaan.

Defense attorney: I know it's hard, but we must know the truth. Take your time and tell the court what happened on the day of the incident.

Ham: Moses tried to tell everybody that it was Canaan who did it. But everyone kept blaming me because I'm his [Canaan's] father.

Defense attorney: How did Moses try to tell them that Canaan was involved?

Ham: Prior to mentioning the incident in the Scripture, he kept mentioning Canaan's name with mine, but no one picked this up. He was trying to tell them that Canaan was involved. You notice he didn't mention any of my other sons nor did he mention my brothers and their sons, only Canaan (Gen. 9:18 & 22). My dad knew that Canaan was the one who committed the act, that's why he cursed him and not me, and still no one picked this up (Gen. 9:25).

Defense attorney: What did Canaan do? Did he see his father without any clothes on?

Ham: No. I guess that's what has confused people all these years. As boys, we had seen our father naked many times. You see, it was very common to bathe in the rivers with our father as boys. After all, we had no private bathrooms in those days. Nudity had nothing to do with it. When Canaan committed this act, my brothers and I were considered old men by your standards today, and had seen our father naked many times. As I stated before, our father started having children when he was 500 years old (Gen. 5:32), but when we went into the ark, he was 600, two months and 17 days old (Gen. 7:11). My brothers and I were almost 100 years old ourselves, which means we had seen our father's nudity for almost 100 years before the flood.

Defense attorney: Then what did Moses mean when he said, you saw your "**father's nakedness**?"

Ham: I did. I saw my **father's nakedness**. In other words, I was an eye witness. I saw exactly what went on and who did what to whom. You see, the term, "**father's nakedness**" has nothing to do with nudity. It's a term used for sexual intercourse. As you know, the Bible used many terms to let us know that someone has had sexual intercourse with another. One common term was "**knew**" (Gen. 4:1). Another common term was "**went in unto**" (Gen. 16:4). Sometimes the Bible used a negative term like "**he knew her not**" (in 1 Kings 1:4) to let us know that sexual intercourse did not take place. All of these terms including "**father's nakedness**" refer to sexual intercourse. Our society, like your society today, had several terms that we used in place of the term sexual intercourse.

Defense attorney: Give us an example of similar terms that we would use today.

Ham: Terms like, "they made love," "they did it," or "they got it on."

Defense attorney: You claim you did nothing, and that you were only an eye witness. Are you trying to say that Canaan, your youngest son, had sex with his father?

Ham: No, this has nothing to do with sex with my father.

Defense attorney: Let me see if I understand you. First you say this has nothing to do with your father's nudity. Then you tell the court that the term "**his father's nakedness**" pertains to sexual intercourse with your father. Now you tell us it has nothing to do with having sex with your father. This is confusing to the court.

Ham: Sir, I never said that the term, "**father's nakedness**" meant having sex with my father. I only said it pertained to sexual intercourse. The term means having sex with my mother, my father's wife.

Defense attorney: Are you trying to tell the court that Canaan had sex with your mother (his grandmother), Mrs. Noah.

Ham: Yes sir. That's why my father said, "**cursed be Canaan**" (Gen. 9:25).

Defense attorney: Is there any evidence to support your claim that the term his "**father's nakedness**" means sexual intercourse with your father's wife and not with him?

Ham: Yes, I do.

Defense attorney: Tell the court where we can find this definition.

Ham: My distant nephew, Moses, wrote the definition of "**father's nakedness**" in the Leviticus Law books in 1490 BC. Under section (chapter) 18 of the Leviticus laws and paragraph (verse) 8, it says, ... "thy father's wife shalt thou not uncover: it is thy **father's nakedness**". And in Leviticus 20:11 it says, "And the man that lieth with his father's wife hath uncovered his **father's nakedness**...." Due. 27:20, also states this. The term uncovering a **relative's nakedness** is used for sexual intercourse throughout the 20th chapter of Leviticus.

Defense attorney: I know it will be difficult for you, but in your own words, will you tell the court what happened on that day?

Ham: After the flood, my father planted a vineyard and made some wine. On this particular day, my father had too much to drink. Mother was in the tent with him. I don't know if she had been drinking or not. When I passed by the tent, I heard some commotion and the voice of my son, Canaan. I knew he wasn't supposed to be in the tent, so I looked inside and there he was, taking advantage of mother, my father's wife. I grabbed him and dragged him out of my father's tent. As I was coming out of the tent, my brothers asked, what was going on. I told them what Canaan had done and asked if they would go back inside and cover mother.

Defense attorney: Then, it was you who told your brothers to cover your mother? Most people thought your brothers covered your father (Gen. 9:22).

Ham: No sir, it was my mother.

Defense attorney: Now that we know it was your mother that they covered, many will want to know why you didn't cover her.

Ham: I was preoccupied with getting Canaan out of the tent. After I was out, I couldn't bear going back inside and seeing my mother in that condition. I felt my immediate responsibility was to deal with my son.

Defense attorney: Many scholars said that when the Scripture says, "you told your brothers without" (Gen. 9:22), you were actually joking with your brothers. They said, "you thought the whole thing was funny." Is that true?

Ham: No, that's not true. If I had, my father would have cursed me, too. My father was a preacher who preached 120 years. He was never at a loss for words and would not have hesitated to curse me if I had dishonored him or participated in anyway, including joking about the matter. My father was an expert on wrong doing, that's what he preached about for 120 years. After evaluating the entire situation, he was confident that I had committed no wrong. When the Scripture says in Gen. 9:22, that I told "my brothers without," Moses meant that I told them what had happened, and told them by the way of a request to go cover mother, and asked them not to look. With respect for our mother, they went in backwards and covered her body. When my father awakened we told him what Canaan had done. Sir, it hurts me to think that these scholars would think that I would joke about something like that. You have to remember, these are the same scholars who didn't even know what the simple term "**father's nakedness**" meant.

Defense attorney: I know this has been hard on you. But could you tell us how they came up with a term "**father's nakedness**" to mean sex with the wife?

Ham: It's difficult, but I'll try. In Genesis 2:22, when God made woman he took her from man and Adam said: "**...she is bone of my bone and flesh of my flesh because she was taken out of man.**" Adam goes on to say "**the two shall become one flesh.**" Because the woman's body was made from man and not from the ground like Adam, we believe she will always be a part of our body. To do something to our wife is like doing something to our own body. That's why in your New Testament, Paul tells Christians in Ephesian 5:28-31, "**...to love your wife even as you love your OWN bodies.**" The wife's body belongs to her husband because her body comes from his body. So in reality, a violation **to** her body is a violation **of** his body. The concept of her body belonging to her husband is not that he owns her as he would own a material possession or slave, but more like the heart belonging to the natural body. It means she is a natural and vital part of him.

Defense attorney: Mr. Ham, it was a terrible thing that your son did. I hope something like this will never happen again.

Ham: Unfortunately, this wasn't the only time something like this has happened.

Defense attorney: What do you mean?

Ham: Our incident took place around 2348 BC, but similar incidents have happened since that time. That's why Moses put these things into the law books.

Defense attorney: You mean you have knowledge of other children taking advantage of their parents and having sex with them?

Ham: Yes, sir. In Genesis 19:30-38, Lot's daughters got their father drunk and had sex with him. In Genesis 35:22, Jacob's oldest son, Reuben, had sex with his father's concubine wife, Bilhah. And in Genesis 38:1-26, Judah had sex with his daughter-in-law, Tamar. These incidents along with ours, is what inspired Moses to write this law.

Defense attorney: If you don't mind, let's go back to the subject of the curse. Why do you think these scholars thought you and your descendants were the ones who were cursed?

Ham: I don't know. My father said, "Cursed be Canaan." He cursed no one else. I don't see how these Bible scholars can take my father's simple statement regarding Canaan and apply it to me and my descendants. According to one of the top Bible concordances (Strong's Concordance), my name (Ham) appears 17 times in the Bible and not one time is my name associated with doing anything wrong, nor is it associated with sin or being cursed. I don't know what Scriptures your scholars were looking at when they reached their conclusion that I was cursed.

Defense attorney: Do you think they said these things about you because they thought you were cursed and turned black?

Ham: Here again there is no Biblical reference of God or anyone else cursing a person and turning them black. Everyone knows that anytime God cursed or approved a curse where skin color was involved, the curse always turned them **White, never Black**. Even though these scholars know this to be Scripturally true, they will never say the White race is cursed, even though there is Biblical evidence that people were cursed and turned White.

Defense attorney: That's a pretty harsh accusation.

Ham: No sir, it is not an accusation. It's the truth. We find evidence of this in Numbers the 12th chapter with Moses' sister Miriam (Num. 12:1-10) and with Gehazi, Elisha's servant, in II Kings 5:1-17. In the situation involving Elisha's curse on Gehazi, the curse not only covered Gehazi but all of his seed [future generations], as well. Sir, I'm not trying to say the White race is cursed. I'm just saying there is much more evidence to reach such a conclusion than there was evidence to support the claim that Black people were cursed. Black people were never cursed. If they were, no one would ever know it, because they would be turned white according to the Bible.

Defense attorney: If the curse did not extend to your descendants can you explain why Blacks became slaves in America?

Ham: Again Sir, I was never cursed, so my descendants could not have been cursed. In my most humble opinion, slavery in America as well as around the world involved all races, not just blacks. I believe slavery had more to do with the sins of the people who enslaved them, more than the sins of slaves themselves. Sir, no one has been in slavery longer nor has any group suffered persecution as much as my brother's (Shem) children, the Jews. My descendants enslaved them in Egypt for almost 400 years. Afterwards they were captives in Babylon for a number of years; not to mention what the Christian Crusades and the Nazi Germans did to them. In my opinion, my nephews, the Jews, suffered more than my descendants. The Bible reveals that even though Canaan was cursed, his descendants lived in a prosperous land flowing with milk and honey long before the land was turned over to the blessed ones (Shem's descendants). While the Canaanites were enjoying their prosperous land, the blessed descendants of Shem were wandering in the wilderness eating manna for 40 long years. And the manna years were preceded by four hundreds years of slavery in Egypt. Over the years, many scholars have tried to overlook the suffering of the Jews, and many of these same scholars are now trying to convince people that the Holocaust did not happen, even though there is a tremendous amount of evidence available to prove them wrong.

Defense attorney: Many scholars thought that you, Canaan's father, should be responsible for your son's sins, that's why they included you in the curse. How do you feel about this?

Ham: Lot wasn't cursed for his daughter's sexual sin. Jesse wasn't cursed for David's sexual sin, and Jacob wasn't cursed for Reuben's sexual sin. Why would God want to curse me for my son's sexual sin? God knew I had suffered enough. This was a very painful experience for me. How would any father feel if he caught his son having sex with his helpless grandmother?

Defense attorney: Did your father's feelings change toward you after this incident?

Ham: It's hard to say. I don't think so. I really loved my mother and father and they both knew it. I think my father felt sorry for me because it was my son that dishonored us both. I think my father was in a dilemma. On one hand, he was glad that I rescued mother from Canaan, so I deserved a blessing for that. But on the other hand, it was my son who committed the act. So he neither blessed me or cursed me. In some ways, perhaps, he felt partly to blame for everything because he allowed himself to become so drunk that he didn't know what was going on in his own tent. We never really talked about it much after that.

Defense attorney: Before we take this case to the jury, what would you like to tell the court?

Ham: First of all, I would like to say I did no wrong neither was I cursed by my father because of my son's sin. If my father, mother, and brothers were here today, they would tell the court that I did what was right at the time, and that was rescue my mother from my son. They would tell the court that my father was the type of preacher who would not hesitate to pronounce a curse on me, if he honestly felt that I had anything to do with dishonoring him.

I was not cursed. Neither were any of my descendants other than those associated with Canaan. Canaan's curse was fulfilled when my brother's [Shem] descendants took over the territory of the Canaan.

My descendants had their share of faults as did my brother's descendants, Shem & Japheth. We all had our shortcomings. We all strayed away from God and we all suffered for it.

These scholars who testified for the prosecution told the court many negative things about me and my descendants, most of which were not true. But what they failed to tell the court is that many of my descendants were married to the most powerful people in Bible History. Let me just name a few of them.

<u>Abraham</u> married a descendant of mine, an Egyptian lady by the name of Hagar. She gave Abram his first son, Ishmael. As you

know, very few children are personally named by God. Not only did God name Hagar's son, **this descendant of Ham** was born before Isaac, named before Isaac, circumcised before Isaac and blessed before Isaac. After Abram was married to Hagar for 13 years, God added my name (Ham) to the "father of faith," changing his name from Abram to Abra**ham**. God did this to include the many nations and kings my seed would produce through my distant grandson, Ishmael (Gen. 16th & 17th chapter; Isaiah. 11:11).

Jacob had four boys with two of my female descendants, Bilhah and Zilpah. The children from these two Canaanite concubines became four of the leaders within the 12 tribes of Israel (Gen. 30th & 49th chapters).

Joseph married one of my descendants, a beautiful young lady by the name of Asenath. He had two sons with her. His sons also became two more leaders of the twelve tribes of Israel (Gen. 41:50-52; Gen. 49th chapter).

Judah had two boys with Shuah, a Canaanite descendant of mine (Gen. 38:1-9).

Abraham, at the age of 140, married another descendant of mine. Her name was Keturah. He had six sons with her. One of her sons founded a country in the east, and named it after himself, Midian. This man was the distant relative of Jethro, the Priest of Midian and the father-in-law of Moses. As I testified earlier, this Godly priest taught Moses for 40 years and the Scripture said (Ex. 18:24), Moses "did everything he said" (Gen. 25:1-6, Exodus chapters 3, 4 & 18).

Moses also married one of my descendants. Her name was Zipporah. She saved Moses' life. God loved Zipporah so much that He [God] cursed her sister-in-law, Miriam, when Miriam was upset with Moses for marrying this Black woman (Exodus chapters 2 & 4 and Numbers chapter 12).

Solomon married my descendant, Abishag, a Black Shunammite beauty queen. He wrote the Song of Solomon about her (I Kings 1-4; Song of Solomon).

Solomon married a Canaanite by the name of Rahab. She became the great great grandmother of David (Joshua 2 & 6:17-23). This Canaanite descendant of mine is only one of four women mentioned in the genealogies of Jesus (Matt 1:5-6). This means both Jesus and David had Canaanite blood in their families. If this is true, then Jesus and David themselves must be cursed because they too are descendants of Canaan, through Rahab.

Many of the greatest men of the Bible were either married or related to my descendants (Abraham, Jacob, Moses, Joseph, Solomon, David and Jesus). My descendants produced six sons who became six leaders of the twelve tribes of Israel. Jesus and David were descendants of a black Canaanite prostitute. According to the prosecutor's key witnesses (scholars), all of these people must be cursed because they are all either direct descendants of Canaan or distant descendants of mine.

History also reveals that my descendants were blessed to build some of the finest cities and countries in the world. In fact, at one time or another the most powerful nations in the world were nations developed and ruled by my people (Gen. 10:8-20).

Finally, history will reveal that God used the talents and gifts of my people to help others when they were in need. My descendants were always available at the most convenient time to help and bless Israel (Gen 12:3). Let me give you just a few examples:

Egypt was available to feed the nation of Israel when there was a worldwide famine (Gen. chapter 43). The lives of the spies who entered Canaan were saved by a Black Canaanite prostitute, who in turned married a Jewish man (Joshua chapter 2); Jeremiah's life was saved by a Black eunuch when he was sentenced to death (Jeremiah 38th Chapter); Moses' life was saved by his Black wife when God sought to kill him (Exodus 4:24-26), and a Black man arrived just in time to help Jesus when He could go no further (Mark 15:21).

Your Honor, an objective view of Bible History will show that God used and blessed my descendants as much as, if not more than my brothers'. This should be of no surprise, because God promised to bless all nations in Genesis 12:3. Evidence of this fact can be found in both the Old and New Testaments. Mark 3:18 tells us that one of Jesus's disciples was a Canaanite, and Mark 15:21 tells us that God selected a Black man to help his son carry out the mission of the cross. In addition to this role, Acts 13:1, identifies this same Black man (Simon of Cyrene) as one of the leaders of the New Testament Church. And Paul, in Romans 16:13, refers to Simon's wife and son (Rufus) as being holy people. Referring to Simon's wife, Paul says she was like a mother to him.

In closing, I just want to say, there is no Biblical evidence that I did anything wrong or that I was cursed. Your honor, I'm not ashamed of my descendants. As a matter of fact, I'm proud of the way many of them submitted to the will of God and allowed Him to use them for His service. However, I must say, I'm not proud of those descendants who sinned against Him. Even though, "**all have sinned and come short of the glory of God**" (Rom. 3:23), the opposition has only focused on the sins of my descendants. This is not fair.

Some may ask, "where did this debate originate?" I really don't know the answer. Perhaps it goes back as far as 1611, when King James had the Bible translated or as far back as 1381, when John Wycliffe introduced the first translation of the English Bible. But whatever the origin, or whatever the reason, this whole issue regarding the curse must be resolved. We may not know who started the debate or when it was started. But we do know this debate has had a devastating affect on my people and has divided the body of Christ. Your Honor, I hope this trial will put this whole issue to rest.

Defense attorney: Mr. Ham, I don't want to take advantage of your patience, but I do have one more question for you. If you are found innocent and acquitted of all charges, do you want to be compensated for damages?

Ham: No, sir. What I want, the court cannot give. I want all mankind to live harmoniously together in peace, with a greater degree of love and respect for each other, as well as a greater appreciation for one another. I sincerely believe this can only happen when nations and individuals are willing to replace the prejudice of men, for the loving peace of God (Isa. 26:3).

Defense Closing Remarks

Defense Attorney: Your honor, ladies and gentlemen of the jury, you have heard the testimony of the most brilliant scholars in Bible History as well as the testimony of my humble client, Ham, the only eye witness to testify in this case. The testimony that he gives is irrefutable, shocking and revealing. Never before has this information been given. And never before have we ever been exposed to the truth, the whole truth, and nothing but the truth.

As we listened to the defendant, none can deny that he spoke with sincerity and conviction as he explained the true meaning of "**his father's nakedness**" and summed up the significant role his descendants played in Bible History. After hearing his inspiring testimony, there should be no doubt in our mind as to what took place in his father's tent and absolutely no doubt as to who was cursed. Ladies and gentlemen of the jury, I ask you to find my client not guilty of the following charges:

1. Not guilty of sexually abusing his parents.
2. Not guilty of dishonoring his parents.
3. Not guilty of being cursed.
4. And not guilty of being cursed black.

Your Honor, the defense rest their case.

Epilog

For the past 300 years Blacks have lived in shame with the accusation that they were cursed and for the past 30 years they have shamefully lived with the accusation that they were worshipping a White man's God. Both accusations were made by people who were influenced by a society of ignorance and prejudice.

The trial of Ham has provided a multitude of answers to many difficult questions and hopefully it has destroyed a multitude of myths and accusations - more particularly, the accusation that Blacks are worshipping a White man's God. This accusation alone has affected an entire generation of Afro-American young people. In an effort to avoid such charges, many have turned their backs on the traditional Black Church, and have joined other groups in an effort to establish their own Black identity.

As implied in the case of Ham, it is impossible to study the Bible with an open mind without recognizing the significant role Blacks played in Bible History. Likewise, it is impossible to study true Black History without acknowledging the powerful role of the Black Church. In the past, Bible scholars have overlooked the significant role Blacks played in the Bible History. Today, professors of Black History are committing the same sin by overlooking a very important part of Black History, the role of the Black Church.

If taught correctly, true Black History will reveal this fact: **unlike any other race on earth, the Black woman and the Black Church have always been the key to the success and survival of the Black race.** The Black woman gained her tremendous strength (to support her husband and family) through her faith in God and the Black Church was the institution that provided her with that faith.

In addition to providing faith, the Black Church provided political leadership, schools, unity, and support for Black businesses. The Black Church gave W.E.B. DuBois his first scholarship to go to school. It gave Booker T. Washington his first position as a school principal. It gave the Negro Baseball League a place to eat every Sunday, and it gave America the Rev. Andrew Young, the Rev. Benjamin Hooks, the Rev. Adam Clayton Powell, the Rev. Jessie Jackson, the Rev. Dr. Martin Luther King Jr. and 60% of all the Black Colleges. In addition to ministers and schools, the church has influenced and inspired a multitude of professionals, among them include: Dr. George Washington Carver, world renown brain surgeon, Dr. Ben Carson and Colin Powell, chairman of the Joint Chiefs of Staff, just to name a few.

If Blacks only knew their true history they would realize that to be truly Black, is to be truly spiritual. They would know that it is easier to remove the blackness from their skin than it is to remove God from their historical past. And finally, they would realize that our only hope for a peaceful and prosperous future, is to go back to the only thing that has worked for us in the past, our faith in God and our support for one another. II Cor. 5:7, Isa. 41:6, St. John 10:10, St. John 15:12, Phil. 4:19.

CHRISTIAN WITNESS OF AFRICAN PEOPLES THROUGH THE AGES IN AFRICA, EUROPE AND THE AMERICAS

by David D. Daniels, Ph.D

Christian Witness of African Peoples Through the Ages in Africa, Europe and the Americas

Africans and people of African descendent have traveled around the world preaching the gospel of Jesus Christ in Europe, Africa, North and South America, Asia, and Australia. The Christian witness of Africans began prior to the crucifixion. The story of Africans in the history of Christianity is a great one of persons, congregations, and movements that demonstrated the power of God to conquer all forms of personal and corporate sin from rebelliousness to racism. While Israel is the place to begin the biblical history of individual African Christians, North Africa is the place to begin the history of African Christian movements.

The Influence in Africa

The Christian witness of Africans in North Africa profoundly affected the future of Christianity. Early great women of the Church included Perpetua and Felicitas, both North Africans. Many of the most influential theologians during the first centuries of the Church were North African: St. Cyril of Alexandria, Origen, Athanasius, Tertullian, St. Cyprian, Augustine. Scholars debate whether the theologians were black or racially mixed Africans. Yet, few would deny that most of these leaders were Africans who lived in Africa, especially in North Africa, a region known as a "crossroads of ethnic groupings, cultures, and civilizations." Although scholars debate the racial identity of these outstanding Christians, it is clear that black Africans did live throughout North Africa during this era.[1]

The Christian witness of black Africans includes the two great kingdoms of Ethiopia and Nubia. These great churches were founded before Christianity entered Anglo-Saxon England, Ireland, Sweden or Russia. Ethiopia received Christianity three centuries

---

[1]   Cyprian Davis, <u>The History of Black Catholics in the United States</u> (New York: Crossroads Publishing Company, 1990), 11.

after Christ during the A.D. 300s. By the year A.D. 100 Ethiopia emerged as a major commercial hub with trading links reaching throughout the Mediterranean Sea, Indian Ocean, and the African interior. The kingdom of Ethiopia extended north of Axum, the capital, to include southern Nubia and across the Red Sea to include parts of southern Arabia.

By late fourth century, Ethiopian Christians were making pilgrimages to the holy city of Jerusalem. And by the early sixth century, Ethiopia's Christian kings established themselves as military protectors of the Christian communities in the neighboring regions.

The Christian Church in Ethiopia engaged in expressive forms of worship. It incorporated the African religious practice of dance and drumming in its formal praise and worship of God. Ethiopian monasteries maintained the Christian practices of prayer, consecration, purity and Bible study as well as the practices of fasting and denying the flesh.

In their artistic depiction of biblical events, Ethiopian Christians presented biblical persons, ranging from Adam and Eve to Abraham to Mary to Jesus, as Ethiopians with afro-hair styles and ebony complexions.[2]

Nubia received the Christian message five centuries after Christ during the A.D. 500s. Nubian Christians testify to the power of the gospel through murals of great Christians and royal families of Nubia. Within their numerous monasteries, they maintained the Christian practices of prayer, consecration, purity and bible study. In 641 the Muslim conquest of North Africa toppled Christian rule and turned Christians into minorities in Egypt and the other kingdoms of North Africa; Nubia and Ethiopia became the only Christian kingdoms left in Africa for many centuries. The Nubian Church remained strong until as late as the 1400s. It is unclear when Christianity lost its vital witness in Nubia, but by the 1700s it had been reduced to isolated villages.[3]

2   C.P. Groves, The Planting of Christianity in Africa, vol. 1 (London: Lutterworth Press, 1948), 109-111; Davis, 7-8; Gamal Mokhter, ed. General History of Africa, vol. 2: Ancient Civilizations in Africa (Berkeley: University of California Press, 1981)

3   Groves, 106-109: Davis, 4-6; Mokhter.

Black Africans also lived throughout Roman-occupied Europe and West Asia. One incident among this population of black Africans in Europe that was immortalized in art and the canonization of the group leader was the witness of St. Maurice and his Theban Legion, a Roman militia. During the third century these Christian soldiers were captured in what is now Switzerland. They were ordered by their captors to deny Christ. They refused and these men were summarily executed for their faith. The power of their witness so impressed future European Christians that accounts of their martyrdom were retold for centuries and artistic depictions of the events were made, displaying them in the beauty of black hue.[4]

Outside the Christian kingdoms of Ethiopia and Nubia, scholars are not aware of Christian communities among black people in Africa until the mid-1400s, prior to the age of Christopher Columbus and the European conquest of the Americas. Around 1457, an African chief, Nomimansa, of the Senegambia area, chose the Christian faith over Islam. He did so after having been lectured on Christianity by Diogo Gomez, a Portuguese Franciscan brother, and on Islam by a Muslim sheikh. In 1489 Behemoi, a chief of the Wolof who lived in the Senegambia area, received baptism in Lisbon, Portugal, along with his 25-member entourage. Earlier, Christian missionaries had informed him of the gospel while he still resided in Senegambia prior to his trip to Europe. When he returned to his chiefdom, he brought with him some Dominican missionaries to bring the Wolof into the Christian faith. However, conflicts arose between Chief Behemoi and the missionaries, which led him to expel them. The culturally sophisticated kingdom of Benin first heard the gospel in 1485 after the king invited missionaries to teach him the Christian faith. While the interest was there, a Christian church was not established until centuries later. [5]

The most vital Christian Church among black Africans in Africa, outside of the ancient Christian Church in Ethiopia and Nubia, had its beginning in 1484. At that time, Diogo Cam, a Portuguese ad-

---

4   Robert E. Hood, Begrimed and Black: Christian Traditions on Blacks and Blackness (Minneapolis: Fortress Press, 1994), 100-101; Davis, 15-16.

5   Groves, 125-127.

venturer, embarked on an exploration to the kingdom of the Kongo in the modern Zaire and Angola region. Cam secured permission to bring some Kongo subjects with him on his return to Portugal so that they could learn Portuguese, thus facilitating their instruction in Christianity. In 1485, upon Cam's return with the Kongoese to Kongo, the king requested that Portuguese missionaries be assigned to his kingdom for the purpose of preaching the gospel. A priest remained in the Kongo as a teacher of the faith for the king and people until the first missionary arrived in 1491. When the missionaries arrived, they met the chief of Sonyo, a chiefdom near the Kongoese kingdom. Upon his request they baptized him. When the missionaries reached the Kongo they also baptized, upon request, the Kongoese king and queen along with their first son, renamed Afonso. The baptismal was held at the royal compound in Mpanzu, the locale of the first church. As instructed, King Nzinga a Nkouwou embraced monogamy. He dismissed all his wives except the queen.

The campaign to make the kingdom Christian produced a backlash from those who held to the old religion. Some of the king's other sons and his former wives were among the dissenters. The opposition convinced the king to cease the campaign and return to the old religion. Thus, the Christian opposition, now with the king's blessings, attacked the small group of Christians and exiled Prince Afonso. A reprise for the Christian minority occurred when the king died. Prince Afonso and his brother Mpanzu battled to determine who would ascend to the throne. According to legend, Afonso won the conflict when a sign, "a solar halo with five flaming swords," appeared confirming to all God's backing of the Christians.[6]

King Afonso reigned over the Kongo from 1506 to 1543. He served Christ throughout his life. He invited more missionaries to the Kongo to teach his people. King Afonso learned Portuguese to better understand the Christian faith and acquaint himself with Portuguese law. A missionary in 1516 commented in a letter to the Portuguese king, Manuel I: "It seems to me that his Christianity is not that of man but of an angel whom the Lord would have sent to

6 Groves, 127-128, Davis 16.

convert his kingdom. I can in fact testify to your Highness that he teaches us and that he knows better than we do the [Bible] prophets, the Gospels...."

King Afonso, according to this missionary, would preach the gospel to the people after the priest had celebrated the mass. Afonso sought to share his great love for God and God's word. Unfortunately, according to Afonso, there existed among the Portuguese some missionaries, some of whom disappointed him with their unrighteousness and immoral lives.

He sponsored the education of his son, Prince Henrique, and other young members of the elite in Lisbon. Like Prince Henrique, some aspired to the ordained ministry. Prior to 1518, Prince Henrique received ordination. In 1521 he was consecrated to the bishopric as an auxiliary to the bishop of Funchal, Madeira Island, with an appointment to Mpanzu, the seat of the Kongo kingdom. The elevation of Afonso's son to the bishopric was an answer to Afonso's prayer that his kingdom would have direct access to the pope without the Portuguese Church as intermediaries. The Christian Church grew under the leadership of ordained Kongoese priests assisting the bishop in the work of the gospel.

During the mid-1500s, four Jesuit missionaries arrived. Within three months of their missionary tour they baptized 5,000 Kongoese. A decade later missionaries reported the existence of whole Christian villages. The Christian Church in Kongo remained vibrant for more than two centuries. While Christianity in the Kongo was hampered by the association of the church with the horrendous slave trade, the Christian church in the Kongo remained vibrant for more than two centuries.[7]

The chiefdom of Angola, a vassal of the Kongoese king, entered the Christian orbit in 1584 with the baptism of the chief and many others. With the settlement of Portuguese in Luanda, Angola, they built a cathedral in Luanda and the bishop was relocated there. Portuguese religious and political attention shifted from Mpanzu to Luanda. During the mid-1500s the Portuguese also participated in the conversion of the chiefs and people in Solafa, Mozamibique,

7   Davis, 16-17; Groves, 129-130.

Sena, and Tete, as well as the king and people of Monomotapa and a kingdom on the east coast of southern Africa.[8]

The Witness in Europe

The second advent of black Africans to Europe occurred sometime before the 1100s in Moslem-occupied Spain and Portugal. They entered as slaves. By the 1400s, some black African Christian men and women in Barcelona and Valencia organized themselves into confraternities. These were lay Christian societies that accepted freed persons and slaves. Confraternities were organizations which white and black Europeans established for "mutual support, mutual security and protection, professional aid, and religious fervor." A few other slaves joined predominately white Christian societies. Listed among these would be Benedict the Moor (1526-1589), the son of Diana and Cristoforo Manassari, who were slaves themselves. As a youth, Benedict's piety was already recognized. After his slaveholder freed him, Benedict first joined a Roman Catholic group of religious men who had dedicated their lives to God. Later he joined a Franciscan order. Benedict was known as a holy man who lived close to God. Although he never became a priest, his gifts as a spiritual counselor led clergy and laity to seek his advise. Even Sicily's governor sought his ministry.[9]

In protestant Europe, African Christians distinguished themselves. One of these was Jacobus Elisa Johannes Capitein, from West Africa, who was enslaved as a mere child. By 1741, he was taken by his slave holder to be educated in Holland. He completed a university education at the University of Leyden by age 25. Afterwards, he received ordination in the Dutch Reformed Church. Among his accomplishments was the translation of some Christian texts into the African language of Fanti. Another commendable African Christian was Anthony William Amo, also of West Africa. His academic career included earning a doctorate from the University at Wittenberg in 1734.[10]

[8] Groves, 130-131.

[9] Davis, 19-20.

[10] Lamin Sanneh, <u>West African Christianity</u>: <u>The Religious Impact</u> (Maryknoll, NY: Orbis Books, 1983), 113.

In the Americas

The presence of African Christians in the Americas began with the arrival of Europeans in 1492. While concentrations of Africans did occur on islands like Cuba and Haiti and in countries like the United States and Brazil, Africans lived throughout the Americas from Argentina to Canada. By the mid-1500s, African Christians were integral members of congregations in such places as the Cathedral in Mexico City. Brazil was the Latin American country where the African Christians had the greatest impact. The Jesuits in Brazil deserve much credit for nurturing Afro-Roman Catholic congregations. They masterfully employed African music and dance to evangelize African slaves. They also relied on African customs to communicate the gospel. This appreciation of African culture encouraged African slaves to adapt their broadly defined culture to Roman Catholic Christianity. The Jesuits committed themselves mostly to establishing black confraternities throughout Brazil during the 1500s. In 1552, they organized Brazil's first black confraternity with newly arrived slaves from West Africa. They received crucial support from the Crown through its 1576 decree "ordering the tithes collected from the newly converted Africans should be used for their churches, lay brotherhoods (confraternities) and their spiritual affairs in Brazil for a space of six years."[11]

The confraternities were autonomous and semi-autonomous organizations that functioned within the Church. Some submitted their charter to the Bishop for approval, while others acted independently. Since most were attached to a parish, we may assume the rector would oversee their activities as he would any other religious activity in his parish. But due to the low priest-parishioner ratio it is doubtful that the priest exercised much control. Confraternities often matched the class and ethnic divisions that society maintained. White, mulattoes, creoles, Africans — free and slave — often joined separate confraternities. Where an African ethnic group like the Angolans or Yorubas was numerous enough to form a confraternity, they did. Confraternities primarily arose in urban Brazil where community life among Africans was more complex

---

[11] Patricia Mulvey, "The Black Lay Brotherhoods of Colonial Brazil, A History," unpub, Ph.D. diss. City University of New York, 1976. 79.

than in the mining regions. Slaves, Brazil's largest African group, constituted the majority of the members in the total confraternity membership of all races.

Confraternities were instrumental in the manumission, or paying for the freedom, of a sizeable minority of slaves. They annually assessed their memberships a designated amount for the "emancipation of members." They offered assistance to freed slaves entering the free African community with clientele for the business of freed members, ranging from barbers to midwives. They also supported members facing expulsion from their craft guilds. Providing pastoral care for their members, especially care for the sick and the aged members, ranked high in the significant services confraternities performed. Since many confraternities had their charters granted by the Portuguese king, they had recourse against injustice. They could petition the king to hear their case. Different Portuguese kings ruled on cases throughout the colonial period. The royal relationship buttressed their advocacy for justice and struggle for the dignity of Africans against slaveholders and clergy. From the 1600s onward, petitions against injustice consistently echoed a theology espousing "the basic equality of all Christians [regardless of race] before the eyes of God."[12]

African Christians in Brazil also organized their Christian life outside of Brazilian society within African-led refugee communities called maroon republics. For instance the refugees in Palmares, the largest maroon settlement in Brazil, erected Catholic churches, "complete with statues of the saints." Palmares was established around 1612 and existed for nearly eighty-three years. Palmares rebuffed "at least twenty major attacks or seizes by the Dutch, the Portuguese and Brazilians before succumbing in 1695." The churches they built served the 20,000 to 30,000 citizens residing in ten areas. Between 1550 and 1822 hundreds of maroon societies were organized in Brazil's forests, mountains, and heaths. These refugees also served as missionaries of sorts introducing the basics of Christianity to Amerindians in the interior, such as the Rio des Mortes during the 1600s and 1700s.[13]

12 Mulvey, 78-79

13 Roger Bastide, The African Religions in Brazil (Baltimore: Johns Hopkins University Press, 1978).

On the North American continent, within the colonies that would later become the United States of America, African Christians appeared, possibly as early as 1618, represented by an African named Angela. Individual Africans were converted until the First Great Awakening. This inter-colony revival resulted in the conversion of a significant number of African slaves in the low country region of South Carolina during the 1740s. By 1758, some scholars note the emergence of the first recorded congregation among African Americans. It was located in Mecklenburg, Virginia. The first noted African American preachers are two Baptists ministers, George Liele and David George. They began preaching between 1773 and 1775 in Silver Bluff, South Carolina, located on the Georgia and South Carolina coast. These preachers were later joined by African American Puritan preacher Lemuel Haynes, Methodist preachers like Richard Allen and Harry Hosier; and, Episcopal preacher Absalom Jones. Lemuel Haynes has the distinction of becoming, in 1782, the first African American to pastor a predominately white congregation. By 1819, Jarena Lee and other women had joined the ranks of the African American preachers. The first African American women, however, would not be ordained until the 1890s.

While the United States advertised itself as a Christian nation, the institution of slavery in the United States undermined this claim. Many African American Christians pondered, like Frederick Douglass, how African slaves could be sold in the slave market as fund-raisers for churches to build edifices, pay clergy, and buy Bibles to send to foreign countries. These African American Christians questioned how a Christian could break up marriages and separate parents from children just to make money. As African American Christians understood more of the gospel, they discovered that slavery was not only unjust, it actually blasphemed God. Slavery's problem, some argued, was that it undid God's creation:[14]

"not robbing a man of his privileges, but of himself;
not loading him with burdens, but making him a beast of
burden; not restraining his liberty, but subverting it;

14 James Melvin Washington, "Origins of the black evangelical Cosmology," Union
Seminary Quarterly Review, 114.

not curtailing rights, but abolishing them; not inflicting
personal injury, but annihilating personality....
uncreating a man, to make him a thing."

During slavery, many African American preachers in the South
were persecuted just because they preached the Gospel. Henry
Evans, Harry Hosier, Andrew Bryan and others endured floggings
and harassment. Some slaveholders were fearful that these preachers were beyond their control, only beholden to God, thus poten-
tially subversive to the social order. After 1831, the limited religious liberty of slaves was repealed by the state governments of
many slave states. These states prohibited African Americans from
preaching and gathering for worship without white supervision.
Many deemed such laws to be anti-biblical and expanded the practice of illegal worship in clandestine meetings where they could
freely pray, preach, sing, dance and praise God.

At the core of the faith of Christian slaves was an affirmation of
life as created by God. Many slave Christians trusted God more
than they feared the terrorism of the slave system. One dimension
of their affirmation of life was a merging of the realm of heaven
with earthly existence. For them, God definitely acted in their world;
Miracles, ranging from personal healing to blinding patrols so run-
away slaves could escape, definitely existed. A second dimension
was a hope against hope, expressed in collective as well as personal terms. Their reading of the Bible taught them that just as
God delivered the Hebrew slaves from Egyptian slavery so would
God deliver African American slaves from American slavery. The
deliverance expected from God was more than personal, it was
collective. A collective or social deliverance from slavery was just
as Bible-based as personal deliverance from sin.

A third expression was the notion of collective innocence. A
doctrine of sin, according to some scholars, was not fully developed among slave Christians. They defined sin in terms of wrongdoing or transgression rather than human depravity. The absence
of an original sin doctrine led them to stress the healing and deliverance capacity of salvation instead of justification and redemption. The lack of an original sin doctrine also had them focus more
on God than on their plight. In Jewish and western Christian traditions the enslavement of a people was often interpreted as a sign of

God's judgment upon a people for their collective sin or violation of God's law. In African American Christianity, however, the enslavement of Africans was interpreted as an evil condition from which God would deliver them. The condition was evil, not them. Their enslavement was not a collective punishment for their collective sin for they were not collectively guilty. Thus, African American Christians declined to blame each other for their plight. Instead, their faith in God freed them to love each other and themselves, as well as to express genuine joy even in the midst of sorrow. Their collective innocence and joy was buttressed by their sense of chosen peoplehood. Their respective African ethnicities — Angolan, Kongoese, Yoruba, Dan, Ashanti — were formed into an identity that became African American.

Integral to the formation of peoplehood among slaves was the biblical concept of chosen people and the slaves's identification with the Hebrew slaves in Egypt and their deliverance from Egyptian slavery. The slaves' sense of peoplehood grounded their identity in God, the Bible, and their humanity. This helped form an alternative identity from that of subhuman and mere property hoisted upon them by slaveholders. They communicated their affirmation of life as created by God through the Christian music genre of spirituals, music that slaves began to compose by the early 1800s. Spirituals, like biblical psalms, captured the full range of human experience — joy, sorrow, delight, anger, praise, fear, awe, anguish, love — and offered it unto God. [15]

During the twentieth century, African American Christians profoundly shaped Christianity in the United States. Pentecostalism as a global movement was born in a small black Holiness congregation, which later became the Apostolic Faith Mission at 312 Azusa Street in Los Angeles, California. Early pentecostalism's commitment to interracial cooperation was a biblical ethic of African American Christianity interjected into the movement. African Americans from other Christian traditions worked to make American Christianity a more just and biblical faith. From leaders such as

15 Albert Raboteau, Slave Religion: The "Invisible Institution" in the Antebellum South (New York and Oxford: Oxford University Press, 1978), 212-288; Sterling Stuckey, Slave Culture: Nationalist Theory & the Foundations of Black America (New York and Oxford; Oxford University Press, 1987), 17-42.

Ida B. Wells and Mary McLeod Bethune to Martin Luther King, Jr. and Jesse Louis Jackson, African American Christians have proclaimed a gospel that can change nations as well as lives. As the twentieth century soon concludes, African American Christianity is recognized for the vitality of its worship noted in its spiritually uplifting gospel music and soul-gripping preaching. It is also noted for the integrity of its Christian witness in urban life and politics, and the relevance of its theology through the writings of black and womanist theologians. These include James Cone, Katie Cannon, Robert Franklin, Cheryl Sanders and Cornel West.[16]

On the African continent, the second wave of missions activity occurred during the late nineteenth century prior to the colonization of Africa by the British, French, Portuguese and Belgians. These colonial powers encouraged the establishment of Protestant, Anglican and Catholic missions, converting a significant portion of the population through their mission schools. Included within the mission activity were African American missionaries from the United States who arrived in the 1800s. From the early 1800s to the early 1900s African American missionaries went to Africa under the auspices of various denominations: Baptist, African Methodist Episcopal, African Methodist Episcopal Zion, and Church of God in Christ.

By the 1890s, some African Christians organized congregations and later denominations distinct from the mission churches because of the racism among the European missionaries. While some of these leaders affiliated their congregations with African American denominations, others founded independent communions, such as the Ethiopian Church, the Kimbanguist Church, the Harrist Church, and the Church of the Lord (Aladura). During the independence struggle within various African countries, Christians led the cry for freedom and justice. According to statisticians, Africa will soon hold the largest concentration of Christians in the world.[17]

---

[16] Gayraud Wilmore, Black Religion and Black Radicalism: An Interpretation of the Religious History of Afro-American People, 2nd ed. (Maryknoll, NY: Orbis Books, 1983)

[17] Sanneh.

While Africans lived in Britain as early as the 1500s and a black community existed as early as the 1700s, congregations of blacks only began to emerge after World War II with the large immigration of Caribbean blacks to the country. Soon after their arrival, these immigrants would be integral in the formation of black British denominations, specifically Pentecostal communions such as the Church of God in Christ, the New Testament Church of God and the Church of God of Prophecy. Musicians in the Church of God in Christ and the New Testament Church of God would be instrumental in the development of gospel choirs in Britain.

During the 1970s as Africans immigrated to Britain in increasing numbers, African-instituted or indigenous churches were formed. These included the Church of the Lord (Aladura) and Celestial Church of Christ. By the 1980s, a cadre of leaders emerged among black churches in Britain. They began to confront white racism in the country and call the churches to a unity in Christ unmarred by the sin of racism. While the largest population of black people and number of black congregations are in Britain, black congregations do exist in Germany, Holland and France.[18]

The Christian witness of Africans and peoples of Africa has extended over the almost two thousand years of the Church. From Africa to the Americas and Asia to Australia, black Christians have preached and lived the gospel of Jesus Christ. Their witness has endured despite persecution, martyrdom, racism, and colonialism, which testifies to the power of the gospel to be heard and lived during oppressive times. From the Nubians and Ethiopians to the African Americans and black Britons, the Christian witness was exhibited in art, music, dance and word. Theirs is a story of faith and struggle working towards the world of justice and peace that God has promised.

---

[18] Bryan Wilson, Religious Sects (New York: Mcgraw-Hill, 1970)

DEVELOPING YOUR RELATIONSHIP WITH GOD

WHO IS GOD

And so we know and rely on the love God has for us. God is love. Whoever lives in love lives in God, and God in him. 1 John 4:16

God is spirit, and his worshipers must worship in spirit and in truth. John 4:24

Moreover, we have all had human fathers who disciplined us and we respected them for it. How much more should we submit to the Father of our spirits and live! Hebrews 12:9

But Moses and Aaron fell facedown and cried out, "O God, God of the spirits of all mankind, will you be angry with the entire assembly when only one man sins?" Numbers 16:22

May the Lord, the God of the spirits of all mankind, appoint a man over this community. Numbers 27:16

GOD IS THE CREATOR OF HEAVEN AND EARTH

In the beginning God created the heavens and the earth. Genesis 1:1

This is what God the Lord says—he who created the heavens and stretched them out, who spread out the earth and all that comes out of it, who gives breath to its people, and life to those who walk on it: Isaiah 42:5

Nature is the art of God. - Sir Thomas Browne

For this is what the Lord says—he who created the heavens, he is God; he who fashioned and made the earth, he founded it; he did

73

not create it to be empty, but formed it to be inhabited—he says: I am the Lord, and there is no other. Isaiah 45:18

GOD IS THE CREATOR OF MANKIND

Then God said, "Let us make man in our image, in our likeness, and let them rule over the fish of the sea and the birds of the air, over the livestock, over all the earth, and over all the creatures that move along the ground." Genesis 1:26

So God created man in his own image, in the image of God he created him; male and female he created them. Genesis 1:27

The Lord God formed the man from the dust of the ground and breathed into his nostrils the breath of life, and the man became a living being. Genesis 2:7

The Lord God said, "It is not good for the man to be alone. I will make a helper suitable for him." Genesis 2:18

So the Lord God caused the man to fall into a deep sleep; and while he was sleeping, he took one of the man's ribs and closed up the place with flesh. Then the Lord God made a woman from the rib he had taken out of the man, and he brought her to the man. The man said, "This is now bone of my bones and flesh of my flesh; she shall be called 'woman,' for she was taken out of man." For this reason a man will leave his father and mother and be united to his wife, and they will become one flesh. Genesis 2:21-24

This is the word of the Lord concerning Israel. The Lord, who stretches out the heavens, who lays the foundation of the earth, and who forms the spirit of man within him, declares. Zechariah 12:1

GOD IS SOVEREIGN AND OMNIPOTENT

His eyes are on the ways of men; he sees their every step.
Job 34:21

How great is God—beyond our understanding! The number of his years is past finding out. Job 36:26

Do you know how the clouds hang poised, those wonders of him who is perfect in knowledge? Job 37:16

He rules forever by his power, his eyes watch the nations—let not the rebellious rise up against him. Selah Psalms 66:7

Lord, you have been our dwelling place throughout all generations. Before the mountains were born or you brought forth the earth and the world, from everlasting to everlasting you are God. You turn men back to dust, saying, Return to dust, O sons of men. For a thousand years in your sight are like a day that has just gone by, or like a watch in the night. Psalms 90:1-4

He makes clouds rise from the ends of the earth; he sends lightning with the rain and brings out the wind from his storehouses.
Psalms 135:7

God is not in time; time is in God. - Myles Munroe

When he thunders, the waters in the heavens roar; he makes clouds rise from the ends of the earth. He sends lightning with the rain and brings out the wind from his storehouses. Jeremiah 10:13

Your kingdom is an everlasting kingdom, and your dominion endures through all generations. The Lord is faithful to all his promises and loving toward all he has made. Psalms 145:13

Great is our Lord and mighty in power; his understanding has no limit. Psalms 147:5

For a man's ways are in full view of the Lord, and he examines all his paths. Proverbs 5:21

The eyes of the Lord are everywhere, keeping watch on the wicked and the good. Proverbs 15:3

The king's heart is in the hand of the Lord; he directs it like a watercourse wherever he pleases. Proverbs 21:1

Before there was a beginning, God was.
- Myles Munroe

Who has gone up to heaven and come down? Who has gathered up the wind in the hollow of his hands? Who has wrapped up the waters in his cloak? Who has established all the ends of the earth? What is his name, and the name of his son? Tell me if you know!
Proverbs 30:4

As you do not know the path of the wind, or how the body is formed in a mother's womb, so you cannot understand the work of God, the Maker of all things. Ecclesiastes 11:5

Before him all the nations are as nothing; they are regarded by him as worthless and less than nothing. To whom, then, will you compare God? What image will you compare him to? Isaiah 40:17-18

"For my thoughts are not your thoughts, neither are your ways my ways," declares the Lord. As the heavens are higher than the earth, so are my ways higher than your ways and my thoughts than your thoughts. Isaiah 55:8-9

This is what the Lord says: "Heaven is my throne, and the earth is my footstool. Where is the house you will build for me? Where will my resting place be? Has not my hand made all these things, and so they came into being?" declares the Lord. This is the one I esteem: he who is humble and contrite in spirit, and trembles at my word. Isaiah 66:1-2

"Am I only a God nearby," declares the Lord, "and not a God far away? Can anyone hide in secret places so that I cannot see him?" declares the Lord. "Do not I fill heaven and earth?" declares the Lord. Jeremiah 23:23-24

He who forms the mountains, creates the wind, and reveals his thoughts to man, he who turns dawn to darkness, and treads the high places of the earth—the Lord God Almighty is his name.
Amos 4:13

For nothing is impossible with God. Luke 1:37

Oh, the depth of the riches of the wisdom and knowledge of God! How unsearchable his judgments, and his paths beyond tracing out!
Romans 11:33

For the foolishness of God is wiser than man's wisdom, and the weakness of God is stronger than man's strength.
1 Corinthians 1:25

When God made his promise to Abraham, since there was no one greater for him to swear by, he swore by himself. Hebrews 6:13

Therefore, since we are receiving a kingdom that cannot be shaken, let us be thankful, and so worship God acceptably with reverence and awe, for our "God is a consuming fire." Hebrews 12:28-29

When I saw him, I fell at his feet as though dead. Then he placed his right hand on me and said: Do not be afraid. I am the First and the Last. I am the Living One; I was dead, and behold I am alive for ever and ever! And I hold the keys of death and Hades.
Revelation 1:17-18

Then I heard what sounded like a great multitude, like the roar of rushing waters and like loud peals of thunder, shouting: Hallelujah! For our Lord God Almighty reigns. Revelation 19:6

I am the Alpha and the Omega, the First and the Last, the Beginning and the End. Revelation 22:13

WHO IS JESUS

He is the image of the invisible God, the firstborn over all creation.
Colossians 1:15

For by him all things were created: things in heaven and on earth, visible and invisible, whether thrones or powers or rulers or authorities; all things were created by him and for him. He is before all things, and in him all things hold together. And he is the head of the body, the church; he is the beginning and the firstborn from among the dead, so that in everything he might have the supremacy. For God was pleased to have all his fullness dwell in him, and through him to reconcile to himself all things, whether things on earth or things in heaven, by making peace through his blood, shed on the cross. Colossians 1:16-19

He was in the world, and though the world was made through him, the world did not recognize him. John 1:10

JESUS IS THE MEDIATOR BETWEEN GOD AND MAN

For there is one God and one mediator between God and men, the man Christ Jesus. 1 Timothy 2:5

77

Jesus answered, "I am the way and the truth and the life. No one comes to the Father except through me." John 14:6

Therefore Jesus said again, I tell you the truth, I am the gate for the sheep. All who ever came before me were thieves and robbers, but the sheep did not listen to them. I am the gate; whoever enters through me will be saved. He will come in and go out, and find pasture. John 10:7-9

No one who denies the Son has the Father; whoever acknowledges the Son has the Father also. 1 John 2:23

And through him to reconcile to himself all things, whether things on earth or things in heaven, by making peace through his blood, shed on the cross. Colossians 1:20

All things have been committed to me by my Father. No one knows the Son except the Father, and no one knows the Father except the Son and those to whom the Son chooses to reveal him.
Matthew 11:27

All that the Father gives me will come to me, and whoever comes to me I will never drive away. For I have come down from heaven not to do my will but to do the will of him who sent me. And this is the will of him who sent me, that I shall lose none of all that he has given me, but raise them up at the last day. For my Father's will is that everyone who looks to the Son and believes in him shall have eternal life, and I will raise him up at the last day. John 6:37-40

JESUS IS THE SON OF GOD

As soon as Jesus was baptized, he went up out of the water. At that moment heaven was opened, and he saw the Spirit of God descending like a dove and lighting on him. And a voice from heaven said, "This is my Son, whom I love; with him I an well pleased.
Matthew 3:16-17

Children born not of natural descent, nor of human decision or a husband's will, but born of God. John 1:13

For the one whom God has sent speaks the words of God, for God gives the Spirit without limit. John 3:34

I came from the Father and entered the world; now I am leaving the world and going back to the Father. John 16:28

And who through the Spirit of holiness was declared with power to be the Son of God by his resurrection from the dead: Jesus Christ our Lord. Romans 1:4

JESUS IS GOD

I and the Father are one. John 10:30

Beyond all question, the mystery of godliness is great: He appeared in a body, was vindicated by the Spirit, was seen by angels, was preached among the nations, was believed on in the world, was taken up in glory. 1 Timothy 3:16

But whoever drinks the water I give him will never thirst. Indeed, the water I give him will become in him a spring of water welling up to eternal life. John 4:14

For this reason the Jews tried all the harder to kill him; not only was he breaking the Sabbath, but he was even calling God his own Father, making himself equal with God. John 5:18

When he looks at me, he sees the one who sent me. John 12:45

Then Jesus declared, I am the bread of life. He who comes to me will never go hungry, and he who believes in me will never be thirsty. John 6:35

But if I do it, even though you do not believe me, believe the miracles, that you may know and understand that the Father is in me, and I in the Father. John 10:38

But in these last days he has spoken to us by his Son, whom he appointed heir of all things, and through whom he made the universe. The Son is the radiance of God's glory and the exact representation of his being, sustaining all things by his powerful word. After he had provided purification for sins, he sat down at the right hand of the Majesty in heaven. Hebrews 1:2-3

JESUS EXISTED AS GOD BEFORE HE CAME TO EARTH

John testifies concerning him. He cries out, saying, "This was he of whom I said, 'He who comes after me has surpassed me because he was before me.'" John 1:15

The one who comes from above is above all; the one who is from the earth belongs to the earth, and speaks as one from the earth. The one who comes from heaven is above all. John 3:31

Who, being in very nature God, did not consider equality with God something to be grasped, but made himself nothing, taking the very nature of a servant, being made in human likeness. And being found in appearance as a man, he humbled himself and became obedient to death—even death on a cross! Therefore God exalted him to the highest place and gave him the name that is above every name,
Philippians 2:6-9

Then God said, "Let us make man in our image, in our likeness, and let them rule over the fish of the sea and the birds of the air, over the livestock, over all the earth, and over all the creatures that move along the ground." Genesis 1:26

But you remain the same, and your years will never end.
Psalms 102:27

In the beginning was the Word, and the Word was with God, and the Word was God. John 1:1

What about the one whom the Father set apart as his very own and sent into the world? Why then do you accuse me of blasphemy because I said, 'I am God's Son'? John 10:36

Through him all things were made; without him nothing was made that has been made. John 1:3

The Word became flesh and made his dwelling among us. We have seen his glory, the glory of the One and Only, who came from the Father, full of grace and truth. John 1:14

Your father Abraham rejoiced at the thought of seeing my day; he saw it and was glad. "You are not yet fifty years old," the Jews said to him, "and you have seen Abraham!" "I tell you the truth," Jesus answered, "before Abraham was born, I am!" John 8:56-58

Father, I want those you have given me to be with me where I am, and to see my glory, the glory you have given me because you loved me before the creation of the world. John 17:24

He is the image of the invisible God, the firstborn over all creation. For by him all things were created: things in heaven and on earth, visible and invisible, whether thrones or powers or rulers or authorities; all things were created by him and for him. He is before all things, and in him all things hold together. Colossians 1:15-17

The Son is the radiance of God's glory and the exact representation of his being, sustaining all things by his powerful word. After he had provided purification for sins, he sat down at the right hand of the Majesty in heaven. Hebrews 1:3

But about the Son he says, "Your throne, O God, will last for ever and ever, and righteousness will be the scepter of your kingdom. You have loved righteousness and hated wickedness; therefore God, your God, has set you above your companions by anointing you with the oil of joy." He also says, "In the beginning, O Lord, you laid the foundations of the earth, and the heavens are the work of your hands. They will perish, but you remain; they will all wear out like a garment. You will roll them up like a robe; like a garment they will be changed. But you remain the same, and your years will never end." Hebrews 1:8-12

Jesus Christ is the same yesterday and today and forever.
Hebrews 13:8

I am the Alpha and the Omega, the First and the Last, the Beginning and the End. Revelation 22:13

JESUS IS THE WORD OF GOD

In the beginning was the Word, and the Word was with God, and the Word was God. John 1:1

The Word became flesh and made his dwelling among us. We have seen his glory, the glory of the One and Only, who came from the Father, full of grace and truth. John 1:14

For there are three that bear record in heaven, the Father, the Word, and the Holy Ghost: and these three are one. 1 John 5:7 KJV

He is dressed in a robe dipped in blood, and his name is the Word of God. Revelation 19:13

JESUS IS WISDOM

But to those whom God has called, both Jews and Greeks, Christ the power of God and the wisdom of God. 1 Corinthians 1:24

It is because of him that you are in Christ Jesus, who has become for us wisdom from God—that is, our righteousness, holiness and redemption. 1 Corinthians 1:30

In whom are hidden all the treasures of wisdom and knowledge.
Colossians 2:3

THE TRINITY (THE FATHER, SON, AND THE HOLY GHOST)

Then God said, "Let **us** make man in our image, in **our** likeness, and let them rule over the fish of the sea and the birds of the air, over the livestock, over all the earth, and over all the creatures that move along the ground." Genesis 1:26

And the Lord God said, "The man has now become like one of **us**, knowing good and evil. He must not be allowed to reach out his hand and take also from the tree of life and eat, and live forever."
Genesis 3:22

"Come near me and listen to this: "From the first announcement I have not spoken in secret; at the time it happens, I am there." And now the Sovereign **Lord** has sent me, with his **Spirit**. Isaiah 48:16

Therefore go and make disciples of all nations, baptizing them in the name of the **Father** and of the **Son** and of the **Holy Spirit**.
Matthew 28:19

For the one whom God has sent speaks the words of God, for God gives the **Spirit** without limit. The **Father** loves the **Son** and has placed everything in his hands. John 3:34-35

I and the **Father** are one. John 10:30

And I will ask the **Father**, and he will give you another Counselor to be with you forever—the **Spirit of truth**. The world cannot accept him, because it neither sees him nor knows him. But you know him, for he lives with you and will be in you. John 14:16-17

But the Counselor, the **Holy Spirit**, whom the **Father** will send in my name, will teach you all things and will remind you of everything I have said to you. John 14:26

When the Counselor comes, whom I will send to you from the **Father**, the **Spirit** of truth who goes out from the Father, he will testify about **me**. John 15:26

Do you not know that your body is a temple of the Holy Spirit, who is in you, whom you have received from God? You are not your own. 1 Corinthians 6:19

Yet for us there is but one God, the **Father**, from whom all things came and for whom we live; and there is but one Lord, **Jesus Christ**, through whom all things came and through whom we live.
1 Corinthians 8:6

The sun, in my opinion, is the best example of the Trinity. God is the sun; Jesus is the light of the sun; and the Holy Ghost is the heat of the sun. - Benny Hinn

Now it is **God** who makes both us and you stand firm in **Christ**. He anointed us, set his seal of ownership on us, and put his **Spirit** in our hearts as a deposit, guaranteeing what is to come.
2 Corinthians 1:21-22

May the grace of the Lord **Jesus Christ**, and the love of **God**, and the fellowship of the **Holy Spirit** be with you all.
2 Corinthians 13:14

But when the time had fully come, **God** sent his **Son**, born of a woman, born under law,   Because you are sons, God sent the **Spirit** of his Son into our hearts, the Spirit who calls out, "Abba, Father."
Galatians 4:4,6

My purpose is that they may be encouraged in heart and united in love, so that they may have the full riches of complete understanding, in order that they may know the mystery of **God**, namely, **Christ**. Colossians 2:2

But we ought always to thank **God** for you, brothers loved by the Lord, because from the beginning God chose you to be saved through the sanctifying work of the **Spirit** and through belief in the truth. He called you to this through our gospel, that you might share in the glory of our Lord **Jesus Christ**.

2 Thessalonians 2:13-14

But when the kindness and love of **God our Savior** appeared, he saved us, not because of righteous things we had done, but because of his mercy. He saved us through the washing of rebirth and renewal by the **Holy Spirit**, whom he poured out on us generously through **Jesus Christ our Savior**. Titus 3:4-6

Who have been chosen according to the foreknowledge of God the **Father**, through the sanctifying work of the **Spirit**, for obedience to **Jesus Christ** and sprinkling by his blood: Grace and peace be yours in abundance. 1 Peter 1:2

For **Christ** died for sins once for all, the righteous for the unrighteous, to bring you to **God**. He was put to death in the body but made alive by the **Spirit**. 1 Peter 3:18

This is the one who came by water and blood—**Jesus Christ**. He did not come by water only, but by water and blood. And it is the Spirit who testifies, because the **Spirit** is the truth. For there are three that testify. 1 John 5:6-7

HOW TO REACH GOD

Jesus answered, "I am the way and the truth and the life. No one comes to the Father except through me." John 14:6

For there is one God and one mediator between God and men, the man Christ Jesus. 1 Timothy 2:5

Therefore Jesus said again, "I tell you the truth, I am the gate for the sheep. All who ever came before me were thieves and robbers, but the sheep did not listen to them. I am the gate; whoever enters through me will be saved. He will come in and go out, and find pasture. John 10:7-9

No one who denies the Son has the Father; whoever acknowledges the Son has the Father also. 1 John 2:23

He who has the Son has life; he who does not have the Son of God does not have life. 1 John 5:12

HOW TO LOVE AND PLEASE GOD

If you love me, you will obey what I command. John 14:15

Whoever has my commands and obeys them, he is the one who loves me. He who loves me will be loved by my Father, and I too will love him and show myself to him. John 14:21

Jesus replied, "If anyone loves me, he will obey my teaching. My Father will love him, and we will come to him and make our home with him. He who does not love me will not obey my teaching. These words you hear are not my own; they belong to the Father who sent me. John 14:23-24

If you obey my commands, you will remain in my love, just as I have obeyed my Father's commands and remain in his love.
John 15:10

You are my friends if you do what I command. John 15:14

This is how we know that we love the children of God: by loving God and carrying out his commands. 1 John 5:2

This is love for God: to obey his commands. And his commands are not burdensome. 1 John 5:3

COMMUNICATING WITH GOD

Yet a time is coming and has now come when the true worshipers will worship the Father in spirit and truth, for they are the kind of worshipers the Father seeks. God is spirit, and his worshipers must worship in spirit and in truth. John 4:23-24

Let us come before him with thanksgiving and extol him with music and song. Psalms 95:2

Enter his gates with thanksgiving and his courts with praise; give thanks to him and praise his name. Psalms 100:4

For through him we both have access to the Father by one Spirit. Ephesians 2:18

In him and through faith in him we may approach God with freedom and confidence. Ephesians 3:12

Life for the Christian is a dialogue with God.
- J . H. Oldham

Let us then approach the throne of grace with confidence, so that we may receive mercy and find grace to help us in our time of need. Hebrews 4:16

Therefore, brothers, since we have confidence to enter the Most Holy Place by the blood of Jesus. Hebrews 10:19

Here I am! I stand at the door and knock. If anyone hears my voice and opens the door, I will come in and eat with him, and he with me. Revelation 3:20

PRAISING GOD

I will give thanks to the Lord because of his righteousness and will sing praise to the name of the Lord Most High. Psalms 7:17

The Lord is my strength and my shield; my heart trusts in him, and I am helped. My heart leaps for joy and I will give thanks to him in song. Psalms 28:7

I will extol the Lord at all times; his praise will always be on my lips. Psalms 34:1

My tongue will speak of your righteousness and of your praises all day long. Psalms 35:28

In God we make our boast all day long, and we will praise your name forever. Selah Psalms 44:8

Great is the Lord, and most worthy of praise, in the city of our God, his holy mountain. Psalms 48:1

O Lord, open my lips, and my mouth will declare your praise.
Psalms 51:15

In God, whose word I praise, in God I trust; I will not be afraid. What can mortal man do to me? Psalms 56:4

In God, whose word I praise, in the Lord, whose word I praise.
Psalms 56:10

Then will I ever sing praise to your name and fulfill my vows day after day. Psalms 61:8

Because your love is better than life, my lips will glorify you.
Psalms 63:3

Shout with joy to God, all the earth! Sing the glory of his name; make his praise glorious! Psalms 66:1-2

May the peoples praise you, O God; may all the peoples praise you. Psalms 67:3

Sing to God, O kingdoms of the earth, sing praise to the Lord, Selah Psalms 68:32

I will praise God's name in song and glorify him with thanksgiving. Psalms 69:30

Let heaven and earth praise him, the seas and all that move in them.
Psalms 69:34

My mouth is filled with your praise, declaring your splendor all day long. Psalms 71:8

But as for me, I will always have hope; I will praise you more and more. Psalms 71:14

I will praise you, O Lord my God, with all my heart; I will glorify your name forever. Psalms 86:12

The heavens praise your wonders, O Lord, your faithfulness too, in the assembly of the holy ones. Psalms 89:5

It is good to praise the Lord and make music to your name, O Most High, to proclaim your love in the morning and your faithfulness at night, to the music of the ten-stringed lyre and the melody of the harp. For you make me glad by your deeds, O Lord; I sing for joy at the works of your hands. Psalms 92:1-4

Shout for joy to the Lord, all the earth, burst into jubilant song with music. Psalms 98:4

Shout for joy to the Lord, all the earth. Worship the Lord with gladness; come before him with joyful songs. Psalms 100:1-2

Enter his gates with thanksgiving and his courts with praise; give thanks to him and praise his name. For the Lord is good and his love endures forever; his faithfulness continues through all generations. Psalms 100:4-5

My heart is steadfast, O God; I will sing and make music with all my soul. Awake, harp and lyre! I will praise you, O Lord, among the nations; I will sing of you among the peoples. Psalms 108:1-3

Praise the Lord. I will extol the Lord with all my heart in the council of the upright and in the assembly. Psalms 111:1

Praise the Lord. Praise, O servants of the Lord, praise the name of the Lord. Let the name of the Lord be praised, both now and forevermore. From the rising of the sun to the place where it sets, the name of the Lord is to be praised. Psalms 113:1-3

Praise the Lord, all you nations; extol him, all you peoples. For great is his love toward us, and the faithfulness of the Lord endures forever. Praise the Lord. Psalms 117:1-2

I will praise you with an upright heart as I learn your righteous laws. Psalms 119:7

Seven times a day I praise you for your righteous laws.
Psalms 119:164

Praise the Lord, for the Lord is good; sing praise to his name, for that is pleasant. Psalms 135:3

I will praise you, O Lord, with all my heart; before the "gods" I will sing your praise. I will bow down toward your holy temple and will praise your name for your love and your faithfulness, for you have exalted above all things your name and your word.
Psalms 138:1-2

May all the kings of the earth praise you, O Lord, when they hear the words of your mouth. Psalms 138:4

Great is the Lord and most worthy of praise; his greatness no one can fathom. Psalms 145:3

Praise the Lord. How good it is to sing praises to our God, how pleasant and fitting to praise him! Psalms 147:1

Praise the Lord. Praise the Lord from the heavens, praise him in the heights above. Praise him, all his angels, praise him, all his heavenly hosts. Praise him, sun and moon, praise him, all you shining stars. Praise him, you highest heavens and you waters above the skies. Let them praise the name of the Lord, for he commanded and they were created. He set them in place for ever and ever; he gave a decree that will never pass away. Praise the Lord from the earth, you great sea creatures and all ocean depths, lightning and hail, snow and clouds, stormy winds that do his bidding, you mountains and all hills, fruit trees and all cedars, wild animals and all cattle, small creatures and flying birds, kings of the earth and all nations, you princes and all rulers on earth, young men and maidens, old men and children. Let them praise the name of the Lord, for his name alone is exalted; his splendor is above the earth and the heavens. Psalms 148:1-13

Praise the Lord. Praise God in his sanctuary; praise him in his mighty heavens. Praise him for his acts of power; praise him for his surpassing greatness. Praise him with the sounding of the trumpet, praise him with the harp and lyre, praise him with tambourine and dancing, praise him with the strings and flute, praise him with the clash of cymbals, praise him with resounding cymbals. Let everything that has breath praise the Lord. Praise the Lord.

Psalms 150:1-6

O Lord, you are my God; I will exalt you and praise your name, for in perfect faithfulness you have done marvelous things, things planned long ago. Isaiah 25:1

And provide for those who grieve in Zion—to bestow on them a crown of beauty instead of ashes, the oil of gladness instead of mourning, and a garment of praise instead of a spirit of despair.

They will be called oaks of righteousness, a planting of the Lord for the display of his splendor. Isaiah 61:3

Do you hear what these children are saying? they asked him. "Yes," replied Jesus, "have you never read, "'From the lips of children and infants you have ordained praise'?" Matthew 21:16

Through Jesus, therefore, let us continually offer to God a sacrifice of praise—the fruit of lips that confess his name. Hebrews 13:15

Then a voice came from the throne, saying: "Praise our God, all you his servants, you who fear him, both small and great!"
Revelation 19:5

WORSHIPPING GOD

Do not worship any other god, for the Lord, whose name is Jealous, is a jealous God. Exodus 34:14

All the ends of the earth will remember and turn to the Lord, and all the families of the nations will bow down before him.
Psalms 22:27

Ascribe to the Lord the glory due his name; worship the Lord in the splendor of his holiness. Psalms 29:2

All the earth bows down to you; they sing praise to you, they sing praise to your name. Selah Psalms 66:4

All the nations you have made will come and worship before you, O Lord; they will bring glory to your name. Psalms 86:9

Come, let us bow down in worship, let us kneel before the Lord our Maker. Psalms 95:6

Exalt the Lord our God and worship at his footstool; he is holy.
Psalms 99:5

Exalt the Lord our God and worship at his holy mountain, for the Lord our God is holy. Psalms 99:9

Let us go to his dwelling place; let us worship at his footstool.
Psalms 132:7

And asked, "Where is the one who has been born king of the Jews? We saw his star in the east and have come to worship him.
Matthew 2:2

Jesus said to him, "Away from me, Satan! For it is written: 'Worship the Lord your God, and serve him only.'" Matthew 4:10

Suddenly Jesus met them. "Greetings," he said. They came to him, clasped his feet and worshiped him. Matthew 28:9

When they saw him, they worshiped him; but some doubted.
Matthew 28:17

Yet a time is coming and has now come when the true worshipers will worship the Father in spirit and truth, for they are the kind of worshipers the Father seeks. God is spirit, and his worshipers must worship in spirit and in truth." John 4:23-24

Our Lord approved neither idol worship or idle worship but ideal worship in Spirit and truth. - Vance Havner

For it is we who are the circumcision, we who worship by the Spirit of God, who glory in Christ Jesus, and who put no confidence in the flesh. Philippians 3:3

The twenty-four elders fall down before him who sits on the throne, and worship him who lives for ever and ever. They lay their crowns before the throne and say: "You are worthy, our Lord and God, to receive glory and honor and power, for you created all things, and by your will they were created and have their being."
Revelation 4:10-11

The four living creatures said, "Amen," and the elders fell down and worshiped. Revelation 5:14

All the angels were standing around the throne and around the elders and the four living creatures. They fell down on their faces before the throne and worshiped God, saying: "Amen! Praise and glory and wisdom and thanks and honor and power and strength be to our God for ever and ever. Amen!" Revelation 7:11-12

And the twenty-four elders, who were seated on their thrones before God, fell on their faces and worshiped God. Revelation 11:16

91

He said in a loud voice, "Fear God and give him glory, because the hour of his judgment has come. Worship him who made the heavens, the earth, the sea and the springs of water." Revelation 14:7

THE FEAR OF THE LORD

The fear of the Lord is pure, enduring forever. The ordinances of the Lord are sure and altogether righteous. Psalms 19:9

The fear of the Lord is the beginning of wisdom; all who follow his precepts have good understanding. To him belongs eternal praise. Psalms 111:10

Then you will understand the fear of the Lord and find the knowledge of God. Proverbs 2:5

The fear of the Lord is the beginning of wisdom, and knowledge of the Holy One is understanding. Proverbs 9:10

The fear of the Lord adds length to life, but the years of the wicked are cut short. Proverbs 10:27

He who fears the Lord has a secure fortress, and for his children it will be a refuge. The fear of the Lord is a fountain of life, turning a man from the snares of death. Proverbs 14:26-27

The fear of the Lord teaches a man wisdom, and humility comes before honor. Proverbs 15:33

To fear the Lord is to hate evil; I hate pride and arrogance, evil behavior and perverse speech. Proverbs 8:13

I fear God, yet I am not afraid of him. - Thomas Browne

Better a little with the fear of the Lord than great wealth with turmoil. Proverbs 15:16

Through love and faithfulness sin is atoned for; through the fear of the Lord a man avoids evil. Proverbs 16:6

The fear of the Lord leads to life: Then one rests content, untouched by trouble. Proverbs 19:23

Humility and the fear of the Lord bring wealth and honor and life.
Proverbs 22:4

Since we have these promises, dear friends, let us purify ourselves
from everything that contaminates body and spirit, perfecting holiness out of reverence for God. 2 Corinthians 7:1

Do not let your heart envy sinners, but always be zealous for the
fear of the Lord. Proverbs 23:17

> *To fear God is to stand in awe of him; to be afraid of
> God is to run away from him. - Carroll E. Simcox*

TRUSTING GOD

My God is my rock, in whom I take refuge, my shield and the horn
of my salvation. He is my stronghold, my refuge and my savior—
from violent men you save me. 2 Samuel 22:3

As for God, his way is perfect; the word of the Lord is flawless. He
is a shield for all who take refuge in him. 2 Samuel 22:31

Will you rely on him for his great strength? Will you leave your
heavy work to him? Job 39:11

Offer right sacrifices and trust in the Lord. Psalms 4:5

But let all who take refuge in you be glad; let them ever sing for
joy. Spread your protection over them, that those who love your
name may rejoice in you. Psalms 5:11

O Lord my God, I take refuge in you; save and deliver me from all
who pursue me. Psalms 7:1

Those who know your name will trust in you, for you, Lord, have
never forsaken those who seek you. Psalms 9:10

But I trust in your unfailing love; my heart rejoices in your salvation. Psalms 13:5

Keep me safe, O God, for in you I take refuge. Psalms 16:1

The Lord is my rock, my fortress and my deliverer; my God is my
rock, in whom I take refuge. He is my shield and the horn of my
salvation, my stronghold. Psalms 18:2

As for God, his way is perfect; the word of the Lord is flawless. He is a shield for all who take refuge in him. Psalms 18:30

Vindicate me, O Lord, for I have led a blameless life; I have trusted in the Lord without wavering. Psalms 26:1

> *We do not usually learn that Christ is all we need until we reach that place where He is all we have!*
> *- Vance Havner*

The Lord is my strength and my shield; my heart trusts in him, and I am helped. My heart leaps for joy and I will give thanks to him in song. Psalms 28:7

In you, O Lord, I have taken refuge; let me never be put to shame; deliver me in your righteousness. Psalms 31:1

Many are the woes of the wicked, but the Lord's unfailing love surrounds the man who trusts in him. Psalms 32:10

Taste and see that the Lord is good; blessed is the man who takes refuge in him. Psalms 34:8

Trust in the Lord and do good; dwell in the land and enjoy safe pasture. Psalms 37:3

Commit your way to the Lord; trust in him and he will do this.
Psalms 37:5

Blessed is the man who makes the Lord his trust, who does not look to the proud, to those who turn aside to false gods.
Psalms 40:4

But I am like an olive tree flourishing in the house of God; I trust in God's unfailing love for ever and ever. Psalms 52:8

When I am afraid, I will trust in you. Psalms 56:3

Trust in him at all times, O people; pour out your hearts to him, for God is our refuge. Selah Psalms 62:8

In you, O Lord, I have taken refuge; let me never be put to shame.
Psalms 71:1

I will say of the Lord, "He is my refuge and my fortress, my God, in whom I trust." Psalms 91:2

Jesus does not say, "There is no storm." He says, "I am here, do not toss but trust." - Vance Havner

Those who trust in the Lord are like Mount Zion, which cannot be shaken but endures forever. Psalms 125:1

Trust in the Lord with all your heart and lean not on your own understanding. Proverbs 3:5

Surely God is my salvation; I will trust and not be afraid. The Lord, is my strength and my song; he has become my salvation.
Isaiah 12:2

FAITH IN GOD AND HIS WORD

GREAT FAITH

Jesus turned and saw her. "Take heart, daughter," he said, "your faith has healed you." And the woman was healed from that moment. Matthew 9:22

Then Jesus answered, "Woman, you have great faith! Your request is granted." And her daughter was healed from that very hour.
Matthew 15:28

He said to her, "Daughter, your faith has healed you. Go in peace and be freed from your suffering." Mark 5:34

When Jesus heard this, he was amazed at him, and turning to the crowd following him, he said, "I tell you, I have not found such great faith even in Israel." Luke 7:9

"Where is your faith?" he asked his disciples. In fear and amazement they asked one another, "Who is this? He commands even the winds and the water, and they obey him." Luke 8:25

As it is written: "I have made you a father of many nations." He is our father in the sight of God, in whom he believed—the God who gives life to the dead and calls things that are not as though they

95

were. Against all hope, Abraham in hope believed and so became the father of many nations, just as it had been said to him, "So shall your offspring be." Without weakening in his faith, he faced the fact that his body was as good as dead—since he was about a hundred years old—and that Sarah's womb was also dead. Yet he did not waver through unbelief regarding the promise of God, but was strengthened in his faith and gave glory to God, being fully persuaded that God had power to do what he had promised.

Romans 4:17-21

By faith Abraham, even though he was past age—and Sarah herself was barren—was enabled to become a father because he considered him faithful who had made the promise. And so from this one man, and he as good as dead, came descendants as numerous as the stars in the sky and as countless as the sand on the seashore. All these people were still living by faith when they died. They did not receive the things promised; they only saw them and welcomed them from a distance. And they admitted that they were aliens and strangers on earth. Hebrews 11:11-13

PRINCIPLES OF FAITH

He replied, "Because you have so little faith. I tell you the truth, if you have faith as small as a mustard seed, you can say to this mountain, 'Move from here to there' and it will move. Nothing will be impossible for you." Matthew 17:20

"Have faith in God," Jesus answered. "I tell you the truth, if anyone says to this mountain, 'Go, throw yourself into the sea,' and does not doubt in his heart but believes that what he says will happen, it will be done for him. Therefore I tell you, whatever you ask for in prayer, believe that you have received it, and it will be yours.

Mark 11:22-24

Then he said to Thomas, "Put your finger here; see my hands. Reach out your hand and put it into my side. Stop doubting and believe."

John 20:27

Then Jesus told him, "Because you have seen me, you have believed; blessed are those who have not seen and yet have believed."

John 20:29

But the man who has doubts is condemned if he eats, because his eating is not from faith; and everything that does not come from faith is sin. Romans 14:23

Nothing is more disastrous than to study faith, analyze faith, make noble resolves of faith, but never actually make the leap of faith. - Vance Havner

So we fix our eyes not on what is seen, but on what is unseen. For what is seen is temporary, but what is unseen is eternal.
2 Corinthians 4:18

We live by faith, not by sight. 2 Corinthians 5:7

Let us hold unswervingly to the hope we profess, for he who promised is faithful. Hebrews 10:23

Now faith is being sure of what we hope for and certain of what we do not see. Hebrews 11:1

By faith we understand that the universe was formed at God's command, so that what is seen was not made out of what was visible.
Hebrews 11:3

Because you know that the testing of your faith develops perseverance. James 1:3

Though you have not seen him, you love him; and even though you do not see him now, you believe in him and are filled with an inexpressible and glorious joy, for you are receiving the goal of your faith, the salvation of your souls. 1 Peter 1:8-9

FAITH IN ACTION

What good is it, my brothers, if a man claims to have faith but has no deeds? Can such faith save him? Suppose a brother or sister is without clothes and daily food. If one of you says to him, "Go, I wish you well; keep warm and well fed," but does nothing about his physical needs, what good is it? In the same way, faith by itself, if it is not accompanied by action, is dead. But someone will say, "You have faith; I have deeds." Show me your faith without deeds, and I will show you my faith by what I do. You believe that there is one God. Good! Even the demons believe that—and shudder. You foolish man, do you want evidence that faith without deeds is useless? Was not our ancestor Abraham considered righteous for what he did when he offered his son Isaac on the altar? You see that his faith and his actions were working together, and his faith was made complete by what he did. And the scripture was fulfilled that says, "Abraham believed God, and it was credited to him as righteousness," and he was called God's friend. You see that a person is justified by what he does and not by faith alone. In the same way, was not even Rahab the prostitute considered righteous for what she did when she gave lodging to the spies and sent them off in a different direction? As the body without the spirit is dead, so faith without deeds is dead. James 2:14-26

It's not how much you know, but it is what you do with what you know. - Ramiro Angulo

Early in the morning, as he was on his way back to the city, he was hungry. Seeing a fig tree by the road, he went up to it but found nothing on it except leaves. Then he said to it, "May you never bear fruit again!" Immediately the tree withered. When the disciples saw this, they were amazed. "How did the fig tree wither so quickly?" they asked. Matthew 21:18-20

Seeing in the distance a fig tree in leaf, he went to find out if it had any fruit. When he reached it, he found nothing but leaves, because it was not the season for figs. Then he said to the tree, "May no one ever eat fruit from you again." And his disciples heard him say it. Mark 11:13-14

In the morning, as they went along, they saw the fig tree withered from the roots. Peter remembered and said to Jesus, "Rabbi, look! The fig tree you cursed has withered!" Mark 11:20-21

In addition to all this, take up the shield of faith, with which you can extinguish all the flaming arrows of the evil one.

Ephesians 6:16

Fight the good fight of the faith. Take hold of the eternal life to which you were called when you made your good confession in the presence of many witnesses. 1 Timothy 6:12

If anyone has material possessions and sees his brother in need but has no pity on him, how can the love of God be in him? Dear children, let us not love with words or tongue but with actions and in truth. 1 John 3:17-18

Faith is a fact. Faith is an act. - Morris Cerrilo

A LIFESTYLE OF FAITH

For in the gospel a righteousness from God is revealed, a righteousness that is by faith from first to last, just as it is written: "The righteous will live by faith." Romans 1:17

Clearly no one is justified before God by the law, because, "The righteous will live by faith." Galatians 3:11

But my righteous one will live by faith. And if he shrinks back, I will not be pleased with him. Hebrews 10:38

THROUGH FAITH

Through whom we have gained access by faith into this grace in which we now stand. And we rejoice in the hope of the glory of God. Romans 5:2

For it is by grace you have been saved, through faith—and this not from yourselves, it is the gift of God. Ephesians 2:8

He redeemed us in order that the blessing given to Abraham might come to the Gentiles through Christ Jesus, so that by faith we might receive the promise of the Spirit. Galatians 3:14

OBTAINING FAITH

Let us fix our eyes on Jesus, the author and perfecter of our faith, who for the joy set before him endured the cross, scorning its shame, and sat down at the right hand of the throne of God. Hebrews 12:2

Consequently, faith comes from hearing the message, and the message is heard through the word of Christ. Romans 10:17

For by the grace given me I say to every one of you: Do not think of yourself more highly than you ought, but rather think of yourself with sober judgment, in accordance with the measure of faith God has given you. Romans 12:3

It is written: "I believed; therefore I have spoken." With that same spirit of faith we also believe and therefore speak.
2 Corinthians 4:13

ACCORDING TO YOUR FAITH

Then he touched their eyes and said, "According to your faith will it be done to you." Matthew 9:29

Then Jesus answered, "Woman, you have great faith! Your request is granted." And her daughter was healed from that very hour.
Matthew 15:28

He said to her, "Daughter, your faith has healed you. Go in peace and be freed from your suffering." Mark 5:34

"Go," said Jesus, "your faith has healed you." Immediately he received his sight and followed Jesus along the road. Mark 10:52

HINDRANCE TO YOUR FAITH

DOUBT AND UNBELIEF

He could not do any miracles there, except lay his hands on a few sick people and heal them. And he was amazed at their lack of faith. Then Jesus went around teaching from village to village.
Mark 6:5-6

Yet he did not waver through unbelief regarding the promise of God, but was strengthened in his faith and gave glory to God,
Romans 4:20

Granted. But they were broken off because of unbelief, and you stand by faith. Do not be arrogant, but be afraid. Romans 11:20

That is true. But they were broken (pruned) off because of their unbelief—their lack of real faith, and you are established through faith—because you do believe. So do not become proud and conceited, but rather stand in awe and be reverently afraid.
Romans 11:20 AMP

See to it, brothers, that none of you has a sinful, unbelieving heart that turns away from the living God. Hebrews 3:12

> *Negative, uncertain, doubtful living poisons the body, mind, and spirit; fills insane asylums, penitentiaries, graves, and hell itself. - Vance Havner*

[Therefore beware,] brethren; take care lest there be in any one of you a wicked, unbelieving heart—which refuses to cleave to, trust in and rely on Him—leading you to turn away and desert or stand aloof from the living God. Hebrews 3:12 AMP

DOUBT AND UNBELIEF STOPS THE POWER OF GOD IN YOUR LIFE

And he did not do many miracles there because of their lack of faith. Matthew 13:58

> *Doubt's number one tactic is to invade your mind with thoughts and imaginations that are contrary to the Word of God or to your prayer of faith. Resist and attack doubt every time it comes to you and audibly confess God's Word.*

Jesus rebuked the demon, and it came out of the boy, and he was healed from that moment. Then the disciples came to Jesus in private and asked, "Why couldn't we drive it out?" He replied, "Because you have so little faith. I tell you the truth, if you have faith as small as a mustard seed, you can say to this mountain, 'Move from here to there' and it will move. Nothing will be impossible for you." Matthew 17:18-20

So we see that they were not able to enter, because of their unbelief. Hebrews 3:19

So we see that they were not able to enter [into His rest] because of their unwillingness to adhere to and trust and rely on God—unbelief had shut them out. Hebrews 3:19 AMP

DOUBT AND UNBELIEF FRUSTRATES GOD

Later Jesus appeared to the Eleven as they were eating; he rebuked them for their lack of faith and their stubborn refusal to believe those who had seen him after he had risen. Mark 16:14

If that is how God clothes the grass of the field, which is here today, and tomorrow is thrown into the fire, how much more will he clothe you, O you of little faith! And do not set your heart on what you will eat or drink; do not worry about it. Luke 12:28-29

But when he asks, he must believe and not doubt, because he who doubts is like a wave of the sea, blown and tossed by the wind. That man should not think he will receive anything from the Lord; he is a double-minded man, unstable in all he does. James 1:6-8

Only it must be in faith that he asks, with no wavering—no hesitating, no doubting. For the one who wavers (hesitates, doubts) is like the billowing surge out at sea, that is blown hither and thither and tossed by the wind. For truly, let not such a person imagine that he will receive anything [he asks for] from the Lord,

[For being as he is] a man of two minds—hesitating, dubious, irresolute—[he is] unstable and unreliable and uncertain about everything (he thinks, feels, decides). James 1:6-8 AMP

Immediately Jesus reached out his hand and caught him. "You of little faith," he said, "why did you doubt?" Matthew 14:31

THE WILL OF GOD

OBEDIENCE TO GOD'S WILL (GOD'S WORD)

Whoever does God's will is my brother and sister and mother.
                                                    Mark 3:35

For whoever does the will of my Father in heaven is my brother and sister and mother." Matthew 12:50

That servant who knows his master's will and does not get ready or does not do what his master wants will be beaten with many blows. Luke 12:47

If anyone chooses to do God's will, he will find out whether my teaching comes from God or whether I speak on my own.
John 7:17

We know that God does not listen to sinners. He listens to the godly man who does his will. John 9:31

Obey them not only to win their favor when their eye is on you, but like slaves of Christ, doing the will of God from your heart.
Ephesians 6:6

You need to persevere so that when you have done the will of God, you will receive what he has promised. Hebrews 10:36

The world and its desires pass away, but the man who does the will of God lives forever. 1 John 2:17

PRAYING IN AGREEMENT WITH HIS WILL (GOD'S WORD)

This is the confidence we have in approaching God: that if we ask anything according to his will, he hears us. And if we know that he hears us—whatever we ask—we know that we have what we asked of him. 1 John 5:14-15

And he who searches our hearts knows the mind of the Spirit, because the Spirit intercedes for the saints in accordance with God's will. Romans 8:27

SUBMITTING TO GOD'S WILL
(PLAN OR DESTINY FOR YOUR LIFE)

Going a little farther, he fell with his face to the ground and prayed, "My Father, if it is possible, may this cup be taken from me. Yet not as I will, but as you will." Matthew 26:39

Your kingdom come, your will be done on earth as it is in heaven.
Matthew 6:10

Then he said to them all: "If anyone would come after me, he must deny himself and take up his cross daily and follow me."
Luke 9:23

103

Do not conform any longer to the pattern of this world, but be transformed by the renewing of your mind. Then you will be able to test and approve what God's will is—his good, pleasing and perfect will. Romans 12:2

And they did not do as we expected, but they gave themselves first to the Lord and then to us in keeping with God's will.

2 Corinthians 8:5

Who gave himself for our sins to rescue us from the present evil age, according to the will of our God and Father. Galatians 1:4

For it is God who works in you to will and to act according to his good purpose. Philippians 2:13

Epaphras, who is one of you and a servant of Christ Jesus, sends greetings. He is always wrestling in prayer for you, that you may stand firm in all the will of God, mature and fully assured.

Colossians 4:12

It is God's will that you should be sanctified: that you should avoid sexual immorality; 1 Thessalonians 4:3

Be joyful always; pray continually; give thanks in all circumstances, for this is God's will for you in Christ Jesus.

1 Thessalonians 5:16-18

For it is God's will that by doing good you should silence the ignorant talk of foolish men. 1 Peter 2:15

As a result, he does not live the rest of his earthly life for evil human desires, but rather for the will of God. 1 Peter 4:2

So then, those who suffer according to God's will should commit themselves to their faithful Creator and continue to do good.

1 Peter 4:19

In His will is our peace. - Dante Alighieri

GOD IS WILLING TO BLESS, HEAL, AND TO SAVE YOU

But I know that even now God will give you whatever you ask.

John 11:22

"What do you want me to do for you?" Jesus asked him. The blind man said, "Rabbi, I want to see." "Go," said Jesus, "your faith has healed you." Immediately he received his sight and followed Jesus along the road. Mark 10:51-52

While Jesus was in one of the towns, a man came along who was covered with leprosy. When he saw Jesus, he fell with his face to the ground and begged him, "Lord, if you are willing, you can make me clean." Jesus reached out his hand and touched the man. "I am wiling," he said. "Be clean!" And immediately the leprosy left him. Luke 5:12-13

Because God wanted to make the unchanging nature of his purpose very clear to the heirs of what was promised, he confirmed it with an oath. Hebrews 6:17

The Lord is not slow in keeping his promise, as some understand slowness. He is patient with you, not wanting anyone to perish, but everyone to come to repentance. 2 Peter 3:9

SALVATION

BELIEVE IN JESUS CHRIST

I tell you the truth, he who believes has everlasting life. John 6:47

Yet to all who received him, to those who believed in his name, he gave the right to become children of God. John 1:12

That everyone who believes in him may have eternal life.
John 3:15

For God so loved the world that he gave his one and only Son, that whoever believes in him shall not perish but have eternal life.
John 3:16

For God did not send his Son into the world to condemn the world, but to save the world through him. Whoever believes in him is not condemned, but whoever does not believe stands condemned already because he has not believed in the name of God's one and only Son. John 3:17-18

Whoever believes in the Son has eternal life, but whoever rejects the Son will not see life, for God's wrath remains on him.
John 3:36

I tell you the truth, whoever hears my word and believes him who sent me has eternal life and will not be condemned; he has crossed over from death to life. John 5:24

Jesus said to them, "I tell you the truth, it is not Moses who has given you the bread from heaven, but it is my Father who gives you the true bread from heaven. For the bread of God is he who comes down from heaven and gives life to the world." "Sir," they said, "from now on give us this bread." Then Jesus declared, "I am the bread of life. He who comes to me will never go hungry, and he who believes in me will never be thirsty. John 6:32-35

I tell you the truth, he who believes has everlasting life. John 6:47

We believe and know that you are the Holy One of God. John 6:69

Whoever believes in me, as the Scripture has said, streams of living water will flow from within him. John 7:38

I told you that you would die in your sins; if you do not believe that I am the one I claim to be, you will indeed die in your sins.
John 8:24

But if I do it, even though you do not believe me, believe the miracles, that you may know and understand that the Father is in me, and I in the Father. John 10:38

But these are written that you may believe that Jesus is the Christ, the Son of God, and that by believing you may have life in his name. John 20:31

For he says, "In the time of my favor I heard you, and in the day of salvation I helped you." I tell you, now is the time of God's favor, now is the day of salvation. 2 Corinthians 6:2

PLAN OF SALVATION

HOW TO OBTAIN ETERNAL LIFE THROUGH JESUS CHRIST

That if you confess with your mouth, "Jesus is Lord," and believe in your heart that God raised him from the dead, you will be saved.
Romans 10:9

IN ORDER TO BE SAVED

1. **Admit that you have sinned and confess (to GOD) and repent.**

2. **Confess (speak aloud) that JESUS CHRIST is the SON of GOD and the LORD and SAVIOR of your life.**

3. **Believe in your heart (inner most being, spirit, the real you) that GOD raised JESUS CHRIST from the dead.**

4. After completing the above three steps (according to the Word of God), you are now saved and have eternal life through JESUS CHRIST.

For it is with your heart that you believe and are justified, and it is with your mouth that you confess and are saved. Romans 10:10

HOW TO KNOW YOU ARE REALLY SAVED

1. Read what God's Word says about your salvation.

For it is with your heart that you believe and are justified, and it is with your mouth that you confess and are saved. Romans 10:10

I tell you the truth, whoever hears my word and believes him who sent me has eternal life and will not be condemned; he has crossed over from death to life. John 5:24

I give them eternal life, and they shall never perish; no one can snatch them out of my hand. John 10:28

I write these things to you who believe in the name of the Son of God so that you may know that you have eternal life. 1 John 5:13

We know also that the Son of God has come and has given us understanding, so that we may know him who is true. And we are in him who is true—even in his Son Jesus Christ. He is the true God and eternal life. 1 John 5:20

For it is with your heart that you believe and are justified, and it is with your mouth that you confess and are saved. Romans 10:10

2. The devil might lie and try to play with your mind and tell you that "you are not saved."

He was a murderer from the beginning, not holding to the truth, for there is no truth in him. When he lies, he speaks his native language, for he is a liar and the father of lies. John 8:44

3. You will obey GOD'S WORD.

If you know that he is righteous, you know that everyone who does what is right has been born of him. 1 John 2:29

No one who lives in him keeps on sinning. No one who continues to sin has either seen him or known him. 1 John 3:6

No one who is born of God will continue to sin, because God's seed remains in him; he cannot go on sinning, because he has been born of God. 1 John 3:9

We know that anyone born of God does not continue to sin; the one who was born of God keeps him safe, and the evil one cannot harm him. 1 John 5:18

NOW THAT YOU ARE SAVED

1. **Get filled with the HOLY GHOST.**

2. **Find a BIBLE BELIEVING Church that is ON FIRE and ALIVE. READ THE BOOK OF ACTS**

3. **PRAY and read GOD'S WORD every single day of your life. Obtain a bible that you can understand (LIVING BIBLE, NIV BIBLE or THE AMPLIFIED BIBLE)**

4. **Learn and know who you are in JESUS CHRIST.**

5. **Obey the Word of GOD.**

6. **Don't be DECEIVED**

7. **Know your authority in JESUS CHRIST**

8. **Tell others what GOD did for you**

SAVED BY GRACE

Made us alive with Christ even when we were dead in transgressions—it is by grace you have been saved. Ephesians 2:5

For it is by grace you have been saved, through faith—and this not from yourselves, it is the gift of God. Ephesians 2:8

For the grace of God that brings salvation has appeared to all men.
Titus 2:11

So that, having been justified by his grace, we might become heirs having the hope of eternal life. Titus 3:7

Who has saved us and called us to a holy life—not because of anything we have done but because of his own purpose and grace. This grace was given us in Christ Jesus before the beginning of time. 2 Timothy 1:9

RESPECTING THE GRACE OF GOD

As God's fellow workers we urge you not to receive God's grace in vain. 2 Corinthians 6:1

I do not set aside the grace of God, for if righteousness could be gained through the law, Christ died for nothing! Galatians 2:21

What shall we say, then? Shall we go on sinning so that grace may increase? Romans 6:1

SANCTIFICATION

Keep my decrees and follow them. I am the Lord, who makes you holy. Leviticus 20:8

To be a minister of Christ Jesus to the Gentiles with the priestly duty of proclaiming the gospel of God, so that the Gentiles might become an offering acceptable to God, sanctified by the Holy Spirit.
Romans 15:16

May God himself, the God of peace, sanctify you through and through. May your whole spirit, soul and body be kept blameless at the coming of our Lord Jesus Christ. 1 Thessalonians 5:23

But we ought always to thank God for you, brothers loved by the Lord, because from the beginning God chose you to be saved through the sanctifying work of the Spirit and through belief in the truth. 2 Thessalonians 2:13

Both the one who makes men holy and those who are made holy are of the same family. So Jesus is not ashamed to call them brothers. Hebrews 2:11

For both He Who sanctifies—making men holy—and those who are sanctified all have one [Father]. For this reason He is not ashamed to call them brethren. Hebrews 2:11 AMP

111

Who have been chosen according to the foreknowledge of God the Father, through the sanctifying work of the Spirit, for obedience to Jesus Christ and sprinkling by his blood: Grace and peace be yours in abundance. 1 Peter 1:2

SANCTIFIED BY THE WORD OF GOD

Sanctify them by the truth; your word is truth. John 17:17

To make her holy, cleansing her by the washing with water through the word. Ephesians 5:26

SANCTIFIED THROUGH JESUS CHRIST

To the church of God in Corinth, to those sanctified in Christ Jesus and called to be holy, together with all those everywhere who call on the name of our Lord Jesus Christ—their Lord and ours:
1 Corinthians 1:2

And that is what some of you were. But you were washed, you were sanctified, you were justified in the name of the Lord Jesus Christ and by the Spirit of our God. 1 Corinthians 6:11

And by that will, we have been made holy through the sacrifice of the body of Jesus Christ once for all. Hebrews 10:10

Because by one sacrifice he has made perfect forever those who are being made holy. Hebrews 10:14

And so Jesus also suffered outside the city gate to make the people holy through his own blood. Hebrews 13:12

To open their eyes and turn them from darkness to light, and from the power of Satan to God, so that they may receive forgiveness of sins and a place among those who are sanctified by faith in me.
Acts 26:18

SET APART FROM THE SINS OF THE WORLD

It is God's will that you should be sanctified: that you should avoid sexual immorality; that each of you should learn to control his own body in a way that is holy and honorable. 1 Thessalonians 4:3-4

If a man cleanses himself from the latter, he will be an instrument for noble purposes, made holy, useful to the Master and prepared to do any good work. 2 Timothy 2:21

Now I commit you to God and to the word of his grace, which can build you up and give you an inheritance among all those who are sanctified. Acts 20:32

RIGHTEOUSNESS

RIGHTEOUS THROUGH JESUS CHRIST

This righteousness from God comes through faith in Jesus Christ to all who believe. There is no difference, for all have sinned and fall short of the glory of God. Romans 3:22-23

For if, by the trespass of the one man, death reigned through that one man, how much more will those who receive God's abundant provision of grace and of the gift of righteousness reign in life through the one man, Jesus Christ. Consequently, just as the result of one trespass was condemnation for all men, so also the result of one act of righteousness was justification that brings life for all men. Romans 5:17-18

The law was added so that the trespass might increase. But where sin increased, grace increased all the more, so that, just as sin reigned in death, so also grace might reign through righteousness to bring eternal life through Jesus Christ our Lord. Romans 5:20-21

But if Christ is in you, your body is dead because of sin, yet your spirit is alive because of righteousness. Romans 8:10

> *This is the mystery of the riches of divine grace for sinners; for by a wonderful exchange our sins are now not ours but Christ's, and Christ's righteousness is not Christ's but ours. - Martin Luther*

It is because of him that you are in Christ Jesus, who has become for us wisdom from God—that is, our righteousness, holiness and redemption. 1 Corinthians 1:30

113

God made him who had no sin to be sin for us, so that in him we might become the righteousness of God. 2 Corinthians 5:21

And to put on the new self, created to be like God in true righteousness and holiness. Ephesians 4:24

Filled with the fruit of righteousness that comes through Jesus Christ—to the glory and praise of God. Philippians 1:11

He himself bore our sins in his body on the tree, so that we might die to sins and live for righteousness; by his wounds you have been healed. 1 Peter 2:24

BELIEVING INTO RIGHTEOUSNESS

What does the Scripture say? "Abraham believed God, and it was credited to him as righteousness." Romans 4:3

For with the heart man believeth unto righteousness; and with the mouth confession is made unto salvation. Romans 10:10 KJV

For it is with your heart that you believe and are justified, and it is with your mouth that you confess and are saved. Romans 10:10

THE WORD OF GOD IS OUR INSTRUCTION FOR RIGHTEOUS LIVING

All Scripture is God-breathed and is useful for teaching, rebuking, correcting and training in righteousness. 2 Timothy 3:16

Anyone who lives on milk, being still an infant, is not acquainted with the teaching about righteousness. Hebrews 5:13

MAN MADE RIGHTEOUSNESS

For I can testify about them that they are zealous for God, but their zeal is not based on knowledge. Since they did not know the righteousness that comes from God and sought to establish their own, they did not submit to God's righteousness. Romans 10:2-3

And be found in him, not having a righteousness of my own that comes from the law, but that which is through faith in Christ—the righteousness that comes from God and is by faith. Philippians 3:9

SELF RIGHTEOUSNESS

But you have said in my hearing—I heard the very words— I am pure and without sin; I am clean and free from guilt. Job 33:8-9

Do you think this is just? You say, 'I will be cleared by God.'
Job 35:2

Everyone has turned away, they have together become corrupt; there is no one who does good, not even one. Psalms 53:3

All a man's ways seem innocent to him, but motives are weighed by the Lord. Proverbs 16:2

There is a way that seems right to a man, but in the end it leads to death. Proverbs 16:25

Woe to those who are wise in their own eyes and clever in their own sight. Isaiah 5:21

All of us have become like one who is unclean, and all our righteous acts are like filthy rags; we all shrivel up like a leaf, and like the wind our sins sweep us away. Isaiah 64:6

He said to them, You are the ones who justify yourselves in the eyes of men, but God knows your hearts. What is highly valued among men is detestable in God's sight. Luke 16:15

The Pharisee stood up and prayed about himself: 'God, I thank you that I am not like other men—robbers, evildoers, adulterers—or even like this tax collector. I fast twice a week and give a tenth of all I get.' "But the tax collector stood at a distance. He would not even look up to heaven, but beat his breast and said, 'God, have mercy on me, a sinner.' "I tell you that this man, rather than the other, went home justified before God. For everyone who exalts himself will be humbled, and he who humbles himself will be exalted." Luke 18:11-14

Jesus said, "If you were blind, you would not be guilty of sin; but now that you claim you can see, your guilt remains. John 9:41

As it is written: "There is no one righteous, not even one.
Romans 3:10

For all have sinned and fall short of the glory of God. Romans 3:23

So, because you are lukewarm—neither hot nor cold—I am about to spit you out of my mouth. You say, 'I am rich; I have acquired wealth and do not need a thing.' But you do not realize that you are wretched, pitiful, poor, blind and naked. Revelation 3:16-17

JUSTIFICATION

JUSTIFICATION THROUGH JESUS CHRIST

Through him everyone who believes is justified from everything you could not be justified from by the law of Moses. Acts 13:39

And are justified freely by his grace through the redemption that came by Christ Jesus. Romans 3:24

He did it to demonstrate his justice at the present time, so as to be just and the one who justifies those who have faith in Jesus.
Romans 3:26

However, to the man who does not work but trusts God who justifies the wicked, his faith is credited as righteousness. Romans 4:5

Therefore, since we have been justified through faith, we have peace with God through our Lord Jesus Christ. Romans 5:1

He was delivered over to death for our sins and was raised to life for our justification. Romans 4:25

Since we have now been justified by his blood, how much more shall we be saved from God's wrath through him! Romans 5:9

Consequently, just as the result of one trespass was condemnation for all men, so also the result of one act of righteousness was justification that brings life for all men. Romans 5:18

And that is what some of you were. But you were washed, you were sanctified, you were justified in the name of the Lord Jesus Christ and by the Spirit of our God. 1 Corinthians 6:11

So the law was put in charge to lead us to Christ that we might be justified by faith. Galatians 3:24

So that, having been justified by his grace, we might become heirs having the hope of eternal life. Titus 3:7

REMAINING IN THE KINGDOM OF GOD

Blessed are the pure in heart, for they will see God. Matthew 5:8

All men will hate you because of me, but he who stands firm to the end will be saved. Matthew 10:22

But he who stands firm to the end will be saved. Matthew 24:13

He who has an ear, let him hear what the Spirit says to the churches. To him who overcomes, I will give the right to eat from the tree of life, which is in the paradise of God. Revelation 2:7

He who has an ear, let him hear what the Spirit says to the churches. He who overcomes will not be hurt at all by the second death.
Revelation 2:11

He who has an ear, let him hear what the Spirit says to the churches. To him who overcomes, I will give some of the hidden manna. I will also give him a white stone with a new name written on it, known only to him who receives it. Revelation 2:17

To him who overcomes and does my will to the end, I will give authority over the nations. Revelation 2:26

He who overcomes will, like them, be dressed in white. I will never blot out his name from the book of life, but will acknowledge his name before my Father and his angels. Revelation 3:5

Him who overcomes I will make a pillar in the temple of my God. Never again will he leave it. I will write on him the name of my God and the name of the city of my God, the new Jerusalem, which is coming down out of heaven from my God; and I will also write on him my new name. Revelation 3:12

To him who overcomes, I will give the right to sit with me on my throne, just as I overcame and sat down with my Father on his throne. Revelation 3:21

He who overcomes will inherit all this, and I will be his God and he will be my son. Revelation 21:7

THE RETURN OF CHRIST (THE RAPTURE)

For the Son of Man is going to come in his Father's glory with his angels, and then he will reward each person according to what he has done. Matthew 16:27

For as lightning that comes from the east is visible even in the west, so will be the coming of the Son of Man. Matthew 24:27

At that time the sign of the Son of Man will appear in the sky, and all the nations of the earth will mourn. They will see the Son of Man coming on the clouds of the sky, with power and great glory.
Matthew 24:30

"I am," said Jesus. "And you will see the Son of Man sitting at the right hand of the Mighty One and coming on the clouds of heaven."
Mark 14:62

I tell you the truth, a time is coming and has now come when the dead will hear the voice of the Son of God and those who hear will live. John 5:25

Do not be amazed at this, for a time is coming when all who are in their graves will hear his voice. John 5:28

And if I go and prepare a place for you, I will come back and take you to be with me that you also may be where I am. John 14:3

You heard me say, 'I am going away and I am coming back to you.' If you loved me, you would be glad that I am going to the Father, for the Father is greater than I. John 14:28

"Men of Galilee," they said, "why do you stand here looking into the sky? This same Jesus, who has been taken from you into heaven, will come back in the same way you have seen him go into heaven."
Acts 1:11

Therefore judge nothing before the appointed time; wait till the Lord comes. He will bring to light what is hidden in darkness and will expose the motives of men's hearts. At that time each will receive his praise from God. 1 Corinthians 4:5

When Christ, who is your life, appears, then you also will appear with him in glory. Colossians 3:4

For the Lord himself will come down from heaven, with a loud command, with the voice of the archangel and with the trumpet call of God, and the dead in Christ will rise first. After that, we who are still alive and are left will be caught up together with them in the clouds to meet the Lord in the air. And so we will be with the Lord forever. 1 Thessalonians 4:16-17

While we wait for the blessed hope—the glorious appearing of our great God and Savior, Jesus Christ. Titus 2:13

So Christ was sacrificed once to take away the sins of many people; and he will appear a second time, not to bear sin, but to bring salvation to those who are waiting for him. Hebrews 9:28

And when the Chief Shepherd appears, you will receive the crown of glory that will never fade away. 1 Peter 5:4

Dear friends, now we are children of God, and what we will be has not yet been made known. But we know that when he appears, we shall be like him, for we shall see him as he is. 1 John 3:2

Look, he is coming with the clouds, and every eye will see him, even those who pierced him; and all the peoples of the earth will mourn because of him. So shall it be! Amen. Revelation 1:7

Behold, I am coming soon! My reward is with me, and I will give to everyone according to what he has done. Revelation 22:12

He who testifies to these things says, "Yes, I am coming soon." Amen. Come, Lord Jesus. Revelation 22:20

ARE YOU READY FOR THE RETURN OF CHRIST (THE RAPTURE)

Therefore keep watch, because you do not know on what day your Lord will come. Matthew 24:42

Be always on the watch, and pray that you may be able to escape all that is about to happen, and that you may be able to stand before the Son of Man. Luke 21:36

Listen, I tell you a mystery: We will not all sleep, but we will all be changed—in a flash, in the twinkling of an eye, at the last trumpet.

For the trumpet will sound, the dead will be raised imperishable, and we will be changed. 1 Corinthians 15:51-52

BACKSLIDER

DEFINITION: A Christian that no longer walks in fellowship with God nor obeys His WORD.

As a dog returns to its vomit, so a fool repeats his folly.
Proverbs 26:11

Your wickedness will punish you; your backsliding will rebuke you. Consider then and realize how evil and bitter it is for you when you forsake the Lord your God and have no awe of me," declares the Lord, the Lord Almighty. Jeremiah 2:19

Go, proclaim this message toward the north: "'Return, faithless Israel,' declares the Lord, 'I will frown on you no longer, for I am merciful,' declares the Lord, 'I will not be angry forever.
Jeremiah 3:12

"Return, faithless people," declares the Lord, "for I am your husband. I will choose you—one from a town and two from a clan—and bring you to Zion. Jeremiah 3:14

"Return, faithless people; I will cure you of backsliding." "Yes, we will come to you, for you are the Lord our God. Jeremiah 3:22

Return, O Israel, to the Lord your God. Your sins have been your downfall! Hosea 14:1

But now that you know God—or rather are known by God—how is it that you are turning back to those weak and miserable principles? Do you wish to be enslaved by them all over again?
Galatians 4:9

Thus they bring judgment on themselves, because they have broken their first pledge. 1 Timothy 5:12

COMPROMISING CHRISTIAN

DEFINITION: A luke warm or uncommitted Christian

They claim to know God, but by their actions they deny him. They are detestable, disobedient and unfit for doing anything good.
Titus 1:16

What shall we say, then? Shall we go on sinning so that grace may increase? Romans 6:1

Salt is good, but if it loses its saltiness, how can you make it salty again? Have salt in yourselves, and be at peace with each other.
Mark 9:50

And do this, understanding the present time. The hour has come for you to wake up from your slumber, because our salvation is nearer now than when we first believed. The night is nearly over; the day is almost here. So let us put aside the deeds of darkness and put on the armor of light. Let us behave decently, as in the daytime, not in orgies and drunkenness, not in sexual immorality and debauchery, not in dissension and jealousy. Rather, clothe yourselves with the Lord Jesus Christ, and do not think about how to gratify the desires of the sinful nature. Romans 13:11-14

A whole new generation of Christians has come up believing that it is possible to "accept" Christ without forsaking the world. - A. W. Tozer

No, I beat my body and make it my slave so that after I have preached to others, I myself will not be disqualified for the prize.
1 Corinthians 9:27

I declare to you, brothers, that flesh and blood cannot inherit the kingdom of God, nor does the perishable inherit the imperishable.
1 Corinthians 15:50

As God's fellow workers we urge you not to receive God's grace in vain. For he says, "In the time of my favor I heard you, and in the day of salvation I helped you." I tell you, now is the time of God's favor, now is the day of salvation. 2 Corinthians 6:1-2

Set your minds on things above, not on earthly things.

Colossians 3:2

The Spirit clearly says that in later times some will abandon the faith and follow deceiving spirits and things taught by demons.

1 Timothy 4:1

It teaches us to say "No" to ungodliness and worldly passions, and to live self-controlled, upright and godly lives in this present age, while we wait for the blessed hope—the glorious appearing of our great God and Savior, Jesus Christ. Titus 2:12-13

We are not here to learn how to live in the dark but to walk in the light. We are not here to get along with evil but to overcome it with good. - Vance Havner

You have not yet struggled and fought agonizingly against sin, nor have you yet resisted and withstood to the point of pouring your [own] blood. Hebrews 12:4 AMP

Religion that God our Father accepts as pure and faultless is this: to look after orphans and widows in their distress and to keep oneself from being polluted by the world. James 1:27

Christians are not just nice people. They're new creatures. If you are what you have always been you are not a Christian. A Christian is something new; old things have passed away and all things are become new.

- Vance Havner

If they have escaped the corruption of the world by knowing our Lord and Savior Jesus Christ and are again entangled in it and overcome, they are worse off at the end than they were at the beginning. It would have been better for them not to have known the way of righteousness, than to have known it and then to turn their backs on the sacred command that was passed on to them. Of them the proverbs are true: "A dog returns to its vomit," and, "A sow that is washed goes back to her wallowing in the mud."

2 Peter 2:20-22

Do not love the world or anything in the world. If anyone loves the world, the love of the Father is not in him. For everything in the world—the cravings of sinful man, the lust of his eyes and the boasting of what he has and does—comes not from the Father but from the world. The world and its desires pass away, but the man who does the will of God lives forever. 1 John 2:15-17

At that time the kingdom of heaven will be like ten virgins who took their lamps and went out to meet the bridegroom. Five of them were foolish and five were wise. The foolish ones took their lamps but did not take any oil with them. The wise, however, took oil in jars along with their lamps. The bridegroom was a long time in coming, and they all became drowsy and fell asleep. At midnight the cry rang out: Here's the bridegroom! Come out to meet him! Then all the virgins woke up and trimmed their lamps. The foolish ones said to the wise, Give us some of your oil; our lamps are going out. No, they replied, there may not be enough for both us and you. Instead, go to those who sell oil and buy some for yourselves. But while they were on their way to buy the oil, the bridegroom arrived. The virgins who were ready went in with him to the wedding banquet. And the door was shut. Later the others also came. 'Sir! Sir!' they said. 'Open the door for us!' But he replied, 'I tell you the truth, I don't know you. Therefore keep watch, because you do not know the day or the hour. Matthew 25:1-13

Is your lifestyle taking the people
around you to heaven or hell?

A WARNING FOR THE BACKSLIDER AND COMPROMISING CHRISTIAN

I know your deeds, that you are neither cold nor hot. I wish you were either one or the other! So, because you are lukewarm—neither hot nor cold—I am about to spit you out of my mouth. You say, 'I am rich; I have acquired wealth and do not need a thing.' But you do not realize that you are wretched, pitiful, poor, blind and naked. Revelation 3:15-17

Enter through the narrow gate. For wide is the gate and broad is the road that leads to destruction, and many enter through it. But small is the gate and narrow the road that leads to life, and only a few find it. Matthew 7:13-14

Not everyone who says to me, 'Lord, Lord,' will enter the kingdom of heaven, but only he who does the will of my Father who is in heaven. Many will say to me on that day, 'Lord, Lord, did we not prophesy in your name, and in your name drive out demons and perform many miracles?' Then I will tell them plainly, 'I never knew you. Away from me, you evildoers!' Matthew 7:21-23

Life is too short and hell is too hot to play games with your eternal future.

Make every effort to enter through the narrow door, because many, I tell you, will try to enter and will not be able to. Once the owner of the house gets up and closes the door, you will stand outside knocking and pleading, 'Sir, open the door for us.' "But he will answer, 'I don't know you or where you come from.' Then you will say, 'We ate and drank with you, and you taught in our streets.' But he will reply, 'I don't know you or where you come from. Away from me, all you evildoers!' There will be weeping there, and gnashing of teeth, when you see Abraham, Isaac and Jacob and all the prophets in the kingdom of God, but you yourselves thrown out. Luke 13:24-28

Yet I hold this against you: You have forsaken your first love. Remember the height from which you have fallen! Repent and do the things you did at first. If you do not repent, I will come to you and remove your lampstand from its place. Revelation 2:4-5

HOLY SPIRIT

RESPECTING THE HOLY SPIRIT

And so I tell you, every sin and blasphemy will be forgiven men, but the blasphemy against the Spirit will not be forgiven. Anyone who speaks a word against the Son of Man will be forgiven, but anyone who speaks against the Holy Spirit will not be forgiven, either in this age or in the age to come. Matthew 12:31-32

And do not grieve the Holy Spirit of God, with whom you were sealed for the day of redemption. Ephesians 4:30

Do not put out the Spirit's fire. 1 Thessalonians 5:19

How much more severely do you think a man deserves to be punished who has trampled the Son of God under foot, who has treated as an unholy thing the blood of the covenant that sanctified him, and who has insulted the Spirit of grace? Hebrews 10:29

> *The first step toward establishing a relationship with the Holy Spirit is to respect and acknowledge Him as God and not as an "it."!*

RECEIVING THE BAPTISM OF THE HOLY SPIRIT

If you then, though you are evil, know how to give good gifts to your children, how much more will your Father in heaven give the Holy Spirit to those who ask him! Luke 11:13

And with that he breathed on them and said, "Receive the Holy Spirit. John 20:22

Do not get drunk on wine, which leads to debauchery. Instead, be filled with the Spirit. Ephesians 5:18

But you, dear friends, build yourselves up in your most holy faith and pray in the Holy Spirit. Jude 1:20

Therefore, my brothers, be eager to prophesy, and do not forbid speaking in tongues. 1 Corinthians 14:39

THE BENEFITS OF PRAYING IN THE HOLY SPIRIT

In the same way, the Spirit helps us in our weakness. We do not know what we ought to pray for, but the Spirit himself intercedes for us with groans that words cannot express. And he who searches our hearts knows the mind of the Spirit, because the Spirit intercedes for the saints in accordance with God's will.

Romans 8:26-27

For anyone who speaks in a tongue does not speak to men but to God. Indeed, no one understands him; he utters mysteries with his spirit. 1 Corinthians 14:2

For if I pray in a tongue, my spirit prays, but my mind is unfruitful. So what shall I do? I will pray with my spirit, but I will also pray with my mind; I will sing with my spirit, but I will also sing with my mind. 1 Corinthians 14:14-15

> *Praying in the Spirit guarantees perfect prayer that is directed by the Holy Spirit; untouched by doubt and fear of the mind; and impossible for the devil to understand or hinder.*

And pray in the Spirit on all occasions with all kinds of prayers and requests. With this in mind, be alert and always keep on praying for all the saints. Ephesians 6:18

EXAMPLES OF BELIEVERS BEING FILLED WITH THE HOLY SPIRIT

All of them were filled with the Holy Spirit and began to speak in other tongues as the Spirit enabled them. Acts 2:4

When the apostles in Jerusalem heard that Samaria had accepted the word of God, they sent Peter and John to them. When they arrived, they prayed for them that they might receive the Holy Spirit, because the Holy Spirit had not yet come upon any of them; they had simply been baptized into the name of the Lord Jesus. Then

Peter and John placed their hands on them, and they received the Holy Spirit. Acts 8:14-17

Then Ananias went to the house and entered it. Placing his hands on Saul, he said, "Brother Saul, the Lord—Jesus, who appeared to you on the road as you were coming here—has sent me so that you may see again and be filled with the Holy Spirit. Acts 9:17

While Peter was still speaking these words, the Holy Spirit came on all who heard the message. The circumcised believers who had come with Peter were astonished that the gift of the Holy Spirit had been poured out even on the Gentiles. For they heard them speaking in tongues and praising God. Then Peter said, "Can anyone keep these people from being baptized with water? They have received the Holy Spirit just as we have." Acts 10:44-47

God, who knows the heart, showed that he accepted them by giving the Holy Spirit to them, just as he did to us. He made no distinction between us and them, for he purified their hearts by faith.
Acts 15:8-9

And asked them, "Did you receive the Holy Spirit when you believed?" They answered, "No, we have not even heard that there is a Holy Spirit." So Paul asked, "Then what baptism did you receive?" "John's baptism," they replied. Paul said, "John's baptism was a baptism of repentance. He told the people to believe in the one coming after him, that is, in Jesus." On hearing this, they were baptized into the name of the Lord Jesus. When Paul placed his hands on them, the Holy Spirit came on them, and they spoke in tongues and prophesied. Acts 19:2-6

HOLY SPIRIT, THE TEACHER, LEADER, GUIDE AND COUNSELOR

For the Holy Spirit will teach you at that time what you should say.
Luke 12:12

By this he meant the Spirit, whom those who believed in him were later to receive. Up to that time the Spirit had not been given, since Jesus had not yet been glorified. John 7:39

But the Counselor, the Holy Spirit, whom the Father will send in my name, will teach you all things and will remind you of everything I have said to you. John 14:26

But when he, the Spirit of truth, comes, he will guide you into all truth. He will not speak on his own; he will speak only what he hears, and he will tell you what is yet to come. John 16:13

Because those who are led by the Spirit of God are sons of God. Romans 8:14

The Spirit himself testifies with our spirit that we are God's children. Romans 8:16

But God has revealed it to us by his Spirit. The Spirit searches all things, even the deep things of God. For who among men knows the thoughts of a man except the man's spirit within him? In the same way no one knows the thoughts of God except the Spirit of God. 1 Corinthians 2:10-11

This is what we speak, not in words taught us by human wisdom but in words taught by the Spirit, expressing spiritual truths in spiritual words. 1 Corinthians 2:13

But if you are led by the Spirit, you are not under law. Galatians 5:18

THE HOLY SPIRIT LIVING INSIDE THE BELIEVER

And I will put my Spirit in you and move you to follow my decrees and be careful to keep my laws. Ezekiel 36:27

The Spirit of truth. The world cannot accept him, because it neither sees him nor knows him. But you know him, for he lives with you and will be in you. John 14:17

Don't you know that you yourselves are God's temple and that God's Spirit lives in you? 1 Corinthians 3:16

Do you not know that your body is a temple of the Holy Spirit, who is in you, whom you have received from God? You are not your own. 1 Corinthians 6:19

Because you are sons, God sent the Spirit of his Son into our hearts, the Spirit who calls out, "Abba, Father." Galatians 4:6

I pray that out of his glorious riches he may strengthen you with power through his Spirit in your inner being. Ephesians 3:16

Guard the good deposit that was entrusted to you—guard it with the help of the Holy Spirit who lives in us. 2 Timothy 1:14

> *If you have been born of the Holy Spirit, you will not have to serve God ...it will become the natural thing to do. - D. L. Moody*

Those who obey his commands live in him, and he in them. And this is how we know that he lives in us: We know it by the Spirit he gave us. 1 John 3:24

We know that we live in him and he in us, because he has given us of his Spirit. 1 John 4:13

SEALED BY THE HOLY SPIRIT

Set his seal of ownership on us, and put his Spirit in our hearts as a deposit, guaranteeing what is to come. 2 Corinthians 1:22

And you also were included in Christ when you heard the word of truth, the gospel of your salvation. Having believed, you were marked in him with a seal, the promised Holy Spirit.

Ephesians 1:13

And do not grieve the Holy Spirit of God, with whom you were sealed for the day of redemption. Ephesians 4:30

THE POWER OF THE HOLY SPIRIT

But you will receive power when the Holy Spirit comes on you; and you will be my witnesses in Jerusalem, and in all Judea and Samaria, and to the ends of the earth. Acts 1:8

In the last days, God says, I will pour out my Spirit on all people. Your sons and daughters will prophesy, your young men will see visions, your old men will dream dreams. Even on my servants, both men and women, I will pour out my Spirit in those days, and they will prophesy. Acts 2:17-18

When they came up out of the water, the Spirit of the Lord suddenly took Philip away, and the eunuch did not see him again, but went on his way rejoicing. Acts 8:39

And if the Spirit of him who raised Jesus from the dead is living in you, he who raised Christ from the dead will also give life to your mortal bodies through his Spirit, who lives in you. Romans 8:11

To be "fervent in spirit" is to be "boiling in spirit," and to boil we must be near the Fire. - Vance Havner

My message and my preaching were not with wise and persuasive words, but with a demonstration of the Spirit's power.
1 Corinthians 2:4

And that is what some of you were. But you were washed, you were sanctified, you were justified in the name of the Lord Jesus Christ and by the Spirit of our God. 1 Corinthians 6:11

Because our gospel came to you not simply with words, but also with power, with the Holy Spirit and with deep conviction. You know how we lived among you for your sake. 1 Thessalonians 1:5

Never let a person or man-made doctrine talk you out of the power of God. The gods of the pagans are dead and powerless but the God of Israel heals, delivers and manifests His glory in Sovereign miracles through His Son Jesus Christ who is the same yesterday, today, and forever.

God also testified to it by signs, wonders and various miracles, and gifts of the Holy Spirit distributed according to his will.
Hebrews 2:4

THE GIFTS OF THE HOLY SPIRIT

There are different kinds of gifts, but the same Spirit. There are different kinds of service, but the same Lord. There are different kinds of working, but the same God works all of them in all men.

Now to each one the manifestation of the Spirit is given for the common good. To one there is given through the Spirit the message of wisdom, to another the message of knowledge by means of the same Spirit, to another faith by the same Spirit, to another gifts of healing by that one Spirit, to another miraculous powers, to another prophecy, to another distinguishing between spirits, to another speaking in different kinds of tongues, and to still another the interpretation of tongues. All these are the work of one and the same Spirit, and he gives them to each one, just as he determines.

1 Corinthians 12:4-11

GOD'S WORD

THE INTEGRITY OF GOD'S WORD

God is not a man, that he should lie, nor a son of man, that he should change his mind. Does he speak and then not act? Does he promise and not fulfill? Numbers 23:19

Know therefore that the Lord your God is God; he is the faithful God, keeping his covenant of love to a thousand generations of those who love him and keep his commands. Deuteronomy 7:9

Now I am about to go the way of all the earth. You know with all your heart and soul that not one of all the good promises the Lord your God gave you has failed. Every promise has been fulfilled; not one has failed. Joshua 23:14

The Lord Almighty has sworn, "Surely, as I have planned, so it will be, and as I have purposed, so it will stand. Isaiah 14:24

He who is the Glory of Israel does not lie or change his mind; for he is not a man, that he should change his mind. 1 Samuel 15:29

The grass withers and the flowers fall, but the word of our God stands forever. Isaiah 40:8

Praise be to the Lord, who has given rest to his people Israel just as he promised. Not one word has failed of all the good promises he gave through his servant Moses. 1 Kings 8:56

By the word of the Lord were the heavens made, their starry host by the breath of his mouth. Psalms 33:6

For he spoke, and it came to be; he commanded, and it stood firm.
Psalms 33:9

I will not violate my covenant or alter what my lips have uttered.
Psalms 89:34

He remembers his covenant forever, the word he commanded, for a thousand generations. Psalms 105:8

He provides food for those who fear him; he remembers his covenant forever. Psalms 111:5

All your commands are trustworthy; help me, for men persecute me without cause. Psalms 119:86

Your word, O Lord, is eternal; it stands firm in the heavens.
Psalms 119:89

I will hasten and not delay to obey your commands. Psalms 119:160

I will bow down toward your holy temple and will praise your name for your love and your faithfulness, for you have exalted above all things your name and your word. Psalms 138:2

Every word of God is flawless; he is a shield to those who take refuge in him. Proverbs 30:5

From the east I summon a bird of prey; from a far-off land, a man to fulfill my purpose. What I have said, that will I bring about; what I have planned, that will I do. Isaiah 46:11

As the rain and the snow come down from heaven, and do not return to it without watering the earth and making it bud and flourish, so that it yields seed for the sower and bread for the eater, so is my word that goes out from my mouth: It will not return to me empty, but will accomplish what I desire and achieve the purpose for which I sent it. Isaiah 55:10-11

"'I the Lord have spoken. The time has come for me to act. I will not hold back; I will not have pity, nor will I relent. You will be judged according to your conduct and your actions, declares the Sovereign Lord.'" Ezekiel 24:14

Heaven and earth will pass away, but my words will never pass away. Mark 13:31

Sanctify them by the truth; your word is truth. John 17:17

Being fully persuaded that God had power to do what he had promised. Romans 4:21

For no matter how many promises God has made, they are "Yes" in Christ. And so through him the "Amen" is spoken by us to the glory of God. 2 Corinthians 1:20

A faith and knowledge resting on the hope of eternal life, which God, who does not lie, promised before the beginning of time.
Titus 1:2

But in these last days he has spoken to us by his Son, whom he appointed heir of all things, and through whom he made the universe. The Son is the radiance of God's glory and the exact representation of his being, sustaining all things by his powerful word. After he had provided purification for sins, he sat down at the right hand of the Majesty in heaven. Hebrews 1:2-3

Being fully persuaded that God had power to do what he had promised. Romans 4:21

God did this so that, by two unchangeable things in which it is impossible for God to lie, we who have fled to take hold of the hope offered to us may be greatly encouraged. Hebrews 6:18

By faith we understand that the universe was formed at God's command, so that what is seen was not made out of what was visible.
Hebrews 11:3

Jesus Christ is the same yesterday and today and forever.
Hebrews 13:8

For you have been born again, not of perishable seed, but of imperishable, through the living and enduring word of God. 1 Peter 1:23

But the word of the Lord stands forever." And this is the word that was preached to you. 1 Peter 1:25

> *His promises are checks to be cashed, not mere mottoes to hang on the wall! - Vance Havner*

The Lord is not slow in keeping his promise, as some understand slowness. He is patient with you, not wanting anyone to perish, but everyone to come to repentance. 2 Peter 3:9

GOD'S WORD IS SPIRITUAL FOOD

Jesus answered, "It is written: 'Man does not live on bread alone, but on every word that comes from the mouth of God.'"

Matthew 4:4

Jesus answered, "It is written: 'Man does not live on bread alone.'"

Luke 4:4

But he said to them, "I have food to eat that you know nothing about." John 4:32

Do not work for food that spoils, but for food that endures to eternal life, which the Son of Man will give you. On him God the Father has placed his seal of approval. John 6:27

Jesus said to them, "I tell you the truth, it is not Moses who has given you the bread from heaven, but it is my Father who gives you the true bread from heaven. For the bread of God is he who comes down from heaven and gives life to the world." "Sir," they said, "from now on give us this bread." Then Jesus declared, "I am the bread of life. He who comes to me will never go hungry, and he who believes in me will never be thirsty." John 6:32-35

Hunger for God's Word is not a natural appetite. We are not born with it. It comes with the new birth when we begin with milk and should go on to meat.

- Vance Havner

I am the living bread that came down from heaven. If anyone eats of this bread, he will live forever. This bread is my flesh, which I will give for the life of the world." John 6:51

This is the bread that came down from heaven. Your forefathers ate manna and died, but he who feeds on this bread will live forever.

John 6:58

When they had finished eating, Jesus said to Simon Peter, "Simon son of John, do you truly love me more than these?" "Yes, Lord," he said, "you know that I love you." Jesus said, "Feed my lambs." Again Jesus said, "Simon son of John, do you truly love me?" He answered, "Yes, Lord, you know that I love you." Jesus said, "Take care of my sheep." John 21:15-16

Brothers, I could not address you as spiritual but as worldly—mere infants in Christ. I gave you milk, not solid food, for you were not yet ready for it. Indeed, you are still not ready. You are still worldly. For since there is jealousy and quarreling among you, are you not worldly? Are you not acting like mere men? 1 Corinthians 3:1-3

They all ate the same spiritual food and drank the same spiritual drink; for they drank from the spiritual rock that accompanied them, and that rock was Christ. 1 Corinthians 10:3-4

In fact, though by this time you ought to be teachers, you need someone to teach you the elementary truths of God's word all over again. You need milk, not solid food! Anyone who lives on milk, being still an infant, is not acquainted with the teaching about righteousness. But solid food is for the mature, who by constant use have trained themselves to distinguish good from evil.

Hebrews 5:12-14

Like newborn babies, crave pure spiritual milk, so that by it you may grow up in your salvation. 1 Peter 2:2

THE WORD OF GOD IN THE HEART

I desire to do your will, O my God; your law is within my heart.
Psalms 40:8

I do not hide your righteousness in my heart; I speak of your faithfulness and salvation. I do not conceal your love and your truth from the great assembly. Psalms 40:10

I have hidden your word in my heart that I might not sin against you. Psalms 119:11

Turn my heart toward your statutes and not toward selfish gain.
Psalms 119:36

My son, do not forget my teaching, but keep my commands in your heart. Proverbs 3:1

He taught me and said, "Lay hold of my words with all your heart; keep my commands and you will live. Proverbs 4:4

My son, pay attention to what I say; listen closely to my words. Do not let them out of your sight, keep them within your heart; for they are life to those who find them and health to a man's whole body. Above all else, guard your heart, for it is the wellspring of life. Proverbs 4:20-23

It is not the Word hidden in the head but in the heart that keeps us from sin. - Vance Havner

My son, keep your father's commands and do not forsake your mother's teaching. Bind them upon your heart forever; fasten them around your neck. Proverbs 6:20-21

My son, keep my words and store up my commands within you. Keep my commands and you will live; guard my teachings as the apple of your eye. Bind them on your fingers; write them on the tablet of your heart. Proverbs 7:1-3

Pay attention and listen to the sayings of the wise; apply your heart to what I teach. Proverbs 22:17

This is the covenant I will make with the house of Israel after that time, declares the Lord. I will put my law in their minds and write it on their hearts. I will be their God, and they will be my people.
Jeremiah 31:33

But what does it say? "The word is near you; it is in your mouth and in your heart," that is, the word of faith we are proclaiming.
Romans 10:8

"This is the covenant I will make with them after that time, says the Lord. I will put my laws in their hearts, and I will write them on their minds." Hebrews 10:16

You yourselves are our letter, written on our hearts, known and read by everybody. You show that you are a letter from Christ, the result of our ministry, written not with ink but with the Spirit of the living God, not on tablets of stone but on tablets of human hearts.
2 Corinthians 3:2-3

DIFFERENT WAYS THE WORD OF GOD IS TAKEN OUT OF THE HEART OF MAN

1. NOT UNDERSTANDING THE WORD OF GOD

When anyone hears the message about the kingdom and does not understand it, the evil one comes and snatches away what was sown in his heart. This is the seed sown along the path. Matthew 13:19

While any one is hearing the Word of the kingdom and does not grasp and comprehend it, the evil one comes and snatches away what is sown in his heart. This is what was sown along the roadside. Matthew 13:19 AMP

2. TRIBULATION AND PERSECUTION

The one who received the seed that fell on rocky places is the man who hears the word and at once receives it with joy. But since he has no root, he lasts only a short time. When trouble or persecution comes because of the word, he quickly falls away.

Matthew 13:20-21

As for what was sown on thin (rocky) soil, this is he who hears the Word and at once welcomes and accepts it with joy. Yet it has no real root in himself, but is temporary—inconstant, lasts but a little while and when affliction or trouble or persecution comes on account of the Word, at once he is caused to stumble—he is repelled and begins to distrust and desert Him Whom he ought to trust and obey, and he falls away. Matthew 13:20-21 AMP

3. THE CARES OF THIS WORLD AND THE DECEITFULNESS OF RICHES

The one who received the seed that fell among the thorns is the man who hears the word, but the worries of this life and the deceitfulness of wealth choke it, making it unfruitful. Matthew 13:22

As for what was sown among thorns, this is he who hears the Word, but the cares of the world and the pleasure and delight and glamour and deceitfulness of riches choke and suffocate the Word and it yields no fruit. Matthew 13:22 AMP

139

4. satan WILL TRY TO STEAL THE WORD OF GOD.

Some people are like seed along the path, where the word is sown. As soon as they hear it, Satan comes and takes away the word that was sown in them. Mark 4:15

The ones along the path are those who have the Word sown [in their hearts], but when they hear, satan comes at once and (by force) takes away the message which is sown in them. Mark 4:15 AMP

A GOOD HEART FOR THE WORD OF GOD

But the one who received the seed that fell on good soil is the man who hears the word and understands it. He produces a crop, yielding a hundred, sixty or thirty times what was sown. Matthew 13:23

Others, like seed sown on good soil, hear the word, accept it, and produce a crop—thirty, sixty or even a hundred times what was sown. Mark 4:20

And those that were sown on the good (wee-adapted) soil are the ones who hear the Word, and receive and accept and welcome it and bear fruit, some thirty times as much as was sown, some sixty times as much, and some [even] a hundred times as much.

Mark 4:20 AMP

MEDITATING ON GOD'S WORD

DEFINITIONS FOR MEDITATING:
- to care for, to attend to, practice, to ponder, or imagine.
- to pass some time thinking in a quiet way; reflect.
- to plan or consider.

Do not let this Book of the Law depart from your mouth; meditate on it day and night, so that you may be careful to do everything written in it. Then you will be prosperous and successful.

Joshua 1:8

But his delight is in the law of the Lord, and on his law he meditates day and night. Psalms 1:2

May the words of my mouth and the meditation of my heart be pleasing in your sight, O Lord, my Rock and my Redeemer.
Psalms 19:14

My mouth will speak words of wisdom; the utterance from my heart will give understanding. Psalms 49:3

On my bed I remember you; I think of you through the watches of the night. Psalms 63:6

I will meditate on all your works and consider all your mighty deeds. Psalms 77:12

May my meditation be pleasing to him, as I rejoice in the Lord.
Psalms 104:34

I meditate on your precepts and consider your ways. Psalms 119:15

God does not give the soul a vacation, He gives it a vocation. - Vance Havner

Though rulers sit together and slander me, your servant will meditate on your decrees. Psalms 119:23

My eyes stay open through the watches of the night, that I may meditate on your promises. Psalms 119:48

May the arrogant be put to shame for wronging me without cause; but I will meditate on your precepts. Psalms 119:78

Oh, how I love your law! I meditate on it all day long.
Psalms 119:97

I have more insight than all my teachers, for I meditate on your statutes. Psalms 119:99

I lift up my hands to your commands, which I love, and I meditate on your decrees. Psalms 119:148

I remember the days of long ago; I meditate on all your works and consider what your hands have done. Psalms 143:5

HOW TO OBTAIN PROMISES FROM GOD'S WORD

1. CONFESS THE WORD OF GOD

Do not snatch the word of truth from my mouth, for I have put my hope in your laws. Psalms 119:43

May my tongue sing of your word, for all your commands are righteous. Psalms 119:172

It is written: "I believed; therefore I have spoken." With that same spirit of faith we also believe and therefore speak.
2 Corinthians 4:13

Fight the good fight of the faith. Take hold of the eternal life to which you were called when you made your good confession in the presence of many witnesses. 1 Timothy 6:12

Therefore, since we have a great high priest who has gone through the heavens, Jesus the Son of God, let us hold firmly to the faith we profess. Hebrews 4:14

Let us hold unswervingly to the hope we profess, for he who promised is faithful. Hebrews 10:23

But what does it say? "The word is near you; it is in your mouth and in your heart," that is, the word of faith we are proclaiming.
Romans 10:8

So tell them, 'As surely as I live, declares the Lord, I will do to you the very things I heard you say. Numbers 14:28

The angels of heaven and the demons of hell bring to past whatever you speak out of your mouth. The angels respond to the Word of God and demons respond to negative, vain, and destructive words.

2. REMAIN PATIENT

But the seed on good soil stands for those with a noble and good heart, who hear the word, retain it, and by persevering produce a crop. Luke 8:15

For everything that was written in the past was written to teach us, so that through endurance and the encouragement of the Scriptures we might have hope. Romans 15:4

Let us not become weary in doing good, for at the proper time we will reap a harvest if we do not give up. Galatians 6:9

We do not want you to become lazy, but to imitate those who through faith and patience inherit what has been promised. Hebrews 6:12

And so after waiting patiently, Abraham received what was promised. Hebrews 6:15

> *Just as faith without works is dead*
> *so is faith without patience.*

So do not throw away your confidence; it will be richly rewarded. You need to persevere so that when you have done the will of God, you will receive what he has promised. For in just a very little while, "He who is coming will come and will not delay.
Hebrews 10:35-37

Who through faith conquered kingdoms, administered justice, and gained what was promised; who shut the mouths of lions.
Hebrews 11:33

3. DO NOT DOUBT THE ABILITY OF GOD AND HIS WORD

But when he asks, he must believe and not doubt, because he who doubts is like a wave of the sea, blown and tossed by the wind. That man should not think he will receive anything from the Lord; he is a double-minded man, unstable in all he does. James 1:6-8

Only it must be in faith that he asks, with no wavering—no hesitating, no doubting. For the one who wavers (hesitates, doubts) is like the billowing surge out at sea, that is blown hither and thither and tossed by the wind. For truly, let not such a person imagine that he will receive anything [he asks for] from the Lord,

[For being as he is] a man of two minds—hesitating, dubious, irresolute—[he is] unstable and unreliable and uncertain about everything (he thinks, feels, decides). James 1:6-8 AMP

"Have faith in God," Jesus answered. "I tell you the truth, if anyone says to this mountain, `Go, throw yourself into the sea,' and does not doubt in his heart but believes that what he says will happen, it will be done for him. Therefore I tell you, whatever you ask for in prayer, believe that you have received it, and it will be yours.
Mark 11:22-24

Yet he did not waver through unbelief regarding the promise of God, but was strengthened in his faith and gave glory to God,
Romans 4:20

Granted. But they were broken off because of unbelief, and you stand by faith. Do not be arrogant, but be afraid. Romans 11:20

That is true. But they were broken (pruned) off because of their unbelief—their lack of real faith, and you are established through faith—because you do believe. So do not become proud and conceited, but rather stand in awe and be reverently afraid.
Romans 11:20 AMP

And he did not do many miracles there because of their lack of faith. Matthew 13:58

THE CLEANSING OF THE WORD OF GOD

How can a young man keep his way pure? By living according to your word. Psalms 119:9

Now that you have purified yourselves by obeying the truth so that you have sincere love for your brothers, love one another deeply, from the heart. 1 Peter 1:22

Since we have these promises, dear friends, let us purify ourselves from everything that contaminates body and spirit, perfecting holiness out of reverence for God. 2 Corinthians 7:1

To make her holy, cleansing her by the washing with water through the word. Ephesians 5:26

Now I commit you to God and to the word of his grace, which can build you up and give you an inheritance among all those who are sanctified. Acts 20:32

MEMORIZING THE WORD OF GOD

Then you will know the truth, and the truth will set you free.
John 8:32

Then you will remember to obey all my commands and will be consecrated to your God. Numbers 15:40

Be careful that you do not forget the Lord your God, failing to observe his commands, his laws and his decrees that I am giving you this day. Deuteronomy 8:11

But from everlasting to everlasting the Lord's love is with those who fear him, and his righteousness with their children's children—with those who keep his covenant and remember to obey his precepts. Psalms 103:17-18

I delight in your decrees; I will not neglect your word. Psalms 119:16

Though I am like a wineskin in the smoke, I do not forget your decrees. Psalms 119:83

I will never forget your precepts, for by them you have preserved my life. Psalms 119:93

Though I am lowly and despised, I do not forget your precepts.
Psalms 119:141

My son, do not forget my teaching, but keep my commands in your heart. Proverbs 3:1

By this gospel you are saved, if you hold firmly to the word I preached to you. Otherwise, you have believed in vain.
1 Corinthians 15:2

But the man who looks intently into the perfect law that gives freedom, and continues to do this, not forgetting what he has heard, but doing it—he will be blessed in what he does. James 1:25

But, dear friends, remember what the apostles of our Lord Jesus Christ foretold. Jude 1:17

GUIDANCE FROM GOD'S WORD

You guide me with your counsel, and afterward you will take me into glory. Psalms 73:24

Your word is a lamp to my feet and a light for my path.
Psalms 119:105

Direct my footsteps according to your word; let no sin rule over me. Psalms 119:133

I have considered my ways and have turned my steps to your statutes. Psalms 119:59

The unfolding of your words gives light; it gives understanding to the simple. Psalms 119:130

All Scripture is God-breathed and is useful for teaching, rebuking, correcting and training in righteousness, so that the man of God may be thoroughly equipped for every good work.
2 Timothy 3:16-17

For everything that was written in the past was written to teach us, so that through endurance and the encouragement of the Scriptures we might have hope. Romans 15:4

THE SPOKEN WORD OF GOD

1. IS THE SWORD OF THE SPIRITUAL REALM

So that the thoughts of many hearts will be revealed. And a sword will pierce your own soul too. Luke 2:35

Take the helmet of salvation and the sword of the Spirit, which is the word of God. Ephesians 6:17

For the word of God is living and active. Sharper than any double-edged sword, it penetrates even to dividing soul and spirit, joints and marrow; it judges the thoughts and attitudes of the heart.
Hebrews 4:12

And then shall that Wicked be revealed, whom the Lord shall consume with the spirit of his mouth, and shall destroy with the brightness of his coming. 2 Thessalonians 2:8 KJV

And then the lawless one will be revealed, whom the Lord Jesus will overthrow with the breath of his mouth and destroy by the splendor of his coming. 2 Thessalonians 2:8

In his right hand he held seven stars, and out of his mouth came a sharp double-edged sword. His face was like the sun shining in all its brilliance. Revelation 1:16

"To the angel of the church in Pergamum write: These are the words of him who has the sharp, double-edged sword. Revelation 2:12

Repent therefore! Otherwise, I will soon come to you and will fight against them with the sword of my mouth. Revelation 2:16

Out of his mouth comes a sharp sword with which to strike down the nations. "He will rule them with an iron scepter." He treads the winepress of the fury of the wrath of God Almighty.
Revelation 19:15

The devil is a spiritual being and the spoken Word of God is the sword of the Spirit. Nothing else cuts, controls, binds, hinders, and defeats the devil and his demons more than a Christian confessing God's Word in faith.

2. GIVES FAITH TO THE BELIEVER

Consequently, faith comes from hearing the message, and the message is heard through the word of Christ. Romans 10:17

3. CONVICTS AND CONVERTS THE UNBELIEVER

For, "Everyone who calls on the name of the Lord will be saved." How, then, can they call on the one they have not believed in? And how can they believe in the one of whom they have not heard? And how can they hear without someone preaching to them?
Romans 10:13-14

When the people heard this, they were cut to the heart and said to Peter and the other apostles, "Brothers, what shall we do?
Acts 2:37

147

4. ANGERS THE SINNER

When they heard this, they were furious and wanted to put them to death. Acts 5:33

When they heard this, they were furious and gnashed their teeth at him. Acts 7:54

5. WILL CAST OUT demon spirits

When evening came, many who were demon-possessed were brought to him, and he drove out the spirits with a word and healed all the sick. Matthew 8:16

6. PUTS satan TO FLIGHT

The tempter came to him and said, "If you are the Son of God, tell these stones to become bread." Jesus answered, "It is written: 'Man does not live on bread alone, but on every word that comes from the mouth of God.'" Then the devil took him to the holy city and had him stand on the highest point of the temple. "If you are the Son of God," he said, "throw yourself down. For it is written: '"He will command his angels concerning you, and they will lift you up in their hands, so that you will not strike your foot against a stone.'" Jesus answered him, "It is also written: 'Do not put the Lord your God to the test.'" Again, the devil took him to a very high mountain and showed him all the kingdoms of the world and their splendor. "All this I will give you," he said, "if you will bow down and worship me." Jesus said to him, "Away from me, Satan! For it is written: 'Worship the Lord your God, and serve him only.'" Then the devil left him, and angels came and attended him.

Matthew 4:3-11

Jesus met the devil not in His own name, not in His own power, but with the Scriptures: "It is written... It is written..." If he could defeat the devil with three verses out of Deuteronomy, we ought to be able to do it with the whole Bible. - Vance Havner

THE NAME OF JESUS

THE DIFFERENT NAMES OF JESUS

EMMANUEL .... Matthew 1:23
ETERNAL LIFE .... 1 John 5:20
EVERLASTING FATHER ....Isaiah 9:6
FAITHFUL, THE .... Revelation 3:14
FAITHFUL WITNESS .... Revelation 1:5
FAITHFUL AND TRUE... Revelation 19:11
FIRST BEGOTTEN .... Hebrews 1:6
FIRST BEGOTTEN OF THE DEAD .... Revelation 1:5
FIRST AND THE LAST.. Revelation 22:13
FIRSTBORN .... Psalms 89:27
FIRSTBORN AMONG MANY BRETHREN .... Romans 8:29
FIRSTBORN FROM THE DEAD .... Colossians 1:18
FIRSTBORN OF EVERY CREATURE.................................... Colossians 1:15
FIRSTFRUITS, THE.. 1 Corinthians 15:23
GLORIOUS LORD ....Isaiah 33:21
GOD .... John 1:1, Isaiah 9:6
GOD WITH US .... Matthew 1:23
GOOD SHEPHERD ....John 10:11
GOVERNOR .... Matthew 2:6
GREAT HIGH PRIEST .... Hebrews 4:14
HEAD OF THE BODY .... Colossians 1:18
HEAD OF THE CHURCH .... Ephesians 5:23
HEAD OVER ALL THINGS.. Ephesians 1:22
HEAD STONE OF THE CORNER .... Psalms 118:22
HEIR OF ALL THINGS .... Hebrews 1:2
HIGH PRIEST.. Hebrews 3:1
HOLY ONE OF ISRAEL..Isaiah 41:14
HOPE OF GLORY .... Colossians 1:27
I AM ....John 8:58
IMAGE OF THE INVISIBLE GOD .... Colossians 1:15
IMMANUEL ....Isaiah 7:14
KING .... Zechariah 9:9
KING ETERNAL .... 1 Timothy 1:17
KING OF GLORY .... Psalms 24:7
KING OF KINGS .... 1 Timothy 6:15
KING OVER ALL THE EARTH .... Zechariah 14:9
LAMB OF GOD..John 1:29
LAST ADAM .... 1 Corinthians 15:45

LIFE, THE ....John 14:6
LIGHT OF THE GENTILES ....Isaiah 42:6
LIGHT OF THE WORLD...John 8:12
LILY OF THE VALLEYS .... Song of Solomon 2:1
LIVING BREAD ....John 6:51
LORD AND SAVIOUR .... 2 Peter 2:20
LORD OF ALL .... Acts 10:36
LORD OF LORDS .... 1 Timothy 6:15
LORD OUR RIGHTEOUSNESS ....Jeremiah 23:6
LORD GOD ALMIGHTY .... Revelation 4:8
LOVE .... 1 John 4:8
MADE PERFECT .... Hebrews 5:9
MAN... 1 Timothy 2:5
MASTER .... Matthew 23:10
MESSIAH.. Daniel 9:25-26, John 1:41
MIGHTY GOD ....Isaiah 9:6
MOST MIGHTY ....Psalms 45:3
NAZARENE.. Matthew 2:23
OFFSPRING OF DAVID.................................... Revelation 22:16
ONLY BEGOTTEN OF THE FATHER ....John 1:14
ONLY WISE GOD, THE.. 1 Timothy 1:17
OUR LORD .... Romans 8:39
OUR PASSOVER .... 1 Corinthians 5:7
OUR PROFESSION .... Hebrews 3:1
PRECIOUS .... 1 Peter 2:6
PRECIOUS CORNER STONE.....................................Isaiah 28:16
PRINCE OF PEACE ....Isaiah 9:6
PRINCE OF THE KINGS OF THE EARTH.......................... Revelation 1:5
PROPITIATION, THE .... Romans 3:25
RABBI ....John 1:49
REDEEMER...Isaiah 41:14
ROOT, THE .... Revelation 22:16
ROOT OF JESSE ....Isaiah 11:10
ROSE OF SHARON .... Song of Solomon 2:1
RESURRECTION, THE ....John 11:25
RIGHTEOUS, THE.. 1 John 2:1
SAVIOUR .... Titus 2:13
SAVIOUR OF THE WORLD ....1 John 4:14

THE NAME ABOVE ALL NAMES

Therefore God exalted him to the highest place and gave him the name that is above every name, that at the name of Jesus every knee should bow, in heaven and on earth and under the earth, and every tongue confess that Jesus Christ is Lord, to the glory of God the Father. Philippians 2:9-11

So he became as much superior to the angels as the name he has inherited is superior to theirs. Hebrews 1:4

PRAYING IN THE NAME OF JESUS

Again, I tell you that if two of you on earth agree about anything you ask for, it will be done for you by my Father in heaven. For where two or three come together in my name, there am I with them." Matthew 18:19-20

And I will do whatever you ask in my name, so that the Son may bring glory to the Father. You may ask me for anything in my name, and I will do it. John 14:13-14

You did not choose me, but I chose you and appointed you to go and bear fruit—fruit that will last. Then the Father will give you whatever you ask in my name. John 15:16

In that day you will no longer ask me anything. I tell you the truth, my Father will give you whatever you ask in my name. Until now you have not asked for anything in my name. Ask and you will receive, and your joy will be complete. John 16:23-24

In that day you will ask in my name. I am not saying that I will ask the Father on your behalf. John 16:26

Is any one of you sick? He should call the elders of the church to pray over him and anoint him with oil in the name of the Lord.
James 5:14

POWER IN THE NAME OF JESUS

And these signs will accompany those who believe: In my name they will drive out demons; they will speak in new tongues; they will pick up snakes with their hands; and when they drink deadly poison, it will not hurt them at all; they will place their hands on sick people, and they will get well. Mark 16:17-18

The seventy-two returned with joy and said, "Lord, even the demons submit to us in your name." Luke 10:17

Yet to all who received him, to those who believed in his name, he gave the right to become children of God. John 1:12

Then Peter said, "Silver or gold I do not have, but what I have I give you. In the name of Jesus Christ of Nazareth, walk." Acts 3:6

By faith in the name of Jesus, this man whom you see and know was made strong. It is Jesus' name and the faith that comes through him that has given this complete healing to him, as you can all see. Acts 3:16

They had Peter and John brought before them and began to question them: "By what power or what name did you do this?" Then Peter, filled with the Holy Spirit, said to them: "Rulers and elders of the people! Then know this, you and all the people of Israel: It is by the name of Jesus Christ of Nazareth, whom you crucified but whom God raised from the dead, that this man stands before you healed. Acts 4:7-8,10

She kept this up for many days. Finally Paul became so troubled that he turned around and said to the spirit, "In the name of Jesus Christ I command you to come out of her!" At that moment the spirit left her. Acts 16:18

The name of the Lord is a strong tower; the righteous run to it and are safe. Proverbs 18:10

The devil respects nothing but force through the name of Jesus.–Iraj Modarressi

BELIEVING IN THE NAME OF JESUS

Whoever believes in him is not condemned, but whoever does not believe stands condemned already because he has not believed in the name of God's one and only Son. John 3:18

But these are written that you may believe that Jesus is the Christ, the Son of God, and that by believing you may have life in his name. John 20:31

And everyone who calls on the name of the Lord will be saved. Acts 2:21

Salvation is found in no one else, for there is no other name under heaven given to men by which we must be saved. Acts 4:12

All the prophets testify about him that everyone who believes in him receives forgiveness of sins through his name. Acts 10:43

For, Everyone who calls on the name of the Lord will be saved.
Romans 10:13

In his name the nations will put their hope. Matthew 12:21

And this is his command: to believe in the name of his Son, Jesus Christ, and to love one another as he commanded us. 1 John 3:23

I write these things to you who believe in the name of the Son of God so that you may know that you have eternal life. 1 John 5:13

Now while he was in Jerusalem at the Passover Feast, many people saw the miraculous signs he was doing and believed in his name.
John 2:23

SERVING IN THE NAME OF JESUS

I tell you the truth, anyone who gives you a cup of water in my name because you belong to Christ will certainly not lose his reward. Mark 9:41

And whatever you do, whether in word or deed, do it all in the name of the Lord Jesus, giving thanks to God the Father through him. Colossians 3:17

SUFFERING FOR THE NAME OF JESUS

And everyone who has left houses or brothers or sisters or father or mother or children or fields for my sake will receive a hundred times as much and will inherit eternal life. Matthew 19:29

Remember the words I spoke to you: 'No servant is greater than his master.' If they persecuted me, they will persecute you also. If they obeyed my teaching, they will obey yours also. They will treat you this way because of my name, for they do not know the One who sent me. John 15:20-21

I tell you the truth, Jesus replied, no one who has left home or brothers or sisters or mother or father or children or fields for me and the gospel will fail to receive a hundred times as much in this present age (homes, brothers, sisters, mothers, children and fields— and with them, persecutions) and in the age to come, eternal life.
Mark 10:29-30

His speech persuaded them. They called the apostles in and had them flogged. Then they ordered them not to speak in the name of Jesus, and let them go. The apostles left the Sanhedrin, rejoicing because they had been counted worthy of suffering disgrace for the Name. Day after day, in the temple courts and from house to house, they never stopped teaching and proclaiming the good news that Jesus is the Christ. Acts 5:40-42

If you are insulted because of the name of Christ, you are blessed, for the Spirit of glory and of God rests on you. 1 Peter 4:14

COMMITTING TO CHRIST

SEEKING GOD

If my people, who are called by my name, will humble themselves and pray and seek my face and turn from their wicked ways, then will I hear from heaven and will forgive their sin and will heal their land. 2 Chronicles 7:14

But if it were I, I would appeal to God; I would lay my cause before him. Job 5:8

Those who know your name will trust in you, for you, Lord, have never forsaken those who seek you. Psalms 9:10

My heart says of you, "Seek his face!" Your face, Lord, I will seek. Psalms 27:8

God looks down from heaven on the sons of men to see if there are any who understand, any who seek God. Psalms 53:2

The poor will see and be glad—you who seek God, may your hearts live! Psalms 69:32

> *Jesus Christ is the first and last, author and finisher, beginning and end, alpha and omega, and by Him all other things hold together. He must be first or nothing. God never comes next! - Vance Havner*

So I turned to the Lord God and pleaded with him in prayer and petition, in fasting, and in sackcloth and ashes. Daniel 9:3

This is what the Lord says to the house of Israel: "Seek me and live. Amos 5:4

Seek the Lord, all you humble of the land, you who do what he commands. Seek righteousness, seek humility; perhaps you will be sheltered on the day of the Lord's anger. Zephaniah 2:3

And many peoples and powerful nations will come to Jerusalem to seek the Lord Almighty and to entreat him. Zechariah 8:22

But seek first his Kingdom and his righteousness, and all these things will be given to you as well. Matthew 6:33

Ask and it will be given to you; seek and you will find; knock and the door will be opened to you. For everyone who asks receives; he who seeks finds; and to him who knocks, the door will be opened.
Matthew 7:7-8

So I say to you: Ask and it will be given to you; seek and you will find; knock and the door will be opened to you. Luke 11:9

For everyone who asks receives; he who seeks finds; and to him who knocks, the door will be opened. Luke 11:10

And do not set your heart on what you will eat or drink; do not worry about it. For the pagan world runs after all such things, and your Father knows that you need them. But seek his kingdom, and these things will be given to you as well. Luke 12:29-31

Yet a time is coming and has now come when the true worshipers will worship the Father in spirit and truth, for they are the kind of worshipers the Father seeks. John 4:23

God did this so that men would seek him and perhaps reach out for him and find him, though he is not far from each one of us.
Acts 17:27

Since, then, you have been raised with Christ, set your hearts on things above, where Christ is seated at the right hand of God.
Colossians 3:1

For the law made nothing perfect, and a better hope is introduced, by which we draw near to God. Hebrews 7:19

Come near to God and he will come near to you. Wash your hands, you sinners, and purify your hearts, you double-minded. James 4:8

SEEK AFTER GOD WITH YOUR WHOLE BEING (SPIRIT, SOUL, AND BODY)

But if from there you seek the Lord your God, you will find him if you look for him with all your heart and with all your soul.
Deuteronomy 4:29

Now devote your heart and soul to seeking the Lord your God. Begin to build the sanctuary of the Lord God, so that you may bring the ark of the covenant of the Lord and the sacred articles belonging to God into the temple that will be built for the Name of the Lord. 1 Chronicles 22:19

They entered into a covenant to seek the Lord, the God of their fathers, with all their heart and soul. 2 Chronicles 15:12

Blessed are they who keep his statutes and seek him with all their heart. Psalms 119:2

You will seek me and find me when you seek me with all your heart. Jeremiah 29:13

SEEK GOD EARLY IN THE MORNING

O God, thou art my God; early will I seek thee: my soul thirsteth for thee, my flesh longeth for thee in a dry and thirsty land, where no water is. Psalms 63:1 KJV

With my soul have I desired thee in the night; yea, with my spirit within me will I seek thee early: for when thy judgments are in the earth, the inhabitants of the world will learn righteousness.
Isaiah 26:9 KJV

I will go and return to my place, till they acknowledge their offence, and seek my face: in their affliction they will seek me early.
Hosea 5:15 KJV

I love them that love me; and those that seek me early shall find me. Proverbs 8:17 KJV

Whatever is your best time in the day, give that to communion with God. - Hudson Taylor

I love those who love me, and those who seek me find me.

Proverbs 8:17

SEEK GOD CONTINUOUSLY

So I came out to meet you; I looked for you and have found you!

Proverbs 7:15

Glory in his holy name; let the hearts of those who seek the Lord rejoice. Look to the Lord and his strength; seek his face always.

1 Chronicles 16:10-11

Look to the Lord and his strength; seek his face always.

Psalms 105:4

Seek the Lord while he may be found; call on him while he is near.

Isaiah 55:6

For day after day they seek me out; they seem eager to know my ways, as if they were a nation that does what is right and has not forsaken the commands of its God. They ask me for just decisions and seem eager for God to come near them. Isaiah 58:2

And without faith it is impossible to please God, because anyone who comes to him must believe that he exists and that he rewards those who earnestly seek him. Hebrews 11:6

THE RESULTS OF CONTINUOUSLY SEEKING GOD

The poor will eat and be satisfied; they who seek the Lord will praise him—may your hearts live forever! Psalms 22:26

The lions may grow weak and hungry, but those who seek the Lord lack no good thing. Psalms 34:10

Evil men do not understand justice, but those who seek the Lord understand it fully. Proverbs 28:5

The Lord is good to those whose hope is in him, to the one who seeks him. Lamentations 3:25

THE CONSEQUENCES OF NOT SEEKING GOD

He did evil because he had not set his heart on seeking the Lord.
2 Chronicles 12:14

OVERCOMING IDOLATRY

DEFINITION: The worship of false gods, whether by means of images or otherwise.

You shall have no other gods before me. Exodus 20:3

Do not make any gods to be alongside me; do not make for yourselves gods of silver or gods of gold. Exodus 20:23

Do not worship any other god, for the Lord, whose name is Jealous, is a jealous God. Exodus 34:14

Do not turn to idols or make gods of cast metal for yourselves. I am the Lord your God. Leviticus 19:4

Do not make idols or set up an image or a sacred stone for yourselves, and do not place a carved stone in your land to bow down before it. I am the Lord your God. Leviticus 26:1

Whatever you put first is your God.

If you ever forget the Lord your God and follow other gods and worship and bow down to them, I testify against you today that you will surely be destroyed. Deuteronomy 8:19

Therefore, my dear friends, flee from idolatry. 1 Corinthians 10:14

THE CONSEQUENCES OF COMMITTING IDOLATRY

Do you not know that the wicked will not inherit the kingdom of God? Do not be deceived: Neither the sexually immoral nor idolaters nor adulterers nor male prostitutes nor homosexual offenders.
1 Corinthians 6:9

For of this you can be sure: No immoral, impure or greedy person—such a man is an idolater—has any inheritance in the kingdom of Christ and of God. Ephesians 5:5

THE WORSHIP OF demon spirits

The rest of mankind that were not killed by these plagues still did not repent of the work of their hands; they did not stop worshiping demons, and idols of gold, silver, bronze, stone and wood—idols that cannot see or hear or walk. Revelation 9:20

But the cowardly, the unbelieving, the vile, the murderers, the sexually immoral, those who practice magic arts, the idolaters and all liars—their place will be in the fiery lake of burning sulfur. This is the second death. Revelation 21:8

MATERIAL AND HUMAN gods

(OCCUPATION, SPORTS, MONEY and PEOPLE)

You shall have no other gods before me. Exodus 20:3

For where your treasure is, there your heart will be also.
Matthew 6:21

SINS RELATED TO IDOLATRY

For rebellion is like the sin of divination, and arrogance like the evil of idolatry. Because you have rejected the word of the Lord, he has rejected you as king. 1 Samuel 15:23

Put to death, therefore, whatever belongs to your earthly nature: sexual immorality, impurity, lust, evil desires and greed, which is idolatry. Colossians 3:5

OBEYING THE WORD OF GOD

Oh, that their hearts would be inclined to fear me and keep all my commands always, so that it might go well with them and their children forever! Deuteronomy 5:29

Do what is right and good in the Lord's sight, so that it may go well with you and you may go in and take over the good land that the Lord promised on oath to your forefathers. Deuteronomy 6:18

If you pay attention to these laws and are careful to follow them, then the Lord your God will keep his covenant of love with you, as he swore to your forefathers. Deuteronomy 7:12

Carefully follow the terms of this covenant, so that you may prosper in everything you do. Deuteronomy 29:9

See, I set before you today life and prosperity, death and destruction. For I command you today to love the Lord your God, to walk in his ways, and to keep his commands, decrees and laws; then you will live and increase, and the Lord your God will bless you in the land you are entering to possess. Deuteronomy 30:15-16

If they obey and serve him, they will spend the rest of their days in prosperity and their years in contentment. Job 36:11

Blessed are they who maintain justice, who constantly do what is right. Psalms 106:3

I will always obey your law, for ever and ever. Psalms 119:44

I will hasten and not delay to obey your commands. Psalms 119:60

I have kept my feet from every evil path so that I might obey your word. Psalms 119:101

Your statutes are wonderful; therefore I obey them. Psalms 119:129

How can a young man keep his way pure? By living according to your word. Psalms 119:9

My son, keep your father's commands and do not forsake your mother's teaching. Bind them upon your heart forever; fasten them around your neck. When you walk, they will guide you; when you sleep, they will watch over you; when you awake, they will speak to you. Proverbs 6:20-22

Anyone who breaks one of the least of these commandments and teaches others to do the same will be called least in the kingdom of heaven, but whoever practices and teaches these commands will be called great in the kingdom of heaven. Matthew 5:19

Not everyone who says to me, 'Lord, Lord,' will enter the kingdom of heaven, but only he who does the will of my Father who is in heaven. Matthew 7:21

For whoever does the will of my Father in heaven is my brother and sister and mother. Matthew 12:50

Jesus said, "Let the little children come to me, and do not hinder them, for the kingdom of heaven belongs to such as these."
Matthew 19:14

I tell you the truth, whoever hears my word and believes him who sent me has eternal life and will not be condemned; he has crossed over from death to life. John 5:24

I tell you the truth, if anyone keeps my word, he will never see death. John 8:51

Now that you know these things, you will be blessed if you do them. John 13:17

If you love me, you will obey what I command. John 14:15

Whoever has my commands and obeys them, he is the one who loves me. He who loves me will be loved by my Father, and I too will love him and show myself to him. John 14:21

Jesus replied, "If anyone loves me, he will obey my teaching. My Father will love him, and we will come to him and make our home with him. He who does not love me will not obey my teaching. These words you hear are not my own; they belong to the Father who sent me. John 14:23-24

If you obey my commands, you will remain in my love, just as I have obeyed my Father's commands and remain in his love.
John 15:10

You are my friends if you do what I command. John 15:14

Everyone must submit himself to the governing authorities, for there is no authority except that which God has established. The authorities that exist have been established by God. Romans 13:1

Whatever you have learned or received or heard from me, or seen in me—put it into practice. And the God of peace will be with you.
Philippians 4:9

And, once made perfect, he became the source of eternal salvation for all who obey him. Hebrews 5:9

We know that we have come to know him if we obey his commands. The man who says, "I know him," but does not do what he commands is a liar, and the truth is not in him. But if anyone obeys his word, God's love is truly made complete in him. This is how we know we are in him: Whoever claims to live in him must walk as Jesus did. 1 John 2:3-6

The world and its desires pass away, but the man who does the will of God lives forever. 1 John 2:17

And receive from him anything we ask, because we obey his commands and do what pleases him. 1 John 3:22

TRUE OBEDIENCE

He replied, "Blessed rather are those who hear the word of God and obey it." Luke 11:28

For it is not those who hear the law who are righteous in God's sight, but it is those who obey the law who will be declared righteous. Romans 2:13

Therefore everyone who hears these words of mine and puts them into practice is like a wise man who built his house on the rock. The rain came down, the streams rose, and the winds blew and beat against that house; yet it did not fall, because it had its foundation on the rock. Matthew 7:24-25

For it is not those who hear the law who are righteous in God's sight, but it is those who obey the law who will be declared righteous. Romans 2:13

But the man who looks intently into the perfect law that gives freedom, and continues to do this, not forgetting what he has heard, but doing it—he will be blessed in what he does. James 1:25

> *We have not learned the commandments until we have learned to do them. - Vance Havner*

SUBMITTING TO THE CORRECTION OF GOD

Blessed is the man whom God corrects; so do not despise the discipline of the Almighty. For he wounds, but he also binds up; he injures, but his hands also heal. Job 5:17-18

Blessed is the man you discipline, O Lord, the man you teach from your law; you grant him relief from days of trouble, till a pit is dug for the wicked. Psalms 94:12-13

My son, do not despise the Lord's discipline and do not resent his rebuke, because the Lord disciplines those he loves, as a father the son he delights in. Proverbs 3:11-12

When we are judged by the Lord, we are being disciplined so that we will not be condemned with the world. 1 Corinthians 11:32

And you have forgotten that word of encouragement that addresses you as sons: "My son, do not make light of the Lord's discipline, and do not lose heart when he rebukes you, because the Lord disciplines those he loves, and he punishes everyone he accepts as a son." Endure hardship as discipline; God is treating you as sons. For what son is not disciplined by his father? If you are not disciplined (and everyone undergoes discipline), then you are illegitimate children and not true sons. Moreover, we have all had human fathers who disciplined us and we respected them for it. How much more should we submit to the Father of our spirits and live! Our fathers disciplined us for a little while as they thought best; but God disciplines us for our good, that we may share in his holiness. No discipline seems pleasant at the time, but painful. Later on, however, it produces a harvest of righteousness and peace for those who have been trained by it. Hebrews 12:5-11

Those whom I love I rebuke and discipline. So be earnest, and repent. Revelation 3:19

DYING TO SELF

Whoever finds his life will lose it, and whoever loses his life for my sake will find it. Matthew 10:39

For whoever wants to save his life will lose it, but whoever loses his life for me and for the gospel will save it. Mark 8:35

Then he said to them all: "If anyone would come after me, he must deny himself and take up his cross daily and follow me. For whoever wants to save his life will lose it, but whoever loses his life for me will save it. What good is it for a man to gain the whole world, and yet lose or forfeit his very self? Luke 9:23-25

Whoever tries to keep his life will lose it, and whoever loses his life will preserve it. Luke 17:33

The man who loves his life will lose it, while the man who hates his life in this world will keep it for eternal life. John 12:25

> *The man who is prepared to die is prepared to live. - Vance Havner*

In the same way, count yourselves dead to sin but alive to God in Christ Jesus. Therefore do not let sin reign in your mortal body so that you obey its evil desires. Romans 6:11-12

Everything is permissible—but not everything is beneficial. Everything is permissible—but not everything is constructive.
1 Corinthians 10:23

For Christ's love compels us, because we are convinced that one died for all, and therefore all died. And he died for all, that those who live should no longer live for themselves but for him who died for them and was raised again. So from now on we regard no one from a worldly point of view. Though we once regarded Christ in this way, we do so no longer. Therefore, if anyone is in Christ, he is a new creation; the old has gone, the new has come!
2 Corinthians 5:14-17

> *In this day of self-exaltation the Bible teaches self-execution. Not that we execute ourselves but that we submit to the death of self by the hand of God. Paul witnessed his own execution, but there came forth a new Paul: "I live, yet not I, but Christ liveth in me.*
> *- Vance Havner*

For to be sure, he was crucified in weakness, yet he lives by God's power. Likewise, we are weak in him, yet by God's power we will live with him to serve you. 2 Corinthians 13:4

I have been crucified with Christ and I no longer live, but Christ lives in me. The life I live in the body, I live by faith in the Son of God, who loved me and gave himself for me. Galatians 2:20

You were taught, with regard to your former way of life, to put off your old self, which is being corrupted by its deceitful desires; to

be made new in the attitude of your minds; and to put on the new self, created to be like God in true righteousness and holiness.
Ephesians 4:22-24

But whatever was to my profit I now consider loss for the sake of Christ. Philippians 3:7

We are always trying to "find ourselves" when that is exactly what we need to lose. -Vance Havner

FOLLOWING CHRIST AND CARRYING YOUR CROSS

And anyone who does not take his cross and follow me is not worthy of me. Matthew 10:38

Then Jesus said to his disciples, "If anyone would come after me, he must deny himself and take up his cross and follow me.
Matthew 16:24

Then he called the crowd to him along with his disciples and said: If anyone would come after me, he must deny himself and take up his cross and follow me. Mark 8:34

Jesus looked at him and loved him. "One thing you lack," he said. "Go, sell everything you have and give to the poor, and you will have treasure in heaven. Then come, follow me." Mark 10:21

May I never boast except in the cross of our Lord Jesus Christ, through which the world has been crucified to me, and I to the world. Galatians 6:14

Then he said to them all: If anyone would come after me, he must deny himself and take up his cross daily and follow me. Luke 9:23

Salvation is free. The gift of God is eternal life. It is not cheap for it cost God his Son and the Son His life, but it is free. However, when we become believers we become disciples and that will cost everything we have.
- Vance Havner

And anyone who does not carry his cross and follow me cannot be my disciple. Luke 14:27

BEING A TRUE REPRESENTATIVE OF GOD IS

LIVING THE LIFE OF CHRIST BEFORE GOD AND MAN

The righteous man leads a blameless life; blessed are his children after him. Proverbs 20:7

In the same way, let your light shine before men, that they may see your good deeds and praise your Father in heaven. Matthew 5:16

You, then, who teach others, do you not teach yourself? You who preach against stealing, do you steal? You who say that people should not commit adultery, do you commit adultery? You who abhor idols, do you rob temples? You who brag about the law, do you dishonor God by breaking the law? As it is written: "God's name is blasphemed among the Gentiles because of you."
Romans 2:21-24

No, I beat my body and make it my slave so that after I have preached to others, I myself will not be disqualified for the prize.
1 Corinthians 9:27

Where one reads the Bible, a hundred read you and me. - D. L. Moody

It teaches us to say "No" to ungodliness and worldly passions, and to live self-controlled, upright and godly lives in this present age.
Titus 2:12

They claim to know God, but by their actions they deny him. They are detestable, disobedient and unfit for doing anything good.
Titus 1:16

Like a muddied spring or a polluted well is a righteous man who gives way to the wicked. Proverbs 25:26

Like a muddied fountain and a polluted spring is a righteous man who yields, falls down and compromises his integrity before the wicked. Proverbs 25:26 AMP

The man who says, "I know him," but does not do what he commands is a liar, and the truth is not in him. 1 John 2:4

We put no stumbling block in anyone's path, so that our ministry will not be discredited. Rather, as servants of God we commend ourselves in every way: in great endurance; in troubles, hardships and distresses; in beatings, imprisonments and riots; in hard work, sleepless nights and hunger; in purity, understanding, patience and kindness; in the Holy Spirit and in sincere love; in truthful speech and in the power of God; with weapons of righteousness in the right hand and in the left; through glory and dishonor, bad report and good report; genuine, yet regarded as impostors; known, yet regarded as unknown; dying, and yet we live on; beaten, and yet not killed; sorrowful, yet always rejoicing; poor, yet making many rich; having nothing, and yet possessing everything.
2 Corinthians 6:3-10

We want to avoid any criticism of the way we administer this liberal gift. For we are taking pains to do what is right, not only in the eyes of the Lord but also in the eyes of men. 2 Corinthians 8:20-21

You and I are human post offices. We are daily giving out messages of some sort to the world. They do not come from us, but through us we do not create, we convey. And they come either from hell or from heaven.
- Vance Havner

BEING A TRUE REPRESENTATIVE OF GOD IS

KNOWING THE WORD OF GOD WHEN SHARING WITH UNBELIEVERS

Then I will teach transgressors your ways, and sinners will turn back to you. Psalms 51:13

The heart of the righteous weighs its answers, but the mouth of the wicked gushes evil. Proverbs 15:28

The fruit of the righteous is a tree of life, and he who wins souls is wise. Proverbs 11:30

That I might make thee know the certainty of the words of truth; that thou mightest answer the words of truth to them that send unto thee? Proverbs 22:21 KJV

Do your best to present yourself to God as one approved, a workman who does not need to be ashamed and who correctly handles the word of truth. 2 Timothy 2:15

I pray that you may be active in sharing your faith, so that you will have a full understanding of every good thing we have in Christ.
Philemon 1:6

But in your hearts set apart Christ as Lord. Always be prepared to give an answer to everyone who asks you to give the reason for the hope that you have. But do this with gentleness and respect, keeping a clear conscience, so that those who speak maliciously against your good behavior in Christ may be ashamed of their slander.
1 Peter 3:15-16

He must hold firmly to the trustworthy message as it has been taught, so that he can encourage others by sound doctrine and refute those who oppose it. Titus 1:9

Not only was the Teacher wise, but also he imparted knowledge to the people. He pondered and searched out and set in order many proverbs. The Teacher searched to find just the right words, and what he wrote was upright and true. The words of the wise are like goads, their collected sayings like firmly embedded nails—given by one Shepherd. Ecclesiastes 12:9-11

BEING A TRUE REPRESENTATIVE OF GOD IS

LOVING EVERYONE FROM YOUR HEART

We know that we have passed from death to life, because we love our brothers. Anyone who does not love remains in death.
1 John 3:14

By this all men will know that you are my disciples, if you love one another. John 13:35

171

BEING A TRUE REPRESENTATIVE OF GOD IS

NEVER DENYING JESUS CHRIST

"Whoever acknowledges me before men, I will also acknowledge him before my Father in heaven. But whoever disowns me before men, I will disown him before my Father in heaven.
Matthew 10:32-33

I tell you, whoever acknowledges me before men, the Son of Man will also acknowledge him before the angels of God. But he who disowns me before men will be disowned before the angels of God.
Luke 12:8-9

If we endure, we will also reign with him. If we disown him, he will also disown us. 2 Timothy 2:12

I know your deeds. See, I have placed before you an open door that no one can shut. I know that you have little strength, yet you have kept my word and have not denied my name. Revelation 3:8

BEING A TRUE REPRESENTATIVE OF GOD IS BEING

A VESSEL FOR GOD'S POWER TO FLOW THROUGH

But you will receive power when the Holy Spirit comes on you; and you will be my witnesses in Jerusalem, and in all Judea and Samaria, and to the ends of the earth. Acts 1:8

And such as do wickedly against the covenant shall he corrupt by flatteries: but the people that do know their God shall be strong, and do exploits. Daniel 11:32 KJV

He said to them, "Go into all the world and preach the good news to all creation. Whoever believes and is baptized will be saved, but whoever does not believe will be condemned. And these signs will accompany those who believe: In my name they will drive out demons; they will speak in new tongues; they will pick up snakes with their hands; and when they drink deadly poison, it will not hurt them at all; they will place their hands on sick people, and they will get well." Mark 16:15-18

I tell you the truth, anyone who has faith in me will do what I have been doing. He will do even greater things than these, because I am going to the Father. John 14:12

I assure you, most solemnly I tell you, if any one steadfastly believes in Me, he will himself be able to do the things that I do, and he will do even greater things than these, because I go to the Father. John 14:12 AMP

FASTING

Is this the kind of fast I have chosen, only a day for a man to humble himself? Is it only for bowing one's head like a reed and for lying on sackcloth and ashes? Is that what you call a fast, a day acceptable to the Lord? "Is not this the kind of fasting I have chosen: to loose the chains of injustice and untie the cords of the yoke, to set the oppressed free and break every yoke? Isaiah 58:5-6

Yet when they were ill, I put on sackcloth and humbled myself with fasting. When my prayers returned to me unanswered.

Psalms 35:13

So I turned to the Lord God and pleaded with him in prayer and petition, in fasting, and in sackcloth and ashes. Daniel 9:3

After fasting forty days and forty nights, he was hungry.

Matthew 4:2

Fasting is the attitude of , "Lord, empty me of self." Prayer is the insistent cry of one's soul, "Lord, fill me with thyself." - H. H. Leavitt

FASTING GIVE YOU POWER OVER satan

When Jesus saw that a crowd was running to the scene, he rebuked the evil spirit. "You deaf and mute spirit," he said, "I command you, come out of him and never enter him again." The spirit shrieked, convulsed him violently and came out. The boy looked so much like a corpse that many said, "He's dead." But Jesus took him by the hand and lifted him to his feet, and he stood up. After Jesus had gone indoors, his disciples asked him privately, "Why couldn't we drive it out?" He replied, "This kind can come out only by prayer." Mark 9:25-29

FASTING WITH PURE MOTIVES

When you fast, do not look somber as the hypocrites do, for they disfigure their faces to show men they are fasting. I tell you the truth, they have received their reward in full. But when you fast, put oil on your head and wash your face, so that it will not be obvious to men that you are fasting, but only to your Father, who is unseen; and your Father, who sees what is done in secret, will reward you. Matthew 6:16-18

The Pharisee stood up and prayed about himself: 'God, I thank you that I am not like other men—robbers, evildoers, adulterers—or even like this tax collector. I fast twice a week and give a tenth of all I get.' "But the tax collector stood at a distance. He would not even look up to heaven, but beat his breast and said, 'God, have mercy on me, a sinner.' Luke 18:11-13

PRAYER

Let us then approach the throne of grace with confidence, so that we may receive mercy and find grace to help us in our time of need. Hebrews 4:16

Therefore, brothers, since we have confidence to enter the Most Holy Place by the blood of Jesus. Hebrews 10:19

If you, then, though you are evil, know how to give good gifts to your children, how much more will your Father in heaven give good gifts to those who ask him! Matthew 7:11

"Ask and it will be given to you; seek and you will find; knock and the door will be opened to you. For everyone who asks receives; he who seeks finds; and to him who knocks, the door will be opened. "Which of you, if his son asks for bread, will give him a stone? Or if he asks for a fish, will give him a snake? If you, then, though you are evil, know how to give good gifts to your children, how much more will your Father in heaven give good gifts to those who ask him! Matthew 7:7-11

> *Prayer moves the hand which moves the world.*
> *- John A. Wallace*

PRAYING IN THE NAME OF JESUS

Again, I tell you that if two of you on earth agree about anything you ask for, it will be done for you by my Father in heaven. For where two or three come together in my name, there am I with them." Matthew 18:19-20

And I will do whatever you ask in my name, so that the Son may bring glory to the Father. You may ask me for anything in my name, and I will do it. John 14:13-14

You did not choose me, but I chose you and appointed you to go and bear fruit—fruit that will last. Then the Father will give you whatever you ask in my name. John 15:16

In that day you will no longer ask me anything. I tell you the truth, my Father will give you whatever you ask in my name. Until now you have not asked for anything in my name. Ask and you will receive, and your joy will be complete. John 16:23-24

In that day you will ask in my name. I am not saying that I will ask the Father on your behalf. John 16:26

Is any one of you sick? He should call the elders of the church to pray over him and anoint him with oil in the name of the Lord.
James 5:14

THE LORD'S PRAYER

This, then, is how you should pray: 'Our Father in heaven, hallowed be your name, your kingdom come, your will be done on earth as it is in heaven. Give us today our daily bread. Forgive us our debts, as we also have forgiven our debtors. And lead us not into temptation, but deliver us from the evil one. Matthew 6:9-13

GOD HEARS YOUR PRAYERS

Am I only a God nearby, declares the LORD, and not a God far away? Jeremiah 23:23

Know that the Lord has set apart the godly for himself; the Lord will hear when I call to him. Psalms 4:3

In the morning, O Lord, you hear my voice; in the morning I lay my requests before you and wait in expectation. Psalms 5:3

I waited patiently for the Lord; he turned to me and heard my cry.
Psalms 40:1

Evening, morning and noon I cry out in distress, and he hears my voice. Psalms 55:17

The Lord is far from the wicked but he hears the prayer of the righteous. Proverbs 15:29

The eyes of the Lord are on the righteous and his ears are attentive to their cry. Psalms 34:15

But as for me, I watch in hope for the Lord, I wait for God my Savior; my God will hear me. Micah 7:7

This is the confidence we have in approaching God: that if we ask anything according to his will, he hears us. And if we know that he hears us—whatever we ask—we know that we have what we asked of him. 1 John 5:14-15

HINDRANCES TO PRAYER

If I had cherished sin in my heart, the Lord would not have listened. Psalms 66:18

If a man shuts his ears to the cry of the poor, he too will cry out and not be answered. Proverbs 21:13

If anyone turns a deaf ear to the law, even his prayers are detestable. Proverbs 28:9

Surely the arm of the Lord is not too short to save, nor his ear too dull to hear. But your iniquities have separated you from your God; your sins have hidden his face from you, so that he will not hear.
Isaiah 59:1-2

Then they will cry out to the Lord, but he will not answer them. At that time he will hide his face from them because of the evil they have done. Micah 3:4

You want something but don't get it. You kill and covet, but you cannot have what you want. You quarrel and fight. You do not have, because you do not ask God. When you ask, you do not receive, because you ask with wrong motives, that you may spend what you get on your pleasures. James 4:2-3

Husbands, in the same way be considerate as you live with your wives, and treat them with respect as the weaker partner and as heirs with you of the gracious gift of life, so that nothing will hinder your prayers. 1 Peter 3:7

For the eyes of the Lord are on the righteous and his ears are attentive to their prayer, but the face of the Lord is against those who do evil. 1 Peter 3:12

PRAYING IN THE RIGHT ATTITUDE AND MOTIVE

And when you pray, do not be like the hypocrites, for they love to pray standing in the synagogues and on the street corners to be seen by men. I tell you the truth, they have received their reward in full. But when you pray, go into your room, close the door and pray to your Father, who is unseen. Then your Father, who sees what is done in secret, will reward you. And when you pray, do not keep on babbling like pagans, for they think they will be heard because of their many words. Do not be like them, for your Father knows what you need before you ask him. Matthew 6:5-8

For if you forgive men when they sin against you, your heavenly Father will also forgive you. But if you do not forgive men their sins, your Father will not forgive your sins. "When you fast, do not look somber as the hypocrites do, for they disfigure their faces to show men they are fasting. I tell you the truth, they have received their reward in full. But when you fast, put oil on your head and wash your face, so that it will not be obvious to men that you are fasting, but only to your Father, who is unseen; and your Father, who sees what is done in secret, will reward you. Matthew 6:14-18

> *Praying only when you are in trouble or when you need something; being thankful only when you get your way; and ignoring God when things are going great, is a terrible way to treat God!*

And when you stand praying, if you hold anything against anyone, forgive him, so that your Father in heaven may forgive you your sins. Mark 11:25

PRAYING FOR YOUR DESIRES

You have granted him the desire of his heart and have not withheld the request of his lips. Selah Psalms 21:2

You open your hand and satisfy the desires of every living thing.
Psalms 145:16

He fulfills the desires of those who fear him; he hears their cry and saves them. Psalms 145:19

What the wicked dreads will overtake him; what the righteous desire will be granted. Proverbs 10:24

And if we know that he hears us—whatever we ask—we know that we have what we asked of him. 1 John 5:15

THE KEY TO RECEIVING YOUR DESIRES

Delight yourself in the Lord and he will give you the desires of your heart. Psalms 37:4

But seek first his kingdom and his righteousness, and all these things will be given to you as well. Matthew 6:33

The lions may grow weak and hungry, but those who seek the Lord lack no good thing. Psalms 34:10

If you remain in me and my words remain in you, ask whatever you wish, and it will be given you. John 15:7

DESIRING THE WORD OF GOD

Surely you desire truth in the inner parts; you teach me wisdom in the inmost place. Psalms 51:6

Like newborn babies, crave pure spiritual milk, so that by it you may grow up in your salvation. 1 Peter 2:2

GOOD DESIRES

The desire of the righteous ends only in good, but the hope of the wicked only in wrath. Proverbs 11:23

What a man desires is unfailing love; better to be poor than a liar.
Proverbs 19:22

I denied myself nothing my eyes desired; I refused my heart no pleasure. My heart took delight in all my work, and this was the reward for all my labor. Ecclesiastes 2:10

Brothers, my heart's desire and prayer to God for the Israelites is that they may be saved. Romans 10:1

Here is a trustworthy saying: If anyone sets his heart on being an overseer, he desires a noble task. 1 Timothy 3:1

EVIL DESIRES

What causes fights and quarrels among you? Don't they come from your desires that battle within you? You want something but don't get it. You kill and covet, but you cannot have what you want. You quarrel and fight. You do not have, because you do not ask God. When you ask, you do not receive, because you ask with wrong motives, that you may spend what you get on your pleasures.
James 4:1-3

The wicked desire the plunder of evil men, but the root of the righteous flourishes. Proverbs 12:12

The wicked man craves evil; his neighbor gets no mercy from him.
Proverbs 21:10

Do not envy wicked men, do not desire their company.
Proverbs 24:1

Let us not be desirous of vain glory, provoking one another, envying one another. Galatians 5:26 KJV

Let us not become conceited, provoking and envying each other.
Galatians 5:26

All of us also lived among them at one time, gratifying the cravings of our sinful nature and following its desires and thoughts. Like the rest, we were by nature objects of wrath. Ephesians 2:3

DIFFERENT KINDS OF PRAYER

So I turned to the Lord God and pleaded with him in prayer and petition, in fasting, and in sackcloth and ashes. Daniel 9:3

And pray in the Spirit on all occasions with all kinds of prayers and requests. With this in mind, be alert and always keep on praying for all the saints. Ephesians 6:18

The measure of any Christian is his prayer life.
- Vance Havner

I urge, then, first of all, that requests, prayers, intercession and thanksgiving be made for everyone. 1 Timothy 2:1

PRAYER OF AGREEMENT

How could one man chase a thousand, or two put ten thousand to flight, unless their Rock had sold them, unless the Lord had given them up? Deuteronomy 32:30

This will be my third visit to you. "Every matter must be established by the testimony of two or three witnesses."
2 Corinthians 13:1

"I tell you the truth, whatever you bind on earth will be bound in heaven, and whatever you loose on earth will be loosed in heaven. "Again, I tell you that if two of you on earth agree about anything you ask for, it will be done for you by my Father in heaven.
Matthew 18:18-19

PRAYING IN FAITH

Jesus replied, "I tell you the truth, if you have faith and do not doubt, not only can you do what was done to the fig tree, but also you can say to this mountain, 'Go, throw yourself into the sea,' and it will be done. If you believe, you will receive whatever you ask for in prayer." Matthew 21:21-22

If you can? said Jesus. "Everything is possible for him who believes." Immediately the boy's father exclaimed, "I do believe; help me overcome my unbelief!" Mark 9:23-24

Therefore I tell you, whatever you ask for in prayer, believe that you have received it, and it will be yours. Mark 11:24

And the prayer offered in faith will make the sick person well; the Lord will raise him up. If he has sinned, he will be forgiven.

James 5:15

WAITING ON GOD IN PRAYER

But they that wait upon the Lord shall renew their strength; they shall mount up with wings as eagles; they shall run, and not be weary; and they shall walk, and not faint. Isaiah 40:31 KJV

But those who hope in the Lord will renew their strength. They will soar on wings like eagles; they will run and not grow weary, they will walk and not be faint. Isaiah 40:31

Call to me and I will answer you and tell you great and unsearchable things you do not know. Jeremiah 33:3

PRAYING IN THE HOLY SPIRIT

In the same way, the Spirit helps us in our weakness. We do not know what we ought to pray for, but the Spirit himself intercedes for us with groans that words cannot express. And he who searches our hearts knows the mind of the Spirit, because the Spirit intercedes for the saints in accordance with God's will.

Romans 8:26-27

For if I pray in a tongue, my spirit prays, but my mind is unfruitful. So what shall I do? I will pray with my spirit, but I will also pray with my mind; I will sing with my spirit, but I will also sing with my mind. 1 Corinthians 14:14-15

But you, dear friends, build yourselves up in your most holy faith and pray in the Holy Spirit. Jude 1:20

Praying in the Spirit guarantees perfect prayer that is directed by the Holy Spirit; untouched by doubt and fear of the mind; and impossible for the devil to understand or hinder.

INTERCESSORY PRAYER

He saw that there was no one, he was appalled that there was no one to intervene; so his own arm worked salvation for him, and his own righteousness sustained him. Isaiah 59:16

I looked for a man among them who would build up the wall and stand before me in the gap on behalf of the land so I would not have to destroy it, but I found none. Ezekiel 22:30

But I have prayed for you, Simon, that your faith may not fail. And when you have turned back, strengthen your brothers. Luke 22:32

In that day you will ask in my name. I am not saying that I will ask the Father on your behalf. John 16:26

I pray for them. I am not praying for the world, but for those you have given me, for they are yours. John 17:9

I urge you, brothers, by our Lord Jesus Christ and by the love of the Spirit, to join me in my struggle by praying to God for me.
Romans 15:30

For this reason, since the day we heard about you, we have not stopped praying for you and asking God to fill you with the knowledge of his will through all spiritual wisdom and understanding.
Colossians 1:9

And pray for us, too, that God may open a door for our message, so that we may proclaim the mystery of Christ, for which I am in chains. Colossians 4:3

With this in mind, we constantly pray for you, that our God may count you worthy of his calling, and that by his power he may fulfill every good purpose of yours and every act prompted by your faith. 2 Thessalonians 1:11

Finally, brothers, pray for us that the message of the Lord may spread rapidly and be honored, just as it was with you. And pray that we may be delivered from wicked and evil men, for not everyone has faith. 2 Thessalonians 3:1-2

Therefore confess your sins to each other and pray for each other so that you may be healed. The prayer of a righteous man is powerful and effective. James 5:16

EXAMPLES OF PRAYER WARRIORS

And then was a widow until she was eighty-four. She never left the temple but worshiped night and day, fasting and praying. Luke 2:37

One of those days Jesus went out to a mountainside to pray, and spent the night praying to God. Luke 6:12

Suddenly a sound like the blowing of a violent wind came from heaven and filled the whole house where they were sitting. They saw what seemed to be tongues of fire that separated and came to rest on each of them. All of them were filled with the Holy Spirit and began to speak in other tongues as the Spirit enabled them.
Acts 2:2-4

PRAYING CONTINUOUSLY

Watch and pray so that you will not fall into temptation. The spirit is willing, but the body is weak. Matthew 26:41

Then Jesus told his disciples a parable to show them that they should always pray and not give up. Luke 18:1

Be always on the watch, and pray that you may be able to escape all that is about to happen, and that you may be able to stand before the Son of Man." Luke 21:36

"Why are you sleeping?" he asked them. "Get up and pray so that you will not fall into temptation." Luke 22:46

Devote yourselves to prayer, being watchful and thankful.
Colossians 4:2

Pray continually. 1 Thessalonians 5:17

The end of all things is near. Therefore be clear minded and self-controlled so that you can pray. 1 Peter 4:7

To be a Christian without prayer is no more possible than to be alive without breathing. - Martin Luther

DEVELOPING THE WHOLE MAN

THE SPIRIT

GOD IS THE CREATOR OF HUMAN SPIRITS

Then God said, "Let us make man in our image, in our likeness, and let them rule over the fish of the sea and the birds of the air, over the livestock, over all the earth, and over all the creatures that move along the ground." So God created man in his own image, in the image of God he created him; male and female he created them.
Genesis 1:26-27

May the Lord, the God of the spirits of all mankind, appoint a man over this community. Numbers 27:16

This is the word of the Lord concerning Israel. The Lord, who stretches out the heavens, who lays the foundation of the earth, and who forms the spirit of man within him, declares. Zechariah 12:1

Moreover, we have all had human fathers who disciplined us and we respected them for it. How much more should we submit to the Father of our spirits and live! Hebrews 12:9

But Moses and Aaron fell facedown and cried out, "O God, God of the spirits of all mankind, will you be angry with the entire assembly when only one man sins?" Numbers 16:22

GOD HAS ULTIMATE CONTROL OVER HUMAN SPIRITS

No man has power over the wind to contain it; so no one has power over the day of his death. As no one is discharged in time of war, so wickedness will not release those who practice it. Ecclesiastes 8:8

185

And the dust returns to the ground it came from, and the spirit returns to God who gave it. Ecclesiastes 12:7

THE BODY IS THE TEMPORARY CONTAINER FOR THE HUMAN SPIRIT

As the body without the spirit is dead, so faith without deeds is dead. James 2:26

Don't you know that you yourselves are God's temple and that God's Spirit lives in you? If anyone destroys God's temple, God will destroy him; for God's temple is sacred, and you are that temple.
1 Corinthians 3:16-17

Do you not know that your body is a temple of the Holy Spirit, who is in you, whom you have received from God? You are not your own; you were bought at a price. Therefore honor God with your body. 1 Corinthians 6:19-20

May God himself, the God of peace, sanctify you through and through. May your whole spirit, soul and body be kept blameless at the coming of our Lord Jesus Christ. 1 Thessalonians 5:23

THE LIFE OF THE HUMAN SPIRIT

He who has the Son has life; he who does not have the Son of God does not have life. 1 John 5:12

The Spirit gives life; the flesh counts for nothing. The words I have spoken to you are spirit and they are life. John 6:63

Because through Christ Jesus the law of the Spirit of life set me free from the law of sin and death. Romans 8:2

So it is written: "The first man Adam became a living being"; the last Adam, a life-giving spirit. 1 Corinthians 15:45

GOD COMMUNICATES WITH YOUR SPIRIT

The Spirit himself testifies with our spirit that we are God's children. Romans 8:16

God is spirit, and his worshipers must worship in spirit and in truth.
John 4:24

SPIRIT OF MAN

But it is the spirit in a man, the breath of the Almighty, that gives him understanding. Job 32:8

A man's spirit sustains him in sickness, but a crushed spirit who can bear? Proverbs 18:14

The lamp of the Lord searches the spirit of a man; it searches out his inmost being. Proverbs 20:27

Through whom also he went and preached to the spirits in prison.
1 Peter 3:19

RENEWED (BORN AGAIN) SPIRIT

But he who unites himself with the Lord is one with him in spirit.
1 Corinthians 6:17

Create in me a pure heart, O God, and renew a steadfast spirit within me. Psalms 51:10

I will give you a new heart and put a new spirit in you; I will remove from you your heart of stone and give you a heart of flesh. And I will put my Spirit in you and move you to follow my decrees and be careful to keep my laws. Ezekiel 36:26-27

In reply Jesus declared, "I tell you the truth, no one can see the kingdom of God unless he is born again." "How can a man be born when he is old?" Nicodemus asked. "Surely he cannot enter a second time into his mother's womb to be born!" Jesus answered, "I tell you the truth, no one can enter the kingdom of God unless he is born again." Flesh gives birth to flesh, but the Spirit gives birth to spirit. You should not be surprised at my saying, You Must be born again. John 3:3-7

God doesn't have any grandchildren. - E. Stanley Jones

Flesh gives birth to flesh, but the Spirit gives birth to spirit.
John 3:6

187

SPIRITUAL FOOD (GOD'S WORD) FOR THE SPIRIT

Jesus answered, "It is written: 'Man does not live on bread alone, but on every word that comes from the mouth of God.'"
Matthew 4:4

Jesus answered, "It is written: 'Man does not live on bread alone.'"
Luke 4:4

But he said to them, "I have food to eat that you know nothing about." John 4:32

Do not work for food that spoils, but for food that endures to eternal life, which the Son of Man will give you. On him God the Father has placed his seal of approval. John 6:27

Jesus said to them, "I tell you the truth, it is not Moses who has given you the bread from heaven, but it is my Father who gives you the true bread from heaven. For the bread of God is he who comes down from heaven and gives life to the world." "Sir," they said, "from now on give us this bread." Then Jesus declared, "I am the bread of life. He who comes to me will never go hungry, and he who believes in me will never be thirsty." John 6:32-35

I am the living bread that came down from heaven. If anyone eats of this bread, he will live forever. This bread is my flesh, which I will give for the life of the world." John 6:51

This is the bread that came down from heaven. Your forefathers ate manna and died, but he who feeds on this bread will live forever.
John 6:58

When they had finished eating, Jesus said to Simon Peter, "Simon son of John, do you truly love me more than these?" "Yes, Lord," he said, "you know that I love you." Jesus said, "Feed my lambs." Again Jesus said, "Simon son of John, do you truly love me?" He answered, "Yes, Lord, you know that I love you." Jesus said, "Take care of my sheep." John 21:15-16

Brothers, I could not address you as spiritual but as worldly—mere infants in Christ. I gave you milk, not solid food, for you were not yet ready for it. Indeed, you are still not ready. You are still worldly.

For since there is jealousy and quarreling among you, are you not worldly? Are you not acting like mere men? 1 Corinthians 3:1-3

They all ate the same spiritual food and drank the same spiritual drink; for they drank from the spiritual rock that accompanied them, and that rock was Christ. 1 Corinthians 10:3-4

In fact, though by this time you ought to be teachers, you need someone to teach you the elementary truths of God's word all over again. You need milk, not solid food! Anyone who lives on milk, being still an infant, is not acquainted with the teaching about righteousness. But solid food is for the mature, who by constant use have trained themselves to distinguish good from evil.

Hebrews 5:12-14

Like newborn babies, crave pure spiritual milk, so that by it you may grow up in your salvation. 1 Peter 2:2

THE WORD OF GOD PLANTED IN THE HEART OF MAN

I desire to do your will, O my God; your law is within my heart.
Psalms 40:8

I do not hide your righteousness in my heart; I speak of your faithfulness and salvation. I do not conceal your love and your truth from the great assembly. Psalms 40:10

I have hidden your word in my heart that I might not sin against you. Psalms 119:11

Turn my heart toward your statutes and not toward selfish gain.
Psalms 119:36

May my heart be blameless toward your decrees, that I may not be put to shame. Psalms 119:80

My son, do not forget my teaching, but keep my commands in your heart. Proverbs 3:1

He taught me and said, "Lay hold of my words with all your heart; keep my commands and you will live. Proverbs 4:4

My son, pay attention to what I say; listen closely to my words. Do not let them out of your sight, keep them within your heart; for they are life to those who find them and health to a man's whole body. Above all else, guard your heart, for it is the wellspring of life. Proverbs 4:20-23

My son, keep your father's commands and do not forsake your mother's teaching. Bind them upon your heart forever; fasten them around your neck. Proverbs 6:20-21

My son, keep my words and store up my commands within you. Keep my commands and you will live; guard my teachings as the apple of your eye. Bind them on your fingers; write them on the tablet of your heart. Proverbs 7:1-3

Pay attention and listen to the sayings of the wise; apply your heart to what I teach. Proverbs 22:17

This is the covenant I will make with the house of Israel after that time, declares the Lord. I will put my law in their minds and write it on their hearts. I will be their God, and they will be my people.
Jeremiah 31:33

If you remain in me and my words remain in you, ask whatever you wish, and it will be given you. John 15:7

But what does it say? "The word is near you; it is in your mouth and in your heart," that is, the word of faith we are proclaiming.
Romans 10:8

"This is the covenant I will make with them after that time, says the Lord. I will put my laws in their hearts, and I will write them on their minds." Hebrews 10:16

You yourselves are our letter, written on our hearts, known and read by everybody. You show that you are a letter from Christ, the result of our ministry, written not with ink but with the Spirit of the living God, not on tablets of stone but on tablets of human hearts.
2 Corinthians 3:2-3

GOD'S WORD DISCERNS THE HEART

So that the thoughts of many hearts will be revealed. And a sword will pierce your own soul too. Luke 2:35

For the word of God is living and active. Sharper than any double-edged sword, it penetrates even to dividing soul and spirit, joints and marrow; it judges the thoughts and attitudes of the heart.

Hebrews 4:12

I have read many books, but the Bible reads me.
- Anonymous

THOUGHTS AND WORDS ORIGINATE IN THE HEART OF MAN

For as he thinketh in his heart, so is he: Eat and drink, saith he to thee; but his heart is not with thee. Proverbs 23:7 KJV

For he is the kind of man who is always thinking about the cost. "Eat and drink," he says to you, but his heart is not with you.

Proverbs 23:7

But the things that come out of the mouth come from the heart, and these make a man 'unclean.' Matthew 15:18

The good man brings good things out of the good stored up in his heart, and the evil man brings evil things out of the evil stored up in his heart. For out of the overflow of his heart his mouth speaks.

Luke 6:45

What we love usually manages to get into our conversation. What is down in the well of the heart will come up in the bucket of the speech. - Vance Havner

LIVING AND WALKING IN THE SPIRIT

In order that the righteous requirements of the law might be fully met in us, who do not live according to the sinful nature but according to the Spirit. Those who live according to the sinful nature have their minds set on what that nature desires; but those who live in accordance with the Spirit have their minds set on what the Spirit desires. Romans 8:4-5

You, however, are controlled not by the sinful nature but by the Spirit, if the Spirit of God lives in you. And if anyone does not have the Spirit of Christ, he does not belong to Christ. But if Christ is in you, your body is dead because of sin, yet your spirit is alive because of righteousness. And if the Spirit of him who raised Jesus from the dead is living in you, he who raised Christ from the dead will also give life to your mortal bodies through his Spirit, who lives in you. Romans 8:9-11

For if you live according to the sinful nature, you will die; but if by the Spirit you put to death the misdeeds of the body, you will live.
Romans 8:13

So I say, live by the Spirit, and you will not gratify the desires of the sinful nature. Galatians 5:16

But if you are led by the Spirit, you are not under law.
Galatians 5:18

Since we live by the Spirit, let us keep in step with the Spirit.
Galatians 5:25

For this is the reason the gospel was preached even to those who are now dead, so that they might be judged according to men in regard to the body, but live according to God in regard to the spirit.
1 Peter 4:6

FRUITS OF THE SPIRIT

But the fruit of the Spirit is love, joy, peace, patience, kindness, goodness, faithfulness, gentleness and self-control. Against such things there is no law. Galatians 5:22-23

For the fruit of the light consists in all goodness, righteousness and truth. Ephesians 5:9

Filled with the fruit of righteousness that comes through Jesus Christ—to the glory and praise of God. Philippians 1:11

THE MIND

RENEWING YOUR MIND

That ye be not soon shaken in mind, or be troubled, neither by spirit, nor by word, nor by letter as from us, as that the day of Christ is at hand. 2 Thessalonians 2:2 KJV

Not to become easily unsettled or alarmed by some prophecy, report or letter supposed to have come from us, saying that the day of the Lord has already come. 2 Thessalonians 2:2

For God did not give us a spirit of timidity, but a spirit of power, of love and of self-discipline. 2 Timothy 1:7

Similarly, encourage the young men to be self-controlled.
Titus 2:6

Therefore, prepare your minds for action; be self-controlled; set your hope fully on the grace to be given you when Jesus Christ is revealed. 1 Peter 1:13

He hath delivered my soul in peace from the battle that was against me: for there were many with me. Psalms 55:18 KJV

He ransoms me unharmed from the battle waged against me, even though many oppose me. Psalms 55:18

FOCUSING YOUR MIND ON THE WORD OF GOD

The law of the Lord is perfect, reviving the soul. The statutes of the Lord are trustworthy, making wise the simple. Psalms 19:7

For wisdom will enter your heart, and knowledge will be pleasant to your soul. Proverbs 2:10

My son, preserve sound judgment and discernment, do not let them out of your sight; they will be life for you, an ornament to grace your neck. Proverbs 3:21-22

Do not conform any longer to the pattern of this world, but be transformed by the renewing of your mind. Then you will be able to test and approve what God's will is—his good, pleasing and perfect will. Romans 12:2

To be made new in the attitude of your minds. Ephesians 4:23

"This is the covenant I will make with them after that time, says the Lord. I will put my laws in their hearts, and I will write them on their minds." Hebrews 10:16

Therefore, get rid of all moral filth and the evil that is so prevalent and humbly accept the word planted in you, which can save you.
James 1:21

Dear friends, this is now my second letter to you. I have written both of them as reminders to stimulate you to wholesome thinking. I want you to recall the words spoken in the past by the holy prophets and the command given by our Lord and Savior through your apostles. 2 Peter 3:1-2

For the word of God is living and active. Sharper than any double-edged sword, it penetrates even to dividing soul and spirit, joints and marrow; it judges the thoughts and attitudes of the heart.
Hebrews 4:12

FOCUSING YOUR MIND ON JESUS

You will keep in perfect peace him whose mind is steadfast, because he trusts in you. Isaiah 26:3

Jesus replied: " 'Love the Lord your God with all your heart and with all your soul and with all your mind.' Matthew 22:37

For who has known the mind of the Lord that he may instruct him?" But we have the mind of Christ. 1 Corinthians 2:16

And the peace of God, which transcends all understanding, will guard your hearts and your minds in Christ Jesus. Philippians 4:7

CONTROLLING IMAGINATIONS AND THOUGHTS

I hate vain thoughts: but thy law do I love. Psalms 119:113

The thoughts of the righteous are right: but the counsels of the wicked are deceit. Proverbs 12:5 KJV

Commit thy works unto the Lord, and thy thoughts shall be established. Proverbs 16:3 KJV

The thought of foolishness is sin: and the scorner is an abomination to men. Proverbs 24:9 KJV

The schemes of folly are sin, and men detest a mocker.
Proverbs 24:9

The weapons we fight with are not the weapons of the world. On the contrary, they have divine power to demolish strongholds. We demolish arguments and every pretension that sets itself up against the knowledge of God, and we take captive every thought to make it obedient to Christ. 2 Corinthians 10:4-5

The mind of sinful man is death, but the mind controlled by the Spirit is life and peace; the sinful mind is hostile to God. It does not submit to God's law, nor can it do so. Romans 8:6-7

Finally, brothers, whatever is true, whatever is noble, whatever is right, whatever is pure, whatever is lovely, whatever is admirable—if anything is excellent or praiseworthy—think about such things.
Philippians 4:8

OVERCOMING LUST

Do not lust in your heart after her beauty or let her captivate you with her eyes. Proverbs 6:25

But I tell you that anyone who looks at a woman lustfully has already committed adultery with her in his heart. Matthew 5:28

But the worries of this life, the deceitfulness of wealth and the desires for other things come in and choke the word, making it unfruitful. Mark 4:19

You belong to your father, the devil, and you want to carry out your father's desire. He was a murderer from the beginning, not holding to the truth, for there is no truth in him. When he lies, he speaks his native language, for he is a liar and the father of lies.
John 8:44

Therefore God gave them over in the sinful desires of their hearts to sexual impurity for the degrading of their bodies with one another. Romans 1:24

Therefore do not let sin reign in your mortal body so that you obey its evil desires. Romans 6:12

Rather, clothe yourselves with the Lord Jesus Christ, and do not think about how to gratify the desires of the sinful nature.
Romans 13:14

Now these things occurred as examples to keep us from setting our hearts on evil things as they did. 1 Corinthians 10:6

So I say, live by the Spirit, and you will not gratify the desires of the sinful nature. For the sinful nature desires what is contrary to the Spirit, and the Spirit what is contrary to the sinful nature. They are in conflict with each other, so that you do not do what you want. Galatians 5:16-17

Those who belong to Christ Jesus have crucified the sinful nature with its passions and desires. Galatians 5:24

In which you used to live when you followed the ways of this world and of the ruler of the kingdom of the air, the spirit who is now at work in those who are disobedient. All of us also lived among them at one time, gratifying the cravings of our sinful nature and following its desires and thoughts. Like the rest, we were by nature objects of wrath. But because of his great love for us, God, who is rich in mercy, made us alive with Christ even when we were dead in transgressions—it is by grace you have been saved. And God raised us up with Christ and seated us with him in the heavenly realms in Christ Jesus. Ephesians 2:2-6

You were taught, with regard to your former way of life, to put off your old self, which is being corrupted by its deceitful desires.
Ephesians 4:22

Flee the evil desires of youth, and pursue righteousness, faith, love and peace, along with those who call on the Lord out of a pure heart. 2 Timothy 2:22

It teaches us to say "No" to ungodliness and worldly passions, and to live self-controlled, upright and godly lives in this present age.

Titus 2:12

When tempted, no one should say, "God is tempting me." For God cannot be tempted by evil, nor does he tempt anyone; but each one is tempted when, by his own evil desire, he is dragged away and enticed. Then, after desire has conceived, it gives birth to sin; and sin, when it is full-grown, gives birth to death. James 1:13-15

What causes fights and quarrels among you? Don't they come from your desires that battle within you? You want something but don't get it. You kill and covet, but you cannot have what you want. You quarrel and fight. You do not have, because you do not ask God. When you ask, you do not receive, because you ask with wrong motives, that you may spend what you get on your pleasures.

James 4:1-3

As obedient children, do not conform to the evil desires you had when you lived in ignorance. 1 Peter 1:14

Dear friends, I urge you, as aliens and strangers in the world, to abstain from sinful desires, which war against your soul.

1 Peter 2:11

As a result, he does not live the rest of his earthly life for evil human desires, but rather for the will of God. 1 Peter 4:2

Through these he has given us his very great and precious promises, so that through them you may participate in the divine nature and escape the corruption in the world caused by evil desires.

2 Peter 1:4

For everything in the world—the cravings of sinful man, the lust of his eyes and the boasting of what he has and does—comes not from the Father but from the world. The world and its desires pass away, but the man who does the will of God lives forever.

1 John 2:16-17

TELEVISION, MOVIE, AND MUSIC GUIDE

Would Jesus listen to this Music, watch this TV program, or Movie?

When Jesus spoke again to the people, he said, "I am the light of the world. Whoever follows me will never walk in darkness, but will have the light of life. John 8:12

I have come into the world as a light, so that no one who believes in me should stay in darkness. John 12:46

Through your TV and music, what kind of people or evil spirits are you inviting into your home?

I have written you in my letter not to associate with sexually immoral people—not at all meaning the people of this world who are immoral, or the greedy and swindlers, or idolaters. In that case you would have to leave this world. But now I am writing you that you must not associate with anyone who calls himself a brother but is sexually immoral or greedy, an idolater or a slanderer, a drunkard or a swindler. With such a man do not even eat.
1 Corinthians 5:9-11

Do not be yoked together with unbelievers. For what do righteousness and wickedness have in common? Or what fellowship can light have with darkness? What harmony is there between Christ and Belial? What does a believer have in common with an unbeliever? 2 Corinthians 6:14-15

Have nothing to do with the fruitless deeds of darkness, but rather expose them. Ephesians 5:11

Is the TV program, movie or music contrary to God's Word?

The thought of foolishness is sin: and the scorner is an abomination to men. Proverbs 24:9

Cease, my son, to hear the instruction that causeth to err from the words of knowledge. Proverbs 19:27 KJV

We demolish arguments and every pretension that sets itself up against the knowledge of God, and we take captive every thought to make it obedient to Christ. 2 Corinthians 10:5

Is the TV program or music bringing you closer to Christ?

You adulterous people, don't you know that friendship with the world is hatred toward God? Anyone who chooses to be a friend of the world becomes an enemy of God. James 4:4

"Everything is permissible for me"—but not everything is beneficial. "Everything is permissible for me"—but I will not be mastered by anything. 1 Corinthians 6:12

"Everything is permissible"—but not everything is beneficial. "Everything is permissible"—but not everything is constructive.
1 Corinthians 10:23

Therefore, since we are surrounded by such a great cloud of witnesses, let us throw off everything that hinders and the sin that so easily entangles, and let us run with perseverance the race marked out for us. Hebrews 12:1

Is it causing you to compromise and sin?

You cannot drink the cup of the Lord and the cup of demons too; you cannot have a part in both the Lord's table and the table of demons. 1 Corinthians 10:21

And if your eye causes you to sin, gouge it out and throw it away. It is better for you to enter life with one eye than to have two eyes and be thrown into the fire of hell. Matthew 18:9

What are you putting in your heart through your eyes and ears?

I will set before my eyes no vile thing. The deeds of faithless men I hate; they will not cling to me. Psalms 101:3

Turn my eyes away from worthless things; preserve my life according to your word. Psalms 119:37

Your eyes will see strange sights and your mind imagine confusing things. Proverbs 23:33

A wicked man listens to evil lips; a liar pays attention to a malicious tongue. Proverbs 17:4

"Consider carefully what you hear," he continued. "With the measure you use, it will be measured to you—and even more.
Mark 4:24

Do not be misled: "Bad company corrupts good character."
1 Corinthians 15:33

Avoid every kind of evil. 1 Thessalonians 5:22

They have become filled with every kind of wickedness, evil, greed and depravity. They are full of envy, murder, strife, deceit and malice. They are gossips, slanderers, God-haters, insolent, arrogant and boastful; they invent ways of doing evil; they disobey their parents; they are senseless, faithless, heartless, ruthless. Although they know God's righteous decree that those who do such things deserve death, they not only continue to do these very things but also approve of those who practice them. Romans 1:29-32

Until they were filled—permeated and saturated—with every kind of unrighteousness, iniquity, grasping and covetous greed, [and] malice. [They were] full of envy and jealousy, murder, strife, deceit and treachery, ill will and cruel ways. [They were] secret back-biters and gossipers, Slanderers, hateful to and hating God, full of insolence, arrogance [and] boasting; inventors of new forms of evil, disobedient and undutiful to parents.

[They were] without understanding, conscienceless and faithless, heartless and loveless [and] merciless.

Though they are fully aware of God's righteous decree that those who do such things deserve to die, they not only do them themselves but approve and applaud others who practice them.
Romans 1:29-32 AMP

Are you wasting time?

Redeeming the time, because the days are evil. Ephesians 5:16 KJV

Making the most of every opportunity, because the days are evil.
Ephesians 5:16

Walk in wisdom toward them that are without, redeeming the time.
Colossians 4:5 KJV

Be wise in the way you act toward outsiders; make the most of every opportunity. Colossians 4:5

And if ye call on the Father, who without respect of persons judgeth according to every man's work, pass the time of your sojourning here in fear. 1 Peter 1:17 KJV

Since you call on a Father who judges each man's work impartially, live your lives as strangers here in reverent fear. 1 Peter 1:17

Qualifying good TV programs, Movies, and Music.

Since, then, you have been raised with Christ, set your hearts on things above, where Christ is seated at the right hand of God.
Colossians 3:1

Finally, brothers, whatever is true, whatever is noble, whatever is right, whatever is pure, whatever is lovely, whatever is admirable—if anything is excellent or praiseworthy—think about such things.
Philippians 4:8

Every good and perfect gift is from above, coming down from the Father of the heavenly lights, who does not change like shifting shadows. James 1:17

THE BODY

THE TEMPLE OF THE HOLY SPIRIT

Don't you know that you yourselves are God's temple and that God's Spirit lives in you? 1 Corinthians 3:16

Do you not know that your body is a temple of the Holy Spirit, who is in you, whom you have received from God? You are not your own; you were bought at a price. Therefore honor God with your body. 1 Corinthians 6:19-20

Because you are sons, God sent the Spirit of his Son into our hearts, the Spirit who calls out, "Abba, Father." Galatians 4:6

I pray that out of his glorious riches he may strengthen you with power through his Spirit in your inner being. Ephesians 3:16

Guard the good deposit that was entrusted to you—guard it with the help of the Holy Spirit who lives in us. 2 Timothy 1:14

SEX BEFORE MARRIAGE

SEXUAL SINS

Instead we should write to them, telling them to abstain from food polluted by idols, from sexual immorality, from the meat of strangled animals and from blood. Acts 15:20

You are to abstain from food sacrificed to idols, from blood, from the meat of strangled animals and from sexual immorality. You will do well to avoid these things. Farewell. Acts 15:29

As for the Gentile believers, we have written to them our decision that they should abstain from food sacrificed to idols, from blood, from the meat of strangled animals and from sexual immorality.
Acts 21:25

But now I am writing you that you must not associate with anyone who calls himself a brother but is sexually immoral or greedy, an idolater or a slanderer, a drunkard or a swindler. With such a man do not even eat. 1 Corinthians 5:11

Do you not know that your bodies are members of Christ himself? Shall I then take the members of Christ and unite them with a prostitute? Never! Do you not know that he who unites himself with a prostitute is one with her in body? For it is said, "The two will become one flesh." 1 Corinthians 6:15-16

Flee from sexual immorality. All other sins a man commits are outside his body, but he who sins sexually sins against his own body. Do you not know that your body is a temple of the Holy Spirit, who is in you, whom you have received from God? You are not your own; you were bought at a price. Therefore honor God with your body. 1 Corinthians 6:18-20

Now for the matters you wrote about: It is good for a man not to marry. But since there is so much immorality, each man should have his own wife, and each woman her own husband.
1 Corinthians 7:1-2

We should not commit sexual immorality, as some of them did—and in one day twenty-three thousand of them died.
1 Corinthians 10:8

But among you there must not be even a hint of sexual immorality, or of any kind of impurity, or of greed, because these are improper for God's holy people. Ephesians 5:3

It is God's will that you should be sanctified: that you should avoid sexual immorality. 1 Thessalonians 4:3

SEX IS ONLY FOR MARRIED COUPLES

But because of the temptation to impurity and to avoid immorality, let each [man] have his own wife and let each [woman] have her own husband. 1 Corinthians 7:2 AMP

The husband should fulfill his marital duty to his wife, and likewise the wife to her husband. The wife's body does not belong to her alone but also to her husband. In the same way, the husband's body does not belong to him alone but also to his wife. Do not deprive each other except by mutual consent and for a time, so that you may devote yourselves to prayer. Then come together again so that Satan will not tempt you because of your lack of self-control.
1 Corinthians 7:3-5

THE CONSEQUENCES OF FORNICATION

The acts of the sinful nature are obvious: sexual immorality, impurity and debauchery; And envy; drunkenness, orgies, and the like. I warn you, as I did before, that those who live like this will not inherit the kingdom of God. Galatians 5:19,21

In a similar way, Sodom and Gomorrah and the surrounding towns gave themselves up to sexual immorality and perversion. They serve as an example of those who suffer the punishment of eternal fire.
Jude 1:7

ADULTERY

You shall not commit adultery. Exodus 20:14

If a man commits adultery with another man's wife—with the wife of his neighbor—both the adulterer and the adulteress must be put to death. Leviticus 20:10

You shall not commit adultery. Deuteronomy 5:18

This is the way of an adulteress: She eats and wipes her mouth and says, 'I've done nothing wrong. Proverbs 30:20

But I tell you that anyone who looks at a woman lustfully has already committed adultery with her in his heart. Matthew 5:28

THE CONSEQUENCES OF ADULTERY

For the prostitute reduces you to a loaf of bread, and the adulteress preys upon your very life. Proverbs 6:26

But a man who commits adultery lacks judgment; whoever does so destroys himself. Proverbs 6:32

Do you not know that the wicked will not inherit the kingdom of God? Do not be deceived: Neither the sexually immoral nor idolaters nor adulterers nor male prostitutes nor homosexual offenders.
1 Corinthians 6:9

Marriage should be honored by all, and the marriage bed kept pure, for God will judge the adulterer and all the sexually immoral.
Hebrews 13:4

HOMOSEXUALITY AND LESBIANISM

Do not lie with a man as one lies with a woman; that is detestable.
Leviticus 18:22

Therefore God gave them over in the sinful desires of their hearts to sexual impurity for the degrading of their bodies with one another. Romans 1:24

Because of this, God gave them over to shameful lusts. Even their women exchanged natural relations for unnatural ones. In the same way the men also abandoned natural relations with women and were inflamed with lust for one another. Men committed indecent acts with other men, and received in themselves the due penalty for their perversion. Furthermore, since they did not think it worthwhile to retain the knowledge of God, he gave them over to a depraved mind, to do what ought not to be done. Romans 1:26-28

Without understanding, covenantbreakers, without natural affection, implacable, unmerciful. Romans 1:31 KJV

Put to death, therefore, whatever belongs to your earthly nature: sexual immorality, impurity, lust, evil desires and greed, which is idolatry. Colossians 3:5

Without natural affection, trucebreakers, false accusers, incontinent, fierce, despisers of those that are good. 2 Timothy 3:3 KJV

GLUTTONY

When you sit to dine with a ruler, note well what is before you, and put a knife to your throat if you are given to gluttony. Do not crave his delicacies, for that food is deceptive. Proverbs 23:1-3

Do not join those who drink too much wine or gorge themselves on meat, for drunkards and gluttons become poor, and drowsiness clothes them in rags. Proverbs 23:20-21

If you find honey, eat just enough—too much of it, and you will vomit. Proverbs 25:16

Like a city whose walls are broken down is a man who lacks self-control. Proverbs 25:28

Blessed are you, O land whose king is of noble birth and whose princes eat at a proper time—for strength and not for drunkenness.
Ecclesiastes 10:17

Their destiny is destruction, their god is their stomach, and their glory is in their shame. Their mind is on earthly things.
Philippians 3:19

DRINKING ALCOHOL

You and your sons are not to drink wine or other fermented drink whenever you go into the Tent of Meeting, or you will die. This is a lasting ordinance for the generations to come. You must distinguish between the holy and the common, between the unclean and the clean. Leviticus 10:9-10

Wine is a mocker and beer a brawler; whoever is led astray by them is not wise. Proverbs 20:1

He who loves pleasure will become poor; whoever loves wine and oil will never be rich. Proverbs 21:17

For drunkards and gluttons become poor, and drowsiness clothes them in rags. Proverbs 23:21

Who has woe? Who has sorrow? Who has strife? Who has complaints? Who has needless bruises? Who has bloodshot eyes? Those who linger over wine, who go to sample bowls of mixed wine. Do not gaze at wine when it is red, when it sparkles in the cup, when it goes down smoothly! In the end it bites like a snake and poisons like a viper. Your eyes will see strange sights and your mind imagine confusing things. You will be like one sleeping on the high seas, lying on top of the rigging. "They hit me," you will say, "but I'm not hurt! They beat me, but I don't feel it! When will I wake up so I can find another drink?" Proverbs 23:29-35

It is not for kings, O Lemuel—not for kings to drink wine, not for rulers to crave beer. Proverbs 31:4

Woe to those who rise early in the morning to run after their drinks, who stay up late at night till they are inflamed with wine.
                                                                Isaiah 5:11

No longer do they drink wine with a song; the beer is bitter to its drinkers. Isaiah 24:9

For he will be great in the sight of the Lord. He is never to take wine or other fermented drink, and he will be filled with the Holy Spirit even from birth. Luke 1:15

Be careful, or your hearts will be weighed down with dissipation, drunkenness and the anxieties of life, and that day will close on you unexpectedly like a trap. Luke 21:34

Let us behave decently, as in the daytime, not in orgies and drunkenness, not in sexual immorality and debauchery, not in dissension and jealousy. Romans 13:13

It is better not to eat meat or drink wine or to do anything else that will cause your brother to fall. Romans 14:21

Do not get drunk on wine, which leads to debauchery. Instead, be filled with the Spirit. Ephesians 5:18

So then, let us not be like others, who are asleep, but let us be alert and self-controlled. For those who sleep, sleep at night, and those who get drunk, get drunk at night. But since we belong to the day, let us be self-controlled, putting on faith and love as a breastplate, and the hope of salvation as a helmet. 1 Thessalonians 5:6-8

Not given to drunkenness, not violent but gentle, not quarrelsome, not a lover of money. 1 Timothy 3:3

BIBLICAL DIET

Then God said, I give you every seed-bearing plant on the face of the whole earth and every tree that has fruit with seed in it. They will be yours for food. Genesis 1:29

> *Give the devil no place in your life; not*
> *even in the food that you eat.*

"'Keep my decrees. "'Do not mate different kinds of animals. "'Do not plant your field with two kinds of seed. "'Do not wear clothing woven of two kinds of material. Leviticus 19:19

Take wheat and barley, beans and lentils, millet and spelt; put them in a storage jar and use them to make bread for yourself. You are to eat it during the 390 days you lie on your side. Ezekiel 4:9

Fruit trees of all kinds will grow on both banks of the river. Their leaves will not wither, nor will their fruit fail. Every month they will bear, because the water from the sanctuary flows to them. Their fruit will serve for food and their leaves for healing. Ezekiel 47:12

"Please test your servants for ten days: Give us nothing but vegetables to eat and water to drink. Then compare our appearance with that of the young men who eat the royal food, and treat your servants in accordance with what you see." So he agreed to this and tested them for ten days. At the end of the ten days they looked healthier and better nourished than any of the young men who ate the royal food. So the guard took away their choice food and the wine they were to drink and gave them vegetables instead.

Daniel 1:12-16

HEALING

PROVISIONS FOR HEALING

But he was pierced for our transgressions, he was crushed for our iniquities; the punishment that brought us peace was upon him, and by his wounds we are healed. Isaiah 53:5

He himself bore our sins in his body on the tree, so that we might die to sins and live for righteousness; by his wounds you have been healed. 1 Peter 2:24

PREVENTIVE MEDICINE

He said, "If you listen carefully to the voice of the Lord your God and do what is right in his eyes, if you pay attention to his commands and keep all his decrees, I will not bring on you any of the diseases I brought on the Egyptians, for I am the Lord, who heals you." Exodus 15:26

Therefore, take care to follow the commands, decrees and laws I give you today. If you pay attention to these laws and are careful to follow them, then the Lord your God will keep his covenant of love with you, as he swore to your forefathers. He will love you and bless you and increase your numbers. He will bless the fruit of your womb, the crops of your land—your grain, new wine and oil—the calves of your herds and the lambs of your flocks in the land that he swore to your forefathers to give you. You will be blessed more than any other people; none of your men or women will be childless, nor any of your livestock without young. The Lord will keep you free from every disease. He will not inflict on you the horrible diseases you knew in Egypt, but he will inflict them on all who hate you. Deuteronomy 7:11-15

Obedience in the spirit brings life
and health to the natural.

Trust in the Lord with all your heart and lean not on your own understanding; in all your ways acknowledge him, and he will make your paths straight. Do not be wise in your own eyes; fear the Lord and shun evil. This will bring health to your body and nourishment to your bones. Proverbs 3:5-8

GOD'S PROMISES FOR HEALING

Worship the Lord your God, and his blessing will be on your food and water. I will take away sickness from among you. Exodus 23:25

Think how you have instructed many, how you have strengthened feeble hands. Your words have supported those who stumbled; you have strengthened faltering knees. Job 4:3-4

O Lord my God, I called to you for help and you healed me.
Psalms 30:2

He protects all his bones, not one of them will be broken.
Psalms 34:20

The Lord will sustain him on his sickbed and restore him from his bed of illness. Psalms 41:3

Surely he will save you from the fowler's snare and from the deadly pestilence. Psalms 91:3

There shall no evil befall thee, neither shall any plague come nigh thy dwelling. Psalms 91:10 KJV

Who forgives all your sins and heals all your diseases, who redeems your life from the pit and crowns you with love and compassion, who satisfies your desires with good things so that your youth is renewed like the eagle's. Psalms 103:3-5

He sent forth his word and healed them; he rescued them from the grave. Psalms 107:20

The Lord upholds all those who fall and lifts up all who are bowed down. Psalms 145:14

The Lord gives sight to the blind, the Lord lifts up those who are bowed down, the Lord loves the righteous. Psalms 146:8

He heals the brokenhearted and binds up their wounds. Psalms 147:3

My son, pay attention to what I say; listen closely to my words. Do not let them out of your sight, keep them within your heart; for they are life to those who find them and health to a man's whole body. Proverbs 4:20-22

A heart at peace gives life to the body, but envy rots the bones.
Proverbs 14:30

Pleasant words are a honeycomb, sweet to the soul and healing to the bones. Proverbs 16:24

Strengthen the feeble hands, steady the knees that give way.
Isaiah 35:3

He gives strength to the weary and increases the power of the weak.
Isaiah 40:29

The Lord will guide you always; he will satisfy your needs in a sun-scorched land and will strengthen your frame. You will be like a well-watered garden, like a spring whose waters never fail.
Isaiah 58:11

Heal me, O Lord, and I will be healed; save me and I will be saved, for you are the one I praise. Jeremiah 17:14

But I will restore you to health and heal your wounds, declares the Lord, because you are called an outcast, Zion for whom no one cares. Jeremiah 30:17

Nevertheless, I will bring health and healing to it; I will heal my people and will let them enjoy abundant peace and security.
Jeremiah 33:6

Who had come to hear him and to be healed of their diseases. Those troubled by evil spirits were cured, and the people all tried to touch him, because power was coming from him and healing them all.
Luke 6:18-19

Christ redeemed us from the curse of the law by becoming a curse for us, for it is written: "Cursed is everyone who is hung on a tree."
Galatians 3:13

Therefore, strengthen your feeble arms and weak knees. "Make level paths for your feet," so that the lame may not be disabled, but rather healed. Hebrews 12:12-13

Dear friend, I pray that you may enjoy good health and that all may go well with you, even as your soul is getting along well.

3 John 1:2

PRAYING FOR HEALING

Is any one of you in trouble? He should pray. Is anyone happy? Let him sing songs of praise. Is any one of you sick? He should call the elders of the church to pray over him and anoint him with oil in the name of the Lord. And the prayer offered in faith will make the sick person well; the Lord will raise him up. If he has sinned, he will be forgiven. Therefore confess your sins to each other and pray for each other so that you may be healed. The prayer of a righteous man is powerful and effective. James 5:13-16

LIVING LONG AND SATISFIED

Walk in all the way that the Lord your God has commanded you, so that you may live and prosper and prolong your days in the land that you will possess. Deuteronomy 5:33

So that you, your children and their children after them may fear the Lord your God as long as you live by keeping all his decrees and commands that I give you, and so that you may enjoy long life.

Deuteronomy 6:2

You will come to the grave in full vigor, like sheaves gathered in season. Job 5:26

Do not cast me away when I am old; do not forsake me when my strength is gone. Psalms 71:9

Since my youth, O God, you have taught me, and to this day I declare your marvelous deeds. Even when I am old and gray, do not forsake me, O God, till I declare your power to the next generation, your might to all who are to come. Psalms 71:17-18

The length of our days is seventy years—or eighty, if we have the strength; yet their span is but trouble and sorrow, for they quickly pass, and we fly away. Psalms 90:10

Teach us to number our days aright, that we may gain a heart of wisdom. Psalms 90:12

With long life will I satisfy him and show him my salvation.
Psalms 91:16

The righteous will flourish like a palm tree, they will grow like a cedar of Lebanon; planted in the house of the Lord, they will flourish in the courts of our God. They will still bear fruit in old age, they will stay fresh and green, proclaiming, "The Lord is upright; he is my Rock, and there is no wickedness in him."
Psalms 92:12-15

Who satisfies your desires with good things so that your youth is renewed like the eagle's. Psalms 103:5

My son, do not forget my teaching, but keep my commands in your heart, for they will prolong your life many years and bring you prosperity. Proverbs 3:1-2

For through me your days will be many, and years will be added to your life. Proverbs 9:11

The fear of the Lord adds length to life, but the years of the wicked are cut short. Proverbs 10:27

Children's children are a crown to the aged, and parents are the pride of their children. Proverbs 17:6

The glory of young men is their strength, gray hair the splendor of the old. Proverbs 20:29

Even to your old age and gray hairs I am he, I am he who will sustain you. I have made you and I will carry you; I will sustain you and I will rescue you. Isaiah 46:4

Therefore we do not lose heart. Though outwardly we are wasting away, yet inwardly we are being renewed day by day. For our light and momentary troubles are achieving for us an eternal glory that far outweighs them all. So we fix our eyes not on what is seen, but on what is unseen. For what is seen is temporary, but what is unseen is eternal. 2 Corinthians 4:16-18

THE BELIEVER'S AUTHORITY

THE SUPERIOR POWER AND AUTHORITY OF CHRIST

It is written: As surely as I live, says the Lord, every knee will bow before me; every tongue will confess to God. Romans 14:11

Then Jesus came to them and said, All authority in heaven and on earth has been given to me. Therefore go and make disciples of all nations, baptizing them in the name of the Father and of the Son and of the Holy Spirit. Matthew 28:18-19

And his incomparably great power for us who believe. That power is like the working of his mighty strength, which he exerted in Christ when he raised him from the dead and seated him at his right hand in the heavenly realms, far above all rule and authority, power and dominion, and every title that can be given, not only in the present age but also in the one to come. And God placed all things under his feet and appointed him to be head over everything for the church, which is his body, the fullness of him who fills everything in every way. Ephesians 1:19-23

He is the image of the invisible God, the firstborn over all creation. For by him all things were created: things in heaven and on earth, visible and invisible, whether thrones or powers or rulers or authorities; all things were created by him and for him. He is before all things, and in him all things hold together. And he is the head of the body, the church; he is the beginning and the firstborn from among the dead, so that in everything he might have the supremacy.
Colossians 1:15-18

And you have been given fullness in Christ, who is the head over every power and authority. Colossians 2:10

And having disarmed the powers and authorities, he made a public spectacle of them, triumphing over them by the cross.
Colossians 2:15

Everyone must submit himself to the governing authorities, for there is no authority except that which God has established. The authorities that exist have been established by God. Romans 13:1

I am the Living One; I was dead, and behold I am alive for ever and ever! And I hold the keys of death and Hades. Revelation 1:18

But when this priest had offered for all time one sacrifice for sins, he sat down at the right hand of God. Since that time he waits for his enemies to be made his footstool. Hebrews 10:12-13

He who does what is sinful is of the devil, because the devil has been sinning from the beginning. The reason the Son of God appeared was to destroy the devil's work. 1 John 3:8

YOU HAVE POWER OVER THE devil

He called his twelve disciples to him and gave them authority to drive out evil spirits and to heal every disease and sickness.
Matthew 10:1

I have given you authority to trample on snakes and scorpions and to overcome all the power of the enemy; nothing will harm you. However, do not rejoice that the spirits submit to you, but rejoice that your names are written in heaven. Luke 10:19-20

When he has done this, then the Son himself will be made subject to him who put everything under him, so that God may be all in all.
1 Corinthians 15:28

For God did not give us a spirit of timidity, but a spirit of power, of love and of self-discipline. 2 Timothy 1:7

Since the children have flesh and blood, he too shared in their humanity so that by his death he might destroy him who holds the power of death—that is, the devil— and free those who all their lives were held in slavery by their fear of death. Hebrews 2:14-15

Submit yourselves, then, to God. Resist the devil, and he will flee from you. James 4:7

Who has gone into heaven and is at God's right hand—with angels, authorities and powers in submission to him. 1 Peter 3:22

And like the heat of the desert. You silence the uproar of foreigners; as heat is reduced by the shadow of a cloud, so the song of the ruthless is stilled. On this mountain he will destroy the shroud that enfolds all peoples, the sheet that covers all nations; Isaiah 25:5,7

The ruthless will vanish, the mockers will disappear, and all who have an eye for evil will be cut down. Isaiah 29:20

No weapon that is formed against thee shall prosper; and every tongue that shall rise against thee in judgment thou shalt condemn. This is the heritage of the servants of the Lord, and their righteousness is of me, saith the Lord. Isaiah 54:17 KJV

No weapon forged against you will prevail, and you will refute every tongue that accuses you. This is the heritage of the servants of the Lord, and this is their vindication from me," declares the Lord. Isaiah 54:17

I am the Living One; I was dead, and behold I am alive for ever and ever! And I hold the keys of death and Hades. Revelation 1:18

SPIRITUAL WARFARE

ARMOR FOR THE SPIRITUAL REALM

LOINS GIRT ABOUT WITH TRUTH
BREASTPLATE OF RIGHTEOUSNESS
FEET SHOD WITH THE PREPARATION OF THE GOSPEL OF PEACE
SHIELD OF FAITH
HELMET OF SALVATION
SWORD OF THE SPIRIT, WHICH IS THE WORD OF GOD

Finally, be strong in the Lord and in his mighty power. Put on the full armor of God so that you can take your stand against the devil's schemes. For our struggle is not against flesh and blood, but against the rulers, against the authorities, against the powers of this dark world and against the spiritual forces of evil in the heavenly realms. Therefore put on the full armor of God, so that when the day of evil comes, you may be able to stand your ground, and after you have done everything, to stand. Stand firm then, with the belt of truth buckled around your waist, with the breastplate of righteousness in place, and with your feet fitted with the readiness that comes from the gospel of peace. In addition to all this, take up the shield of faith, with which you can extinguish all the flaming arrows of the evil one. Take the helmet of salvation and the sword of the Spirit, which is the word of God. Ephesians 6:10-17

THE WEAPONS OF THE SPIRITUAL REALM

1. THE NAME OF JESUS

The seventy-two returned with joy and said, Lord, even the demons submit to us in your name. Luke 10:18

Therefore God exalted him to the highest place and gave him the name that is above every name, that at the name of Jesus every knee should bow, in heaven and on earth and under the earth.
Philippians 2:9-10

2. THE BLOOD OF JESUS

They overcame him by the blood of the Lamb and by the word of their testimony; they did not love their lives so much as to shrink from death. Revelation 12:11

3. THE SWORD OF THE SPIRIT (THE WORD OF GOD)

So that the thoughts of many hearts will be revealed. And a sword will pierce your own soul too. Luke 2:35

Take the helmet of salvation and the sword of the Spirit, which is the word of God. Ephesians 6:17

And then shall that Wicked be revealed, whom the Lord shall consume with the spirit of his mouth, and shall destroy with the brightness of his coming. 2 Thessalonians 2:8 KJV

For the word of God is living and active. Sharper than any double-edged sword, it penetrates even to dividing soul and spirit, joints and marrow; it judges the thoughts and attitudes of the heart.
Hebrews 4:12

In his right hand he held seven stars, and out of his mouth came a sharp double-edged sword. His face was like the sun shining in all its brilliance. Revelation 1:16

> *The devil is a spiritual being and the spoken Word of God is the sword of the Spirit. Nothing else cuts, controls, binds, hinders, and defeats the devil and his demons more than a Christian confessing God's Word in faith.*

To the angel of the church in Pergamum write: These are the words of him who has the sharp, double-edged sword. Revelation 2:12

Repent therefore! Otherwise, I will soon come to you and will fight against them with the sword of my mouth. Revelation 2:16

Out of his mouth comes a sharp sword with which to strike down the nations. He will rule them with an iron scepter. He treads the winepress of the fury of the wrath of God Almighty.
Revelation 19:15

> *"Submit yourselves therefore to God. Resist the devil, and he will flee from you" (James 4:7). You have to say "yes" to God first before you can effectively say "no" to the devil.*

BINDING AND LOOSING

I tell you the truth, whatever you bind on earth will be bound in heaven, and whatever you loose on earth will be loosed in heaven.
Matthew 18:18

Or again, how can anyone enter a strong man's house and carry off his possessions unless he first ties up the strong man? Then he can rob his house. Matthew 12:29

GOD'S END TIME ARMY

You, dear children, are from God and have overcome them, because the one who is in you is greater than the one who is in the world. 1 John 4:4

217

They charge like warriors; they scale walls like soldiers. They all march in line, not swerving from their course. They do not jostle each other; each marches straight ahead. They plunge through defenses without breaking ranks. They rush upon the city; they run along the wall. They climb into the houses; like thieves they enter through the windows. Before them the earth shakes, the sky trembles, the sun and moon are darkened, and the stars no longer shine. The Lord thunders at the head of his army; his forces are beyond number, and mighty are those who obey his command. The day of the Lord is great; it is dreadful. Who can endure it?

Joel 2:7-11

SPIRITUAL ENEMIES

For though we live in the world, we do not wage war as the world does. The weapons we fight with are not the weapons of the world. On the contrary, they have divine power to demolish strongholds. We demolish arguments and every pretension that sets itself up against the knowledge of God, and we take captive every thought to make it obedient to Christ. 2 Corinthians 10:3-5

For our struggle is not against flesh and blood, but against the rulers, against the authorities, against the powers of this dark world and against the spiritual forces of evil in the heavenly realms.

Ephesians 6:12

ATTACKING THE ENEMY

And they blessed Rebekah and said to her, Our sister, may you increase to thousands upon thousands; may your offspring possess the gates of their enemies. Genesis 24:60

And I tell you that you are Peter, and on this rock I will build my church, and the gates of Hades will not overcome it. Matthew 16:18

And I tell you, you are Peter [petros, masculine, a large piece of rock], and on this rock [petra, feminine, a huge rock like Gibraltar] I will build My church, and the gates of Hades (the powers of the infernal region shall not overpower it—or be strong to its detriment, or hold out against it. Matthew 16:18 AMP

218

From the days of John the Baptist until now, the kingdom of heaven has been forcefully advancing, and forceful men lay hold of it.
Matthew 11:12

And from the days of John the Baptist until the present time the kingdom of heaven has endured violent assault, and violent men seize it by force [as a precious prize]- a share in the heavenly kingdom is sought for with most ardent zeal and intense exertion.
Matthew 11:12 AMP

You will pursue your enemies, and they will fall by the sword before you. Five of you will chase a hundred, and a hundred of you will chase ten thousand, and your enemies will fall by the sword before you. I will look on you with favor and make you fruitful and increase your numbers, and I will keep my covenant with you.
Leviticus 26:7-9

How could one man chase a thousand, or two put ten thousand to flight, unless their Rock had sold them, unless the Lord had given them up? Deuteronomy 32:30

Quenched the fury of the flames, and escaped the edge of the sword; whose weakness was turned to strength; and who became powerful in battle and routed foreign armies. Hebrews 11:34

One of you routs a thousand, because the Lord your God fights for you, just as he promised. Joshua 23:10

A thousand may fall at your side, ten thousand at your right hand, but it will not come near you. Psalms 91:7

SPIRITUAL DISCERNMENT

The man without the Spirit does not accept the things that come from the Spirit of God, for they are foolishness to him, and he cannot understand them, because they are spiritually discerned.
1 Corinthians 2:14

To another miraculous powers, to another prophecy, to another distinguishing between spirits, to another speaking in different kinds of tongues, and to still another the interpretation of tongues.
1 Corinthians 12:10

In order that Satan might not outwit us. For we are not unaware of his schemes. 2 Corinthians 2:11

DISCERNING GOOD AND EVIL

So give your servant a discerning heart to govern your people and to distinguish between right and wrong. For who is able to govern this great people of yours? 1 Kings 3:9

They are to teach my people the difference between the holy and the common and show them how to distinguish between the unclean and the clean. Ezekiel 44:23

And you will again see the distinction between the righteous and the wicked, between those who serve God and those who do not.
Malachi 3:18

But solid food is for the mature, who by constant use have trained themselves to distinguish good from evil. Hebrews 5:14

DISCERNMENT FROM GOD'S WORD

My son, preserve sound judgment and discernment, do not let them out of your sight; they will be life for you, an ornament to grace your neck. Then you will go on your way in safety, and your foot will not stumble; when you lie down, you will not be afraid; when you lie down, your sleep will be sweet. Proverbs 3:21-24

For the word of God is living and active. Sharper than any double-edged sword, it penetrates even to dividing soul and spirit, joints and marrow; it judges the thoughts and attitudes of the heart.
Hebrews 4:12

SPIRITUAL EYES AND EARS

Open my eyes that I may see wonderful things in your law.
Psalms 119:18

Let me understand the teaching of your precepts; then I will meditate on your wonders. Psalms 119:27

Give me understanding, and I will keep your law and obey it with all my heart. Psalms 119:34

Your hands made me and formed me; give me understanding to learn your commands. Psalms 119:73

In that day the deaf will hear the words of the scroll, and out of gloom and darkness the eyes of the blind will see. Isaiah 29:18

Those who are wayward in spirit will gain understanding; those who complain will accept instruction. Isaiah 29:24

I will lead the blind by ways they have not known, along unfamiliar paths I will guide them; I will turn the darkness into light before them and make the rough places smooth. These are the things I will do; I will not forsake them. Isaiah 42:16

He replied, "The knowledge of the secrets of the kingdom of heaven has been given to you, but not to them. Matthew 13:11

But blessed are your eyes because they see, and your ears because they hear. For I tell you the truth, many prophets and righteous men longed to see what you see but did not see it, and to hear what you hear but did not hear it. Matthew 13:16-17

I keep asking that the God of our Lord Jesus Christ, the glorious Father, may give you the Spirit of wisdom and revelation, so that you may know him better. I pray also that the eyes of your heart

may be enlightened in order that you may know the hope to which he has called you, the riches of his glorious inheritance in the saints.
Ephesians 1:17-18

He who has an ear, let him hear what the Spirit says to the churches. To him who overcomes, I will give the right to eat from the tree of life, which is in the paradise of God. Revelation 2:7

DECEPTION

BEING DECEIVED BY OTHERS

For many will come in my name, claiming, 'I am the Christ,' and will deceive many. Jesus answered: Watch out that no one deceives you. Matthew 24:4-5

Who plots evil with deceit in his heart—he always stirs up dissension. Proverbs 6:14

The plans of the righteous are just, but the advice of the wicked is deceitful. Proverbs 12:5

Be careful, or you will be enticed to turn away and worship other gods and bow down to them. Deuteronomy 11:16

There is deceit in the hearts of those who plot evil, but joy for those who promote peace. Proverbs 12:20

Is a man who deceives his neighbor and says, "I was only joking!"
Proverbs 26:19

A malicious man disguises himself with his lips, but in his heart he harbors deceit. Proverbs 26:24

And many false prophets will appear and deceive many people.
Matthew 24:11

For false Christs and false prophets will appear and perform great signs and miracles to deceive even the elect—if that were possible.
Matthew 24:24

Jesus said to them: "Watch out that no one deceives you. Many will come in my name, claiming, 'I am he,' and will deceive many.
Mark 13:5-6

He replied: "Watch out that you are not deceived. For many will come in my name, claiming, 'I am he,' and, 'The time is near.' Do not follow them. Luke 21:8

> *satan has a false gospel, a false repentance, a false dedication, a false faith, a false everything. Weak Christians, not well read in the scriptures, will easily fall prey to modern magicians. - Vance Havner*

For such people are not serving our Lord Christ, but their own appetites. By smooth talk and flattery they deceive the minds of naive people. Romans 16:18

Do not be misled: Bad company corrupts good character.
1 Corinthians 15:33

Do you not know that the wicked will not inherit the kingdom of God? Do not be deceived: Neither the sexually immoral nor idolaters nor adulterers nor male prostitutes nor homosexual offenders.
1 Corinthians 6:9

Then we will no longer be infants, tossed back and forth by the waves, and blown here and there by every wind of teaching and by the cunning and craftiness of men in their deceitful scheming.
Ephesians 4:14

Let no one deceive you with empty words, for because of such things God's wrath comes on those who are disobedient.
Ephesians 5:6

Don't let anyone deceive you in any way, for that day will not come until the rebellion occurs and the man of lawlessness is revealed, the man doomed to destruction. 2 Thessalonians 2:3

While evil men and impostors will go from bad to worse, deceiving and being deceived. 2 Timothy 3:13

For there are many rebellious people, mere talkers and deceivers, especially those of the circumcision group. Titus 1:10

Dear children, do not let anyone lead you astray. He who does what is right is righteous, just as he is righteous. 1 John 3:7

Many deceivers, who do not acknowledge Jesus Christ as coming in the flesh, have gone out into the world. Any such person is the deceiver and the antichrist. 2 John 1:7

Wine is a mocker and beer a brawler; whoever is led astray by them is not wise. Proverbs 20:1

Do not testify against your neighbor without cause, or use your lips to deceive. Proverbs 24:28

SELF-DECEPTION

This is what the Lord says: Do not deceive yourselves, thinking, The Babylonians will surely leave us.' They will not!
Jeremiah 37:9

Do not deceive yourselves. If any one of you thinks he is wise by the standards of this age, he should become a "fool" so that he may become wise. 1 Corinthians 3:18

If anyone thinks he is something when he is nothing, he deceives himself. Galatians 6:3

Do not merely listen to the word, and so deceive yourselves. Do what it says. James 1:22

> *We are challenged these days, but not changed, convicted, but not converted. We hear, but do not and thereby we deceive ourselves. - Vance Havner*

If anyone considers himself religious and yet does not keep a tight rein on his tongue, he deceives himself and his religion is worthless. James 1:26

And shall receive the reward of unrighteousness, as they that count it pleasure to riot in the day time. Spots they are and blemishes, sporting themselves with their own deceivings while they feast with you. 2 Peter 2:13 KJV

If we claim to have fellowship with him yet walk in the darkness, we lie and do not live by the truth. 1 John 1:6

If we claim to be without sin, we deceive ourselves and the truth is not in us. 1 John 1:8

He who does what is sinful is of the devil, because the devil has been sinning from the beginning. The reason the Son of God appeared was to destroy the devil's work. No one who is born of God will continue to sin, because God's seed remains in him; he cannot go on sinning, because he has been born of God. This is how we know who the children of God are and who the children of the devil are: Anyone who does not do what is right is not a child of God; nor is anyone who does not love his brother. 1 John 3:8-10

Do not be deceived: God cannot be mocked. A man reaps what he sows. Galatians 6:7

> *There is one thing worse than not coming to church, and that is to come and do nothing about the message one hears. James tells us that hearing without doing means self-deception. - Vance Havner*

DECEIVED BY DARKNESS

The great dragon was hurled down—that ancient serpent called the devil, or Satan, who leads the whole world astray. He was hurled to the earth, and his angels with him. Revelation 12:9

Because of the signs he was given power to do on behalf of the first beast, he deceived the inhabitants of the earth. He ordered them to set up an image in honor of the beast who was wounded by the sword and yet lived. Revelation 13:14

The light of a lamp will never shine in you again. The voice of bridegroom and bride will never be heard in you again. Your merchants were the world's great men. By your magic spell all the nations were led astray. Revelation 18:23

But the beast was captured, and with him the false prophet who had performed the miraculous signs on his behalf. With these signs he had deluded those who had received the mark of the beast and worshiped his image. The two of them were thrown alive into the fiery lake of burning sulfur. Revelation 19:20

He threw him into the Abyss, and locked and sealed it over him, to keep him from deceiving the nations anymore until the thousand

years were ended. After that, he must be set free for a short time.
Revelation 20:3

And will go out to deceive the nations in the four corners of the earth—Gog and Magog—to gather them for battle. In number they are like the sand on the seashore. Revelation 20:8

And the devil, who deceived them, was thrown into the lake of burning sulfur, where the beast and the false prophet had been thrown. They will be tormented day and night for ever and ever.
Revelation 20:10

STRATEGIES OF satan (devil)

1. satan's most infamous strategy is LYING

You belong to your father, the devil, and you want to carry out your father's desire. He was a murderer from the beginning, not holding to the truth, for there is no truth in him. When he lies, he speaks his native language, for he is a liar and the father of lies.
John 8:44

2. satan seeks to steal from, kill, and destroy anybody that will let him.

The thief comes only to steal and kill and destroy; I have come that they may have life, and have it to the full. John 10:10

Be self-controlled and alert. Your enemy the devil prowls around like a roaring lion looking for someone to devour. 1 Peter 5:8

3. satan is the inventor of sin, and he is constantly tempting mankind to sin against GOD.

He who does what is sinful is of the devil, because the devil has been sinning from the beginning. The reason the Son of God appeared was to destroy the devil's work. 1 John 3:8

4. satan tries to steal and choke the Word of God out of the heart of man.

The one who received the seed that fell among the thorns is the man who hears the word, but the worries of this life and the deceitfulness of wealth choke it, making it unfruitful. Matthew 13:22

For everything in the world—the cravings of sinful man, the lust of his eyes and the boasting of what he has and does—comes not from the Father but from the world. 1 John 2:16

Those along the path are the ones who hear, and then the devil comes and takes away the word from their hearts, so that they may not believe and be saved. Luke 8:12

5. satan will try to put evil, vile, crazy, doubtful, and fearful thoughts into your mind.

We demolish arguments and every pretension that sets itself up against the knowledge of God, and we take captive every thought to make it obedient to Christ. 2 Corinthians 10:5

6. satan tries to deceive believers and unbelievers into new and old doctrines of devils, false religions, cults, and the occult, by using false christs, false teachers, false prophets, gurus, etc....

Jesus answered: "Watch out that no one deceives you. For many will come in my name, claiming, 'I am the Christ,' and will deceive many. Matthew 24:4-5

And many false prophets will appear and deceive many people.
Matthew 24:11

For false Christs and false prophets will appear and perform great signs and miracles to deceive even the elect—if that were possible.
Matthew 24:24

Jesus said to them: "Watch out that no one deceives you. Many will come in my name, claiming, 'I am he,' and will deceive many.
Mark 13:5-6

He replied: "Watch out that you are not deceived. For many will come in my name, claiming, 'I am he,' and, 'The time is near.' Do not follow them. Luke 21:8

For such men are false apostles, deceitful workmen, masquerading as apostles of Christ. And no wonder, for Satan himself masquerades as an angel of light. It is not surprising, then, if his servants masquerade as servants of righteousness. Their end will be what their actions deserve. 2 Corinthians 11:13-15

I am astonished that you are so quickly deserting the one who called you by the grace of Christ and are turning to a different gospel—which is really no gospel at all. Evidently some people are throwing you into confusion and are trying to pervert the gospel of Christ. But even if we or an angel from heaven should preach a gospel other than the one we preached to you, let him be eternally condemned! As we have already said, so now I say again: If anybody is preaching to you a gospel other than what you accepted, let him be eternally condemned! Galatians 1:6-9

Then we will no longer be infants, tossed back and forth by the waves, and blown here and there by every wind of teaching and by the cunning and craftiness of men in their deceitful scheming.
Ephesians 4:14

Let no one deceive you with empty words, for because of such things God's wrath comes on those who are disobedient.
Ephesians 5:6

I tell you this so that no one may deceive you by fine-sounding arguments. Colossians 2:4

Dear children, do not let anyone lead you astray. He who does what is right is righteous, just as he is righteous. 1 John 3:7

7. satan and his forces work overtime to lure, trick and trap mankind with various sinful temptations.

Put on the full armor of God so that you can take your stand against the devil's schemes. Ephesians 6:11

Wiles is a craft, deceit, a cunning device. W.E. Vine Expos. Dictionary

Wiles is a clever trick used to fool or lure someone. Webster's Dictionary

8. satan tries to condemn believers of their past and present lifestyles.

For the accuser of our brothers, who accuses them before our God day and night, has been hurled down. Revelation 12:10

9. satan tries to convince sinners and believers that God is mad at them and that He condemns them for their sins.

The thief comes only to steal and kill and destroy; I have come that they may have life, and have it to the full. John 10:10

229

For God did not send his Son into the world to condemn the world, but to save the world through him. John 3:17

I tell you the truth, whoever hears my word and believes him who sent me has eternal life and will not be condemned; he has crossed over from death to life. John 5:24

Therefore, there is now no condemnation for those who are in Christ Jesus. Romans 8:1

Jesus straightened up and asked her, "Woman, where are they? Has no one condemned you?" "No one, sir," she said. "Then neither do I condemn you," Jesus declared. "Go now and leave your life of sin." John 8:10-11

Whenever our hearts condemn us. For God is greater than our hearts, and he knows everything. 1 John 3:20

Dear friends, if our hearts do not condemn us, we have confidence before God. 1 John 3:21

10. satan tries to control the minds of mankind and hinder them from hearing and accepting the Gospel of Christ.

And even if our gospel is veiled, it is veiled to those who are perishing. The god of this age has blinded the minds of unbelievers, so that they cannot see the light of the gospel of the glory of Christ, who is the image of God. 2 Corinthians 4:3-4

11. satan tries to control the lifestyle of mankind on the earth.

In which you used to live when you followed the ways of this world and of the ruler of the kingdom of the air, the spirit who is now at work in those who are disobedient. Ephesians 2:2

12. satan and his forces try to delay believers' prayers from being answered on time, and satan tries to control the governments of nations around the world.

But the prince of the Persian kingdom resisted me twenty-one days. Then Michael, one of the chief princes, came to help me, because I was detained there with the king of Persia. Daniel 10:13

So he said, Do you know why I have come to you? Soon I will return to fight against the prince of Persia, and when I go, the prince of Greece will come. Daniel 10:20

13. satan and his forces and human servants try to hinder normal citizens and leaders (especially) from hearing and receiving the gospel of Jesus Christ.

But Elymas the sorcerer (for that is what his name means) opposed them and tried to turn the proconsul from the faith. Then Saul, who was also called Paul, filled with the Holy Spirit, looked straight at Elymas and said, "You are a child of the devil and an enemy of everything that is right! You are full of all kinds of deceit and trickery. Will you never stop perverting the right ways of the Lord? Now the hand of the Lord is against you. You are going to be blind, and for a time you will be unable to see the light of the sun." Immediately mist and darkness came over him, and he groped about, seeking someone to lead him by the hand. Acts 13:8-11

14. satan and his forces are highly organized, and they are in constant spiritual battle with God's army around the world.

If Satan drives out Satan, he is divided against himself. How then can his kingdom stand? Matthew 12:26

For our struggle is not against flesh and blood, but against the rulers, against the authorities, against the powers of this dark world and against the spiritual forces of evil in the heavenly realms.
Ephesians 6:12

15. Any sickness, death, tragedy, calamity, temptation, all forms of natural disasters, or any problem or situation contrary to the Word of GOD can always be in some way, shape, or form undoubtedly linked or traced directly to satan and his evil forces.

satan is never happier than when he has convinced people that he is non-existent. The very popular modern denial of the existence of a personal devil is one of satan's major triumphs. We have a real enemy on our hands and we shall greatly weaken our position by blissfully disregarding his presence and power.
- Vance Havner

The thief comes only to steal and kill and destroy; I have come that they may have life, and have it to the full. John 10:10

CASTING OUT devils

EXAMPLES OF JESUS CASTING OUT devils

News about him spread all over Syria, and people brought to him all who were ill with various diseases, those suffering severe pain, the demon-possessed, those having seizures, and the paralyzed, and he healed them. Matthew 4:24

When evening came, many who were demon-possessed were brought to him, and he drove out the spirits with a word and healed all the sick. Matthew 8:16

While they were going out, a man who was demon-possessed and could not talk was brought to Jesus. And when the demon was driven out, the man who had been mute spoke. The crowd was amazed and said, "Nothing like this has ever been seen in Israel." Matthew 9:32-33

Then they brought him a demon-possessed man who was blind and mute, and Jesus healed him, so that he could both talk and see. Matthew 12:22

A Canaanite woman from that vicinity came to him, crying out, "Lord, Son of David, have mercy on me! My daughter is suffering terribly from demon-possession." Then Jesus answered, "Woman, you have great faith! Your request is granted." And her daughter was healed from that very hour. Matthew 15:22,28

Jesus rebuked the demon, and it came out of the boy, and he was healed from that moment. Matthew 17:18

When Jesus got out of the boat, a man with an evil spirit came from the tombs to meet him. This man lived in the tombs, and no one could bind him any more, not even with a chain. For he had often been chained hand and foot, but he tore the chains apart and broke the irons on his feet. No one was strong enough to subdue him. Night and day among the tombs and in the hills he would cry out and cut himself with stones. When he saw Jesus from a distance, he ran and fell on his knees in front of him. He shouted at the top of his voice, "What do you want with me, Jesus, Son of the Most High God? Swear to God that you won't torture me!" For Jesus had said to him, "Come out of this man, you evil spirit!" Then Jesus asked him, "What is your name?" "My name is Legion," he replied, "for we are many." And he begged Jesus again and again not to send them out of the area. A large herd of pigs was feeding on the nearby hillside. The demons begged Jesus, "Send us among the pigs; allow us to go into them." He gave them permission, and the evil spirits came out and went into the pigs. The herd, about two thousand in number, rushed down the steep bank into the lake and were drowned. Those tending the pigs ran off and reported this in the town and countryside, and the people went out to see what had happened. When they came to Jesus, they saw the man who had been possessed by the legion of demons, sitting there, dressed and in his right mind; and they were afraid. Mark 5:2-15

That evening after sunset the people brought to Jesus all the sick and demon-possessed. The whole town gathered at the door, and Jesus healed many who had various diseases. He also drove out many demons, but he would not let the demons speak because they knew who he was. Mark 1:32-34

So he traveled throughout Galilee, preaching in their synagogues and driving out demons. Mark 1:39

The woman was a Greek, born in Syrian Phoenicia. She begged Jesus to drive the demon out of her daughter. Mark 7:26

Then he told her, "For such a reply, you may go; the demon has left your daughter." She went home and found her child lying on the bed, and the demon gone. Mark 7:29-30

When Jesus rose early on the first day of the week, he appeared first to Mary Magdalene, out of whom he had driven seven demons. Mark 16:9

In the synagogue there was a man possessed by a demon, an evil spirit. He cried out at the top of his voice, "Ha! What do you want with us, Jesus of Nazareth? Have you come to destroy us? I know who you are—the Holy One of God!" "Be quiet!" Jesus said sternly.

"Come out of him!" Then the demon threw the man down before them all and came out without injuring him. Luke 4:33-35

Moreover, demons came out of many people, shouting, "You are the Son of God!" But he rebuked them and would not allow them to speak, because they knew he was the Christ. Luke 4:41

And also some women who had been cured of evil spirits and diseases: Mary (called Magdalene) from whom seven demons had come out. Luke 8:2

Even while the boy was coming, the demon threw him to the ground in a convulsion. But Jesus rebuked the evil spirit, healed the boy and gave him back to his father. Luke 9:42

Jesus was driving out a demon that was mute. When the demon left, the man who had been mute spoke, and the crowd was amazed. Luke 11:14

How God anointed Jesus of Nazareth with the Holy Spirit and power, and how he went around doing good and healing all who were under the power of the devil, because God was with him. Acts 10:38

THE DISCIPLES CASTING OUT devils

Heal the sick, raise the dead, cleanse those who have leprosy, drive out demons. Freely you have received, freely give. Matthew 10:8

He appointed twelve—designating them apostles—that they might be with him and that he might send them out to preach and to have authority to drive out demons. Mark 3:14-15

They went out and preached that people should repent. They drove out many demons and anointed many sick people with oil and healed them. Mark 6:12-13

When Jesus had called the Twelve together, he gave them power and authority to drive out all demons and to cure diseases. Luke 9:1

The seventy-two returned with joy and said, "Lord, even the demons submit to us in your name." Luke 10:17

YOU CAN CAST OUT devils

And these signs will accompany those who believe: In my name they will drive out demons; they will speak in new tongues.
Mark 16:17

I have given you authority to trample on snakes and scorpions and to overcome all the power of the enemy; nothing will harm you.
Luke 10:19

I tell you the truth, anyone who has faith in me will do what I have been doing. He will do even greater things than these, because I am going to the Father. John 14:12

The devil respects nothing but force through the name of Jesus. –Iraj Modarressi

BEFORE CASTING OUT devils

And we will be ready to punish every act of disobedience, once your obedience is complete. 2 Corinthians 10:6

Submit yourselves, then, to God. Resist the devil, and he will flee from you. James 4:7

But this kind does not go out except by prayer and fasting.
Matthew 17:21

Submit yourselves therefore to God. Resist the devil, and he will flee from you. James 4:7

You have to say "yes" to God first before you can effectively say "no" to the devil. - Vance Havner

WHEN CASTING OUT devils

Use the Name of JESUS, the blood of Jesus, and the Sword of the spirit (Word of God).

But even the archangel Michael, when he was disputing with the devil about the body of Moses, did not dare to bring a slanderous accusation against him, but said, "The Lord rebuke you!" Jude 1:9

So he said to me, "This is the word of the Lord to Zerubbabel: 'Not by might nor by power, but by my Spirit,' says the Lord Almighty.
Zechariah 4:6

After casting out devils advise the person to receive Christ into their spirit, and to study and obey God's Word.

When an evil spirit comes out of a man, it goes through arid places seeking rest and does not find it. Then it says, 'I will return to the house I left.' When it arrives, it finds the house unoccupied, swept clean and put in order. Then it goes and takes with it seven other spirits more wicked than itself, and they go in and live there. And the final condition of that man is worse than the first. That is how it will be with this wicked generation." Matthew 12:43-45

"When an evil spirit comes out of a man, it goes through arid places seeking rest and does not find it. Then it says, 'I will return to the house I left.' When it arrives, it finds the house swept clean and put in order. Then it goes and takes seven other spirits more wicked than itself, and they go in and live there. And the final condition of that man is worse than the first." Luke 11:24-26

Later Jesus found him at the temple and said to him, "See, you are well again. Stop sinning or something worse may happen to you."
John 5:14

Since we have these promises, dear friends, let us purify ourselves from everything that contaminates body and spirit, perfecting holiness out of reverence for God. 2 Corinthians 7:1

LAYING ON OF HANDS

MIRACLES OF JESUS THROUGH THE LAYING ON OF HANDS

Jesus reached out his hand and touched the man. "I am willing," he said. "Be clean!" Immediately he was cured of his leprosy.
Matthew 8:3

He touched her hand and the fever left her, and she got up and began to wait on him. Matthew 8:15

While he was saying this, a ruler came and knelt before him and said, "My daughter has just died. But come and put your hand on her, and she will live." Matthew 9:18

And pleaded earnestly with him, "My little daughter is dying. Please come and put your hands on her so that she will be healed and live." Mark 5:23

SPIRITUAL GIFTS GIVEN THROUGH THE LAYING ON OF HANDS

Then Peter and John placed their hands on them, and they received the Holy Spirit. When Simon saw that the Spirit was given at the laying on of the apostles' hands, he offered them money.
Acts 8:17-18

And Ananias went his way, and entered into the house; and putting his hands on him said, Brother Saul, the Lord, even Jesus, that appeared unto thee in the way as thou camest, hath sent me, that thou mightest receive thy sight, and be filled with the Holy Ghost.
Acts 9:17 KJV

And asked them, "Did you receive the Holy Spirit when you believed?" They answered, "No, we have not even heard that there is a Holy Spirit." So Paul asked, "Then what baptism did you receive?" "John's baptism," they replied. Paul said, "John's baptism was a baptism of repentance. He told the people to believe in the one coming after him, that is, in Jesus." On hearing this, they were baptized into the name of the Lord Jesus. When Paul placed his hands on them, the Holy Spirit came on them, and they spoke in tongues and prophesied. Acts 19:2-6

I long to see you so that I may impart to you some spiritual gift to make you strong. Romans 1:11

Do not neglect your gift, which was given you through a prophetic message when the body of elders laid their hands on you.
1 Timothy 4:14

For this reason I remind you to fan into flame the gift of God, which is in you through the laying on of my hands. 2 Timothy 1:6

237

Instruction about baptisms, the laying on of hands, the resurrection of the dead, and eternal judgment. Hebrews 6:2

BLESSINGS THROUGH THE LAYING ON OF HAND

And Joseph took both of them, Ephraim on his right toward Israel's left hand and Manasseh on his left toward Israel's right hand, and brought them close to him. But Israel reached out his right hand and put it on Ephraim's head, though he was the younger, and crossing his arms, he put his left hand on Manasseh's head, even though Manasseh was the firstborn. Genesis 48:13-14

When Joseph saw his father placing his right hand on Ephraim's head he was displeased; so he took hold of his father's hand to move it from Ephraim's head to Manasseh's head. Joseph said to him, "No, my father, this one is the firstborn; put your right hand on his head." But his father refused and said, "I know, my son, I know. He too will become a people, and he too will become great. Nevertheless, his younger brother will be greater than he, and his descendants will become a group of nations." He blessed them that day and said, "In your name will Israel pronounce this blessing: 'May God make you like Ephraim and Manasseh.'" So he put Ephraim ahead of Manasseh. Genesis 48:17-20

MIRACLES OF THE DISCIPLES THROUGH THE LAYING ON OF HANDS

Long time therefore abode they speaking boldly in the Lord, which gave testimony unto the word of his grace, and granted signs and wonders to be done by their hands. Acts 14:3 KJV

So Paul and Barnabas spent considerable time there, speaking boldly for the Lord, who confirmed the message of his grace by enabling them to do miraculous signs and wonders. Acts 14:3

They will pick up snakes with their hands; and when they drink deadly poison, it will not hurt them at all; they will place their hands on sick people, and they will get well. Mark 16:18

God did extraordinary miracles through Paul. Acts 19:11

TRANSFERENCE OF SPIRITS

The Lord said to Moses: "Bring me seventy of Israel's elders who are known to you as leaders and officials among the people. Have them come to the Tent of Meeting, that they may stand there with you. I will come down and speak with you there, and I will take of the Spirit that is on you and put the Spirit on them. They will help you carry the burden of the people so that you will not have to carry it alone. Numbers 11:16-17

Then the Lord came down in the cloud and spoke with him, and he took of the Spirit that was on him and put the Spirit on the seventy elders. When the Spirit rested on them, they prophesied, but they did not do so again. Numbers 11:25

So the Lord said to Moses, "Take Joshua son of Nun, a man in whom is the spirit, and lay your hand on him. Have him stand before Eleazar the priest and the entire assembly and commission him in their presence. Give him some of your authority so the whole Israelite community will obey him. Numbers 27:18-20

WARNING! BE CAREFUL ABOUT WHO YOU LAY YOUR HANDS UPON, ALSO BE CAUTIOUS ABOUT LETTING ANYONE AT RANDOM LAY THEIR HANDS UPON YOU.

Do not be hasty in the laying on of hands, and do not share in the sins of others. Keep yourself pure. 1 Timothy 5:22

Read "Seductions Exposed" by Gary Greenwald (available from Eagle's Nest Ministries, P.O. Box 15000, Santa Ana, CA 92705

Read "Transference of Spirits" by Alexander William Ness (available from Agapre Publication INC., P.O. BOX 89 PEFFERLAW, ONTARIO LOE INO)

FALSE BROTHERS

For such men are false apostles, deceitful workmen, masquerading as apostles of Christ. And no wonder, for Satan himself masquerades as an angel of light. It is not surprising, then, if his servants masquerade as servants of righteousness. Their end will be what their actions deserve. 2 Corinthians 11:13-15

RECOGNIZING FALSE BROTHERS

1. THEY CLAIM AND BOAST TO HAVE POWER BUT THEY ARE POWERLESS

Like clouds and wind without rain is a man who boasts of gifts he does not give. Proverbs 25:14

These men are blemishes at your love feasts, eating with you without the slightest qualm—shepherds who feed only themselves. They are clouds without rain, blown along by the wind; autumn trees, without fruit and uprooted—twice dead. They are wild waves of the sea, foaming up their shame; wandering stars, for whom blackest darkness has been reserved forever. Jude 1:12-13

2. THEY WILL DENY CHRIST

Who is the liar? It is the man who denies that Jesus is the Christ. Such a man is the antichrist—he denies the Father and the Son. No one who denies the Son has the Father; whoever acknowledges the Son has the Father also. 1 John 2:22-23

For certain men whose condemnation was written about long ago have secretly slipped in among you. They are godless men, who change the grace of our God into a license for immorality and deny Jesus Christ our only Sovereign and Lord. Jude 1:4

3. CHECK OUT THEIR LIFESTYLES

By their fruit you will recognize them. Do people pick grapes from thornbushes, or figs from thistles? Matthew 7:16

Thus, by their fruit you will recognize them. Matthew 7:20

Anyone who runs ahead and does not continue in the teaching of Christ does not have God; whoever continues in the teaching has both the Father and the Son. 2 John 1:9

4. UNSOUND DOCTRINE

But there were also false prophets among the people, just as there will be false teachers among you. They will secretly introduce destructive heresies, even denying the sovereign Lord who bought them—bringing swift destruction on themselves. 2 Peter 2:1

I urge you, brothers, to watch out for those who cause divisions and put obstacles in your way that are contrary to the teaching you have learned. Keep away from them. For such people are not serving our Lord Christ, but their own appetites. By smooth talk and flattery they deceive the minds of naive people. Romans 16:17-18

I am astonished that you are so quickly deserting the one who called you by the grace of Christ and are turning to a different gospel—which is really no gospel at all. Evidently some people are throwing you into confusion and are trying to pervert the gospel of Christ. But even if we or an angel from heaven should preach a gospel other than the one we preached to you, let him be eternally condemned! As we have already said, so now I say again: If anybody is preaching to you a gospel other than what you accepted, let him be eternally condemned! Galatians 1:6-9

For the time will come when men will not put up with sound doctrine. Instead, to suit their own desires, they will gather around them a great number of teachers to say what their itching ears want to hear. They will turn their ears away from the truth and turn aside to myths. 2 Timothy 4:3-4

He must hold firmly to the trustworthy message as it has been taught, so that he can encourage others by sound doctrine and refute those who oppose it. For there are many rebellious people, mere talkers and deceivers, especially those of the circumcision group. They must be silenced, because they are ruining whole households by teaching things they ought not to teach—and that for the sake of dishonest gain. Titus 1:9-11

If anyone comes to you and does not bring this teaching, do not take him into your house or welcome him. Anyone who welcomes him shares in his wicked work. 2 John 1:10-11

5. THEY PROMOTE RELIGION, TRADITIONS, RITUALS RATHER THAN CHRIST

Jesus replied, "And why do you break the command of God for the sake of your tradition? Matthew 15:3

He is not to 'honor his father' with it. Thus you nullify the word of God for the sake of your tradition. Matthew 15:6

You have let go of the commands of God and are holding on to the traditions of men." And he said to them: "You have a fine way of setting aside the commands of God in order to observe your own traditions! Mark 7:8-9

Thus you nullify the word of God by your tradition that you have handed down. And you do many things like that. Mark 7:13

See to it that no one takes you captive through hollow and deceptive philosophy, which depends on human tradition and the basic principles of this world rather than on Christ. Colossians 2:8

Forasmuch as ye know that ye were not redeemed with corruptible things, as silver and gold, from your vain conversation received by tradition from your fathers; 1 Peter 1:18 KJV

For you know that it was not with perishable things such as silver or gold that you were redeemed from the empty way of life handed down to you from your forefathers. 1 Peter 1:18

6. THEY ARE SMOOTH TALKERS THAT SPEAK DECEPTIVE WORDS

Let no one deceive you with empty words, for because of such things God's wrath comes on those who are disobedient.

Ephesians 5:6

I tell you this so that no one may deceive you by fine-sounding arguments. Colossians 2:4

As I urged you when I went into Macedonia, stay there in Ephesus so that you may command certain men not to teach false doctrines any longer nor to devote themselves to myths and endless genealogies. These promote controversies rather than God's work—which is by faith. 1 Timothy 1:3-4

TEST AND CONFRONT FALSE BROTHERS

Who is the liar? It is the man who denies that Jesus is the Christ. Such a man is the antichrist—he denies the Father and the Son. No one who denies the Son has the Father; whoever acknowledges the Son has the Father also. 1 John 2:22-23

Dear friends, do not believe every spirit, but test the spirits to see whether they are from God, because many false prophets have gone out into the world. 1 John 4:1

This is how you can recognize the Spirit of God: Every spirit that acknowledges that Jesus Christ has come in the flesh is from God, but every spirit that does not acknowledge Jesus is not from God. This is the spirit of the antichrist, which you have heard is coming and even now is already in the world. 1 John 4:2-3

We are from God, and whoever knows God listens to us; but whoever is not from God does not listen to us. This is how we recognize the Spirit of truth and the spirit of falsehood. 1 John 4:6

Many deceivers, who do not acknowledge Jesus Christ as coming in the flesh, have gone out into the world. Any such person is the deceiver and the antichrist. 2 John 1:7

FALSE PROPHETS

Then the Lord said to me, "The prophets are prophesying lies in my name. I have not sent them or appointed them or spoken to them. They are prophesying to you false visions, divinations, idolatries and the delusions of their own minds. Therefore, this is what the Lord says about the prophets who are prophesying in my name: I did not send them, yet they are saying, 'No sword or famine will touch this land.' Those same prophets will perish by sword and famine. Jeremiah 14:14-15

In the Old Testament, prophets were stoned if their prophecies were not true. In the New Testament prophecies are examined in light of the word of God, accepted if they are true, and ignored if they are false.

"Both prophet and priest are godless; even in my temple I find their wickedness," declares the Lord. "Therefore their path will become slippery; they will be banished to darkness and there they will fall. I will bring disaster on them in the year they are punished," declares the Lord. "Among the prophets of Samaria I saw this repulsive thing: They prophesied by Baal and led my people Israel astray. And among the prophets of Jerusalem I have seen something horrible: They commit adultery and live a lie. They strengthen the hands of evildoers, so that no one turns from his wickedness. They are all like Sodom to me; the people of Jerusalem are like Gomorrah." Therefore, this is what the Lord Almighty says concerning the prophets: "I will make them eat bitter food and drink poisoned water, because from the prophets of Jerusalem ungodliness has spread throughout the land." This is what the Lord Almighty says: "Do not listen to what the prophets are prophesying to you; they fill you with false hopes. They speak visions from their own minds, not from the mouth of the Lord.

Jeremiah 23:11-16

I did not send these prophets, yet they have run with their message; I did not speak to them, yet they have prophesied. Jeremiah 23:21

"I have heard what the prophets say who prophesy lies in my name. They say, 'I had a dream! I had a dream!' How long will this continue in the hearts of these lying prophets, who prophesy the delusions of their own minds? They think the dreams they tell one another will make my people forget my name, just as their fathers forgot my name through Baal worship. Let the prophet who has a dream tell his dream, but let the one who has my word speak it faithfully. For what has straw to do with grain?" declares the Lord. "Is not my word like fire," declares the Lord, "and like a hammer that breaks a rock in pieces? Jeremiah 23:25-29

Yes," declares the Lord, "I am against the prophets who wag their own tongues and yet declare, 'The Lord declares.' Indeed, I am against those who prophesy false dreams," declares the Lord. "They tell them and lead my people astray with their reckless lies, yet I did not send or appoint them. They do not benefit these people in the least," declares the Lord. Jeremiah 23:31-32

From early times the prophets who preceded you and me have prophesied war, disaster and plague against many countries and great kingdoms. But the prophet who prophesies peace will be recognized as one truly sent by the Lord only if his prediction comes true." Jeremiah 28:8-9

Yes, this is what the Lord Almighty, the God of Israel, says: "Do not let the prophets and diviners among you deceive you. Do not listen to the dreams you encourage them to have. They are prophesying lies to you in my name. I have not sent `them," declares the Lord. Jeremiah 29:8-9

> *A prophecy spoken to you and for you should always confirm what God has already been speaking to your spirit.*

Son of man, prophesy against the prophets of Israel who are now prophesying. Say to those who prophesy out of their own imagination: 'Hear the word of the Lord! This is what the Sovereign Lord says: Woe to the foolish prophets who follow their own spirit and have seen nothing! Your prophets, O Israel, are like jackals among ruins. You have not gone up to the breaks in the wall to repair it for the house of Israel so that it will stand firm in the battle on the day of the Lord. Their visions are false and their divinations a lie. They say, "The Lord declares," when the Lord has not sent them; yet they expect their words to be fulfilled. Have you not seen false visions and uttered lying divinations when you say, "The Lord declares," though I have not spoken? Therefore this is what the Sovereign Lord says: Because of your false words and lying visions, I am against you, declares the Sovereign Lord. My hand will be against the prophets who see false visions and utter lying divinations. They will not belong to the council of my people or be listed in the records of the house of Israel, nor will they enter the land of Israel. Then you will know that I am the Sovereign Lord.

Ezekiel 13:2-9

> *When a person starts prophesying over you and you know that it is contrary to God's Word and that it is a false prophecy coming from their flesh or the devil, Stop them immediately. Tell them, in the spirit of love and boldness, that their prophecy is false and you will not receive it. It's better for them to be confronted with truth and publicly embarrassed than for you to be cursed and deceived.*

And if anyone still prophesies, his father and mother, to whom he was born, will say to him, 'You must die, because you have told lies in the Lord's name.' When he prophesies, his own parents will stab him. "On that day every prophet will be ashamed of his prophetic vision. He will not put on a prophet's garment of hair in order to deceive. He will say, 'I am not a prophet. I am a farmer; the land has been my livelihood since my youth.'

Zechariah 13:3-5

Watch out for false prophets. They come to you in sheep's clothing, but inwardly they are ferocious wolves. Matthew 7:15

ALWAYS TEST AND COMPARE PROPHECIES TO THE WORD OF GOD

Dear friends, do not believe every spirit, but test the spirits to see whether they are from God, because many false prophets have gone out into the world. 1 John 4:1

The word of God is the measuring rod by which we judge every prophetic utterance. - Rick Godwin

A simple man believes anything, but a prudent man gives thought to his steps. Proverbs 14:15

OCCULT, WITCHCRAFT AND IDOLATRY

So Moses and Aaron went to Pharaoh and did just as the Lord commanded. Aaron threw his staff down in front of Pharaoh and his officials, and it became a snake. Pharaoh then summoned wise men and sorcerers, and the Egyptian magicians also did the same things by their secret arts: Each one threw down his staff and it became a snake. But Aaron's staff swallowed up their staffs.

Exodus 7:10-12

Do not allow a sorceress to live. Exodus 22:18

Do not turn to mediums or seek out spiritists, for you will be defiled by them. I am the Lord your God. Leviticus 19:31

I will set my face against the person who turns to mediums and spiritists to prostitute himself by following them, and I will cut him off from his people. Leviticus 20:6

A man or woman who is a medium or spiritist among you must be put to death. You are to stone them; their blood will be on their own heads. Leviticus 20:27

The elders of Moab and Midian left, taking with them the fee for divination. When they came to Balaam, they told him what Balak had said. Numbers 22:7

Let no one be found among you who sacrifices his son or daughter in the fire, who practices divination or sorcery, interprets omens, engages in witchcraft, or casts spells, or who is a medium or spiritist or who consults the dead. Deuteronomy 18:10-11

The nations you will dispossess listen to those who practice sorcery or divination. But as for you, the Lord your God has not permitted you to do so. Deuteronomy 18:14

For rebellion is like the sin of divination, and arrogance like the evil of idolatry. Because you have rejected the word of the Lord, he has rejected you as king. 1 Samuel 15:23

They sacrificed their sons and daughters in the fire. They practiced divination and sorcery and sorcery and sold themselves to do evil in the eyes of the Lord, provoking him to anger. 2 Kings 17:17

He sacrificed his own son in the fire, practiced sorcery and divination, and consulted mediums and spiritists. He did much evil in the eyes of the Lord, provoking him to anger. 2 Kings 21:6

Saul died because he was unfaithful to the Lord; he did not keep the word of the Lord and even consulted a medium for guidance.
1 Chronicles 10:13

When men tell you to consult mediums and spiritists, who whisper and mutter, should not a people inquire of their God? Why consult the dead on behalf of the living? Isaiah 8:19

Who foils the signs of false prophets and makes fools of diviners, who overthrows the learning of the wise and turns it into nonsense.
Isaiah 44:25

Then the Lord said to me, "The prophets are prophesying lies in my name. I have not sent them or appointed them or spoken to them. They are prophesying to you false visions, divinations, idolatries and the delusions of their own minds. Jeremiah 14:14

So do not listen to your prophets, your diviners, your interpreters of dreams, your mediums or your sorcerers who tell you, You will not serve the king of Babylon. Jeremiah 27:9

Yes, this is what the Lord Almighty, the God of Israel, says: Do not let the prophets and diviners among you deceive you. Do not listen to the dreams you encourage them to have. Jeremiah 29:8

For there will be no more false visions or flattering divinations among the people of Israel. Ezekiel 12:24

The seers will be ashamed and the diviners disgraced. They will all cover their faces because there is no answer from God. Micah 3:7

I will destroy your witchcraft and you will no longer cast spells.
Micah 5:12

All because of the wanton lust of a harlot, alluring, the mistress of sorceries, who enslaved nations by her prostitution and peoples by her witchcraft. Nahum 3:4

The idols speak deceit, diviners see visions that lie; they tell dreams that are false, they give comfort in vain. Therefore the people wander like sheep oppressed for lack of a shepherd. Zechariah 10:2

So I will come near to you for judgment. I will be quick to testify against sorcerers, adulterers and perjurers, against those who defraud laborers of their wages, who oppress the widows and the fatherless, and deprive aliens of justice, but do not fear me, says the Lord Almighty. Malachi 3:5

Now for some time a man named Simon had practiced sorcery in the city and amazed all the people of Samaria. He boasted that he was someone great. Acts 8:9

They traveled through the whole island until they came to Paphos. There they met a Jewish sorcerer and false prophet named Bar-Jesus, who was an attendant of the proconsul, Sergius Paulus. The proconsul, an intelligent man, sent for Barnabas and Saul because he wanted to hear the word of God. But Elymas the sorcerer (for that is what his name means) opposed them and tried to turn the proconsul from the faith. Then Saul, who was also called Paul, filled with the Holy Spirit, looked straight at Elymas and said, "You are a child of the devil and an enemy of everything that is right! You are full of all kinds of deceit and trickery. Will you never stop perverting the right ways of the Lord? Now the hand of the Lord is against you. You are going to be blind, and for a time you will be unable to see the light of the sun." Immediately mist and darkness came over him, and he groped about, seeking someone to lead him by the hand. Acts 13:6-11

Once when we were going to the place of prayer, we were met by a slave girl who had a spirit by which she predicted the future. She earned a great deal of money for her owners by fortune-telling. This girl followed Paul and the rest of us, shouting, "These men are servants of the Most High God, who are telling you the way to be saved." She kept this up for many days. Finally Paul became so troubled that he turned around and said to the spirit, "In the name of Jesus Christ I command you to come out of her!" At that moment the spirit left her. Acts 16:16-18

The acts of the sinful nature are obvious: sexual immorality, impurity and debauchery; idolatry and witchcraft; hatred, discord, jealousy, fits of rage, selfish ambition, dissensions, factions and envy; drunkenness, orgies, and the like. I warn you, as I did before, that those who live like this will not inherit the kingdom of God.
Galatians 5:19-21

Nor did they repent of their murders, their magic arts, their sexual immorality or their thefts. Revelation 9:21

The light of a lamp will never shine in you again. The voice of bridegroom and bride will never be heard in you again. Your merchants were the world's great men. By your magic spell all the nations were led astray. Revelation 18:23

But the cowardly, the unbelieving, the vile, the murderers, the sexually immoral, those who practice magic arts, the idolaters and all liars—their place will be in the fiery lake of burning sulfur. This is the second death. Revelation 21:8

Outside are the dogs, those who practice magic arts, the sexually immoral, the murderers, the idolaters and everyone who loves and practices falsehood. Revelation 22:15

MATURING IN CHRIST

FORGIVING OTHERS

Do not seek revenge or bear a grudge against one of your people, but love your neighbor as yourself. I am the Lord. Leviticus 19:18

Therefore, if you are offering your gift at the altar and there remember that your brother has something against you, leave your gift there in front of the altar. First go and be reconciled to your brother; then come and offer your gift. Matthew 5:23-24

But I tell you: Love your enemies and pray for those who persecute you. Matthew 5:44

Forgive us our debts, as we also have forgiven our debtors.
Matthew 6:12

For if you forgive men when they sin against you, your heavenly Father will also forgive you. But if you do not forgive men their sins, your Father will not forgive your sins. Matthew 6:14-15

"I can forgive, but I cannot forget," is only another way of saying, "I cannot forgive." - Henry Ward Beecher

Then Peter came to Jesus and asked, "Lord, how many times shall I forgive my brother when he sins against me? Up to seven times?" Jesus answered, "I tell you, not seven times, but seventy-seven times. Matthew 18:21-22

Do not judge, and you will not be judged. Do not condemn, and you will not be condemned. Forgive, and you will be forgiven.
Luke 6:37

If you forgive anyone his sins, they are forgiven; if you do not forgive them, they are not forgiven. John 20:23

If you forgive anyone, I also forgive him. And what I have forgiven—if there was anything to forgive—I have forgiven in the sight of Christ for your sake, in order that Satan might not outwit us. For we are not unaware of his schemes. 2 Corinthians 2:10-11

Get rid of all bitterness, rage and anger, brawling and slander, along with every form of malice. Be kind and compassionate to one another, forgiving each other, just as in Christ God forgave you.
Ephesians 4:31-32

Grudge not one against another, brethren, lest ye be condemned: behold, the judge standeth before the door. James 5:9 KJV

Don't grumble against each other, brothers, or you will be judged. The Judge is standing at the door! James 5:9

Use hospitality one to another without grudging. 1 Peter 4:9 KJV

Offer hospitality to one another without grumbling. 1 Peter 4:9

Bear with each other and forgive whatever grievances you may have against one another. Forgive as the Lord forgave you.
Colossians 3:13

Forgiving your offenders sets you free more than it does anyone else.

PATIENCE

Wait for the Lord; be strong and take heart and wait for the Lord.
Psalms 27:14

Be still before the Lord and wait patiently for him; do not fret when men succeed in their ways, when they carry out their wicked schemes. Refrain from anger and turn from wrath; do not fret—it leads only to evil. For evil men will be cut off, but those who hope in the Lord will inherit the land. Psalms 37:7-9

Wait for the Lord and keep his way. He will exalt you to inherit the land; when the wicked are cut off, you will see it. Psalms 37:34

I waited patiently for the Lord; he turned to me and heard my cry.
Psalms 40:1

The end of a matter is better than its beginning, and patience is better than pride. Ecclesiastes 7:8

These wait all upon thee; that thou mayest give them their meat in due season. Psalms 104:27 KJV

These wait all upon thee; that thou mayest give them their meat in due season. Psalms 104:27 KJV

> *Impatience and doubt are thieves of the perfect will of God and His greatest blessings.*

Do not say, "I'll pay you back for this wrong!" Wait for the Lord, and he will deliver you. Proverbs 20:22

And it shall be said in that day, Lo, this is our God; we have waited for him, and he will save us: this is the Lord; we have waited for him, we will be glad and rejoice in his salvation. Isaiah 25:9

It is good to wait quietly for the salvation of the Lord.
Lamentations 3:26

By standing firm you will gain life. Luke 21:19

To those who by persistence in doing good seek glory, honor and immortality, he will give eternal life. Romans 2:7

But if we hope for what we do not yet have, we wait for it patiently.
Romans 8:25

> *Just as faith without works is dead so is faith without patience.*

Being strengthened with all power according to his glorious might so that you may have great endurance and patience, and joyfully.
Colossians 1:11

And we urge you, brothers, warn those who are idle, encourage the timid, help the weak, be patient with everyone.
1 Thessalonians 5:14

And the Lord direct your hearts into the love of God, and into the patient waiting for Christ. 2 Thessalonians 3:5 KJV

May the Lord direct your hearts into God's love and Christ's perseverance. 2 Thessalonians 3:5

Wherefore seeing we also are compassed about with so great a cloud of witnesses, let us lay aside every weight, and the sin which doth so easily beset us, and let us run with patience the race that is set before us, Hebrews 12:1 KJV

Therefore, since we are surrounded by such a great cloud of witnesses, let us throw off everything that hinders and the sin that so easily entangles, and let us run with perseverance the race marked out for us. Hebrews 12:1

Be patient, then, brothers, until the Lord's coming. See how the farmer waits for the land to yield its valuable crop and how patient he is for the autumn and spring rains. You too, be patient and stand firm, because the Lord's coming is near. James 5:7-8

Brothers, as an example of patience in the face of suffering, take the prophets who spoke in the name of the Lord. James 5:10

Whereby are given unto us exceeding great and precious promises: that by these ye might be partakers of the divine nature, having escaped the corruption that is in the world through lust.
2 Peter 1:4

And to knowledge temperance; and to temperance patience; and to patience godliness. 2 Peter 1:6 KJV

And to knowledge, self-control; and to self-control, perseverance; and to perseverance, godliness. 2 Peter 1:6

The Lord is not slow in keeping his promise, as some understand slowness. He is patient With you, not wanting anyone to perish, but everyone to come to repentance. 2 Peter 3:9

Since you have kept my command to endure patiently, I will also keep you from the hour of trial that is going to come upon the whole world to test those who live on the earth. Revelation 3:10

This calls for patient endurance on the part of the saints who obey God's commandments and remain faithful to Jesus.
Revelation 14:12

REMAINING PATIENT IN TRIBULATIONS

Not only so, but we also rejoice in our sufferings, because we know that suffering produces perseverance; perseverance, character; and character, hope. And hope does not disappoint us, because God has poured out his love into our hearts by the Holy Spirit, whom he has given us. Romans 5:3-5

Be joyful in hope, patient in affliction, faithful in prayer.
Romans 12:12

Knowing this, that the trying of your faith worketh patience. But let patience have her perfect work, that ye may be perfect and entire, wanting nothing. James 1:3-4 KJV

Because you know that the testing of your faith develops perseverance. Perseverance must finish its work so that you may be mature and complete, not lacking anything. James 1:3-4

> *Some experiences may not contribute to happiness, but all can be made to contribute to the development of patience.*

LIVING IN HOLINESS

I am the Lord your God; consecrate yourselves and be holy, because I am holy. Do not make yourselves unclean by any creature that moves about on the ground. I am the Lord who brought you up out of Egypt to be your God; therefore be holy, because I am holy.
Leviticus 11:44-45

In the last days the mountain of the Lord's temple will be established as chief among the mountains; it will be raised above the hills, and all nations will stream to it. 1 Samuel 2:2

To rescue us from the hand of our enemies, and to enable us to serve him without fear in holiness and righteousness before him all our days. Luke 1:74-75

I put this in human terms because you are weak in your natural selves. Just as you used to offer the parts of your body in slavery to impurity and to ever-increasing wickedness, so now offer them in slavery to righteousness leading to holiness. Romans 6:19

But now that you have been set free from sin and have become slaves to God, the benefit you reap leads to holiness, and the result is eternal life. Romans 6:22

The essence of true holiness consists in conformity to the nature and will of God. - Samuel Lucas

Therefore, I urge you, brothers, in view of God's mercy, to offer your bodies as living sacrifices, holy and pleasing to God—this is your spiritual act of worship. Romans 12:1

Since we have these promises, dear friends, let us purify ourselves from everything that contaminates body and spirit, perfecting holiness out of reverence for God. 2 Corinthians 7:1

For he chose us in him before the creation of the world to be holy and blameless in his sight. In love. Ephesians 1:4

And to put on the new self, created to be like God in true righteousness and holiness. Ephesians 4:24

And to present her to himself as a radiant church, without stain or wrinkle or any other blemish, but holy and blameless.
Ephesians 5:27

May he strengthen your hearts so that you will be blameless and holy in the presence of our God and Father when our Lord Jesus comes with all his holy ones. 1 Thessalonians 3:13

For God did not call us to be impure, but to live a holy life.
1 Thessalonians 4:7

The aged women likewise, that they be in behaviour as becometh holiness, not false accusers, not given to much wine, teachers of good things; Titus 2:3 KJV

A man ought to live so that everybody knows he is a Christian.... and most of all, his family ought to know.
- D. L. Moody

Our fathers disciplined us for a little while as they thought best; but God disciplines us for our good, that we may share in his holiness. Hebrews 12:10

Make every effort to live in peace with all men and to be holy; without holiness no one will see the Lord. Hebrews 12:14

But just as he who called you is holy, so be holy in all you do; for it is written: "Be holy, because I am holy." 1 Peter 1:15-16

FRUITFUL LIVING

Produce fruit in keeping with repentance. Matthew 3:8

The ax is already at the root of the trees, and every tree that does not produce good fruit will be cut down and thrown into the fire.
Matthew 3:10

By their fruit you will recognize them. Do people pick grapes from thornbushes, or figs from thistles? Likewise every good tree bears good fruit, but a bad tree bears bad fruit. A good tree cannot bear bad fruit, and a bad tree cannot bear good fruit. Every tree that does not bear good fruit is cut down and thrown into the fire. Thus, by their fruit you will recognize them. Matthew 7:16-20

All the people were astonished and said, "Could this be the Son of David?" Matthew 12:23

Make a tree good and its fruit will be good, or make a tree bad and its fruit will be bad, for a tree is recognized by its fruit.
Matthew 12:33

I am the true vine, and my Father is the gardener. He cuts off every branch in me that bears no fruit, while every branch that does bear fruit he prunes so that it will be even more fruitful. You are already clean because of the word I have spoken to you. Remain in me, and I will remain in you. No branch can bear fruit by itself; it must remain in the vine. Neither can you bear fruit unless you remain in me. I am the vine; you are the branches. If a man remains in me and I in him, he will bear much fruit; apart from me you can do nothing. John 15:1-5

This is to my Father's glory, that you bear much fruit, showing yourselves to be my disciples. John 15:8

You did not choose me, but I chose you and appointed you to go and bear fruit—fruit that will last. Then the Father will give you whatever you ask in my name. John 15:16

But just as you excel in everything—in faith, in speech, in knowledge, in complete earnestness and in your love for us—see that you also excel in this grace of giving. 2 Corinthians 8:7

If I am to go on living in the body, this will mean fruitful labor for me. Yet what shall I choose? I do not know! Philippians 1:22

That has come to you. All over the world this gospel is bearing fruit and growing, just as it has been doing among you since the day you heard it and understood God's grace in all its truth.
Colossians 1:6

And we pray this in order that you may live a life worthy of the Lord and may please him in every way: bearing fruit in every good work, growing in the knowledge of God. Colossians 1:10

Now no chastening for the present seemeth to be joyous, but grievous: nevertheless afterward it yieldeth the peaceable fruit of righteousness unto them which are exercised thereby.
Hebrews 12:11 KJV

Faith makes a Christian.

Life proves a Christian.

Trial confirms a Christian.

Death crowns a Christian.

-Anonymous

For if these things be in you, and abound, they make you that ye shall neither be barren nor unfruitful in the knowledge of our Lord Jesus Christ. 2 Peter 1:8 KJV

For if you possess these qualities in increasing measure, they will keep you from being ineffective and unproductive in your knowledge of our Lord Jesus Christ. 2 Peter 1:8

PEACEMAKER

Hatred stirs up dissension, but love covers over all wrongs.
Proverbs 10:12

A gentle answer turns away wrath, but a harsh word stirs up anger.
Proverbs 15:1

A hot-tempered man stirs up dissension, but a patient man calms a quarrel. Proverbs 15:18

He who covers over an offense promotes love, but whoever repeats the matter separates close friends. Proverbs 17:9

A gift given in secret soothes anger, and a bribe concealed in the cloak pacifies great wrath. Proverbs 21:14

Through patience a ruler can be persuaded, and a gentle tongue can break a bone. Proverbs 25:15

By long forbearing and calmness of spirit a judge or ruler is persuaded, and soft speech breaks down the most bonelike resistance.
Proverbs 25:15 AMP

Mockers stir up a city, but wise men turn away anger.
Proverbs 29:8

If a ruler's anger rises against you, do not leave your post; calmness can lay great errors to rest. Ecclesiastes 10:4

Blessed are the peacemakers, for they will be called sons of God.
Matthew 5:9

If it is possible, as far as it depends on you, live at peace with everyone. Romans 12:18

Hold them in the highest regard in love because of their work. Live in peace with each other. 1 Thessalonians 5:13

Make every effort to live in peace with all men and to be holy; without holiness no one will see the Lord. Hebrews 12:14

He must turn from evil and do good; he must seek peace and pursue it. 1 Peter 3:11

Peacemakers who sow in peace raise a harvest of righteousness.
James 3:18

OVERCOMING AND COVETOUSNESS

Covetousness - To long for, lust after; whether things good or bad.

You shall not covet your neighbor's house. You shall not covet your neighbor's wife, or his manservant or maidservant, his ox or donkey, or anything that belongs to your neighbor. Exodus 20:17

Incline my heart unto thy testimonies, and not to covetousness.
Psalms 119:36 KJV

Turn my heart toward your statutes and not toward selfish gain.
Psalms 119:36

Then he said to them, "Watch out! Be on your guard against all kinds of greed; a man's life does not consist in the abundance of his possessions. And he told them this parable: "The ground of a certain rich man produced a good crop. He thought to himself, 'What shall I do? I have no place to store my crops.' "Then he said, 'This is what I'll do. I will tear down my barns and build bigger ones, and there I will store all my grain and my goods. And I'll say to myself, "You have plenty of good things laid up for many years. Take life easy; eat, drink and be merry." "But God said to him, 'You fool! This very night your life will be demanded from you. Then who will get what you have prepared for yourself?' "This is how it will be with anyone who stores up things for himself but is not rich toward God." Luke 12:15-21

Let your conversation be without covetousness; and be content with such things as ye have: for he hath said, I will never leave thee, nor forsake thee. Hebrews 13:5 KJV

Keep your lives free from the love of money and be content with what you have, because God has said, "Never will I leave you; never will I forsake you." Hebrews 13:5

The prince that wanteth understanding is also a great oppressor: but he that hateth covetousness shall prolong his days.
Proverbs 28:16 KJV

A tyrannical ruler lacks judgment, but he who hates ill-gotten gain will enjoy a long life. Proverbs 28:16

THE CONSEQUENCES OF COVETOUSNESS

Nor thieves, nor covetous, nor drunkards, nor revilers, nor extortioners, shall inherit the kingdom of God. 1 Corinthians 6:10 KJV

Nor thieves nor the greedy nor drunkards nor slanderers nor swindlers will inherit the kingdom of God. 1 Corinthians 6:10

For this ye know, that no whoremonger, nor unclean person, nor covetous man, who is an idolater, hath any inheritance in the kingdom of Christ and of God. Ephesians 5:5 KJV

For of this you can be sure: No immoral, impure or greedy person—such a man is an idolater—has any inheritance in the kingdom of Christ and of God. Ephesians 5:5

OVERCOMING THE FEAR OF MAN

When I am afraid, I will trust in you. In God, whose word I praise, in God I trust; I will not be afraid. What can mortal man do to me?
Psalms 56:3-4

The Lord is with me; I will not be afraid. What can man do to me?
Psalms 118:6

Fear of man will prove to be a snare, but whoever trusts in the Lord is kept safe. Proverbs 29:25

So we say with confidence, "The Lord is my helper; I will not be afraid. What can man do to me?" Hebrews 13:6

Do not be afraid of those who kill the body but cannot kill the soul. Rather, be afraid of the One who can destroy both soul and body in hell. Matthew 10:28

> *There is one guaranteed formula for failure, and that is to try to please everyone - John Mason*

Who is going to harm you if you are eager to do good? But even if you should suffer for what is right, you are blessed. Do not fear what they fear; do not be frightened. 1 Peter 3:13-14

BECOMING BOLD IN CHRIST

I will speak of your statutes before kings and will not be put to shame. Psalms 119:46

The wicked man flees though no one pursues, but the righteous are as bold as a lion. Proverbs 28:1

If anyone is ashamed of me and my words in this adulterous and sinful generation, the Son of Man will be ashamed of him when he comes in his Father's glory with the holy angels. Mark 8:38

In him and through faith in him we may approach God with freedom and confidence. Ephesians 3:12

Pray also for me, that whenever I open my mouth, words may be given me so that I will fearlessly make known the mystery of the gospel, for which I am an ambassador in chains. Pray that I may declare it fearlessly, as I should. Ephesians 6:19-20

Because of my chains, most of the brothers in the Lord have been encouraged to speak the word of God more courageously and fearlessly. Philippians 1:14

Therefore, although in Christ I could be bold and order you to do what you ought to do. Philemon 1:8

Let us then approach the throne of grace with confidence, so that we may receive mercy and find grace to help us in our time of need. Hebrews 4:16

Therefore, brothers, since we have confidence to enter the Most Holy Place by the blood of Jesus. Hebrews 10:19

So we say with confidence, "The Lord is my helper; I will not be afraid. What can man do to me?" Hebrews 13:6

A boldness in Christ should always be accompanied by wisdom, divine timing, and a spirit of love.

LOVE

LOVE

And so we know and rely on the love God has for us. God is love. Whoever lives in love lives in God, and God in him. 1 John 4:16

There is no fear in love. But perfect love drives out fear, because fear has to do with punishment. The one who fears is not made perfect in love. 1 John 4:18

Love is patient, love is kind. It does not envy, it does not boast, it is not proud. It is not rude, it is not self-seeking, it is not easily angered, it keeps no record of wrongs. Love does not delight in evil but rejoices with the truth. It always protects, always trusts, always hopes, always perseveres. Love never fails. But where there are prophecies, they will cease; where there are tongues, they will be stilled; where there is knowledge, it will pass away.
1 Corinthians 13:4-8

If I speak in the tongues of men and of angels, but have not love, I am only a resounding gong or a clanging cymbal. If I have the gift of prophecy and can fathom all mysteries and all knowledge, and if I have a faith that can move mountains, but have not love, I am nothing. If I give all I possess to the poor and surrender my body to the flames, but have not love, I gain nothing. 1 Corinthians 13:1-3

And now these three remain: faith, hope and love. But the greatest of these is love. 1 Corinthians 13:13

GOD'S LOVE

The Lord gives sight to the blind, the Lord lifts up those who are bowed down, the Lord loves the righteous. Psalms 146:8

As a young man marries a maiden, so will your sons marry you; as a bridegroom rejoices over his bride, so will your God rejoice over you. Isaiah 62:5

The Lord appeared to us in the past, saying: "I have loved you with an everlasting love; I have drawn you with loving-kindness.
Jeremiah 31:3

I will heal their waywardness and love them freely, for my anger has turned away from them. Hosea 14:4

For God so loved the world that he gave his one and only Son, that whoever believes in him shall not perish but have eternal life.
John 3:16

No, the Father himself loves you because you have loved me and have believed that I came from God. John 16:27

I have given them the glory that you gave me, that they may be one as we are one: I in them and you in me. May they be brought to complete unity to let the world know that you sent me and have loved them even as you have loved me. John 17:22-23

I have made you known to them, and will continue to make you known in order that the love you have for me may be in them and that I myself may be in them. John 17:26

But God demonstrates his own love for us in this: While we were still sinners, Christ died for us. Romans 5:8

But because of his great love for us, God, who is rich in mercy, made us alive with Christ even when we were dead in transgressions—it is by grace you have been saved. And God raised us up with Christ and seated us with him in the heavenly realms in Christ Jesus, in order that in the coming ages he might show the incomparable riches of his grace, expressed in his kindness to us in Christ Jesus. Ephesians 2:4-7

And to know this love that surpasses knowledge—that you may be filled to the measure of all the fullness of God. Ephesians 3:19

May our Lord Jesus Christ himself and God our Father, who loved us and by his grace gave us eternal encouragement and good hope, encourage your hearts and strengthen you in every good deed and word. 2 Thessalonians 2:16-17

How great is the love the Father has lavished on us, that we should be called children of God! And that is what we are! The reason the world does not know us is that it did not know him. 1 John 3:1

Dear friends, let us love one another, for love comes from God. Everyone who loves has been born of God and knows God. Whoever does not love does not know God, because God is love. This is how God showed his love among us: He sent his one and only Son into the world that we might live through him. This is love: not that we loved God, but that he loved us and sent his Son as an atoning sacrifice for our sins. Dear friends, since God so loved us, we also ought to love one another. 1 John 4:7-11

And so we know and rely on the love God has for us. God is love. Whoever lives in love lives in God, and God in him. 1 John 4:16

We love him, because he first loved us. 1 John 4:19

LOVING GOD

However, as it is written: "No eye has seen, no ear has heard, no mind has conceived what God has prepared for those who love him." 1 Corinthians 2:9

Know therefore that the Lord your God is God; he is the faithful God, keeping his covenant of love to a thousand generations of those who love him and keep his commands. Deuteronomy 7:9

Delight yourself in the Lord and he will give you the desires of your heart. Psalms 37:4

Whom have I in heaven but you? And earth has nothing I desire besides you. Psalms 73:25

"Because he loves me," says the Lord, "I will rescue him; I will protect him, for he acknowledges my name. Psalms 91:14

The Lord watches over all who love him, but all the wicked he will destroy. Psalms 145:20

I love those who love me, and those who seek me find me.
Proverbs 8:17

Bestowing wealth on those who love me and making their treasuries full. Proverbs 8:21

Whoever has my commands and obeys them, he is the one who loves me. He who loves me will be loved by my Father, and I too will love him and show myself to him. John 14:21

Grace to all who love our Lord Jesus Christ with an undying love.
Ephesians 6:24

LOVING OTHERS

How good and pleasant it is when brothers live together in unity!
Psalms 133:1

But I tell you: Love your enemies and pray for those who persecute you. Matthew 5:44

So in everything, do to others what you would have them do to you, for this sums up the Law and the Prophets. Matthew 7:12

Love the Lord your God with all your heart and with all your soul and with all your mind and with all your strength. The second is this: Love your neighbor as yourself. There is no commandment greater than these. Mark 12:30-31

My command is this: Love each other as I have loved you. Greater love has no one than this, that he lay down his life for his friends.
John 15:12-13

Be devoted to one another in brotherly love. Honor one another above yourselves. Romans 12:10

Love does no harm to its neighbor. Therefore love is the fulfillment of the law. Romans 13:10

Finally, brothers, good-by. Aim for perfection, listen to my appeal, be of one mind, live in peace. And the God of love and peace will be with you. 2 Corinthians 13:11

Now that you have purified yourselves by obeying the truth so that you have sincere love for your brothers, love one another deeply, from the heart. 1 Peter 1:22

Finally, all of you, live in harmony with one another; be sympathetic, love as brothers, be compassionate and humble. Do not repay evil with evil or insult with insult, but with blessing, because to this you were called so that you may inherit a blessing.

1 Peter 3:8-9

Whoever loves his brother lives in the light, and there is nothing in him to make him stumble. 1 John 2:10

We know that we have passed from death to life, because we love our brothers. Anyone who does not love remains in death.

1 John 3:14

Dear children, let us not love with words or tongue but with actions and in truth. This then is how we know that we belong to the truth, and how we set our hearts at rest in his presence.

1 John 3:18-19

Dear friends, let us love one another, for love comes from God. Everyone who loves has been born of God and knows God. Whoever does not love does not know God, because God is love.

1 John 4:7-8

Dear friends, since God so loved us, we also ought to love one another. No one has ever seen God; but if we love one another, God lives in us and his love is made complete in us. 1 John 4:11-12

If anyone says, "I love God," yet hates his brother, he is a liar. For anyone who does not love his brother, whom he has seen, cannot love God, whom he has not seen. And he has given us this command: Whoever loves God must also love his brother.

1 John 4:20-21

And now, dear lady, I am not writing you a new command but one we have had from the beginning. I ask that we love one another.

2 John 1:5

PART II

Culture, Heritage and Identity

Articles

Understanding the Power of Culture
Racism: Death of the Gods
Understanding

UNDERSTANDING THE POWER OF CULTURE

by Wayne Perryman

Understanding the Power of Culture

Every culture is built on a foundation of beliefs. These beliefs shape the culture, the culture shapes the people, and the people shape their lives. The powerful influence of culture will affect factors such as the following:

1. The people's way of thinking
2. How they approach problem solving
3. How they raise their children
4. How they view their spouse and how children view their parents
5. How they communicate
6. How they worship
7. Their sense of humor
8. Their diet
9. Their values
10. Their standards of beauty
11. Their laws and household policies, and
12. How they view others.

One of the most effective (nonviolent) ways to destroy a nation of people is first to destroy its culture. The two most effective ways to destroy the culture are by attacking or eliminating the belief system on which the culture was built, and by letting the stronger culture co-habitat with a weaker culture. In time, the stronger one will overpower the weaker and destroy it.

God Recognizes The Power of Cultures

In Deuteronomy 7:2-7 (Living Bible) the Lord instructs Israel to use both force and separatism to destroy the heathen culture and their belief system (their gods).

"When the Lord your God delivers them over to you to be destroyed, do a complete job of it — don't make any treaties or show them mercy; utterly wipe them out. Do not intermarry with them, nor let your sons or daughters marry their sons and daughters. That would surely result in your young people beginning to worship their gods. . . You must break down the heathen altars and shatter the obelisks and cut up the shameful images and burn the idols. For you are a holy people, dedicated to the Lord your God. . . . "

273

Because Israel's culture and beliefs were so intimately tied to their relationship with God, its cultural preservation was of the utmost importance. However, cultural preservation would not be an easy task. Wars, captivity, stubbornness and disobedience presented a constant threat to the much valued relationship. But the Lord never gave up. The Lord knew if the Israelites lost their culture, they would also lose their identity. If they lost their identity, they would lose their sense of direction, and if they lost their sense of direction, their people would eventually be destroyed.

All contact with the heathens presented such a tremendous threat to the destruction of the Israeli culture and their relationship with God that the Lord reduced the risk factors by not permitting voluntary cohabitation and intermarriage. He wanted all opposition and risk factors completely destroyed.

Very few Jews had the power to resist the powerful influence of heathen cultures. However, Daniel and the Hebrew boys were an exception.

"But Daniel purposed in his heart that he would not defile himself with the portion of the King's meat, nor with the wine which he drank; therefore he requested of the prince of the eunuchs that he might not defile himself" (Daniel 1:8). This was an example of culture associated with diet.

An example of a militant attitude toward resistance to cultural influence is seen in Daniel 3:16-18: "O Nebuchadnezzar, we are not careful to answer thee in this matter. If it be so, our God whom we serve is able to deliver us from the burning fiery furnace and he will deliver us out of thine hand, O king, But if not, be it known unto thee, O king, that we will not serve thy gods, nor worship the golden image which thou hast set up." The book of Daniel also provides an example of preserving the culture at all cost: "Now when Daniel knew that the writing was signed, he went into his house; and his windows being open in his chamber toward Jerusalem, he kneeled upon his knees three times a day, and prayed, and gave thanks before his God, as he did aforetime" (Daniel 6:10).

Note the number of times the word "his" was used, thus claiming ownership. Unlike Ruth (although we applaud her decision to choose the God and life-style of her mother-in-law in Ruth 1:8-16), Daniel would not voluntarily give up the values and traditions that he had been taught since childhood. He also would not let any opposing forces or elements destroy it.

Destruction of Cultures

Cultural destruction was also a subject in the September 23, 1991 issue of *Time* magazine. The cover story carried the following title and sub-title, "Lost Tribes - Lost Knowledge," "When native cultures disappear, so does a trove of scientific and medical wisdom."

The article deals with two ways native cultures have been destroyed: through property acquisition (under the name of modern development) and through cohabitation.

The author of the article, reporter Eugene Linden said, "This largely undocumented knowledge base is humanity's lifeline to a time when people accepted nature's authority and learned through trial, error and observation. But the world's tribes are dying out or being absorbed into modern civilization. As they vanish, so does their irreplaceable knowledge. . .

Until quite recently, few in the developed world cared much about this cultural holocaust. The prevailing attitude has been that Western science, with its powerful analytical tools, has little to learn from tribal knowledge."

(Such was the case with the African slave and the American slave owner. The slave owners did not respect the ideas, wisdom or the cultural ways of their slaves. The slaves' cultural ways were considered to be primitive and inferior to the western culture.)

"Indigenous people have been threatened for centuries as development encroaches on their land and traditions. What is different about the present situation, however, is that it goes beyond basic questions of native land rights into more ambiguous issues, such as the prerogative of individuals to decide between traditional and modern ways. Indigenous knowledge disappears when natives are stripped of their lands, but in many parts of the globe, knowledge also disappears because the young who are in contact with the outside world have embraced the view that traditional ways are illegitimate, and irrelevant."

Most cultures today are not destroyed by violent, forceful take-overs by an opposing nation. They are destroyed because their ways and ideas (through cohabitation) are considered to be illegitimate and irrelevant by the stronger and more powerful culture. Again, such was the case of the African slave. His language, values, traditions, and beliefs were considered to be primitive, illegitimate and irrelevant and was thus, for the most part, destroyed.

The process of cultural destruction through cohabitation is a long, gradual process that's achieved through a variety of changes. Such changes are caused and brought about by many factors including modern legislation, economic depravity, destruction of old communities by new development, biased education, new trends, biased media, intimidation, racism, and the loss of knowledge of traditional ways.

Methods of Preserving Cultures

The Jews, though a constant struggle, protected and preserved their culture and its belief system by establishing their own schools and community, forming their own community papers, developing their own synagogues (churches), manufacturing their types of food, and never forgetting their history.

In Deuteronomy 6:7-9 (Living Bible), Israel was instructed to maintain their cultural beliefs by teaching their children Jewish history, Jewish values, and Jewish beliefs. "You must teach them to your children and talk about them when you are at home or out for a walk; at bedtime and the first thing in the morning. Tie them on your finger, wear them on your forehead, and write them on the doorposts of your house!"

In Proverbs 22:6 (King James), the Jews were also instructed to "Train up a child in the way he should go: and when he is old, he will not depart from it."

God knew that cultures are preserved and maintained in the hearts and minds of young people. In her book, *Bar Mitzvah*, Sarah

Silberstein Swartz writes, ". . . A [Jewish] boy is first taught the Hebrew alphabet at age three, studies the bible at age five, and learns rabbinical commentaries at age ten. He is taken to the synagogue on a regular basis by age four, and, from then on, is formally educated in Jewish culture and values. . ." If such cultural traditions and practices are not passed on to, and practiced by, the younger generation the traditions and practices will be lost.

Dominant Culture Rules

Case Study: A Struggle For Respect And Cultural Survival

In 1970, Rev. Willie Jenison, a black graduate of Moody Bible Institute, took over Oakdale Covenant Church, a Swedish church located in the heart of a black community in Chicago. At the time, the church congregation was made up of one-third black and two-thirds Swedes.

One of the biggest challenges facing the new black pastor was, what type of worship service would be needed to reach the community. Could he continue to rely on the old Swedish Hymns or would the mother church allow him to resort to a style of worship that blacks could identify with? The question was answered eight months later when Rev. Jenison protested by submitting his resignation. The mother church relented and gave him the freedom to formulate a ministry that would be effective in reaching the community it served. Today his congregation is 99% Black.

Can different cultures survive side by side? During the Civil Rights movement of the 60's and 70's, the theme was to integrate. Many were and still are confused about what this means. Does it mean living side by side in peace and harmony with respect for our differences? Or does it mean that I now have to transform my way of living to conform to the ways of the dominate culture? I think many have interpreted it to mean the latter.

In our society, it is very difficult to maintain and preserve our own culture while living in a multi-cultural society because we have not been trained to respect, appreciate, and understand cultures that are different than our own. This is particularly true with the black culture. Since the time of slavery, the black culture has been discounted and classified as inferior and unimportant.

Most studies of human behavior, such as psychology, are based on the white western culture and value system. Very few white psychologists familiarize themselves with books such as "Counseling the Culturally Different," "Ethnicity & Family Therapy" and "Black Families in Therapy." Instead, their concentration usually focuses on studies that address the needs of the western white culture and its standards. These western cultural standards are used to determined what is or is not a functional family; what is abusive and what is not. They are used to establish the proper standards for raising children and the appropriate or inappropriate discipline for children.

Such standards influence how we view biblical theology and interpret the Bible. They dictate what should or should not be placed in text books and determine what is ethical or unethical behavior. Moreover, they define physical beauty — which is usually a person with European features, white with blonde hair and blue eyes.

None of these standards were designed or developed with the Black, Asian, Hispanic or Native American cultures in mind. Because the dominate culture assumes authority and takes control, other cultures can no longer take it for granted that their culture will continue to exist, they must struggle just to keep it alive.

Relaxing and taking culture for granted was also the concern of Rabbi Hayim Halevy Donin, author of *To Raise A Jewish Child.* In his book he tells his readers, ". . .Today, raising a child to feel, think, and live the life of a Jew cannot be taken for granted. The environment in which most Jewish children are raised today differs radically from that which nurtured their parents and grandparents even if they were born or grew up in the United States...Many [Jews] judge the worth of their own religious faith on the basis of its compatibility with American principles and values, instead of assessing the worth of American values in terms of their own traditions. . . . The Jew became so integrated into the life of America, so thoroughly had he absorbed the culture of the secular-Christian country, so accepted a citizen had he become in an atmosphere relatively free of anti-Semitism, and so little did he give expression of his own Jewish heritage, that the Jewish problem today is to undo the consequences of their own success in the great effort to become real' Americans... In addition, it cannot be denied that the rapidly changing mores of American society, increasingly conducive to the breakdown of family life, has also affected Jewish life.... Jewish influence on the spiritual history of mankind has always been greatest when Jews were true to themselves and to their own heritage. The Judaization of the Jew, consistent with traditional values, will provide the Jew with the means by which to overcome those problems of the spirit that engulf Western society. It will serve to give our children not only what they need to live with, but what to live for. . ."

Christianity and Cultures

It is clear from Genesis 11 that God produced our different languages. From these languages came our different cultures. Thus, indirectly, God developed and is responsible for our different cultures. "So God scattered them aboard from thence upon the face of all the earth. . . ." (Gen. 11:8)

If God indeed is the Creator and is the giver of culture, then culture must be good because God only gives that which is good for us. Therefore, we must all embrace and be proud of our own culture. Keep in mind that Jesus and Paul, two of the greatest New Testament figures, were people who proudly embraced and practiced the traditions of their culture.

In Matthew 26:17-18 (Living Bible), Jesus prepares for the Jewish Passover meal. "On the first day of the Passover ceremonies, when bread made with yeast was purged from every Jewish home, the disciples came to Jesus and asked, Where shall we plan to eat the Passover? He replied, Go into the city and see Mr. So-and-So, and tell him, Our Master says, my time has come, and I will eat the Passover meal with my disciples at your house."

The Apostle Paul discusses his Jewish heritage in Philippians 3:5 (Living Bible). "For I went through the Jewish initiation ceremony when I was eight days old, having been born into a pure-blooded Jewish home that was a branch of the old original Benjamin family. So I was a real Jew if there ever was one. What's more, I was a member of the Pharisees who demanded the strictest obedience to every Jewish law and custom." The Apostle Paul later denounced those things that would be considered unrighteous elements of his culture, he did not denounce the culture itself. We must all do the same.

Speaking Their Language

Language is important, as is seen in Genesis 11:7 (Living Bible): "Come let us go down and give them different languages, so that they won't understand each other's words."

From this Scripture we learn that it is difficult to live with a culture that we do not understand or find it difficult to communicate with. Communication is a key factor in living peacefully with other cultures. If we can't understand them, how will we know how to treat them or please them?

People are impressed when people of another culture can understand and communicate with a culture other than their own. Being able to communicate with others from another culture was one of the miracles performed on the day of Pentecost in Acts 2:6-8. Witnesses ". . . were confounded because that every man heard them speak in his own language. And they were all amazed and marvelled, saying one to another, Behold are not all these which speak Galileans? And how hear we every man in our own tongue, wherein we were born?"

Some 2,281 years earlier, God scattered people by changing their language. In 34 A.D., in Acts 8:1, he scattered Galileans with the ability to speak these same languages to reach these people.

Respect For Different Cultures

These and other Scriptures prove that God recognizes and respects other cultures. Such was the case in Galatians 2:3, 5 (Living Bible) ". . . they did not even demand that Titus, my companion, should be circumcised, though he was a Gentile. . . For we did not want to confuse you into thinking that salvation can be earned by being circumcised and by obeying Jewish laws."

If our culture does not violate God's law, then our cultures and their traditions should be proudly practiced. As Paul told his Jewish brothers, no one has a right to discount and disrespect another man's cultural traditions and beliefs if those beliefs and practices, however strange, do not violate God's laws.

RACISM: DEATH OF
THE GODS

by Leonard Lovett, Ph.D

Racism: Death of the Gods

Fueled by the twin gods of idolatry and complacency, racism as a spiritual problem is a distortion of the Creator's grand "rainbow" design and a perversion of His intent that there be variety among His creation. Racism is idolatrous self-worship of the worst kind that violates the First Commandment. Racism is pervasive and exists when one group intentionally or unintentionally refuses to share power and resources with another group, thus resulting in oppression. Racism exists when persons are subjugated on the basis of the pigmentation of their skin. Racism is prejudice linked with power. Racism as a faith for the racist is rooted in pride (hubris), often grounded in the twin gods of complacency and idolatry. These twin gods must die if racism is to be annihilated.

In ancient biblical times, (Genesis 9: 1-17), the Jewish beneficiaries of this special relationship--that stressed the equality of all persons before God--viewed their own exclusivity in racial terms. Oppressive nations were denounced throughout the Old Testament. In specific instances, God promised vengeance on all who oppressed the Israelites, His chosen people (Isa. 34: 1-10). God participated in the Exodus deliverance on behalf of His chosen people by "taking off the chariot wheels" of the pursuing Egyptian oppressors. As God's chosen people, the Jews were forbidden to oppress non-Jews (Exodus 22:21, 23:9). Having been "slaves" in Egypt for over four hundred years, the Israelites well understood that oppression of any kind was not an appropriate response to anyone who possessed the gift of life.

The descendants of Cush (which means "black"), children of Ham and grandchildren of Noah, have always posed a problem to others even in ancient biblical times. Ancient Ethiopia included the Egyptian territory south of Aswan Syene, sometimes called Nubia or Cush. Ethiopia literally means "land of the sun burnt faces." It is among the oldest kingdoms in the world having been in existence many centuries prior to the birth of Christ. In the days when Axum (originally the capital), was the center of the kingdom, the name Ethiopia designated Nubia. The Arabs called the land Habasha from which the name Abyssinia is derived. This was the name used in Anglo Saxon countries, while the Latin countries called it Ethiopia.

Ethiopia came to be known for its rivers, the Blue Nile and the White Nile (Isa. 18:10), and its precious topaz gems (Job 28:19). Ethiopians were known for their black skin (Jer. 13:23), their tallness, smooth skin (Isa. 18:2), and their ferocity in battle (Jer. 46:9). Would history have been different were it not for the incident in Numbers 12:1? Miriam and Aaron began to talk against Moses because of his marriage to an Ethiopian woman. Both Miriam and Aaron were rebuked by God for their complaint against Moses. Miriam also suffered a short period of leprosy.

For ancient societies, race, as we have come to understand it in the West, did not exist as an intellectual construct. From a scientific perspective, race has no biological validity; Genetic analysis has demonstrated that some African-Americans share more of their genes with European-Americans than either do with members of their own race. Pure races do not exist as such. Within the human family, where many physical differences are present it is difficult to make clear distinctions on the basis of race. For example, Jews form an ethnic rather than a racial group. It is not uncommon to find many non-European Jews with dark ruddy features, while many Jews from Northern Europe have light eyes and blonde hair. Several mutable factors account for this. Such factors impacting various human communities may include environment, politics, and cultural, social and biological factors that when linked together may serve to make any group distinctive.

Racism as we have come to experience it in modern times was reinforced and sanctioned by nineteenth century slavery proponents who used philosophical, theological and biblical justification to develop arguments in support of slavery. Pro-slavery proponents drew heavily upon Aristotle for philosophical justification of slavery. Aristotle stated, "some men are born slaves and some men are born free." Aristotle's reference was to class slavery, which was prevalent during the Greek Hellenistic period. Such reasoning was transposed to the demonic institution of chattel slavery imposed upon peoples of African descent in the New World.

For biblical justification, pro-slavery proponents drew from the "curse of Ham" theory deduced from Gen. 9: 22-25 to support their view of slavery--and later segregation during the antebellum period in American history. After Noah's overindulgence with wine finds him naked and in a drunken stupor, "Ham the father of Canaan, saw the nakedness of his father . . . And Noah awoke from his wine and knew what his younger son had done unto him. And he said, cursed be Canaan, a servant of servants shall he be unto his brethren."

We must ask candidly, should God be held responsible for a curse pronounced by a drunken man (Noah) upon Canaan, not Ham, one of the ancestors of peoples of African descent? Does Scripture sanction the condemnation of one generation for the sins of another? Not according to Ezekiel 18:20, "The son shall not bear the iniquity of the father: the righteousness of the righteous shall be upon him, and the wickedness of the wicked shall be upon him." Finally would it take seventeen centuries for a curse to take effect? Proponents of these views were wrong then and are wrong now.

After years of marshaling mountains of evidence from ancient documents, archeological finds, and cultural linguistics, several anthropologists now trace humankind's origins to East Africa. Recently, Allan Wilson, a molecular biologist from the University of California, Berkeley, reported what he considered "conclusive genetic evidence that demonstrates that all living persons today are descended from a single African woman." Such conclusions are perceived as drastically erroneous by those who have viewed history through the eyes of Eurocentric lenses.

The first intellectual defense of modern racism was provided during the nineteenth century by a Frenchman, Count Gobineau in his four volume work, "Essay on the Inequality of the Human Races." Gobineau contended that color of skin determines mental and spiritual differences and that mixture of blood produces degeneracy and the fall of civilizations. This intellectual rationalization of racism reinforced cultural racism, thus giving it vitality in our time. Culture is not a fixed condition, but rather a process, the product of interaction between the past and the present. During the African Diaspora, which has roots in the fifteenth century, Por-

287

tuguese and Spanish invaders rationalized that it was God's will to bring heathens into contact with Christianity, even if it meant a life of enforced servitude.

With approval of their governments and the Catholic church, these traders of human cargo maintained that "Christianized" slaves were better off than free heathens. In the name of God, many slaves were transported to the New World. We now know that during the seventeenth century, slaves who were purchased for twenty-five dollars were sold in the Americas for one hundred and fifty dollars. The goal was to provide a cheap source of labor in the New World. African slaves brought to the New World a continuity of perspective that enabled them to survive cultural genocide.

Institutional racism has been defined as the conscious manipulation of institutions to achieve racist objectives. To this end, racist institutions are but extensions of individual racist thought. Cultural racism has generally been defined as the individual and institutional expression of the superiority of one race's cultural heritage over that of another race. For example, when Europeans first encountered Africans during the Colonialists' rape and scramble for Africa, they sought to impose their culture upon Africans.

The Portuguese spoke of African religion as fetish (object of superstition), while the French regarded African religion as jou jou (play toy or thing). The Europeans did not know that on that same great continent, the Yorubas of Nigeria in West Africa, had a high view of God for centuries comparable to and in many respects similar to the Hebrew concept of Yaweh. The French created a policy of assimilation and instituted direct rule that lasted for nearly a hundred years. Today, in parts of French West Africa, there are many Africans who perceive themselves as French and not African. Consequently, European invaders reasoned that African religion is heathen, polytheistic and superstitious, while Western religion is monotheistic and rational. Europeans did not institute oral tradition among Africans as another way of teaching, communicating and preserving the past; they saw it as a sign of basic illiteracy. Cultural racism ignores the achievements of a race and allows the expression of cultural differences either to go unrewarded or erroneously interpreted.

The Church in our time must be indicted for having selectively practiced "birth control" with regards to racism and must be indicted for such a misdeed in the name of God. If racism is to be dealt a death blow in our time, the Church should lead the way in word and deed. There will be no deep structural change apart from radical repentance by followers of the Lamb. It must be a thorough act within the Church for systemic change to take place within the structures of society. We are said to be the "salt of the earth."

The Euro-American Church must be indicted for its silence and denial; for its complicity in the sins of blatant, subtle and unconscious racism.

The African-American Church must be taken to task for not having collectively supported such leaders as Martin Luther King, Jr., Malcolm X, and others who made prophetic indictments of racism in our time. There is no room for "token, self-serving, plantation-mentality, buck dancing, safe Negroes", to even show up as the final battle against the twin gods of racism takes place. The worst betrayal is that of "selling out for a few bucks under the table." For authentic reconciliation to occur, each of us must go inward and purge ourselves of that which offends our Creator, namely self-deification, which in its purest form, is racism. Racism alone claims ultimacy for humankind (Kelsey).

There are several things that can be done to ensure that the twin gods of racism die:

1) Be sensitive and confess personal racial sin.

2) The Church must put its own house in order (I Peter 4:17-18).

3) Consciously decide that all conferences and policy-making entities of the church will reflect diversity.

4) Discrimination must be broken through group action and just laws.

5) Seek to cultivate interracial fellowship at all times.

6) Proclaim in word and demonstrate in deed an inclusive Gospel.

7) Allow love to be the guiding norm in all relationships.

Notes On Sources: For an excellent critical discussion of biblical and theological issues on the Black presence in the Bible see: "Black Biblical Studies" An Anthology of Charles B. Copher, Chicago: Black Light Fellowship, 1993; "Stony the Road We Trod, (ed)" Cain H. Felder, Minn.: Fortress Press, 1991. On Hamitic Theory see Everett Tilson's "Segregation and the Bible," Nashville: Abingdon, 1958. On racism as a spiritual problem see George Kelsey's "Racism and the Christian Understanding of Man," N.Y.: Charles Scribner & Sons, 1965; also Joseph Barndt's "Dismantling Racism," Minn.: Augsburg, 1991. For a critical discussion of racism and prejudice see James M. Jones', "Prejudice and Racism," Mass, London, Calif: Addison Wesley Pub. Co., 1972.

UNDERSTANDING

by Mensa Otabil

Understanding

When I was a little boy, I heard this story about how God created the different races of the world. It is said that at the time of the creation of mankind, God Almighty had a big pond into which He threw His creation.

The first beings to be thrown into the pond were fully submerged in the water of the pond and as such, came out totally washed, cleansed and lily-white.

The second batch did not turn out very white but came out a bit yellowish.

The third batch got in when the water in the pond was quite depleted and muddied so they came out brownish-red and by the time the last batch had their turn they could only touch the water with the soles of their feet and their palms, so they came out very dark on their body with only the soles of their feet and their palms partially cleansed.

Well, you can guess who came out lily-white and who only got their palms and soles cleansed! I don't know how that story gained popularity, but I can remember that amongst us kids, at least in my neighborhood, it was somehow our standard explanation for the differences between the races.

The essence of that myth was to create racial superiority for one group and inferiority for another. It made one group appear as God's first choice and another as beneficiaries of the leftover of humanity. When people distort history, they can easily isolate you in order to dominate you.

The spirit of racism thrives on misinformation and stereotyping. Instead of portraying people in the likeness of God, it seeks to devalue the worth of people who are different from us as not being as good as we are. Just because somebody does not talk the way you talk, dress the way you dress and look the way you look, does not, in any way, imply that they are inferior or superior to you. Different does not mean better.

See, Hear, Understand and Know

Job said in Chapter 13:1 and 2 of his book, "Lo, mine eye hath seen all this, mine ear hath heard and understood it, What ye know, the same do I know also; I am not inferior unto you."

That is an awesome statement! Inferiority is developed when you do not see what someone else sees, hear what he hears, understand what he understands or know what he knows. So then, if any individual or group of people meant to dominate you, they would endeavor to manipulate what you see, hear and understand.

That has been the method used by all oppressive human institutions, be they governments, religious organizations, or corporations. That is why the media represents the most potent force for either the control or the liberation of a people. When someone controls what you see, hear, understand and know, he can make you feel inferior about yourself and develop a sense of self-hatred and alienation.

The world's power structures perpetuate themselves through a meticulous and systematic network, designed to keep their subjects in total ignorance. Even in the church world, until the Great Reformation of the 16th Century, the Word of God remained chained and unavailable to the body of Believers. The entrance of God's Word, into an individual, brings to that one the light of liberation and thereby frees the individual. A free man can never be bound.

In 1832, the U.S. Senator Henry Berry made this often quoted, revealing statement to the Virginia House of delegates, concerning the state of the Negro slaves, he said, "We have as far as possible, closed every avenue by which light may enter the slave's mind. If we could extinguish the capacity to see the light, our work would be complete. They would then be on the level with the beast of the field and we should be safe."

Senator Berry died a long time ago but the structures his generation put into place to further its agenda, are still being used to keep our people from being enlightened. Friend, this statement was not an isolated one but a fair representation of the logic of the powers that be in that era. It still is the logic of this era!

The images we see on the TV screens are constantly influencing our attitudes either for good or for evil. As a black man, I have observed this war being waged, from all fronts, to portray our people in a very negative light.

Several years ago, I watched the movie, "The Wild Geese" which dramatized a mercenary maneuver to liberate an imprisoned ex-president from a fictionalized African State. Being one to admire precise execution of military operations, the movie naturally had my full emotional attention when I was viewing it. From the beginning of the movie, you are made to identify with the mission of the mercenaries.

Your sympathies would be for those European-trained commandos, who were depicted as the heroes in their efforts to outsmart the hordes of African "natives," who were the villains.

Surprisingly, during the time I was viewing the movie, I never stopped to think that the commandos were just paid soldiers of fortune doing the dirty job for a ruthless, multinational investor, whose only interest in the whole operation was his money. Several times during the screening of the movie, I found myself hoping for the foreign intruders to decimate the sons of the soil.

Later on, in reflection, I did a mental playback of events in some of the scenes in the movie and realized how the tools of manipulation had been employed to make me hate my own. I enthusiastically watched the European butcher--the African--and actually felt saddened when one of the "heroes" died just before the commando airplane took off.

To me, these sentiments reflect the brutal effects of self-negation and alienation that has plagued Africans and people of African descent over the years. As liberated as I thought I was, the effect of that movie brought into sharp focus, the subtle and subliminal attempt to condition my mind to accept as normal the supremacy of one race over another.

These same methods are used to reconstruct and change historical facts to smooth over the mistakes of one people against another, as had been done through the cowboy and Indian movies. Somehow, I think, as children, we have innocently imbibed images and concepts which have together made us vulnerable to foreign control and domination.

The average black person will, for almost all his life, read books which were not written by his people. He will watch films that portray another race as the heroes. His children will play with "white" dolls, which then become the standard of beauty, and watch cartoon scenes that are not relevant to his identity. Even our Bible Colleges have little or no materials written by our own people.

What you see, hear, understand and know has been so tightly controlled that when you grow up, you could spend all your life unconsciously trying to be like somebody else. With this condition, why would you not feel inferior about yourself?

The Truth Liberates

To counteract this negative situation, the words of Jesus Christ in John 8:32 prove very valuable. In a sense it reechoes the words of Job. Jesus said:

"And ye shall know the truth, and the truth shall make you free" (John 8:32).

The opposite of Jesus' words are also true; "You shall know the lie and the lie will keep you in bondage."

You cannot effectively battle lies with lies. That simply compounds the bondage. The Truth, experienced and known, is the key to the total liberation of any oppressed people.

Jesus did not say that knowing the Bible will set you free, because a lot of misinformation has been fed into the world through a misrepresentation of the Bible's total revelation.

Just memorizing and quoting Bible verses will not set anyone free. Knowing the Bible does not necessarily mean you know the truth! Jesus also did not say, "You shall know religion and religion shall set you free" because much of what religion does is keep people under bondage. That is why Jesus always had problems with the Pharisees and the religious leaders of His time. He did not bring us a "religion"; He brought us the liberating truth about God and man!

Many of us Christians have been religiously brain washed. So much so that we are bound by what our religious denomination says instead of what the Spirit of Truth is revealing. I think the Muslims are worse off in this regard. They give their converts Arabic names and let them pray in Arabic, facing an Arabic land!

It is amazing that in this modern 20th Century, there are still people who persist in believing that Africa is Tarzan's jungle domain with people living in trees and fighting lions and elephants. That is how the world's misinformation apparatus has portrayed a part of God's people.

African-Americans have been led to believe that their motherland is a jungle and that slavery was a favor done them because it brought them into civilization. Sad to say, many have bought into that lie. If this stereotyped image is portrayed to anyone who does not really know the truth, it creates a negative response in that individual.

On the other hand, some parts of the world are portrayed as the ultimate in human comfort and pleasure until you discover the truth about the rape, murder, and destitution in those societies. In this case, both the deceiver and the deceived become captives in their own little isolated corners. It is only the Truth that will set us free, to be what God wants us to be.

I strongly believe that God is sovereignly changing the times and seasons of the world to bring about a visitation of His power through the Spirit of Truth. His first stop will be the Church, because judgement begins in the House of God.

DEVELOPING CHARACTER

KEEPING YOUR WORD (PROMISES, VOWS, COMMITMENTS)

When a man makes a vow to the Lord or takes an oath to obligate himself by a pledge, he must not break his word but must do everything he said. Numbers 30:2

If you make a vow to the Lord your God, do not be slow to pay it, for the Lord your God will certainly demand it of you and you will be guilty of sin. Deuteronomy 23:21

Whatever your lips utter you must be sure to do, because you made your vow freely to the Lord your God with your own mouth.
Deuteronomy 23:23

Do not say to your neighbor, "Come back later; I'll give it tomorrow"—when you now have it with you. Proverbs 3:28

It is a trap for a man to dedicate something rashly and only later to consider his vows. Proverbs 20:25

It is a snare to a man to utter a vow [of consecration] rashly, and not until afterward inquire [whether he can fulfill it].
Proverbs 20:25 AMP

When you make a vow to God, do not delay in fulfilling it. He has no pleasure in fools; fulfill your vow. It is better not to vow than to make a vow and not fulfill it. Ecclesiastes 5:4-5

HONESTY

He whose walk is blameless and who does what is righteous, who speaks the truth from his heart. Psalms 15:2

These are the things you are to do: Speak the truth to each other, and render true and sound judgment in your courts. Zechariah 8:16

Do not repay anyone evil for evil. Be careful to do what is right in the eyes of everybody. Proverbs 12:17

But the seed on good soil stands for those with a noble and good heart, who hear the word, retain it, and by persevering produce a crop. Luke 8:15

Wherefore, brethren, look ye out among you seven men of honest report, full of the Holy Ghost and wisdom, whom we may appoint over this business. Acts 6:3 KJV

Brothers, choose seven men from among you who are known to be full of the Spirit and wisdom. We will turn this responsibility over to them. Acts 6:3

Your lifestyle may be the only Christ that some people may ever see or read about.

A truthful witness gives honest testimony, but a false witness tells lies. Romans 12:17

Let us walk honestly, as in the day; not in rioting and drunkenness, not in chambering and wantonness, not in strife and envying.
Romans 13:13 KJV

Let us behave decently, as in the daytime, not in orgies and drunkenness, not in sexual immorality and debauchery, not in dissension and jealousy. Romans 13:13

Now we pray to God that you will not do anything wrong. Not that people will see that we have stood the test but that you will do what is right even though we may seem to have failed.
2 Corinthians 13:7

Honesty is doing what is right when no one else is around.

For we are taking pains to do what is right, not only in the eyes of the Lord but also in the eyes of men. 2 Corinthians 8:21

So that your daily life may win the respect of outsiders and so that you will not be dependent on anybody. 1 Thessalonians 4:12

Pray for us. We are sure that we have a clear conscience and desire to live honorably in every way. Hebrews 13:18

Live such good lives among the pagans that, though they accuse you of doing wrong, they may see your good deeds and glorify God on the day he visits us. 1 Peter 2:12

BEING HONEST WITH YOURSELF

Take heed to yourselves, that your heart be not deceived, and ye turn aside, and serve other gods, and worship them.
Deuteronomy 11:16 KJV

This is what the Lord says: Do not deceive yourselves, thinking, The Babylonians will surely leave us.' They will not!
Jeremiah 37:9

Do not deceive yourselves. If any one of you thinks he is wise by the standards of this age, he should become a "fool" so that he may become wise. 1 Corinthians 3:18

If anyone thinks he is something when he is nothing, he deceives himself. Galatians 6:3

Do not merely listen to the word, and so deceive yourselves. Do what it says. James 1:22

If anyone considers himself religious and yet does not keep a tight rein on his tongue, he deceives himself and his religion is worthless. James 1:26

If we claim to have fellowship with him yet walk in the darkness, we lie and do not live by the truth. 1 John 1:6

If we claim to be without sin, we deceive ourselves and the truth is not in us. 1 John 1:8

He who does what is sinful is of the devil, because the devil has been sinning from the beginning. The reason the Son of God appeared was to destroy the devil's work. No one who is born of God will continue to sin, because God's seed remains in him; he cannot go on sinning, because he has been born of God. This is how we know who the children of God are and who the children of the devil are: Anyone who does not do what is right is not a child of God; nor is anyone who does not love his brother. 1 John 3:8-10

Do not be deceived: God cannot be mocked. A man reaps what he sows. Galatians 6:7

ACCEPTING ADVICE AND POSITIVE CRITICISM

Let the wise listen and add to their learning, and let the discerning get guidance. Proverbs 1:5

But whoever listens to me will live in safety and be at ease, without fear of harm. Proverbs 1:33

Listen, my son, accept what I say, and the years of your life will be many. Proverbs 4:10

Listen to my instruction and be wise; do not ignore it.
Proverbs 8:33

He who heeds discipline shows the way to life, but whoever ignores correction leads others astray. Proverbs 10:17

Whoever loves discipline loves knowledge, but he who hates correction is stupid. Proverbs 12:1

He who ignores discipline comes to poverty and shame, but whoever heeds correction is honored. Proverbs 13:18

He who listens to a life-giving rebuke will be at home among the wise. He who ignores discipline despises himself, but whoever heeds correction gains understanding. Proverbs 15:31-32

A rebuke impresses a man of discernment more than a hundred lashes a fool. Proverbs 17:10

Listen to advice and accept instruction, and in the end you will be wise. Proverbs 19:20

Buy the truth and do not sell it; get wisdom, discipline and understanding. Proverbs 23:23

For these commands are a lamp, this teaching is a light, and the corrections of discipline are the way to life. Proverbs 6:23

LEARN TO CONTROL THE WORDS THAT YOU SPEAK

Set a guard over my mouth, O Lord; keep watch over the door of my lips. Psalms 141:3

I said, "I will watch my ways and keep my tongue from sin; I will put a muzzle on my mouth as long as the wicked are in my presence." Psalms 39:1

When words are many, sin is not absent, but he who holds his tongue is wise. Proverbs 10:19

He who guards his lips guards his life, but he who speaks rashly will come to ruin. Proverbs 13:3

Though you probe my heart and examine me at night, though you test me, you will find nothing; I have resolved that my mouth will not sin. Psalms 17:3

A gentle answer turns away wrath, but a harsh word stirs up anger.
Proverbs 15:1

> *The secret of a governable tongue is not self-control but Christ-control. - G. S.*

AVOID SPEAKING EVIL, USELESS AND MEANINGLESS WORDS

As long as I have life within me, the breath of God in my nostrils, my lips will not speak wickedness, and my tongue will utter no deceit. Job 27:3-4

Truthful lips endure forever, but a lying tongue lasts only a moment. Proverbs 12:19

Keep your tongue from evil and your lips from speaking lies.
Psalms 34:13

For, Whoever would love life and see good days must keep his tongue from evil and his lips from deceitful speech. 1 Peter 3:10

That ye put off concerning the former conversation the old man, which is corrupt according to the deceitful lusts.
Ephesians 4:22 KJV

You were taught, with regard to your former way of life, to put off your old self, which is being corrupted by its deceitful desires.
Ephesians 4:22

Get rid of all bitterness, rage and anger, brawling and slander, along with every form of malice. Ephesians 4:31

Nor should there be obscenity, foolish talk or coarse joking, which are out of place, but rather thanksgiving. Ephesians 5:4

Timothy, guard what has been entrusted to your care. Turn away from godless chatter and the opposing ideas of what is falsely called knowledge, which some have professed and in so doing have wandered from the faith. Grace be with you. 1 Timothy 6:20-21

Avoid godless chatter, because those who indulge in it will become more and more ungodly. 2 Timothy 2:16

Brothers, do not slander one another. Anyone who speaks against his brother or judges him speaks against the law and judges it. When you judge the law, you are not keeping it, but sitting in judgment on it. James 4:11

Be not deceived: evil communications corrupt good manners.
1 Corinthians 15:33 KJV

Do not be misled: "Bad company corrupts good character."
1 Corinthians 15:33

EVIL WORDS ARE DESTRUCTIVE

Real spiritual maturity is evident by a controlled tongue. But hypocrisy can be disguised by fluent scripture quotation, spiritual cliches, religious mannerism and emotionalism.

With his mouth the godless destroys his neighbor, but through knowledge the righteous escape. Proverbs 11:9

An evil man is trapped by his sinful talk, but a righteous man escapes trouble. Proverbs 12:13

Reckless words pierce like a sword, but the tongue of the wise brings healing. Proverbs 12:18

DON'T TALK TOO MUCH

A man of knowledge uses words with restraint, and a man of understanding is even-tempered. Even a fool is thought wise if he keeps silent, and discerning if he holds his tongue.
Proverbs 17:27-28

He who guards his mouth and his tongue keeps himself from calamity. Proverbs 21:23

Simply let your 'Yes' be 'Yes,' and your 'No,' 'No'; anything beyond this comes from the evil one. Matthew 5:37

The best time for you to hold your tongue is the time you feel you must say something or bust. - Josh Billings

A FOOL TALKS TOO MUCH

A fool gives full vent to his anger, but a wise man keeps himself under control. Proverbs 29:11

The discerning heart seeks knowledge, but the mouth of a fool feeds on folly. Proverbs 15:14

A fool's lips bring him strife, and his mouth invites a beating. A fool's mouth is his undoing, and his lips are a snare to his soul.
Proverbs 18:6-7

Better to remain silent and be thought a fool than to speak and to remove all doubt. - Abraham Lincoln

Words from a wise man's mouth are gracious, but a fool is consumed by his own lips. At the beginning his words are folly; at the end they are wicked madness—and the fool multiplies words. No one knows what is coming—who can tell him what will happen after him? Ecclesiastes 10:12-14

YOU WILL BE JUDGED BY THE WORDS THAT YOU SPEAK

But I tell you that men will have to give account on the day of judgment for every careless word they have spoken. For by your words you will be acquitted, and by your words you will be condemned. Matthew 12:36-37

In times like the present, men should utter nothing for which the would not willingly be responsible through time and eternity. - Abraham Lincoln

THINK BEFORE YOU SPEAK

The heart of the righteous weighs its answers, but the mouth of the wicked gushes evil. Proverbs 15:28

A wise man's heart guides his mouth, and his lips promote instruction. Proverbs 16:23

He who answers before listening—that is his folly and his shame.
Proverbs 18:13

Do you see a man who speaks in haste? There is more hope for a fool than for him. Proverbs 29:20

Do not be quick with your mouth, do not be hasty in your heart to utter anything before God. God is in heaven and you are on earth, so let your words be few. Ecclesiastes 5:2

Besser stumm als dumm—Better silent than stupid.
- German Proverb

SPEAK POSITIVE WORDS

Listen, for I have worthy things to say; I open my lips to speak what is right. My mouth speaks what is true, for my lips detest wickedness. All the words of my mouth are just; none of them is crooked or perverse. Proverbs 8:6-8

The mouth of the righteous is a fountain of life, but violence overwhelms the mouth of the wicked. Proverbs 10:11

When words are many, sin is not absent, but he who holds his tongue is wise. The tongue of the righteous is choice silver, but the heart of the wicked is of little value. The lips of the righteous nourish many, but fools die for lack of judgment. Proverbs 10:19-21

The mouth of the righteous brings forth wisdom, but a perverse tongue will be cut out. Proverbs 10:31

An anxious heart weighs a man down, but a kind word cheers him up. Proverbs 12:25

The tongue that brings healing is a tree of life, but a deceitful tongue crushes the spirit. Proverbs 15:4

Pleasant words are a honeycomb, sweet to the soul and healing to the bones. Proverbs 16:24

The angels of heaven and the demons of hell bring to past whatever you speak out of your mouth. The angels respond to the Word of God and demons respond to negative, vain, and destructive words.

SPEAKING WORDS OF WISDOM AND INTEGRITY

The quiet words of the wise are more to be heeded than the shouts of a ruler of fools. Ecclesiastes 9:17

Words from a wise man's mouth are gracious, but a fool is consumed by his own lips. Ecclesiastes 10:12

For I will give you words and wisdom that none of your adversaries will be able to resist or contradict. Luke 21:15

And soundness of speech that cannot be condemned, so that those who oppose you may be ashamed because they have nothing bad to say about us. Titus 2:8

Who is a wise man and endued with knowledge among you? let him show out of a good conversation his works with meekness of wisdom. James 3:13 KJV

Blessed is the man who, having nothing to say, abstains from giving wordy evidence of the fact. - George Eliot

Who is wise and understanding among you? Let him show it by his good life, by deeds done in the humility that comes from wisdom.
James 3:13

SPEAKING THE RIGHT WORDS AT THE APPROPRIATE TIME

The lips of the righteous know what is fitting, but the mouth of the wicked only what is perverse. Proverbs 10:32

A man finds joy in giving an apt reply—and how good is a timely word! Proverbs 15:23

My son, if your heart is wise, then my heart will be glad; my inmost being will rejoice when your lips speak what is right.
Proverbs 23:15-16

A word aptly spoken is like apples of gold in settings of silver.
Proverbs 25:11

There is a time for everything, and a season for every activity under heaven. Ecclesiastes 3:1

A time to tear and a time to mend, a time to be silent and a time to speak. Ecclesiastes 3:7

The Sovereign Lord has given me an instructed tongue, to know the word that sustains the weary. He wakens me morning by morning, wakens my ear to listen like one being taught. Isaiah 50:4

Let your conversation be always full of grace, seasoned with salt, so that you may know how to answer everyone. Colossians 4:6

SPEAKING KNOWLEDGEABLE WORDS

The tongue of the wise commends knowledge, but the mouth of the fool gushes folly. Proverbs 15:2

The lips of the wise spread knowledge; not so the hearts of fools.
Proverbs 15:7

Gold there is, and rubies in abundance, but lips that speak knowledge are a rare jewel. Proverbs 20:15

Would a wise man answer with empty notions or fill his belly with the hot east wind? Job 15:2

My words come from an upright heart; my lips sincerely speak what I know. Job 33:3

Job speaks without knowledge; his words lack insight. Job 34:35

So Job opens his mouth with empty talk; without knowledge he multiplies words. Job 35:16

Be assured that my words are not false; one perfect in knowledge is with you. Job 36:4

That you may maintain discretion and your lips may preserve knowledge. Proverbs 5:2

For the lips of a priest ought to preserve knowledge, and from his mouth men should seek instruction—because he is the messenger of the Lord Almighty. Malachi 2:7

Who is a wise man and endued with knowledge among you? let him show out of a good conversation his works with meekness of wisdom. James 3:13 KJV

DEVELOPING A GOOD ATTITUDE

HUMILITY

My heart is not proud, O Lord, my eyes are not haughty; I do not concern myself with great matters or things too wonderful for me. But I have stilled and quieted my soul; like a weaned child with its mother, like a weaned child is my soul within me. Psalms 131:1-2

Though the Lord is on high, he looks upon the lowly, but the proud he knows from afar. Psalms 138:6

> *True humility is not an abject, groveling, self-despising spirit; it is but a right estimate of ourselves as God sees us. - Tryon Edwards*

The Lord sustains the humble but casts the wicked to the ground.
Psalms 147:6

For the Lord takes delight in his people; he crowns the humble with salvation. Psalms 149:4

The fear of the Lord teaches a man wisdom, and humility comes before honor. Proverbs 15:33

Has not my hand made all these things, and so they came into being? declares the Lord. This is the one I esteem: he who is humble and contrite in spirit, and trembles at my word. Isaiah 66:2

> *True and pure humility is believing and obeying God's Word.*

He has showed you, O man, what is good. And what does the Lord require of you? To act justly and to love mercy and to walk humbly with your God. Micah 6:8

Blessed are the poor in spirit, for theirs is the kingdom of heaven.
Matthew 5:3

Not so with you. Instead, whoever wants to become great among you must be your servant, and whoever wants to be first must be your slave Matthew 20:26-27

For whoever exalts himself will be humbled, and whoever humbles himself will be exalted. Matthew 23:12

He has brought down rulers from their thrones but has lifted up the humble. Luke 1:52

But when you are invited, take the lowest place, so that when your host comes, he will say to you, 'Friend, move up to a better place.' Then you will be honored in the presence of all your fellow guests.
Luke 14:10

But the tax collector stood at a distance. He would not even look up to heaven, but beat his breast and said, 'God, have mercy on me, a sinner.' I tell you that this man, rather than the other, went home justified before God. For everyone who exalts himself will be humbled, and he who humbles himself will be exalted.
Luke 18:13-14

Also a dispute arose among them as to which of them was considered to be greatest. Jesus said to them, "The kings of the Gentiles lord it over them; and those who exercise authority over them call themselves Benefactors. But you are not to be like that. Instead, the greatest among you should be like the youngest, and the one who rules like the one who serves. For who is greater, the one who is at the table or the one who serves? Is it not the one who is at the table? But I am among you as one who serves. Luke 22:24-27

The man who is to take a high place before his fellows must take a low place before his God. - Anonymous

He must become greater; I must become less. John 3:30

Live in harmony with one another. Do not be proud, but be willing to associate with people of low position. Do not be conceited.
Romans 12:16

But by the grace of God I am what I am, and his grace to me was not without effect. No, I worked harder than all of them—yet not I, but the grace of God that was with me. 1 Corinthians 15:10

Be completely humble and gentle; be patient, bearing with one another in love. Ephesians 4:2

The brother in humble circumstances ought to take pride in his high position. But the one who is rich should take pride in his low position, because he will pass away like a wild flower.
James 1:9-10

Humble yourselves before the Lord, and he will lift you up.
James 4:10

Young men, in the same way be submissive to those who are older. All of you, clothe yourselves with humility toward one another, because, God opposes the proud but gives grace to the humble. Humble yourselves, therefore, under God's mighty hand, that he may lift you up in due time. 1 Peter 5:5-6

When confidence comes, strive for humility:
- Robert G. Lee

MEEKNESS

Now Moses was a very humble man, more humble than anyone else on the face of the earth. Numbers 12:3

The poor will eat and be satisfied; they who seek the Lord will praise him—may your hearts live forever! Psalms 22:26

He guides the humble in what is right and teaches them his way.
Psalms 25:9

But the meek will inherit the land and enjoy great peace.
Psalms 37:11

Meekness is not weakness; it's controlled strength.

The Lord sustains the humble but casts the wicked to the ground.
Psalms 147:6

For the Lord takes delight in his people; he crowns the humble with salvation. Psalms 149:4

Once more the humble will rejoice in the Lord; the needy will rejoice in the Holy One of Israel. Isaiah 29:19

313

Seek the Lord, all you humble of the land, you who do what he commands. Seek righteousness, seek humility; perhaps you will be sheltered on the day of the Lord's anger. Zephaniah 2:3

Blessed are the meek, for they will inherit the earth. Matthew 5:5

By the meekness and gentleness of Christ, I appeal to you—I, Paul, who am "timid" when face to face with you, but "bold" when away!
2 Corinthians 10:1

But the fruit of the Spirit is love, joy, peace, patience, kindness, goodness, faithfulness, gentleness and self-control. Against such things there is no law. Galatians 5:22-23

Brothers, if someone is caught in a sin, you who are spiritual should restore him gently. But watch yourself, or you also may be tempted.
Galatians 6:1

Be completely humble and gentle; be patient, bearing with one another in love. Ephesians 4:2

Therefore, as God's chosen people, holy and dearly loved, clothe yourselves with compassion, kindness, humility, gentleness and patience. Colossians 3:12

But you, man of God, flee from all this, and pursue righteousness, godliness, faith, love, endurance and gentleness. 1 Timothy 6:11

To slander no one, to be peaceable and considerate, and to show true humility toward all men. Titus 3:2

Instead, it should be that of your inner self, the unfading beauty of a gentle and quiet spirit, which is of great worth in God's sight.
1 Peter 3:4

But in your hearts set apart Christ as Lord. Always be prepared to give an answer to everyone who asks you to give the reason for the hope that you have. But do this with gentleness and respect.
1 Peter 3:15

Humility is the foundation of logical thinking and confidence is the foundation for great exploits.

OVERCOMING PRIDE

Hear and pay attention, do not be arrogant, for the Lord has spoken. Jeremiah 13:15

Look at every proud man and humble him, crush the wicked where they stand. Job 40:12

You rebuke the arrogant, who are cursed and who stray from your commands. Psalms 119:21

Haughty eyes and a proud heart, the lamp of the wicked, are sin!
Proverbs 21:4

Do you see a man wise in his own eyes? There is more hope for a fool than for him. Proverbs 26:12

> *Pride hardens the spirit and mind and leads it's victim to insanity. Satan, King Herod, and Nebuchadnezzar are all prime examples.*

Woe to those who are wise in their own eyes and clever in their own sight. Isaiah 5:21

He called a little child and had him stand among them. And he said: I tell you the truth, unless you change and become like little children, you will never enter the kingdom of heaven. Therefore, whoever humbles himself like this child is the greatest in the kingdom of heaven. Matthew 18:2-4

The greatest among you will be your servant. For whoever exalts himself will be humbled, and whoever humbles himself will be exalted. Matthew 23:11-12

Sitting down, Jesus called the Twelve and said, "If anyone wants to be first, he must be the very last, and the servant of all."
Mark 9:35

For by the grace given me I say to every one of you: Do not think of yourself more highly than you ought, but rather think of yourself with sober judgment, in accordance with the measure of faith God has given you. Romans 12:3

Live in harmony with one another. Do not be proud, but be willing to associate with people of low position. Do not be conceited.
Romans 12:16

Therefore, as it is written: "Let him who boasts boast in the Lord."
1 Corinthians 1:31

Do not deceive yourselves. If any one of you thinks he is wise by the standards of this age, he should become a "fool" so that he may become wise. 1 Corinthians 3:18

Love is patient, love is kind. It does not envy, it does not boast, it is not proud. 1 Corinthians 13:4

> *God knows best; he hasn't arranged your anatomy so as to make it easy for you to pat yourself on the back.*
> *- Anonymous*

Not that we are competent in ourselves to claim anything for ourselves, but our competence comes from God. 2 Corinthians 3:5

But we have this treasure in jars of clay to show that this all-surpassing power is from God and not from us. 2 Corinthians 4:7

If I must boast, I will boast of the things that show my weakness.
2 Corinthians 11:30

May I never boast except in the cross of our Lord Jesus Christ, through which the world has been crucified to me, and I to the world. Galatians 6:14

> *Don't talk about yourself; it will be done when you leave.*
> *- Wilson Mizner*

Do nothing out of selfish ambition or vain conceit, but in humility consider others better than yourselves. Philippians 2:3

GOD HATES PRIDE

Though the Lord is on high, he looks upon the lowly, but the proud he knows from afar. Psalms 138:6

To fear the Lord is to hate evil; I hate pride and arrogance, evil behavior and perverse speech. Proverbs 8:13

He said to them, You are the ones who justify yourselves in the eyes of men, but God knows your hearts. What is highly valued among men is detestable in God's sight. Luke 16:15

But he gives us more grace. That is why Scripture says: "God opposes the proud but gives grace to the humble." Submit yourselves, then, to God. Resist the devil, and he will flee from you.
James 4:6-7

Young men, in the same way be submissive to those who are older. All of you, clothe yourselves with humility toward one another, because, "God opposes the proud but gives grace to the humble."
1 Peter 5:5

God sends no one away empty except those who are full of themselves. - D. L. Moody

PRIDE WILL CAUSE YOU TO FAIL

Pride goes before destruction, a haughty spirit before a fall. Better to be lowly in spirit and among the oppressed than to share plunder with the proud. Proverbs 16:18-19

Before his downfall a man's heart is proud, but humility comes before honor. Proverbs 18:12

A man's pride brings him low, but a man of lowly spirit gains honor.
Proverbs 29:23

So, if you think you are standing firm, be careful that you don't fall! 1 Corinthians 10:12

BEING PRIDEFUL STARTS TROUBLE

Pride only breeds quarrels, but wisdom is found in those who take advice. Proverbs 13:10

A greedy man stirs up dissension, but he who trusts in the Lord will prosper. He who trusts in himself is a fool, but he who walks in wisdom is kept safe. Proverbs 28:25-26

CONTROLLING ANGER

A patient man has great understanding, but a quick-tempered man displays folly. Proverbs 14:29

A hot-tempered man stirs up dissension, but a patient man calms a quarrel. Proverbs 15:18

Better a patient man than a warrior, a man who controls his temper than one who takes a city. Proverbs 16:32

Even a fool is thought wise if he keeps silent, and discerning if he holds his tongue. Proverbs 17:28

A man's wisdom gives him patience; it is to his glory to overlook an offense. Proverbs 19:11

Mockers stir up a city, but wise men turn away anger.
Proverbs 29:8

A fool gives full vent to his anger, but a wise man keeps himself under control. Proverbs 29:11

Do not be quickly provoked in your spirit, for anger resides in the lap of fools. Ecclesiastes 7:9

Do not take revenge, my friends, but leave room for God's wrath, for it is written: "It is mine to avenge; I will repay," says the Lord. On the contrary: "If your enemy is hungry, feed him; if he is thirsty, give him something to drink. In doing this, you will heap burning coals on his head." Do not be overcome by evil, but overcome evil with good. Romans 12:19-21

Get rid of all bitterness, rage and anger, brawling and slander, along with every form of malice. Be kind and compassionate to one another, forgiving each other, just as in Christ God forgave you.
Ephesians 4:31-32

It is better to avoid strife than to appear justified.

But now you must rid yourselves of all such things as these: anger, rage, malice, slander, and filthy language from your lips.
Colossians 3:8

My dear brothers, take note of this: Everyone should be quick to listen, slow to speak and slow to become angry, for man's anger does not bring about the righteous life that God desires.

James 1:19-20

He who forgives ends the quarrel. - African Proverb

OVERCOMING AN ENVIOUS HEART

DEFINITION: - Is the feeling of displeasure produced by witnessing or hearing of the advantage or prosperity of others.

Do not envy a violent man or choose any of his ways.

Proverbs 3:31

Do not let your heart envy sinners, but always be zealous for the fear of the Lord. Proverbs 23:17

Do not envy wicked men, do not desire their company.

Proverbs 24:1

Do not fret because of evil men or be envious of the wicked.

Proverbs 24:19

Let us behave decently, as in the daytime, not in orgies and drunkenness, not in sexual immorality and debauchery, not in dissension and jealousy. Romans 13:13

Let us not become conceited, provoking and envying each other.

Galatians 5:26

For where you have envy and selfish ambition, there you find disorder and every evil practice. James 3:16

Therefore, rid yourselves of all malice and all deceit, hypocrisy, envy, and slander of every kind. 1 Peter 2:1

It is wiser to join success rather than to fight success. Most successful people are willing to share with you how God prospered them and how God will also prosper you.

A heart at peace gives life to the body, but envy rots the bones.

Proverbs 14:30

319

Anger is cruel and fury overwhelming, but who can stand before jealousy? Proverbs 27:4

OVERCOMING A JUDGMENTAL ATTITUDE

JUDGING OTHERS

"Do not judge, or you too will be judged. For in the same way you judge others, you will be judged, and with the measure you use, it will be measured to you. "Why do you look at the speck of sawdust in your brother's eye and pay no attention to the plank in your own eye? How can you say to your brother, 'Let me take the speck out of your eye,' when all the time there is a plank in your own eye? You hypocrite, first take the plank out of your own eye, and then you will see clearly to remove the speck from your brother's eye. Matthew 7:1-5

Do not judge, and you will not be judged. Do not condemn, and you will not be condemned. Forgive, and you will be forgiven.
Luke 6:37

So when you, a mere man, pass judgment on them and yet do the same things, do you think you will escape God's judgment?
Romans 2:3

How rarely we weigh our neighbor in the same balance in which we weigh ourselves! - Thomas A Kempis

You, then, why do you judge your brother? Or why do you look down on your brother? For we will all stand before God's judgment seat. Romans 14:10

JUDGING OTHERS BY MONEY, RACE, OR BACKGROUND

Do not pervert justice; do not show partiality to the poor or favoritism to the great, but judge your neighbor fairly. Leviticus 19:15

Wherefore now let the fear of the Lord be upon you; take heed and do it: for there is no iniquity with the Lord our God, nor respect of persons, nor taking of gifts. 2 Chronicles 19:7 KJV

Now let the fear of the Lord be upon you. Judge carefully, for with the Lord our God there is no injustice or partiality or bribery.
2 Chronicles 19:7

Who shows no partiality to princes and does not favor the rich over the poor, for they are all the work of his hands? Job 34:19

To show partiality is not good—yet a man will do wrong for a piece of bread. Proverbs 28:21

These also are sayings of the wise: To show partiality in judging is not good. Proverbs 24:23

I have seen something else under the sun: The race is not to the swift or the battle to the strong, nor does food come to the wise or wealth to the brilliant or favor to the learned; but time and chance happen to them all. Ecclesiastes 9:11

No longer will a man teach his neighbor, or a man his brother, saying, 'Know the Lord,' because they will all know me, from the least of them to the greatest, declares the Lord. "For I will forgive their wickedness and will remember their sins no more."
Jeremiah 31:34

Do not judge, and you will not be judged. Do not condemn, and you will not be condemned. Forgive, and you will be forgiven.
Luke 6:37

People will come from east and west and north and south, and will take their places at the feast in the kingdom of God. Indeed there are those who are last who will be first, and first who will be last.
Luke 13:29-30

Stop judging by mere appearances, and make a right judgment.
John 7:24

This righteousness from God comes through faith in Jesus Christ to all who believe. There is no difference. Romans 3:22

Therefore, if you have disputes about such matters, appoint as judges even men of little account in the church! 1 Corinthians 6:4

But to each one of us grace has been given as Christ apportioned it.
Ephesians 4:7

My brothers, as believers in our glorious Lord Jesus Christ, don't show favoritism. Suppose a man comes into your meeting wearing a gold ring and fine clothes, and a poor man in shabby clothes also comes in. If you show special attention to the man wearing fine clothes and say, "Here's a good seat for you," but say to the poor man, "You stand there" or "Sit on the floor by my feet," have you not discriminated among yourselves and become judges with evil thoughts? Listen, my dear brothers: Has not God chosen those who are poor in the eyes of the world to be rich in faith and to inherit the kingdom he promised those who love him? But you have insulted the poor. Is it not the rich who are exploiting you? Are they not the ones who are dragging you into court? Are they not the ones who are slandering the noble name of him to whom you belong? If you really keep the royal law found in Scripture, "Love your neighbor as yourself," you are doing right. But if you show favoritism, you sin and are convicted by the law as lawbreakers. James 2:1-9

OVERCOMING GOSSIPING AND SLANDER

GOSSIP

Keep your tongue from evil and your lips from speaking lies.
Psalms 34:13

Your tongue plots destruction; it is like a sharpened razor, you who practice deceit. Psalms 52:2

A gossip betrays a confidence, but a trustworthy man keeps a secret. Proverbs 11:13

A perverse man stirs up dissension, and a gossip separates close friends. Proverbs 16:28

He who covers over an offense promotes love, but whoever repeats the matter separates close friends. Proverbs 17:9

Whoever gossips to you will gossip of you.
- Spanish proverb

The words of a gossip are like choice morsels; they go down to a man's inmost parts. Proverbs 26:22

The words of a whisperer or slanderer are as dainty morsels or words of sport [to some, but to others are as deadly wound], and they go down into the innermost parts of the body [or of the victim's nature]. Proverbs 26:22 AMP

A gossip betrays a confidence; so avoid a man who talks too much.
Proverbs 20:19

As a north wind brings rain, so a sly tongue brings angry looks.
Proverbs 25:23

Without wood a fire goes out; without gossip a quarrel dies down. As charcoal to embers and as wood to fire, so is a quarrelsome man for kindling strife. The words of a gossip are like choice morsels; they go down to a man's inmost parts. Proverbs 26:20-22

But I tell you that men will have to give account on the day of judgment for every careless word they have spoken. Matthew 12:36

Besides, they get into the habit of being idle and going about from house to house. And not only do they become idlers, but also gossips and busybodies, saying things they ought not to.
1 Timothy 5:13

You will not become a saint through other people's sins.
- Anton Chekhov

Make it your ambition to lead a quiet life, to mind your own business and to work with your hands, just as we told you.
1 Thessalonians 4:11

SLANDER

Do not go about spreading slander among your people. Do not do anything that endangers your neighbor's life. I am the Lord.
Leviticus 19:16

You will be protected from the lash of the tongue, and need not fear when destruction comes. Job 5:21

And has no slander on his tongue, who does his neighbor no wrong and casts no slur on his fellow man. Psalms 15:3

In the shelter of your presence you hide them from the intrigues of men; in your dwelling you keep them safe from accusing tongues. Psalms 31:20

He who conceals his hatred has lying lips, and whoever spreads slander is a fool. Proverbs 10:18

A perverse man stirs up dissension, and a gossip separates close friends. Proverbs 16:28

Hear me, you who know what is right, you people who have my law in your hearts: Do not fear the reproach of men or be terrified by their insults. Isaiah 51:7

People who are criticized are usually doing something so great and significant that their criticizers wish they had the commitment and discipline to do themselves.

Blessed are you when people insult you, persecute you and falsely say all kinds of evil against you because of me. Rejoice and be glad, because great is your reward in heaven, for in the same way they persecuted the prophets who were before you. Matthew 5:11-12

If you keep on biting and devouring each other, watch out or you will be destroyed by each other. Galatians 5:15

If you are insulted because of the name of Christ, you are blessed, for the Spirit of glory and of God rests on you. 1 Peter 4:14

BUILDING YOUR SELF-CONFIDENCE THROUGH CHRIST

You will be blessed when you come in and blessed when you go out. Deuteronomy 28:6

The Lord will make you the head, not the tail. If you pay attention to the commands of the Lord your God that I give you this day and carefully follow them, you will always be at the top, never at the bottom. Deuteronomy 28:13

Jesus looked at them and said, "With man this is impossible, but with God all things are possible." Matthew 19:26

For nothing is impossible with God. Luke 1:37

And those he predestined, he also called; those he called, he also justified; those he justified, he also glorified. Romans 8:30

But thanks be to God, who always leads us in triumphal procession in Christ and through us spreads everywhere the fragrance of the knowledge of him. 2 Corinthians 2:14

I can do everything through him who gives me strength.
                                                    Philippians 4:13

You also, like living stones, are being built into a spiritual house to be a holy priesthood, offering spiritual sacrifices acceptable to God through Jesus Christ. 1 Peter 2:5

You, dear children, are from God and have overcome them, because the one who is in you is greater than the one who is in the world. 1 John 4:4

BUILDING YOUR SELF-IMAGE THROUGH GOD'S WORD

Then God said, "Let us make man in our image, in our likeness, and let them rule over the fish of the sea and the birds of the air, over the livestock, over all the earth, and over all the creatures that move along the ground." So God created man in his own image, in the image of God he created him; male and female he created them.
                                                    Genesis 1:26-27

But Moses and Aaron fell facedown and cried out, "O God, God of the spirits of all mankind, will you be angry with the entire assembly when only one man sins?" Numbers 16:22

May the Lord, the God of the spirits of all mankind, appoint a man over this community. Numbers 27:16

From the lips of children and infants you have ordained praise because of your enemies, to silence the foe and the avenger. When I consider your heavens, the work of your fingers, the moon and the stars, which you have set in place, what is man that you are mindful of him, the son of man that you care for him? You made him a little lower than the heavenly beings and crowned him with glory and honor. You made him ruler over the works of your hands; you put everything under his feet. Psalms 8:2-6

I said, 'You are "gods"; you are all sons of the Most High.
Psalms 82:6

This is the word of the Lord concerning Israel. The Lord, who stretches out the heavens, who lays the foundation of the earth, and who forms the spirit of man within him, declares. Zechariah 12:1

Therefore, if anyone is in Christ, he is a new creation; the old has gone, the new has come! 2 Corinthians 5:17

We are therefore Christ's ambassadors, as though God were making his appeal through us. We implore you on Christ's behalf: Be reconciled to God. 2 Corinthians 5:20

I pray also that the eyes of your heart may be enlightened in order that you may know the hope to which he has called you, the riches of his glorious inheritance in the saints. Ephesians 1:18

Made us alive with Christ even when we were dead in transgressions—it is by grace you have been saved. And God raised us up with Christ and seated us with him in the heavenly realms in Christ Jesus. Ephesians 2:5-6

For we are God's workmanship, created in Christ Jesus to do good works, which God prepared in advance for us to do.
Ephesians 2:10

Consequently, you are no longer foreigners and aliens, but fellow citizens with God's people and members of God's household.
Ephesians 2:19

Do not lie to each other, since you have taken off your old self with its practices and have put on the new self, which is being renewed in knowledge in the image of its Creator. Colossians 3:9-10

Moreover, we have all had human fathers who disciplined us and we respected them for it. How much more should we submit to the Father of our spirits and live! Hebrews 12:9

But the man who looks intently into the perfect law that gives freedom, and continues to do this, not forgetting what he has heard, but doing it—he will be blessed in what he does. James 1:25

In this way, love is made complete among us so that we will have confidence on the day of judgment, because in this world we are like him. 1 John 4:17

THE KEYS OF SUCCESS

WISDOM

The fear of the Lord is the beginning of wisdom; all who follow his precepts have good understanding. To him belongs eternal praise.
Psalms 111:10

Wisdom calls aloud in the street, she raises her voice in the public squares. Proverbs 1:20

HOW TO OBTAIN WISDOM

If any of you lacks wisdom, he should ask God, who gives generously to all without finding fault, and it will be given to him.
James 1:5

If you lack knowledge, go to school. If you lack wisdom, get on your knees! Knowledge is not wisdom. Wisdom is proper use of knowledge. - Vance Havner

WISDOM COMES FROM GOD

For the Lord gives wisdom, and from his mouth come knowledge and understanding. He holds victory in store for the upright, he is a shield to those whose walk is blameless. Proverbs 2:6-7

To the man who pleases him, God gives wisdom, knowledge and happiness, but to the sinner he gives the task of gathering and storing up wealth to hand it over to the one who pleases God. This too is meaningless, a chasing after the wind. Ecclesiastes 2:26

That he lavished on us with all wisdom and understanding.
Ephesians 1:8

I keep asking that the God of our Lord Jesus Christ, the glorious Father, may give you the Spirit of wisdom and revelation, so that you may know him better. Ephesians 1:17

His intent was that now, through the church, the manifold wisdom of God should be made known to the rulers and authorities in the heavenly realms. Ephesians 3:10

In whom are hidden all the treasures of wisdom and knowledge.
Colossians 2:3

But to those whom God has called, both Jews and Greeks, Christ the power of God and the wisdom of God. 1 Corinthians 1:24

It is because of him that you are in Christ Jesus, who has become for us wisdom from God—that is, our righteousness, holiness and redemption. 1 Corinthians 1:30

TRUE WISDOM

But the wisdom that comes from heaven is first of all pure; then peace-loving, considerate, submissive, full of mercy and good fruit, impartial and sincere. James 3:17

PURSUE WISDOM

Turning your ear to wisdom and applying your heart to understanding. Proverbs 2:2

Blessed is the man who finds wisdom, the man who gains understanding. Proverbs 3:13

Get wisdom, get understanding; do not forget my words or swerve from them. Proverbs 4:5

Wisdom is supreme; therefore get wisdom. Though it cost all you have, get understanding. Proverbs 4:7

Know also that wisdom is sweet to your soul; if you find it, there is a future hope for you, and your hope will not be cut off.
Proverbs 24:14

WISDOM ENTERS THE HEART

Who endowed the heart with wisdom or gave understanding to the mind? Job 38:36

Surely you desire truth in the inner parts; you teach me wisdom in the inmost place. Psalms 51:6

For wisdom will enter your heart, and knowledge will be pleasant to your soul. Proverbs 2:10

Wisdom reposes in the heart of the discerning and even among fools she lets herself be known. Proverbs 14:33

So I turned my mind to understand, to investigate and to search out wisdom and the scheme of things and to understand the stupidity of wickedness and the madness of folly. Ecclesiastes 7:25

Let the word of Christ dwell in you richly as you teach and admonish one another with all wisdom, and as you sing psalms, hymns and spiritual songs with gratitude in your hearts to God.
Colossians 3:16

WISDOM IS VALUABLE

For wisdom is more precious than rubies, and nothing you desire can compare with her. I, wisdom, dwell together with prudence; I possess knowledge and discretion. Proverbs 8:11-12

WISDOM IS FOUND IN COUNSEL

Counsel and sound judgment are mine; I have understanding and power. Proverbs 8:14

Pride only breeds quarrels, but wisdom is found in those who take advice. Proverbs 13:10

THE BENEFITS OF WISDOM

Is not wisdom found among the aged? Does not long life bring understanding? To God belong wisdom and power; counsel and understanding are his. Job 12:12-13

Your commands make me wiser than my enemies, for they are ever with me. Psalms 119:98

Instruct a wise man and he will be wiser still; teach a righteous man and he will add to his learning. Proverbs 9:9

Wisdom, like an inheritance, is a good thing and benefits those who see the sun. Wisdom is a shelter as money is a shelter, but the advantage of knowledge is this: that wisdom preserves the life of its possessor. Ecclesiastes 7:11-12

Wisdom makes one wise man more powerful than ten rulers in a city. Ecclesiastes 7:19

So I said, "Wisdom is better than strength." But the poor man's wisdom is despised, and his words are no longer heeded.
Ecclesiastes 9:16

Blessed is the man who finds wisdom, the man who gains understanding. Proverbs 3:13

If the ax is dull and its edge unsharpened, more strength is needed but skill will bring success. Ecclesiastes 10:10

Oh, the depth of the riches of the wisdom and knowledge of God! How unsearchable his judgments, and his paths beyond tracing out!
Romans 11:33

And how from infancy you have known the holy Scriptures, which are able to make you wise for salvation through faith in Christ Jesus. 2 Timothy 3:15

The fear of the Lord is the beginning of wisdom, and knowledge of the Holy One is understanding. Proverbs 9:10

WISDOM IN ACTION

Who is wise and understanding among you? Let him show it by his good life, by deeds done in the humility that comes from wisdom.
James 3:13

Be wise in the way you act toward outsiders; make the most of every opportunity. Colossians 4:5

The wisdom of the prudent is to give thought to their ways, but the folly of fools is deception. Proverbs 14:8

KNOWLEDGE

GOD IS THE SOURCE OF KNOWLEDGE

The eyes of the Lord keep watch over knowledge, but he frustrates the words of the unfaithful. Proverbs 22:12

To the man who pleases him, God gives wisdom, knowledge and happiness, but to the sinner he gives the task of gathering and storing up wealth to hand it over to the one who pleases God. This too is meaningless, a chasing after the wind. Ecclesiastes 2:26

For in him you have been enriched in every way—in all your speaking and in all your knowledge. 1 Corinthians 1:5

To one there is given through the Spirit the message of wisdom, to another the message of knowledge by means of the same Spirit.
1 Corinthians 12:8

For God, who said, "Let light shine out of darkness," made his light shine in our hearts to give us the light of the knowledge of the glory of God in the face of Christ. 2 Corinthians 4:6

In whom are hidden all the treasures of wisdom and knowledge.
Colossians 2:3

PURSUE KNOWLEDGE

The fear of the Lord is the beginning of knowledge, but fools despise wisdom and discipline. Proverbs 1:7

Then you will understand the fear of the Lord and find the knowledge of God. For the Lord gives wisdom, and from his mouth come knowledge and understanding. Proverbs 2:5-6

Wise men store up knowledge, but the mouth of a fool invites ruin.
Proverbs 10:14

It is not good to have zeal without knowledge, nor to be hasty and miss the way. Proverbs 19:2

I myself am convinced, my brothers, that you yourselves are full of goodness, complete in knowledge and competent to instruct one another. Romans 15:14

For this very reason, make every effort to add to your faith goodness; and to goodness, knowledge; and to knowledge, self-control; and to self-control, perseverance; and to perseverance, godliness.
2 Peter 1:5-6

Fortune favors the prepared mind. - Louis Pasteur

THE BENEFITS OF OBTAINING KNOWLEDGE

For wisdom will enter your heart, and knowledge will be pleasant to your soul. Proverbs 2:10

Through knowledge its rooms are filled with rare and beautiful treasures. Proverbs 24:4

A wise man has great power, and a man of knowledge increases strength. Proverbs 24:5

Wisdom is a shelter as money is a shelter, but the advantage of knowledge is this: that wisdom preserves the life of its possessor.
Ecclesiastes 7:12

He will be the sure foundation for your times, a rich store of salvation and wisdom and knowledge; the fear of the Lord is the key to this treasure. Isaiah 33:6

THE CONSEQUENCES OF LACKING KNOWLEDGE

My people are destroyed from lack of knowledge. "Because you have rejected knowledge, I also reject you as my priests; because you have ignored the law of your God, I also will ignore your children. Hosea 4:6

Furthermore, since they did not think it worthwhile to retain the knowledge of God, he gave them over to a depraved mind, to do what ought not to be done. Romans 1:28

Come back to your senses as you ought, and stop sinning; for there are some who are ignorant of God—I say this to your shame.
1 Corinthians 15:34

KNOWLEDGE FROM GOD'S WORD

Teach me knowledge and good judgment, for I believe in your commands. Psalms 119:66

Choose my instruction instead of silver, knowledge rather than choice gold. Proverbs 8:10

Stop listening to instruction, my son, and you will stray from the words of knowledge. Proverbs 19:27

What is more, I consider everything a loss compared to the surpassing greatness of knowing Christ Jesus my Lord, for whose sake I have lost all things. I consider them rubbish, that I may gain Christ.
Philippians 3:8

Pay attention and listen to the sayings of the wise; apply your heart to what I teach. Proverbs 22:17

Have I not written thirty sayings for you, sayings of counsel and knowledge. Proverbs 22:20

Apply your heart to instruction and your ears to words of knowledge. Proverbs 23:12

In reading this, then, you will be able to understand my insight into the mystery of Christ. Ephesians 3:4

And this is my prayer: that your love may abound more and more in knowledge and depth of insight. Philippians 1:9

If we deliberately keep on sinning after we have received the knowledge of the truth, no sacrifice for sins is left. Hebrews 10:26

But grow in the grace and knowledge of our Lord and Savior Jesus Christ. To him be glory both now and forever! Amen. 2 Peter 3:18

UNDERSTANDING

Discretion will protect you, and understanding will guard you.
Proverbs 2:11

Good understanding wins favor, but the way of the unfaithful is hard. Proverbs 13:15

Understanding is a fountain of life to those who have it, but folly brings punishment to fools. Proverbs 16:22

By wisdom a house is built, and through understanding it is established. Proverbs 24:3

By your wisdom and understanding you have gained wealth for yourself and amassed gold and silver in your treasuries.
Ezekiel 28:4

GODLY UNDERSTANDING

But it is the spirit in a man, the breath of the Almighty, that gives him understanding. Job 32:8

Who endowed the heart with wisdom or gave understanding to the mind? Job 38:36

For the Lord gives wisdom, and from his mouth come knowledge and understanding. Proverbs 2:6

The fear of the Lord is the beginning of wisdom, and knowledge of the Holy One is understanding. Proverbs 9:10

There is no wisdom, no insight, no plan that can succeed against the Lord. Proverbs 21:30

I pray also that the eyes of your heart may be enlightened in order that you may know the hope to which he has called you, the riches of his glorious inheritance in the saints. Ephesians 1:18

If a great man says something that seems illogical, don't laugh; try to understand it. -The Talmud

Reflect on what I am saying, for the Lord will give you insight into all this. 2 Timothy 2:7

We know also that the Son of God has come and has given us understanding, so that we may know him who is true. And we are in him who is true—even in his Son Jesus Christ. He is the true God and eternal life. 1 John 5:20

OBTAINING UNDERSTANDING

The fear of the Lord is the beginning of wisdom; all who follow his precepts have good understanding. To him belongs eternal praise.
Psalms 111:10

I gain understanding from your precepts; therefore I hate every wrong path. Psalms 119:104

The unfolding of your words gives light; it gives understanding to the simple. Psalms 119:130

Turning your ear to wisdom and applying your heart to understanding, Proverbs 2:2

Let love and faithfulness never leave you; bind them around your neck, write them on the tablet of your heart. Then you will win favor and a good name in the sight of God and man. Trust in the Lord with all your heart and lean not on your own understanding.
Proverbs 3:3-5

DIRECTION

You have made known to me the path of life; you will fill me with joy in your presence, with eternal pleasures at your right hand. Psalms 16:11

Show me your ways, O Lord, teach me your paths; guide me in your truth and teach me, for you are God my Savior, and my hope is in you all day long. Psalms 25:4-5

He guides the humble in what is right and teaches them his way. All the ways of the Lord are loving and faithful for those who keep the demands of his covenant. Psalms 25:9-10

I will instruct you and teach you in the way you should go; I will counsel you and watch over you. Psalms 32:8

If the Lord delights in a man's way, he makes his steps firm; though he stumble, he will not fall, for the Lord upholds him with his hand. Psalms 37:23-24

For this God is our God for ever and ever; he will be our guide even to the end. Psalms 48:14

Yet I am always with you; you hold me by my right hand. You guide me with your counsel, and afterward you will take me into glory. Psalms 73:23-24

Once God speaks to you, do not confer with negative people. Share the vision God has given you with people who have spiritual eyes to see and spiritual ears to ear. In the multitude of wise and spiritual counsel there is safety.

And David shepherded them with integrity of heart; with skillful hands he led them. Psalms 78:72

For he will command his angels concerning you to guard you in all your ways. Psalms 91:11

The Lord will watch over your coming and going both now and forevermore. Psalms 121:8

For he guards the course of the just and protects the way of his faithful ones. Proverbs 2:8

Trust in the Lord with all your heart and lean not on your own understanding; in all your ways acknowledge him, and he will make your paths straight. Proverbs 3:5-6

The integrity of the upright guides them, but the unfaithful are destroyed by their duplicity. Proverbs 11:3

Plans fail for lack of counsel, but with many advisers they succeed.
Proverbs 15:22

Commit to the Lord whatever you do, and your plans will succeed.
Proverbs 16:3

In his heart a man plans his course, but the Lord determines his steps. Proverbs 16:9

Blessed is the man who finds out which way God is moving and then gets going in the same direction.
- Anonymous.

A man's steps are directed by the Lord. How then can anyone understand his own way? Proverbs 20:24

His God instructs him and teaches him the right way. Isaiah 28:26

Whether you turn to the right or to the left, your ears will hear a voice behind you, saying, "This is the way; walk in it." Isaiah 30:21

I will lead the blind by ways they have not known, along unfamiliar paths I will guide them; I will turn the darkness into light before them and make the rough places smooth. These are the things I will do; I will not forsake them. Isaiah 42:16

I will go before you and will level the mountains; I will break down gates of bronze and cut through bars of iron. Isaiah 45:2

This is what the Lord says—your Redeemer, the Holy One of Israel: I am the Lord your God, who teaches you what is best for you, who directs you in the way you should go. Isaiah 48:17

I have seen his ways, but I will heal him; I will guide him and restore comfort to him. Isaiah 57:18

But seek first his kingdom and his righteousness, and all these things will be given to you as well. Matthew 6:33

When he has brought out all his own, he goes on ahead of them, and his sheep follow him because they know his voice. But they will never follow a stranger; in fact, they will run away from him because they do not recognize a stranger's voice. John 10:4-5

My sheep listen to my voice; I know them, and they follow me.
John 10:27

But when he, the Spirit of truth, comes, he will guide you into all truth. He will not speak on his own; he will speak only what he hears, and he will tell you what is yet to come. John 16:13

So I say, live by the Spirit, and you will not gratify the desires of the sinful nature. Galatians 5:16

For it is God who works in you to will and to act according to his good purpose. Philippians 2:13

But you have an anointing from the Holy One, and all of you know the truth. 1 John 2:20

I know your deeds. See, I have placed before you an open door that no one can shut. I know that you have little strength, yet you have kept my word and have not denied my name. Revelation 3:8

FAVOR FROM GOD

And the boy Samuel continued to grow in stature and in favor with the Lord and with men. Isaiah 2:26

For surely, O Lord, you bless the righteous; you surround them with your favor as with a shield. Psalms 5:12

For his anger lasts only a moment, but his favor lasts a lifetime; weeping may remain for a night, but rejoicing comes in the morning. Psalms 30:5

O Lord, when you favored me, you made my mountain stand firm; but when you hid your face, I was dismayed. Psalms 30:7

I know that you are pleased with me, for my enemy does not triumph over me. Psalms 41:11

I entreated thy favour with my whole heart: be merciful unto me according to thy word. Psalms 119:58 KJV

For whoever finds me finds life and receives favor from the Lord.
Proverbs 8:35

A good man obtains favor from the Lord, but the Lord condemns a crafty man. Proverbs 12:2

Then you will win favor and a good name in the sight of God and man. Proverbs 3:4

And Jesus grew in wisdom and stature, and in favor with God and men. Luke 2:52

DECISIONS

Let the peace of Christ rule in your hearts, since as members of one body you were called to peace. And be thankful.

Colossians 3:15

SAY NO WHEN IT'S CONTRARY TO GOD'S WORD

SAY NO WHEN YOU HAVE PRAYED AND GOD HAS SAID NO

SAY NO WHEN YOU FEEL MANIPULATED

SAY NO WHEN YOU FEEL INTIMIDATED

SAY NO WHEN YOU FEEL UNEASY

SAY NO WHEN YOU FEEL HESITANT

SAY NO WHEN YOU FEEL PUSHED

SAY NO WHEN YOU FEEL USED

SAY NO WHEN YOU FEEL RUSHED

SAY NO WHEN YOU FEEL UNSURE

SAY NO WHEN IT'S AN UNREALISTIC OFFER

SAY NO WHEN YOU FEEL CONDEMNED

SAY NO WHEN YOU FEEL GUILTY

SAY NO WHEN YOU FEEL CONVICTED

SAY NO WHEN YOU HAVEN'T SOUGHT GODLY COUNSEL

SAY YES WHEN IT'S IN AGREEMENT WITH GOD'S WORD

SAY YES WHEN YOU HAVE PRAYED AND RECEIVED A CONFIRMATION FROM GOD SAY YES WHEN YOU FEEL AT PEACE IN YOUR SPIRIT

SAY YES WHEN YOU HAVE THOROUGHLY THOUGHT OUT THE CONSEQUENCES

SAY YES WHEN YOU HAVE SOUGHT GODLY COUNSEL

DILIGENCE

Diligent hands will rule, but laziness ends in slave labor.

Proverbs 12:24

Destiny is not a matter of chance, it is a matter of choice; it is not a thing to be waited for, it is a thing to be achieved. - William Jennings Bryan

The lazy man does not roast his game, but the diligent man prizes his possessions. Proverbs 12:27

The sluggard craves and gets nothing, but the desires of the diligent are fully satisfied. Proverbs 13:4

The plans of the diligent lead to profit as surely as haste leads to poverty. Proverbs 21:5

Seest thou a man diligent in his business? he shall stand before kings; he shall not stand before mean men. Proverbs 22:29 KJV

Do you see a man skilled in his work? He will serve before kings; he will not serve before obscure men. Proverbs 22:29

Be sure you know the condition of your flocks, give careful attention to your herds; for riches do not endure forever, and a crown is not secure for all generations. Proverbs 27:23-24

People can be divided into three groups: Those who make things happen, those who watch things happen, and those who wonder what happened.
- John W. Newbern

FAITHFULNESS

Love the Lord, all his saints! The Lord preserves the faithful, but the proud he pays back in full. Psalms 31:23

My eyes will be on the faithful in the land, that they may dwell with me; he whose walk is blameless will minister to me.
Psalms 101:6

A gossip betrays a confidence, but a trustworthy man keeps a secret. Proverbs 11:13

A wicked messenger falls into trouble, but a trustworthy envoy brings healing. Proverbs 13:17

Many a man claims to have unfailing love, but a faithful man who can find? Proverbs 20:6

The ability to accept responsibility is the measure of the man. - Roy L. Smith

Like a bad tooth or a lame foot is reliance on the unfaithful in times of trouble. Proverbs 25:19

A faithful man will be richly blessed, but one eager to get rich will not go unpunished. Proverbs 28:20

"His master replied, 'Well done, good and faithful servant! You have been faithful with a few things; I will put you in charge of many things. Come and share your master's happiness!'
Matthew 25:23

The Lord answered, "Who then is the faithful and wise manager, whom the master puts in charge of his servants to give them their food allowance at the proper time? It will be good for that servant whom the master finds doing so when he returns. Luke 12:42-43

So if you have not been trustworthy in handling worldly wealth, who will trust you with true riches? And if you have not been trustworthy with someone else's property, who will give you property of your own? Luke 16:11-12

The greatest ability is dependability. - Vance Havner

Be joyful in hope, patient in affliction, faithful in prayer.
Romans 12:12

God, who has called you into fellowship with his Son Jesus Christ our Lord, is faithful. 1 Corinthians 1:9

Now it is required that those who have been given a trust must prove faithful. 1 Corinthians 4:2

I thank Christ Jesus our Lord, who has given me strength, that he considered me faithful, appointing me to his service.
1 Timothy 1:12

He was faithful to the one who appointed him, just as Moses was faithful in all God's house. Hebrews 3:2

Moses was faithful as a servant in all God's house, testifying to what would be said in the future. But Christ is faithful as a son over God's house. And we are his house, if we hold on to our courage and the hope of which we boast. Hebrews 3:5-6

343

Dear friend, you are faithful in what you are doing for the brothers, even though they are strangers to you. 3 John 1:5

This calls for patient endurance on the part of the saints who obey God's commandments and remain faithful to Jesus.
Revelation 14:12

Few ever die from commitment, perseverance, faith, and achievement, but many die from neglected responsibilities, impatience, doubt and unfulfilled dreams.

WORK

Six days you shall labor and do all your work. Exodus 20:9

Better to be a nobody and yet have a servant than pretend to be somebody and have no food. Proverbs 12:9

Better is he who is lightly esteemed but works for his own support, than he who assumes honor for himself and lacks bread.
Proverbs 12:9 AMP

The laborer's appetite works for him; his hunger drives him on.
Proverbs 16:26

The appetite of the laborer works for him, for the need of his mouth urges him on. Proverbs 16:26 AMP

Whatever your hand finds to do, do it with all your might, for in the grave, where you are going, there is neither working nor planning nor knowledge nor wisdom. Ecclesiastes 9:10

Working hard is a good ethic to practice; but working smart with goals, direction and purpose is better.

Whatever you do, work at it with all your heart, as working for the Lord, not for men. Colossians 3:23

Stay in that house, eating and drinking whatever they give you, for the worker deserves his wages. Do not move around from house to house. Luke 10:7

As long as it is day, we must do the work of him who sent me. Night is coming, when no one can work. John 9:4

For we are God's fellow workers; you are God's field, God's building. 1 Corinthians 3:9

One who is slack in his work is brother to one who destroys.
Proverbs 18:9

BENEFITS OF WORKING

Moreover, when God gives any man wealth and possessions, and enables him to enjoy them, to accept his lot and be happy in his work—this is a gift of God. Ecclesiastes 5:19

He who works his land will have abundant food, but he who chases fantasies lacks judgment. Proverbs 12:11

His work will be shown for what it is, because the Day will bring it to light. It will be revealed with fire, and the fire will test the quality of each man's work. If what he has built survives, he will receive his reward. If it is burned up, he will suffer loss; he himself will be saved, but only as one escaping through the flames.
1 Corinthians 3:13-15

COMMANDED TO WORK

And we pray this in order that you may live a life worthy of the Lord and may please him in every way: bearing fruit in every good work, growing in the knowledge of God. Colossians 1:10

Make it your ambition to lead a quiet life, to mind your own business and to work with your hands, just as we told you, so that your daily life may win the respect of outsiders and so that you will not be dependent on anybody. 1 Thessalonians 4:11-12

For even when we were with you, we gave you this rule: "If a man will not work, he shall not eat." 2 Thessalonians 3:10

CONSEQUENCES OF NOT WORKING

Laziness brings on deep sleep, and the shiftless man goes hungry.
Proverbs 19:15

GOOD WORKS

In the same way, let your light shine before men, that they may see your good deeds and praise your Father in heaven. Matthew 5:16

And God is able to make all grace abound to you, so that in all things at all times, having all that you need, you will abound in every good work. 2 Corinthians 9:8

And we pray this in order that you may live a life worthy of the Lord and may please him in every way: bearing fruit in every good work, growing in the knowledge of God. Colossians 1:10

And whatever you do, whether in word or deed, do it all in the name of the Lord Jesus, giving thanks to God the Father through him. Colossians 3:17

Slaves, obey your earthly masters in everything; and do it, not only when their eye is on you and to win their favor, but with sincerity of heart and reverence for the Lord. Whatever you do, work at it with all your heart, as working for the Lord, not for men.
Colossians 3:22-23

When people do not mean business with Christ in their hearts they will not do business for Christ with their hands.
- Vance Havner

For we are God's workmanship, created in Christ Jesus to do good works, which God prepared in advance for us to do.
Ephesians 2:10

In the same way, good deeds are obvious, and even those that are not cannot be hidden. 1 Timothy 5:25

Command them to do good, to be rich in good deeds, and to be generous and willing to share. 1 Timothy 6:18

Attempt something so impossible that unless God is in it, it is doomed to failure. - John Haggai

If a man cleanses himself from the latter, he will be an instrument for noble purposes, made holy, useful to the Master and prepared to do any good work. 2 Timothy 2:21

So that the man of God may be thoroughly equipped for every good work. 2 Timothy 3:17

In everything set them an example by doing what is good. In your teaching show integrity, seriousness. Titus 2:7

Our people must learn to devote themselves to doing what is good, in order that they may provide for daily necessities and not live unproductive lives. Titus 3:14

> *O Lord, let us not live to be useless, for Christ's sake.*
> *- John Wesley*

And let us consider how we may spur one another on toward love and good deeds. Hebrews 10:24

Equip you with everything good for doing his will, and may he work in us what is pleasing to him, through Jesus Christ, to whom be glory for ever and ever. Amen. Hebrews 13:21

Live such good lives among the pagans that, though they accuse you of doing wrong, they may see your good deeds and glorify God on the day he visits us. 1 Peter 2:12

For it is God's will that by doing good you should silence the ignorant talk of foolish men. 1 Peter 2:15

For it is God's will and intention that be doing right [your] good and honest lives should silence (muzzle, gag) the ignorant charges and ill-informed criticisms of foolish persons. 1 Peter 2:15 AMP

YOUR GOOD WORKS WILL BE JUDGED BY CHRIST

For the Son of Man is going to come in his Father's glory with his angels, and then he will reward each person according to what he has done. Matthew 16:27

His work will be shown for what it is, because the Day will bring it to light. It will be revealed with fire, and the fire will test the quality of each man's work. If what he has built survives, he will receive his reward. If it is burned up, he will suffer loss; he himself will be saved, but only as one escaping through the flames.
1 Corinthians 3:13-15

The work of each [one] will become (plainly, openly known-shown for what it is; for the day (of Christ) will disclose and declare it, because it will be revealed with fire, and the fire will test and critically appraise the character and worth of the work each person has done.

If the work which any person has built on this Foundation—any product of his efforts whatever—survives (this test), he will get his reward. But if any person's work is burned up [under the test], he will get his reward.

But if any person's work is burned up [under the test], he will suffer the loss (of it all, losing his reward), though he himself will be saved, but only as [one who has passed] through fire.
1 Corinthians 3:13-15 AMP

When God crowns our merits, it is nothing other than his own gifts that he crowns. - Augustine of Hippo

For the Son of Man is going to come in his Father's glory with his angels, and then he will reward each person according to what he has done. Matthew 16:27

Behold, I am coming soon! My reward is with me, and I will give to everyone according to what he has done. Revelation 22:12

DEVELOPING RELATIONSHIPS

FAMILY OF GOD

Because those who are led by the Spirit of God are sons of God. For you did not receive a spirit that makes you a slave again to fear, but you received the Spirit of sonship. And by him we cry, "Abba, Father." The Spirit himself testifies with our spirit that we are God's children. Now if we are children, then we are heirs—heirs of God and co-heirs with Christ, if indeed we share in his sufferings in order that we may also share in his glory. Romans 8:14-17

"I will be a Father to you, and you will be my sons and daughters, says the Lord Almighty." 2 Corinthians 6:18

Because you are sons, God sent the Spirit of his Son into our hearts, the Spirit who calls out, "Abba, Father." So you are no longer a slave, but a son; and since you are a son, God has made you also an heir. Galatians 4:6-7

He predestined us to be adopted as his sons through Jesus Christ, in accordance with his pleasure and will. Ephesians 1:5

For this reason I kneel before the Father, from whom his whole family in heaven and on earth derives its name. Ephesians 3:14-15

But you are a chosen people, a royal priesthood, a holy nation, a people belonging to God, that you may declare the praises of him who called you out of darkness into his wonderful light. 1 Peter 2:9

FELLOWSHIP WITH GOD

Yet a time is coming and has now come when the true worshipers will worship the Father in spirit and truth, for they are the kind of worshipers the Father seeks. God is spirit, and his worshipers must worship in spirit and in truth. John 4:23-24

Let us come before him with thanksgiving and extol him with music and song. Psalms 95:2

Enter his gates with thanksgiving and his courts with praise; give thanks to him and praise his name. Psalms 100:4

For through him we both have access to the Father by one Spirit. Ephesians 2:18

In him and through faith in him we may approach God with freedom and confidence. Ephesians 3:12

Let us then approach the throne of grace with confidence, so that we may receive mercy and find grace to help us in our time of need. Hebrews 4:16

God has no favorites but He does have intimates.
- Vance Havner

Therefore, brothers, since we have confidence to enter the Most Holy Place by the blood of Jesus. Hebrews 10:19

Here I am! I stand at the door and knock. If anyone hears my voice and opens the door, I will come in and eat with him, and he with me. Revelation 3:20

ANGELS

ANGELS PROTECT THE CHILDREN OF GOD

With the coming of dawn, the angels urged Lot, saying, "Hurry! Take your wife and your two daughters who are here, or you will be swept away when the city is punished." When he hesitated, the men grasped his hand and the hands of his wife and of his two daughters and led them safely out of the city, for the Lord was merciful to them. Genesis 19:15-16

For he will command his angels concerning you to guard you in all your ways; Psalms 91:11

For it is written: "'He will command his angels concerning you to guard you carefully; Luke 4:10

ANGELS TRAVEL BACK AND FORTH FROM HEAVEN TO EARTH

He had a dream in which he saw a stairway resting on the earth, with its top reaching to heaven, and the angels of God were ascending and descending on it. Genesis 28:12

He then added, "I tell you the truth, you shall see heaven open, and the angels of God ascending and descending on the Son of Man."
John 1:51

ANGELS RESPOND TO THE SPOKEN WORD OF GOD

Praise the Lord, you his angels, you mighty ones who do his bidding, who obey his word. Psalms 103:20

The devil is a spiritual being and the spoken Word of God is the sword of the Spirit. Nothing else cuts, controls, binds, hinders, and defeats the devil and his demons more than a Christian confessing God's Word in faith.

ANGELS ARE ASSIGNED TO DIFFERENT BELIEVERS

"See that you do not look down on one of these little ones. For I tell you that their angels in heaven always see the face of my Father in heaven. Matthew 18:10

ANGELS ENGAGE IN SPIRITUAL WARFARE

And there was war in heaven. Michael and his angels fought against the dragon, and the dragon and his angels fought back.
Revelation 12:7

The great dragon was hurled down—that ancient serpent called the devil, or Satan, who leads the whole world astray. He was hurled to the earth, and his angels with him. Revelation 12:9

ANGELS WILL ACCOMPANY CHRIST WHEN HE RETURNS TO EARTH

"When the Son of Man comes in his glory, and all the angels with him, he will sit on his throne in heavenly glory. Matthew 25:31

If anyone is ashamed of me and my words in this adulterous and sinful generation, the Son of Man will be ashamed of him when he comes in his Father's glory with the holy angels." Mark 8:38

ANGELS ARE INFINITE IN NUMBER

Praise him, all his angels, praise him, all his heavenly hosts.
Psalms 148:2

Do you think I cannot call on my Father, and he will at once put at my disposal more than twelve legions of angels? Matthew 26:53

But you have come to Mount Zion, to the heavenly Jerusalem, the city of the living God. You have come to thousands upon thousands of angels in joyful assembly, Hebrews 12:22

Then I looked and heard the voice of many angels, numbering thousands upon thousands, and ten thousand times ten thousand. They encircled the throne and the living creatures and the elders.
Revelation 5:11

The chariots of God are tens of thousands and thousands of thousands; the Lord has come from Sinai into his sanctuary.
Psalms 68:17

ANGELS MINISTER TO GOD'S CHILDREN

And he was in the desert forty days, being tempted by Satan. He was with the wild animals, and angels attended him. Mark 1:13

He makes winds his messengers, flames of fire his servants.
Psalms 104:4

Then the devil left him, and angels came and attended him.
Matthew 4:11

In speaking of the angels he says, "He makes his angels winds, his servants flames of fire." Hebrews 1:7

ANGELS ARE NOT TO BE WORSHIPED

Do not let anyone who delights in false humility and the worship of angels disqualify you for the prize. Such a person goes into great detail about what he has seen, and his unspiritual mind puffs him up with idle notions. Colossians 2:18

ANGELS CAN DISGUISE THEMSELVES AS HUMAN BEINGS

Do not forget to entertain strangers, for by so doing some people have entertained angels without knowing it. Hebrews 13:2

ANGELS ARE UNDER THE AUTHORITY OF GOD

Who has gone into heaven and is at God's right hand—with angels, authorities and powers in submission to him. 1 Peter 3:22

ANGELS WILL SEPARATE THE BELIEVERS FROM THE UNBELIEVERS

And the enemy who sows them is the devil. The harvest is the end of the age, and the harvesters are angels. Matthew 13:39

The Son of Man will send out his angels, and they will weed out of his kingdom everything that causes sin and all who do evil.
Matthew 13:41

This is how it will be at the end of the age. The angels will come and separate the wicked from the righteous. Matthew 13:49

And he will send his angels and gather his elect from the four winds, from the ends of the earth to the ends of the heavens. Mark 13:27

FELLOWSHIP WITH BELIEVERS

How good and pleasant it is when brothers live together in unity!
Psalms 133:1

I appeal to you, brothers, in the name of our Lord Jesus Christ, that all of you agree with one another so that there may be no divisions among you and that you may be perfectly united in mind and thought. 1 Corinthians 1:10

So if the whole church comes together and everyone speaks in tongues, and some who do not understand or some unbelievers come in, will they not say that you are out of your mind?
1 Corinthians 14:23

You, my brothers, were called to be free. But do not use your freedom to indulge the sinful nature; rather, serve one another in love.
Galatians 5:13

Until we all reach unity in the faith and in the knowledge of the Son of God and become mature, attaining to the whole measure of the fullness of Christ. Ephesians 4:13

Be kind and compassionate to one another, forgiving each other, just as in Christ God forgave you. Ephesians 4:32

Submit to one another out of reverence for Christ. Ephesians 5:21

Then make my joy complete by being like-minded, having the same love, being one in spirit and purpose. Philippians 2:2

Let the peace of Christ rule in your hearts, since as members of one body you were called to peace. And be thankful. Colossians 3:15

May the Lord make your love increase and overflow for each other and for everyone else, just as ours does for you.
1 Thessalonians 3:12

Now about brotherly love we do not need to write to you, for you yourselves have been taught by God to love each other.
1 Thessalonians 4:9

Therefore encourage one another and build each other up, just as in fact you are doing. 1 Thessalonians 5:11

Now that you have purified yourselves by obeying the truth so that you have sincere love for your brothers, love one another deeply, from the heart. 1 Peter 1:22

Finally, all of you, live in harmony with one another; be sympathetic, love as brothers, be compassionate and humble. 1 Peter 3:8

Offer hospitality to one another without grumbling. 1 Peter 4:9

But if we walk in the light, as he is in the light, we have fellowship with one another, and the blood of Jesus, his Son, purifies us from all sin. 1 John 1:7

UNITY IN THE BODY OF CHRIST

The body is a unit, though it is made up of many parts; and though all its parts are many, they form one body. So it is with Christ. For we were all baptized by one Spirit into one body—whether Jews or Greeks, slave or free—and we were all given the one Spirit to drink. Now the body is not made up of one part but of many. If the foot should say, "Because I am not a hand, I do not belong to the body," it would not for that reason cease to be part of the body. And if the ear should say, "Because I am not an eye, I do not belong to the body," it would not for that reason cease to be part of the body. If the whole body were an eye, where would the sense of hearing be? If the whole body were an ear, where would the sense of smell be? But in fact God has arranged the parts in the body, every one of them, just as he wanted them to be. If they were all one part, where would the body be? As it is, there are many parts, but one body. The eye cannot say to the hand, "I don't need you!" And the head cannot say to the feet, "I don't need you!" On the contrary, those parts of the body that seem to be weaker are indispensable, and the parts that we think are less honorable we treat with special honor. And the parts that are unpresentable are treated with special modesty, while our presentable parts need no special treatment. But God has combined the members of the body and has given greater honor to the parts that lacked it, so that there should be no division in the body, but that its parts should have equal concern for each other. If one part suffers, every part suffers with it; if one part is honored, every part rejoices with it. Now you are the body of Christ, and each one of you is a part of it. 1 Corinthians 12:12-27

Make every effort to keep the unity of the Spirit through the bond of peace. There is one body and one Spirit—just as you were called to one hope when you were called. Ephesians 4:3-4

From him the whole body, joined and held together by every supporting ligament, grows and builds itself up in love, as each part does its work. Ephesians 4:16

Therefore each of you must put off falsehood and speak truthfully to his neighbor, for we are all members of one body.
Ephesians 4:25

He has lost connection with the Head, from whom the whole body, supported and held together by its ligaments and sinews, grows as God causes it to grow. Colossians 2:19

MARRIAGE

For this reason a man will leave his father and mother and be united to his wife, and they will become one flesh. Genesis 2:24

But at the beginning of creation God made them male and female. For this reason a man will leave his father and mother and be united to his wife, and the two will become one flesh. So they are no longer two, but one. Therefore what God has joined together, let man not separate. Mark 10:6-9

> *Husband and wives who would live happily ever after learn early to give and take, to reach agreements by mutual consent. - Vance Havner*

HUSBANDS

May your fountain be blessed, and may you rejoice in the wife of your youth. A loving doe, a graceful deer—may her breasts satisfy you always, may you ever be captivated by her love.
Proverbs 5:18-19

He who finds a wife finds what is good and receives favor from the Lord. Proverbs 18:22

Houses and wealth are inherited from parents, but a prudent wife is from the Lord. Proverbs 19:14

A wife of noble character who can find? She is worth far more than rubies. Proverbs 31:10

Give her the reward she has earned, and let her works bring her praise at the city gate. Proverbs 31:31

When the husband commits, the wife submits.
- Myles Munroe

Enjoy life with your wife, whom you love, all the days of this meaningless life that God has given you under the sun—all your meaningless days. For this is your lot in life and in your toilsome labor under the sun. Ecclesiastes 9:9

You ask, "Why?" It is because the Lord is acting as the witness between you and the wife of your youth, because you have broken faith with her, though she is your partner, the wife of your marriage covenant. Has not the Lord made them one? In flesh and spirit they are his. And why one? Because he was seeking godly offspring. So guard yourself in your spirit, and do not break faith with the wife of your youth. "I hate divorce," says the Lord God of Israel, "and I hate a man's covering himself with violence as well as with his garment," says the Lord Almighty. So guard yourself in your spirit, and do not break faith. Malachi 2:14-16

The husband should fulfill his marital duty to his wife, and likewise the wife to her husband. The wife's body does not belong to her alone but also to her husband. In the same way, the husband's body does not belong to him alone but also to his wife. Do not deprive each other except by mutual consent and for a time, so that you may devote yourselves to prayer. Then come together again so that Satan will not tempt you because of your lack of self-control. I say this as a concession, not as a command. 1 Corinthians 7:3-6

Success in marriage consist not only in finding the right
mate, but also in being the right mate. - Anonymous

Now I want you to realize that the head of every man is Christ, and the head of the woman is man, and the head of Christ is God.
1 Corinthians 11:3

Wives, submit to your husbands as to the Lord. For the husband is the head of the wife as Christ is the head of the church, his body, of which he is the Savior. Ephesians 5:22-23

Wives, submit to your husbands, as is fitting in the Lord. Husbands, love your wives and do not be harsh with them.

Colossians 3:18-19

WIVES

A wife of noble character is her husband's crown, but a disgraceful wife is like decay in his bones. Proverbs 12:4

The wise woman builds her house, but with her own hands the foolish one tears hers down. Proverbs 14:1

He who finds a wife finds what is good and receives favor from the Lord. Proverbs 18:22

Houses and wealth are inherited from parents, but a prudent wife is from the Lord. Proverbs 19:14

A wife of noble character who can find? She is worth far more than rubies. Proverbs 31:10

Give her the reward she has earned, and let her works bring her praise at the city gate. Proverbs 31:31

> *Husbands should express in words what they are thinking, and wives should express in words what they are feeling.- Myles Munroe*

The husband should fulfill his marital duty to his wife, and likewise the wife to her husband. The wife's body does not belong to her alone but also to her husband. In the same way, the husband's body does not belong to him alone but also to his wife. Do not deprive each other except by mutual consent and for a time, so that you may devote yourselves to prayer. Then come together again so that Satan will not tempt you because of your lack of self-control. I say this as a concession, not as a command. 1 Corinthians 7:3-6

Now I want you to realize that the head of every man is Christ, and the head of the woman is man, and the head of Christ is God.

1 Corinthians 11:3

Wives, submit to your husbands as to the Lord. For the husband is the head of the wife as Christ is the head of the church, his body, of which he is the Savior. Ephesians 5:22-23

Wives, submit to your husbands, as is fitting in the Lord. Husbands, love your wives and do not be harsh with them.
Colossians 3:18-19

DIVORCE

It has been said, Anyone who divorces his wife must give her a certificate of divorce. But I tell you that anyone who divorces his wife, except for marital unfaithfulness, causes her to become an adulteress, and anyone who marries the divorced woman commits adultery. Matthew 5:31-32

Haven't you read, he replied, that at the beginning the Creator 'made them male and female, and said, For this reason a man will leave his father and mother and be united to his wife, and the two will become one flesh'? So they are no longer two, but one. Therefore what God has joined together, let man not separate.
Matthew 19:4-6

But at the beginning of creation God 'made them male and female. For this reason a man will leave his father and mother and be united to his wife, and the two will become one flesh. So they are no longer two, but one. Therefore what God has joined together, let man not separate. When they were in the house again, the disciples asked Jesus about this. He answered, "Anyone who divorces his wife and marries another woman commits adultery against her. And if she divorces her husband and marries another man, she commits adultery. Mark 10:6-12

Anyone who divorces his wife and marries another woman commits adultery, and the man who marries a divorced woman commits adultery. Luke 16:18

To the married I give this command (not I, but the Lord): A wife must not separate from her husband. But if she does, she must remain unmarried or else be reconciled to her husband. And a husband must not divorce his wife. 1 Corinthians 7:10-11

But if the unbeliever leaves, let him do so. A believing man or woman is not bound in such circumstances; God has called us to live in peace. 1 Corinthians 7:15

Divorcing your mate may look like it's the answer to your problems and the way out of pain and misery. However, most of the time it only leads to more pain and misery, not only for you, but also for your children and relatives. God created the institution of marriage and God can heal and revive it.

Are you married? Do not seek a divorce. Are you unmarried? Do not look for a wife. 1 Corinthians 7:27

A woman is bound to her husband as long as he lives. But if her husband dies, she is free to marry anyone she wishes, but he must belong to the Lord. In my judgment, she is happier if she stays as she is—and I think that I too have the Spirit of God.

1 Corinthians 7:39-40

UNSAVED MARRIAGE PARTNER

To the rest I say this (I, not the Lord): If any brother has a wife who is not a believer and she is willing to live with him, he must not divorce her. And if a woman has a husband who is not a believer and he is willing to live with her, she must not divorce him. For the unbelieving husband has been sanctified through his wife, and the unbelieving wife has been sanctified through her believing husband. Otherwise your children would be unclean, but as it is, they are holy. How do you know, wife, whether you will save your husband? Or, how do you know, husband, whether you will save your wife? 1 Corinthians 7:12-16

Wives, in the same way be submissive to your husbands so that, if any of them do not believe the word, they may be won over without words by the behavior of their wives, when they see the purity and reverence of your lives. Your beauty should not come from outward adornment, such as braided hair and the wearing of gold jewelry and fine clothes. Instead, it should be that of your inner self, the unfading beauty of a gentle and quiet spirit, which is of great worth in God's sight. For this is the way the holy women of the past who put their hope in God used to make themselves beautiful. They were submissive to their own husbands, like Sarah, who obeyed Abraham and called him her master. You are her daughters if you do what is right and do not give way to fear. Husbands, in the same way be considerate as you live with your wives, and treat them with respect as the weaker partner and as heirs with you of the gracious gift of life, so that nothing will hinder your prayers.

1 Peter 3:1-7

CHILD-PARENT RELATIONSHIP

RAISING CHILDREN

A good man leaves an inheritance for his children's children, but a sinner's wealth is stored up for the righteous. Proverbs 13:22

Children's children are a crown to the aged, and parents are the pride of their children. Proverbs 17:6

The father of a righteous man has great joy; he who has a wise son delights in him. Proverbs 23:24

He must manage his own family well and see that his children obey him with proper respect. If anyone does not know how to manage his own family, how can he take care of God's church?

1 Timothy 3:4-5

The most important thing a father can do for his children is to love their mother. -Theodore M. Hesburgh

If anyone does not provide for his relatives, and especially for his immediate family, he has denied the faith and is worse than an unbeliever. 1 Timothy 5:8

PHYSICALLY CORRECTING YOUR CHILDREN

He who spares the rod hates his son, but he who loves him is careful to discipline him. Proverbs 13:24

Folly is bound up in the heart of a child, but the rod of discipline will drive it far from him. Proverbs 22:15

Do not withhold discipline from a child; if you punish him with the rod, he will not die. Punish him with the rod and save his soul from death. Proverbs 23:13-14

The rod of correction imparts wisdom, but a child left to himself disgraces his mother. Proverbs 29:15

Discipline your son, and he will give you peace; he will bring delight to your soul. Proverbs 29:17

BEING FAIR TO YOUR CHILDREN

Fathers, do not exasperate your children; instead, bring them up in the training and instruction of the Lord. Ephesians 6:4

Fathers, do not embitter your children, or they will become discouraged. Colossians 3:21

TEACHING YOUR CHILDREN THE WORD OF GOD

These commandments that I give you today are to be upon your hearts. Impress them on your children. Talk about them when you sit at home and when you walk along the road, when you lie down and when you get up. Tie them as symbols on your hands and bind them on your foreheads. Write them on the doorframes of your houses and on your gates. Deuteronomy 6:6-9

For I have chosen him, so that he will direct his children and his household after him to keep the way of the Lord by doing what is right and just, so that the Lord will bring about for Abraham what he has promised him. Genesis 18:19

On that day tell your son, 'I do this because of what the Lord did for me when I came out of Egypt.' Exodus 13:8

Only be careful, and watch yourselves closely so that you do not forget the things your eyes have seen or let them slip from your heart as long as you live. Teach them to your children and to their children after them. Remember the day you stood before the Lord your God at Horeb, when he said to me, "Assemble the people before me to hear my words so that they may learn to revere me as long as they live in the land and may teach them to their children."
Deuteronomy 4:9-10

Teach them to your children, talking about them when you sit at home and when you walk along the road, when you lie down and when you get up. Deuteronomy 11:19

My father could talk it, and, by the grace of God, he lived it. He had not only a talking but a "walking" knowledge of the Scriptures. - Vance Havner

But if serving the Lord seems undesirable to you, then choose for yourselves this day whom you will serve, whether the gods your forefathers served beyond the River, or the gods of the Amorites, in whose land you are living. But as for me and my household, we will serve the Lord. Joshua 24:15

Train your child in the way in which you know you should have gone yourself. - Charles H. Spurgeon

We will not hide them from their children; we will tell the next generation the praiseworthy deeds of the Lord, his power, and the wonders he has done. He decreed statutes for Jacob and established the law in Israel, which he commanded our forefathers to teach their children, so the next generation would know them, even the children yet to be born, and they in turn would tell their children. Then they would put their trust in God and would not forget his deeds but would keep his commands. Psalms 78:4-7

Train a child in the way he should go, and when he is old he will not turn from it. Proverbs 22:6

All your sons will be taught by the Lord, and great will be your children's peace. Isaiah 54:13

CHILDREN AND TEENAGERS

Honor your father and your mother, as the Lord your God has commanded you, so that you may live long and that it may go well with you in the land the Lord your God is giving you.

Deuteronomy 5:16

Each of you must respect his mother and father, and you must observe my Sabbaths. I am the Lord your God. Leviticus 19:3

Cursed is the man who dishonors his father or his mother. Then all the people shall say, Amen! Deuteronomy 27:16

My son, keep your father's commands and do not forsake your mother's teaching. Proverbs 6:20

Now then, my sons, listen to me; blessed are those who keep my ways. Proverbs 8:32

The proverbs of Solomon: A wise son brings joy to his father, but a foolish son grief to his mother. Proverbs 10:1

A wise son heeds his father's instruction, but a mocker does not listen to rebuke. Proverbs 13:1

A fool spurns his father's discipline, but whoever heeds correction shows prudence. Proverbs 15:5

Even a child is known by his actions, by whether his conduct is pure and right. Proverbs 20:11

Listen to your father, who gave you life, and do not despise your mother when she is old. Proverbs 23:22

The father of a righteous man has great joy; he who has a wise son delights in him. May your father and mother be glad; may she who gave you birth rejoice! My son, give me your heart and let your eyes keep to my ways. Proverbs 23:24-26

He who keeps the law is a discerning son, but a companion of gluttons disgraces his father. Proverbs 28:7

You know the commandments: Do not commit adultery, do not murder, do not steal, do not give false testimony, honor your father and mother. Luke 18:20

Children, obey your parents in the Lord, for this is right. Honor your father and mother—which is the first commandment with a promise—that it may go well with you and that you may enjoy long life on the earth. Ephesians 6:1-3

Children, obey your parents in everything, for this pleases the Lord.
Colossians 3:20

DATING AND ENGAGEMENTS

QUESTIONS TO THINK ABOUT OR ASK

1. Are they really committed to a personal relationship with JESUS CHRIST?

Do not be yoked together with unbelievers. For what do righteousness and wickedness have in common? Or what fellowship can light have with darkness? What harmony is there between Christ and Belial? What does a believer have in common with an unbeliever? 2 Corinthians 6:14-15

What agreement is there between the temple of God and idols? For we are the temple of the living God. As God has said: "I will live with them and walk among them, and I will be their God, and they will be my people." "Therefore come out from them and be separate, says the Lord. Touch no unclean thing, and I will receive you." "I will be a Father to you, and you will be my sons and daughters, says the Lord Almighty." 2 Corinthians 6:16-18

Blessed is the man who does not walk in the counsel of the wicked or stand in the way of sinners or sit in the seat of mockers.
Psalms 1:1

You cannot drink the cup of the Lord and the cup of demons too; you cannot have a part in both the Lord's table and the table of demons. 1 Corinthians 10:21

Do not be misled: "Bad company corrupts good character."
1 Corinthians 15:33

Have nothing to do with the fruitless deeds of darkness, but rather expose them. Ephesians 5:11

Since, then, you have been raised with Christ, set your hearts on things above, where Christ is seated at the right hand of God.
Colossians 3:1

You adulterous people, don't you know that friendship with the world is hatred toward God? Anyone who chooses to be a friend of the world becomes an enemy of God. James 4:4

2. **Who created your relationship? Was it GOD or you?**

3. **Is your relationship a result of impatience or loneliness?**

4. **Do they have a contentious spirit?**

5. **Are they lazy or do they have a poverty-stricken mentality?**

6. **Do they have good common sense (understanding)?**

7. **Do they have generational sins or curses that could affect your relationship?**

8. **Will this relationship hinder or distract you from your relationship with JESUS CHRIST?**

9. **Did you ask GOD before making your decision for marriage?**

> *You can live happily married ever after or un-happily married ever after. It all depends on if you listen and obey God's direction in choosing the right mate to marry.*

FRIENDS

A friend loves at all times, and a brother is born for adversity.
Proverbs 17:17

A man of many companions may come to ruin, but there is a friend who sticks closer than a brother. Proverbs 18:24

The man of many friends [a friend of all the world will prove himself a bad friend, but there is a friend who sticks closer than a brother.
Proverbs 18:24 AMP

A man of many companions may come to ruin, but there is a friend who sticks closer than a brother. Proverbs 18:24 NIV

Wealth brings many friends, but a poor man's friend deserts him.
Proverbs 19:4

> *A friend is the one who comes in when the whole world has gone out. - Anonymous*

Two are better than one, because they have a good return for their work: If one falls down, his friend can help him up. But pity the man who falls and has no one to help him up! Also, if two lie down together, they will keep warm. But how can one keep warm alone? Though one may be overpowered, two can defend themselves. A cord of three strands is not quickly broken. Ecclesiastes 4:9-12

Many curry favor with a ruler, and everyone is the friend of a man who gives gifts. Proverbs 19:6

A despairing man should have the devotion of his friends, even though he forsakes the fear of the Almighty. Job 6:14

He who loves a pure heart and whose speech is gracious will have the king for his friend. Proverbs 22:11

Wounds from a friend can be trusted, but an enemy multiplies kisses.
Proverbs 27:6

A real friend covers your sins and protects your reputation in public and rebukes and admonishes you in private.

Perfume and incense bring joy to the heart, and the pleasantness of one's friend springs from his earnest counsel. Do not forsake your friend and the friend of your father, and do not go to your brother's house when disaster strikes you—better a neighbor nearby than a brother far away. Proverbs 27:9-10

As iron sharpens iron, so one man sharpens another. Proverbs 27:17

Greater love has no one than this, that he lay down his life for his friends. You are my friends if you do what I command. I no longer call you servants, because a servant does not know his master's business. Instead, I have called you friends, for everything that I learned from my Father I have made known to you. John 15:13-14

I no longer call you servants, because a servant does not know his master's business. Instead, I have called you friends, for everything that I learned from my Father I have made known to you.
John 15:15

And the scripture was fulfilled that says, "Abraham believed God, and it was credited to him as righteousness," and he was called God's friend. James 2:23

AVOIDING OR BREAKING BAD RELATIONSHIPS

Blessed is the man who does not walk in the counsel of the wicked or stand in the way of sinners or sit in the seat of mockers.
Psalms 1:1

Away from me, you evildoers, that I may keep the commands of my God! Psalms 119:115

Leave your simple ways and you will live; walk in the way of understanding. Proverbs 9:6

The plans of the righteous are just, but the advice of the wicked is deceitful. Proverbs 12:5

He who walks with the wise grows wise, but a companion of fools suffers harm. Proverbs 13:20

Stay away from a foolish man, for you will not find knowledge on his lips. Proverbs 14:7

Better to be lowly in spirit and among the oppressed than to share plunder with the proud. Proverbs 16:19

A violent man entices his neighbor and leads him down a path that is not good. Proverbs 16:29

A man who strays from the path of understanding comes to rest in the company of the dead. Proverbs 21:16

Do not make friends with a hot-tempered man, do not associate with one easily angered, or you may learn his ways and get yourself ensnared. Proverbs 22:24-25

Do not envy wicked men, do not desire their company;
Proverbs 24:1

Fear the Lord and the king, my son, and do not join with the rebellious, for those two will send sudden destruction upon them, and who knows what calamities they can bring? Proverbs 24:21-22

He who keeps the law is a discerning son, but a companion of gluttons disgraces his father. Proverbs 28:7

A man who loves wisdom brings joy to his father, but a companion of prostitutes squanders his wealth. Proverbs 29:3

I never sat in the company of revelers, never made merry with them; I sat alone because your hand was on me and you had filled me with indignation. Jeremiah 15:17

Blessed are you when men hate you, when they exclude you and insult you and reject your name as evil, because of the Son of Man.
Luke 6:22

When Jesus spoke again to the people, he said, "I am the light of the world. Whoever follows me will never walk in darkness, but will have the light of life." John 8:12

I have come into the world as a light, so that no one who believes in me should stay in darkness. John 12:46

I have written you in my letter not to associate with sexually immoral people—not at all meaning the people of this world who are immoral, or the greedy and swindlers, or idolaters. In that case you would have to leave this world. But now I am writing you that you must not associate with anyone who calls himself a brother but is sexually immoral or greedy, an idolater or a slanderer, a drunkard or a swindler. With such a man do not even eat.
1 Corinthians 5:9-11

You cannot drink the cup of the Lord and the cup of demons too; you cannot have a part in both the Lord's table and the table of demons. 1 Corinthians 10:21

Do not be misled: "Bad company corrupts good character."
1 Corinthians 15:33

Do not be yoked together with unbelievers. For what do righteousness and wickedness have in common? Or what fellowship can light have with darkness? What harmony is there between Christ and Belial? What does a believer have in common with an unbeliever? 2 Corinthians 6:14-15

What agreement is there between the temple of God and idols? For we are the temple of the living God. As God has said: "I will live with them and walk among them, and I will be their God, and they will be my people. Therefore come out from them and be separate, says the Lord. Touch no unclean thing, and I will receive you. I will be a Father to you, and you will be my sons and daughters, says the Lord Almighty." 2 Corinthians 6:16-18

Have nothing to do with the fruitless deeds of darkness, but rather expose them. Ephesians 5:11

Since, then, you have been raised with Christ, set your hearts on things above, where Christ is seated at the right hand of God.
Colossians 3:1

Avoid every kind of evil. 1 Thessalonians 5:22

You adulterous people, don't you know that friendship with the world is hatred toward God? Anyone who chooses to be a friend of the world becomes an enemy of God. James 4:4

Salt seasons, purifies and preserves: But somebody ought to remind us that salt also irritates. Real living Christianity rubs this world the wrong way. - Vance Havner

PREPARING THE MIND AND HEART TO RECEIVE GOD'S BLESSING

GOD WANTS YOU TO PROSPER FINANCIALLY

But remember the Lord your God, for it is he who gives you the ability to produce wealth, and so confirms his covenant, which he swore to your forefathers, as it is today. Deuteronomy 8:18

For the Lord your God will bless you as he has promised, and you will lend to many nations but will borrow from none. You will rule over many nations but none will rule over you. Deuteronomy 15:6

The Lord will open the heavens, the storehouse of his bounty, to send rain on your land in season and to bless all the work of your hands. You will lend to many nations but will borrow from none.
Deuteronomy 28:12

If they obey and serve him, they will spend the rest of their days in prosperity and their years in contentment. Job 36:11

You prepare a table before me in the presence of my enemies. You anoint my head with oil; my cup overflows. Psalms 23:5

Let them shout for joy, and be glad, that favour my righteous cause: yea, let them say continually, Let the Lord be magnified, which hath pleasure in the prosperity of his servant. Psalms 35:27 KJV

May those who delight in my vindication shout for joy and gladness; may they always say, The Lord be exalted, who delights in the well-being of his servant. Psalms 35:27

For the Lord God is a sun and shield; the Lord bestows favor and honor; no good thing does he withhold from those whose walk is blameless. Psalms 84:11

Bestowing wealth on those who love me and making their treasuries full. Proverbs 8:21

371

I know that there is nothing better for men than to be happy and do good while they live. That everyone may eat and drink, and find satisfaction in all his toil—this is the gift of God.

Ecclesiastes 3:12-13

So I saw that there is nothing better for a man than to enjoy his work, because that is his lot. For who can bring him to see what will happen after him? Ecclesiastes 3:22

Do not be afraid, little flock, for your Father has been pleased to give you the kingdom. Luke 12:32

The thief comes only to steal and kill and destroy; I have come that they may have life, and have it to the full. John 10:10

He who did not spare his own Son, but gave him up for us all—how will he not also, along with him, graciously give us all things?

Romans 8:32

The biggest lie ever told; is that
God wants his children to be poor.

And God is able to make all grace abound to you, so that in all things at all times, having all that you need, you will abound in every good work. 2 Corinthians 9:8

Now to him who is able to do immeasurably more than all we ask or imagine, according to his power that is at work within us.

Ephesians 3:20

For you know the grace of our Lord Jesus Christ, that though he was rich, yet for your sakes he became poor, so that you through his poverty might become rich. 2 Corinthians 8:9

God has given us two hands - one for receiving and
the other for giving. - Billy Graham

His divine power has given us everything we need for life and godliness through our knowledge of him who called us by his own glory and goodness. 2 Peter 1:3

GIVING IN THE RIGHT ATTITUDE

Each man should give what he has decided in his heart to give, not reluctantly or under compulsion, for God loves a cheerful giver.
2 Corinthians 9:7

Let each one [give] as he has made up his own mind and purposed in his heart, not reluctantly or sorrowfully or under compulsion, for God loves (that is, He takes pleasure in, prizes above other things, and is unwilling to abandon or to do without) a cheerful (joyous, prompt-to-do-it) giver—whose heart is in his giving.
2 Corinthians 9:7 AMP

Whoever watches the wind will not plant; whoever looks at the clouds will not reap. Ecclesiastes 11:4

He who observes the wind [and waits for all conditions to be favorable] will not sow, and he who regards the clouds will not reap.
Ecclesiastes 11:4 AMP

Be careful not to do your 'acts of righteousness' before men, to be seen by them. If you do, you will have no reward from your Father in heaven. So when you give to the needy, do not announce it with trumpets, as the hypocrites do in the synagogues and on the streets, to be honored by men. I tell you the truth, they have received their reward in full. But when you give to the needy, do not let your left hand know what your right hand is doing, so that your giving may be in secret. Then your Father, who sees what is done in secret, will reward you. Matthew 6:1-4

From what you have, take an offering for the Lord. Everyone who is willing is to bring to the Lord an offering of gold, silver and bronze; Exodus 35:5

And everyone who was willing and whose heart moved him came and brought an offering to the Lord for the work on the Tent of Meeting, for all its service, and for the sacred garments. All who were willing, men and women alike, came and brought gold jewelry of all kinds: brooches, earrings, rings and ornaments. They all presented their gold as a wave offering to the Lord.
Exodus 35:21-22

All the Israelite men and women who were willing brought to the Lord freewill offerings for all the work the Lord through Moses had commanded them to do. Exodus 35:29

TRUE RICHES

Do not store up for yourselves treasures on earth, where moth and rust destroy, and where thieves break in and steal. But store up for yourselves treasures in heaven, where moth and rust do not destroy, and where thieves do not break in and steal. For where your treasure is, there your heart will be also. Matthew 6:19-21

Humility and the fear of the Lord bring wealth and honor and life.
Proverbs 22:4

A faithful man will be richly blessed, but one eager to get rich will not go unpunished. Proverbs 28:20

You must have accurate and honest weights and measures, so that you may live long in the land the Lord your God is giving you. For the Lord your God detests anyone who does these things, anyone who deals dishonestly. Deuteronomy 25:15-16

You really save in this life only that which you spend for the Lord. Under the guidance of the Holy Spirit every expenditure is an investment. The Bank of heaven is sound and pays eternal dividends. - Vance Havner

Wisdom, like an inheritance, is a good thing and benefits those who see the sun. Wisdom is a shelter as money is a shelter, but the advantage of knowledge is this: that wisdom preserves the life of its possessor. Ecclesiastes 7:11-12

DO NOT PUT YOUR TRUST OR HOPE IN MONEY

For the love of money is a root of all kinds of evil. Some people, eager for money, have wandered from the faith and pierced themselves with many griefs. 1 Timothy 6:10

Command those who are rich in this present world not to be arrogant nor to put their hope in wealth, which is so uncertain, but to put their hope in God, who richly provides us with everything for our enjoyment. Command them to do good, to be rich in good deeds, and to be generous and willing to share. In this way they will lay up treasure for themselves as a firm foundation for the coming age, so that they may take hold of the life that is truly life.

1 Timothy 6:17-19

Those who trust in their wealth and boast of their great riches? No man can redeem the life of another or give to God a ransom for him. Psalms 49:6-7

> *Fortune does not so much change men as it unmasks them.- Anonymous*

Do not trust in extortion or take pride in stolen goods; though your riches increase, do not set your heart on them. Psalms 62:10

Wealth is worthless in the day of wrath, but righteousness delivers from death. Proverbs 11:4

Whoever trusts in his riches will fall, but the righteous will thrive like a green leaf. Proverbs 11:28

One man pretends to be rich, yet has nothing; another pretends to be poor, yet has great wealth. Proverbs 13:7

Whoever loves money never has money enough; whoever loves wealth is never satisfied with his income. This too is meaningless. As goods increase, so do those who consume them. And what benefit are they to the owner except to feast his eyes on them? The sleep of a laborer is sweet, whether he eats little or much, but the abundance of a rich man permits him no sleep.

Ecclesiastes 5:10-12

> *Money is a terrible master but an excellent servant.*
> *- P. T. Barnum*

Two things I ask of you, O Lord; do not refuse me before I die: Keep falsehood and lies far from me; give me neither poverty nor riches, but give me only my daily bread. Otherwise, I may have too much and disown you and say, 'Who is the Lord?' Or I may become poor and steal, and so dishonor the name of my God.

Proverbs 30:7-9

CONTENTMENT

Better a little with the fear of the Lord than great wealth with turmoil. Proverbs 15:16

Do not wear yourself out to get rich; have the wisdom to show restraint. Cast but a glance at riches, and they are gone, for they will surely sprout wings and fly off to the sky like an eagle.

Proverbs 23:4-5

Keep your lives free from the love of money and be content with what you have, because God has said, "Never will I leave you; never will I forsake you." Hebrews 13:5

THE PURPOSE FOR FINANCES

TO SPREAD THE GOSPEL OF JESUS CHRIST

In the last days the mountain of the Lord's temple will be established as chief among the mountains; it will be raised above the hills, and all nations will stream to it. Isaiah 2:2

And this gospel of the kingdom will be preached in the whole world as a testimony to all nations, and then the end will come.
Matthew 24:14

Therefore go and make disciples of all nations, baptizing them in the name of the Father and of the Son and of the Holy Spirit,
Matthew 28:19

He said to them, Go into all the world and preach the good news to all creation. Mark 16:15

Then the disciples went out and preached everywhere, and the Lord worked with them and confirmed his word by the signs that accompanied it. Mark 16:20

We can go to the mission field in person, by prayer, by provision, or by proxy as we help send someone else.
- Vance Havner

He told them, The harvest is plentiful, but the workers are few. Ask the Lord of the harvest, therefore, to send out workers into his harvest field. Luke 10:2

Then the master told his servant, Go out to the roads and country lanes and make them come in, so that my house will be full.
Luke 14:23

And repentance and forgiveness of sins will be preached in his name to all nations, beginning at Jerusalem. You are witnesses of these things. Luke 24:47-48

But I, when I am lifted up from the earth, will draw all men to myself. John 12:32

But you will receive power when the Holy Spirit comes on you; and you will be my witnesses in Jerusalem, and in all Judea and Samaria, and to the ends of the earth. Acts 1:8

How, then, can they call on the one they have not believed in? And how can they believe in the one of whom they have not heard? And how can they hear without someone preaching to them? And how can they preach unless they are sent? As it is written, "How beautiful are the feet of those who bring good news!" Romans 10:14-15

But I ask: Did they not hear? Of course they did: Their voice has gone out into all the earth, their words to the ends of the world.
Romans 10:18

We must plunder hell to populate heaven.
- Reinhart Bunkie

Preach the Word; be prepared in season and out of season; correct, rebuke and encourage—with great patience and careful instruction. 2 Timothy 4:2

TO HELP THE POOR

There will always be poor people in the land. Therefore I command you to be openhanded toward your brothers and toward the poor and needy in your land. Deuteronomy 15:11

He who despises his neighbor sins, but blessed is he who is kind to the needy. Proverbs 14:21

Defend the cause of the weak and fatherless; maintain the rights of the poor and oppressed. Rescue the weak and needy; deliver them from the hand of the wicked. Psalms 82:3-4

The Bible is very clear on the point that if we have money enough to live well, and do not share with others in need, it is questionable whether God's love is in us at all. - G. S.

If a man shuts his ears to the cry of the poor, he too will cry out and not be answered. Proverbs 21:13

And if you spend yourselves in behalf of the hungry and satisfy the needs of the oppressed, then your light will rise in the darkness, and your night will become like the noonday. Isaiah 58:10

John answered, "The man with two tunics should share with him who has none, and the one who has food should do the same."
Luke 3:11

Then Jesus said to his host, "When you give a luncheon or dinner, do not invite your friends, your brothers or relatives, or your rich neighbors; if you do, they may invite you back and so you will be repaid. But when you give a banquet, invite the poor, the crippled, the lame, the blind, and you will be blessed. Although they cannot repay you, you will be repaid at the resurrection of the righteous."
Luke 14:12-14

Suppose a brother or sister is without clothes and daily food. If one of you says to him, "Go, I wish you well; keep warm and well fed," but does nothing about his physical needs, what good is it? In the same way, faith by itself, if it is not accompanied by action, is dead.
James 2:15-17

When you commit to giving finances for the spreading of the gospel of Christ and feeding the poor, God will supply all of your needs over and above.

GOD'S FINANCIAL BUSINESS PLAN FOR YOU

TITHING AND OFFERINGS

A tithe of everything from the land, whether grain from the soil or fruit from the trees, belongs to the Lord; it is holy to the Lord. If a man redeems any of his tithe, he must add a fifth of the value to it.
Leviticus 27:30-31

When you have entered the land the Lord your God is giving you as an inheritance and have taken possession of it and settled in it, take some of the firstfruits of all that you produce from the soil of the land the Lord your God is giving you and put them in a basket. Then go to the place the Lord your God will choose as a dwelling for his Name Deuteronomy 26:1-2

He brought us to this place and gave us this land, a land flowing with milk and honey; and now I bring the firstfruits of the soil that you, O Lord, have given me. Place the basket before the Lord your God and bow down before him. And you and the Levites and the aliens among you shall rejoice in all the good things the Lord your God has given to you and your household. Deuteronomy 26:9-11

Will a man rob God? Yet you rob me. But you ask, How do we rob you? In tithes and offerings. You are under a curse—the whole nation of you—because you are robbing me. Bring the whole tithe into the storehouse, that there may be food in my house. Test me in this, says the Lord Almighty, and see if I will not throw open the floodgates of heaven and pour out so much blessing that you will not have room enough for it. Malachi 3:8-10

SOWING SEEDS

As the rain and the snow come down from heaven, and do not return to it without watering the earth and making it bud and flourish, so that it yields seed for the sower and bread for the eater, so is my word that goes out from my mouth: It will not return to me empty, but will accomplish what I desire and achieve the purpose for which I sent it. Isaiah 55:10-11

He who goes out weeping, carrying seed to sow, will return with songs of joy, carrying sheaves with him. Psalms 126:6

Give, and it will be given to you. A good measure, pressed down, shaken together and running over, will be poured into your lap. For with the measure you use, it will be measured to you. Luke 6:38

Remember this: Whoever sows sparingly will also reap sparingly, and whoever sows generously will also reap generously.
2 Corinthians 9:6

Sow your financial seeds as soon as you receive your increase. Faster sowers have a faster harvest.
- Dr. John Avanzini

Now he who supplies seed to the sower and bread for food will also supply and increase your store of seed and will enlarge the harvest of your righteousness. You will be made rich in every way so that you can be generous on every occasion, and through us your generosity will result in thanksgiving to God.
2 Corinthians 9:10-11

Do not be deceived: God cannot be mocked. A man reaps what he sows. Galatians 6:7

Know the spirit of the person that toils the soil that you plant your seed into.

Sow your seed in the morning, and at evening let not your hands be idle, for you do not know which will succeed, whether this or that, or whether both will do equally well. Ecclesiastes 11:6

One man gives freely, yet gains even more; another withholds unduly, but comes to poverty. Proverbs 11:24

Cast your bread upon the waters, for after many days you will find it again. Ecclesiastes 11:1

REAPING THE HARVEST

Let us not become weary in doing good, for at the proper time we will reap a harvest if we do not give up. Galatians 6:9

I tell you the truth, Jesus replied, no one who has left home or brothers or sisters or mother or father or children or fields for me and the gospel will fail to receive a hundred times as much in this present age (homes, brothers, sisters, mothers, children and fields—and with them, persecutions) and in the age to come, eternal life.

Mark 10:29-30

The Dead Sea is a dead sea because it continually receives and never gives. -Anonymous

END TIME TRANSFER OF WEALTH TO CHRISTIANS

For I envied the arrogant when I saw the prosperity of the wicked. They have no struggles; their bodies are healthy and strong. They are free from the burdens common to man; they are not plagued by human ills. Therefore pride is their necklace; they clothe themselves with violence. From their callous hearts comes iniquity; the evil conceits of their minds know no limits. They scoff, and speak with malice; in their arrogance they threaten oppression. Their mouths lay claim to heaven, and their tongues take possession of the earth. Therefore their people turn to them and drink up waters in abundance. They say, "How can God know? Does the Most High have knowledge?" This is what the wicked are like—always carefree, they increase in wealth. Surely in vain have I kept my heart pure; in vain have I washed my hands in innocence. All day long I have been plagued; I have been punished every morning. If I had said, "I will speak thus," I would have betrayed your children. When I tried to understand all this, it was oppressive to me till I entered the sanctuary of God; then I understood their final destiny. Surely you place them on slippery ground; you cast them down to ruin. How suddenly are they destroyed, completely swept away by terrors! Psalms 73:3-19

383

Here is the fate God allots to the wicked, the heritage a ruthless man receives from the Almighty: However many his children, their fate is the sword; his offspring will never have enough to eat. The plague will bury those who survive him, and their widows will not weep for them. Though he heaps up silver like dust and clothes like piles of clay, what he lays up the righteous will wear, and the innocent will divide his silver. Job 27:13-17

In order for God to intrust you with the task of distributing the wealth of the wicked into God ordained gospel preaching ministries and legitimate feeding programs for starving nations, you must be proven faithful in the giving of your tithes and offering. Whoever can be trusted with very little can also be trusted with much, and whoever is dishonest with very little will also be dishonest with much. Luke 16:10

He who increases his wealth by exorbitant interest amasses it for another, who will be kind to the poor. Proverbs 28:8

To the man who pleases him, God gives wisdom, knowledge and happiness, but to the sinner he gives the task of gathering and storing up wealth to hand it over to the one who pleases God. This too is meaningless, a chasing after the wind. Ecclesiastes 2:26

If God can get it through you, God will give it to you.
- E. V. Hill

Now listen, you rich people, weep and wail because of the misery that is coming upon you. Your wealth has rotted, and moths have eaten your clothes. Your gold and silver are corroded. Their corrosion will testify against you and eat your flesh like fire. You have hoarded wealth in the last days. James 5:1-3

LOANS

Let no debt remain outstanding, except the continuing debt to love one another, for he who loves his fellowman has fulfilled the law.
Romans 13:8

The rich rule over the poor, and the borrower is servant to the lender.
Proverbs 22:7

For the Lord your God will bless you as he has promised, and you will lend to many nations but will borrow from none. You will rule over many nations but none will rule over you. Deuteronomy 15:6

If you lend money to one of my people among you who is needy, do not be like a moneylender; charge him no interest. Exodus 22:25

You must not lend him money at interest or sell him food at a profit.
Leviticus 25:37

Do not charge your brother interest, whether on money or food or anything else that may earn interest. You may charge a foreigner interest, but not a brother Israelite, so that the Lord your God may bless you in everything you put your hand to in the land you are entering to possess. Deuteronomy 23:19-20

The Lord will open the heavens, the storehouse of his bounty, to send rain on your land in season and to bless all the work of your hands. You will lend to many nations but will borrow from none.
Deuteronomy 28:12

The wicked borrow and do not repay, but the righteous give generously; Psalms 37:21

CO-SIGNING FOR OTHERS

My son, if you have put up security for your neighbor, if you have struck hands in pledge for another, if you have been trapped by what you said, ensnared by the words of your mouth, then do this, my son, to free yourself, since you have fallen into your neighbor's hands: Go and humble yourself; press your plea with your neighbor! Allow no sleep to your eyes, no slumber to your eyelids. Free yourself, like a gazelle from the hand of the hunter, like a bird from the snare of the fowler. Proverbs 6:1-5

He who puts up security for another will surely suffer, but whoever refuses to strike hands in pledge is safe. Proverbs 11:15

A man lacking in judgment strikes hands in pledge and puts up security for his neighbor. Proverbs 17:18

Take the garment of one who puts up security for a stranger; hold it in pledge if he does it for a wayward woman. Proverbs 20:16

385

THE AFRICAN CULTURAL HERITAGE TOPICAL BIBLE

The rich rule over the poor, and the borrower is servant to the lender.
Proverbs 22:7

Do not be a man who strikes hands in pledge or puts up security for debts; if you lack the means to pay, your very bed will be snatched from under you. Proverbs 22:26-27

Take the garment of one who puts up security for a stranger; hold it in pledge if he does it for a wayward woman. Proverbs 27:13

OVERCOMING SIN

SIN

All wrongdoing is sin, and there is sin that does not lead to death.
1 John 5:17

Jesus replied, "I tell you the truth, everyone who sins is a slave to sin. John 8:34

There are six things the Lord hates, seven that are detestable to him: haughty eyes, a lying tongue, hands that shed innocent blood, a heart that devises wicked schemes, feet that are quick to rush into evil, a false witness who pours out lies and a man who stirs up dissension among brothers. Proverbs 6:16-19

The acts of the sinful nature are obvious: sexual immorality, impurity and debauchery; idolatry and witchcraft; hatred, discord, jealousy, fits of rage, selfish ambition, dissensions, factions and envy; drunkenness, orgies, and the like. I warn you, as I did before, that those who live like this will not inherit the kingdom of God.
Galatians 5:19-21

He who does what is sinful is of the devil, because the devil has been sinning from the beginning. The reason the Son of God appeared was to destroy the devil's work. No one who is born of God will continue to sin, because God's seed remains in him; he cannot go on sinning, because he has been born of God. This is how we know who the children of God are and who the children of the devil are: Anyone who does not do what is right is not a child of God; nor is anyone who does not love his brother. 1 John 3:8-10

No one who lives in him keeps on sinning. No one who continues to sin has either seen him or known him. 1 John 3:6

No one who is born of God will continue to sin, because God's seed remains in him; he cannot go on sinning, because he has been born of God. 1 John 3:9

We know that anyone born of God does not continue to sin; the one who was born of God keeps him safe, and the evil one cannot harm him. 1 John 5:18

There is a way that seems right to a man, but in the end it leads to death. Proverbs 16:25

> *The Bible will keep you from sin, or sin will keep you from the Bible. -D. L. Moody*

But the man who has doubts is condemned if he eats, because his eating is not from faith; and everything that does not come from faith is sin. Romans 14:23

But the man who has doubts-misgivings, an uneasy conscience-about eating, and then eats [perhaps because of you], stands condemned [before God], because he is not true to his convictions and he does not act from faith. For whatever does not originate and proceed from faith is sin—that is, whatever is done without a conviction of its approval by God is sinful. Romans 14:23 AMP

SECRET SINS

But if you fail to do this, you will be sinning against the Lord; and you may be sure that your sin will find you out. Numbers 32:23

He who conceals his sins does not prosper, but whoever confesses and renounces them finds mercy. Proverbs 28:13

For God will bring every deed into judgment, including every hidden thing, whether it is good or evil. Ecclesiastes 12:14

For whatever is hidden is meant to be disclosed, and whatever is concealed is meant to be brought out into the open. Mark 4:22

For there is nothing hidden that will not be disclosed, and nothing concealed that will not be known or brought out into the open.
Luke 8:17

There is nothing concealed that will not be disclosed, or hidden that will not be made known. What you have said in the dark will be heard in the daylight, and what you have whispered in the ear in the inner rooms will be proclaimed from the roofs. Luke 12:2-3

This will take place on the day when God will judge men's secrets through Jesus Christ, as my gospel declares. Romans 2:16

THE PLEASURE OF SIN IS ONLY TEMPORARY

He chose to be mistreated along with the people of God rather than to enjoy the pleasures of sin for a short time. Hebrews 11:25

DELIBERATE AND WILLFUL SIN

What shall we say, then? Shall we go on sinning so that grace may increase? Romans 6:1

No one who lives in him keeps on sinning. No one who continues to sin has either seen him or known him. 1 John 3:6

No one who is born of God will continue to sin, because God's seed remains in him; he cannot go on sinning, because he has been born of God. 1 John 3:9

We know that anyone born of God does not continue to sin; the one who was born of God keeps him safe, and the evil one cannot harm him. 1 John 5:18

> *We are not to tolerate evil but abhor it. The mood of the age is to put up with evil, allow it, and then move easily to play with it and finally practice it.*
> *- Vance Havner*

Anyone who runs ahead and does not continue in the teaching of Christ does not have God; whoever continues in the teaching has both the Father and the Son. 2 John 1:9

SOWING SIN AND REAPING THE CONSEQUENCES OF SIN

Anyone who does wrong will be repaid for his wrong, and there is no favoritism. Colossians 3:25

As I have observed, those who plow evil and those who sow trouble reap it. Job 4:8

THE AFRICAN CULTURAL HERITAGE TOPICAL BIBLE

Misfortune pursues the sinner, but prosperity is the reward of the righteous. Proverbs 13:21

If a man pays back evil for good, evil will never leave his house. Proverbs 17:13

He who sows wickedness reaps trouble, and the rod of his fury will be destroyed. Proverbs 22:8

If a man digs a pit, he will fall into it; if a man rolls a stone, it will roll back on him. Proverbs 26:27

He who leads the upright along an evil path will fall into his own trap, but the blameless will receive a good inheritance. Proverbs 28:10

Whoever digs a pit may fall into it; whoever breaks through a wall may be bitten by a snake. Ecclesiastes 10:8

They sow the wind and reap the whirlwind. The stalk has no head; it will produce no flour. Were it to yield grain, foreigners would swallow it up. Hosea 8:7

But you have planted wickedness, you have reaped evil, you have eaten the fruit of deception. Because you have depended on your own strength and on your many warriors. Hosea 10:13

For the wages of sin is death, but the gift of God is eternal life in Christ Jesus our Lord. Romans 6:23

Do not be deceived: God cannot be mocked. A man reaps what he sows. The one who sows to please his sinful nature, from that nature will reap destruction; the one who sows to please the Spirit, from the Spirit will reap eternal life. Galatians 6:7-8

A sinful lifestyle is spiritual insanity.

SIN GIVES satan ENTRANCE INTO YOUR LIFE

In your anger do not sin": Do not let the sun go down while you are still angry, and do not give the devil a foothold. Ephesians 4:26-27

I will not speak with you much longer, for the prince of this world is coming. He has no hold on me. John 14:30

Later Jesus found him at the temple and said to him, "See, you are well again. Stop sinning or something worse may happen to you."
John 5:14

If you forgive anyone, I also forgive him. And what I have forgiven—if there was anything to forgive—I have forgiven in the sight of Christ for your sake, in order that Satan might not outwit us. For we are not unaware of his schemes. 2 Corinthians 2:10-11

He must not be a recent convert, or he may become conceited and fall under the same judgment as the devil. He must also have a good reputation with outsiders, so that he will not fall into disgrace and into the devil's trap. 1 Timothy 3:6-7

And that they will come to their senses and escape from the trap of the devil, who has taken them captive to do his will.
2 Timothy 2:26

Nevertheless, I have a few things against you: You have people there who hold to the teaching of Balaam, who taught Balak to entice the Israelites to sin by eating food sacrificed to idols and by committing sexual immorality. Revelation 2:14

Then Peter came to Jesus and asked, "Lord, how many times shall I forgive my brother when he sins against me? Up to seven times?" Jesus answered, "I tell you, not seven times, but seventy-seven times. Therefore, the kingdom of heaven is like a king who wanted to settle accounts with his servants. Then the master called the servant in. 'You wicked servant,' he said, 'I canceled all that debt of yours because you begged me to. shouldn't you have had mercy on your fellow servant just as I had on you?' In anger his master turned him over to the jailers to be tortured, until he should pay back all he owed. "This is how my heavenly Father will treat each of you unless you forgive your brother from your heart."
Matthew 18:21-23,32-35

A LIFE OF SIN IS HARD

Stern discipline awaits him who leaves the path; he who hates correction will die. Proverbs 15:10

391

For the wages of sin is death, but the gift of God is eternal life in Christ Jesus our Lord. Romans 6:23

All his days the wicked man suffers torment, the ruthless through all the years stored up for him. Job 15:20

But all sinners will be destroyed; the future of the wicked will be cut off. Psalms 37:38

Some became fools through their rebellious ways and suffered affliction because of their iniquities. Psalms 107:17

In the paths of the wicked lie thorns and snares, but he who guards his soul stays far from them. Proverbs 22:5

But the wicked will be cut off from the land, and the unfaithful will be torn from it. Proverbs 2:22

Good understanding wins favor, but the way of the unfaithful is hard. Proverbs 13:15

An evil man is snared by his own sin, but a righteous one can sing and be glad. Proverbs 29:6

WHAT SHOULD I DO WHEN I SIN

1. REPENT

DEFINITION: - Repent means change of mind with regard to sin, a sorrow for sin.

Or do you show contempt for the riches of his kindness, tolerance and patience, not realizing that God's kindness leads you toward repentance? Romans 2:4

The Lord is not slow in keeping his promise, as some understand slowness. He is patient with you, not wanting anyone to perish, but everyone to come to repentance. 2 Peter 3:9

I tell you, no! But unless you repent, you too will all perish.
Luke 13:3

Therefore, O house of Israel, I will judge you, each one according to his ways, declares the Sovereign Lord. Repent! Turn away from all your offenses; then sin will not be your downfall. Ezekiel 18:30

Godly sorrow brings repentance that leads to salvation and leaves no regret, but worldly sorrow brings death. 2 Corinthians 7:10

Say to them, 'As surely as I live, declares the Sovereign Lord, I take no pleasure in the death of the wicked, but rather that they turn from their ways and live. Turn! Turn from your evil ways! Why will you die, O house of Israel?' Ezekiel 33:11

"The time has come," he said. "The kingdom of God is near. Repent and believe the good news!" Mark 1:15

And saying, "Repent, for the kingdom of heaven is near."
Matthew 3:2

Repent, then, and turn to God, so that your sins may be wiped out, that times of refreshing may come from the Lord. Acts 3:19

From that time on Jesus began to preach, "Repent, for the kingdom of heaven is near." Matthew 4:17

I tell you that in the same way there will be more rejoicing in heaven over one sinner who repents than over ninety-nine righteous persons who do not need to repent. Luke 15:7

True repentance has a double aspect; it looks upon things past with a weeping eye, and upon the future with a watchful eye.- Robert Smith

When Jesus heard it, he saith unto them, They that are whole have no need of the physician, but they that are sick: I came not to call the righteous, but sinners to repentance. Mark 2:17 KJV

In the past God overlooked such ignorance, but now he commands all people everywhere to repent. Acts 17:30

I have not come to call the righteous, but sinners to repentance.
Luke 5:32

In the same way, I tell you, there is rejoicing in the presence of the angels of God over one sinner who repents. Luke 15:10

God exalted him to his own right hand as Prince and Savior that he might give repentance and forgiveness of sins to Israel. Acts 5:31

PROOF OF REPENTANCE

I have considered my ways and have turned my steps to your statutes. Psalms 119:59

Produce fruit in keeping with repentance. Matthew 3:8

First to those in Damascus, then to those in Jerusalem and in all Judea, and to the Gentiles also, I preached that they should repent and turn to God and prove their repentance by their deeds.
Acts 26:20

They claim to know God, but by their actions they deny him. They are detestable, disobedient and unfit for doing anything good.
Titus 1:16

True repentance is proceeded by a passionate commitment to obey God's Word.

2. CONFESS THE SIN

He who conceals his sins does not prosper, but whoever confesses and renounces them finds mercy. Proverbs 28:13

When anyone is guilty in any of these ways, he must confess in what way he has sinned. Leviticus 5:5

If we confess our sins, he is faithful and just and will forgive us our sins and purify us from all unrighteousness. 1 John 1:9

Those of Israelite descent had separated themselves from all foreigners. They stood in their places and confessed their sins and the wickedness of their fathers. Nehemiah 9:2

Then I acknowledged my sin to you and did not cover up my iniquity. I said, "I will confess my transgressions to the Lord"—and you forgave the guilt of my sin. Selah Psalms 32:5

Before you were even born God knew every sin that you would commit throughout your lifetime, therefore it is useless to run and hide from God. When you sin, run to God, repent, confess the sin, and humbly receive God's merciful forgiveness through the shed blood of his son Jesus Christ.

Confessing their sins, they were baptized by him in the Jordan River.
Matthew 3:6

Many of those who believed now came and openly confessed their evil deeds. Acts 19:18

Therefore confess your sins to each other and pray for each other so that you may be healed. The prayer of a righteous man is powerful and effective. James 5:16

3. STOP SINNING

In your struggle against sin, you have not yet resisted to the point of shedding your blood. Hebrews 12:4

You have not yet struggled and fought agonizingly against sin, nor have you yet resisted and withstood to the point of pouring our your [own] blood. Hebrews 12:4 AMP

If you put away the sin that is in your hand and allow no evil to dwell in your tent. Job 11:14

The night is nearly over; the day is almost here. So let us put aside the deeds of darkness and put on the armor of light. Romans 13:12

Therefore, O king, be pleased to accept my advice: Renounce your sins by doing what is right, and your wickedness by being kind to the oppressed. It may be that then your prosperity will continue.
Daniel 4:27

"No one, sir," she said. "Then neither do I condemn you," Jesus declared. "Go now and leave your life of sin." John 8:11

Put to death, therefore, whatever belongs to your earthly nature: sexual immorality, impurity, lust, evil desires and greed, which is idolatry. Colossians 3:5

Do not lie to each other, since you have taken off your old self with its practices. Colossians 3:9

Get rid of all bitterness, rage and anger, brawling and slander, along with every form of malice. Ephesians 4:31

Nor should there be obscenity, foolish talk or coarse joking, which are out of place, but rather thanksgiving. For of this you can be

sure: No immoral, impure or greedy person—such a man is an idolater—has any inheritance in the kingdom of Christ and of God.
Ephesians 5:4-5

Nevertheless, God's solid foundation stands firm, sealed with this inscription: "The Lord knows those who are his," and, "Everyone who confesses the name of the Lord must turn away from wickedness." 2 Timothy 2:19

Therefore, get rid of all moral filth and the evil that is so prevalent and humbly accept the word planted in you, which can save you.
James 1:21

Blunders we shall make and failures will shame our faces and dampen our eyes. But if we can manage not to remember what we ought to forget and not to forget what we ought to remember, then forgetting the things behind and stirring up our minds by way of remembrance, we shall press on for the prize. - Vance Havner

DELIVERANCE FROM SIN

She will give birth to a son, and you are to give him the name Jesus, because he will save his people from their sins.
Matthew 1:21

The next day John saw Jesus coming toward him and said, Look, the Lamb of God, who takes away the sin of the world! John 1:29

God made him who had no sin to be sin for us, so that in him we might become the righteousness of God. 2 Corinthians 5:21

You see, at just the right time, when we were still powerless, Christ died for the ungodly. Romans 5:6

But God demonstrates his own love for us in this: While we were still sinners, Christ died for us. Romans 5:8

Because through Christ Jesus the law of the Spirit of life set me free from the law of sin and death. Romans 8:2

Prayer will make a man cease from sin, or sin will entice a man to cease from prayer. - John Bunyan

That God was reconciling the world to himself in Christ, not counting men's sins against them. And he has committed to us the message of reconciliation. 2 Corinthians 5:19

Who gave himself for our sins to rescue us from the present evil age, according to the will of our God and Father. Galatians 1:4

And through him to reconcile to himself all things, whether things on earth or things in heaven, by making peace through his blood, shed on the cross. Colossians 1:20

GENERATIONAL (HEREDITARY) SINS

You shall not bow down to them or worship them; for I, the Lord your God, am a jealous God, punishing the children for the sin of the fathers to the third and fourth generation of those who hate me.
Exodus 20:5

The Lord is slow to anger, abounding in love and forgiving sin and rebellion. Yet he does not leave the guilty unpunished; he punishes the children for the sin of the fathers to the third and fourth generation. Numbers 14:18

You shall not bow down to them or worship them; for I, the Lord your God, am a jealous God, punishing the children for the sin of the fathers to the third and fourth generation of those who hate me, but showing love to a thousand generations of those who love me and keep my commandments. Deuteronomy 5:9-10

If a man denounces his friends for reward, the eyes of his children will fail. Job 17:5

In those days people will no longer say, 'The fathers have eaten sour grapes, and the children's teeth are set on edge.'
Jeremiah 31:29

But suppose this son has a son who sees all the sins his father commits, and though he sees them, he does not do such things: He withholds his hand from sin and takes no usury or excessive interest. He keeps my laws and follows my decrees. He will not die for his father's sin; he will surely live. But his father will die for his own sin, because he practiced extortion, robbed his brother and did what was wrong among his people. Ezekiel 18:14,17-18

Yet you ask, 'Why does the son not share the guilt of his father?' Since the son has done what is just and right and has been careful to keep all my decrees, he will surely live. The soul who sins is the one who will die. The son will not share the guilt of the father, nor will the father share the guilt of the son. The righteousness of the righteous man will be credited to him, and the wickedness of the wicked will be charged against him. Ezekiel 18:19-20

CURSES

DEFINITION 1:   A curse (from God) is righteous judgement against disobedience.

DEFINITION 2:   To Curse is to pray against, or wish evil against a person or thing.

I will bless those who bless you, and whoever curses you I will curse; and all peoples on earth will be blessed through you.
Genesis 12:3

How can I curse those whom God has not cursed? How can I denounce those whom the Lord has not denounced? Numbers 23:8

If a man curses his father or mother, his lamp will be snuffed out in pitch darkness. Proverbs 20:20

He who gives to the poor will lack nothing, but he who closes his eyes to them receives many curses. Proverbs 28:27

This is what the Lord says: Cursed is the one who trusts in man, who depends on flesh for his strength and whose heart turns away from the Lord. Jeremiah 17:5

Peter remembered and said to Jesus, "Rabbi, look! The fig tree you cursed has withered!" Mark 11:21

CURSES ACTIVATED BY DISOBEDIENCE TO GOD'S WORD

The curse if you disobey the commands of the Lord your God and turn from the way that I command you today by following other gods, which you have not known. Deuteronomy 11:28

The Lord's curse is on the house of the wicked, but he blesses the home of the righteous. Proverbs 3:33

Tell them that this is what the Lord, the God of Israel, says: Cursed is the man who does not obey the terms of this covenant.
Jeremiah 11:3

CURSES ACTIVATED BY WORDS

With the tongue we praise our Lord and Father, and with it we curse men, who have been made in God's likeness. Out of the same mouth come praise and cursing. My brothers, this should not be.
James 3:9-10

The tongue has the power of life and death, and those who love it will eat its fruit. Proverbs 18:21

HOW TO BREAK CURSES

Christ redeemed us from the curse of the law by becoming a curse for us, for it is written: "Cursed is everyone who is hung on a tree."
Galatians 3:13

1. Obey God's Word

See, I am setting before you today a blessing and a curse—the blessing if you obey the commands of the Lord your God that I am giving you today. Deuteronomy 11:26-27

This day I call heaven and earth as witnesses against you that I have set before you life and death, blessings and curses. Now choose life, so that you and your children may live. Deuteronomy 30:19

The Lord's curse is on the house of the wicked, but he blesses the home of the righteous. Proverbs 3:33

2. Pray blessings on your enemies.

But I tell you: Love your enemies and pray for those who persecute you. Matthew 5:44

Bless those who curse you, pray for those who mistreat you.
Luke 6:28

Bless those who persecute you; bless and do not curse.
Romans 12:14

RECEIVING GOD'S FORGIVENESS FOR YOUR SINS

SINS CLEANSED BY THE BLOOD OF JESUS

But now in Christ Jesus you who once were far away have been brought near through the blood of Christ. Ephesians 2:13

In whom we have redemption through his blood, even the forgiveness of sins. Colossians 1:14 KJV

In whom we have redemption, the forgiveness of sins.
Colossians 1:14

This is my blood of the covenant, which is poured out for many for the forgiveness of sins. Matthew 26:28

He did not enter by means of the blood of goats and calves; but he entered the Most Holy Place once for all by his own blood, having obtained eternal redemption. Hebrews 9:12

In fact, the law requires that nearly everything be cleansed with blood, and without the shedding of blood there is no forgiveness.
Hebrews 9:22

And from Jesus Christ, who is the faithful witness, the firstborn from the dead, and the ruler of the kings of the earth. To him who loves us and has freed us from our sins by his blood.
Revelation 1:5

GOD WILL FORGIVE YOUR SINS

If you return to the Lord, then your brothers and your children will be shown compassion by their captors and will come back to this land, for the Lord your God is gracious and compassionate. He will not turn his face from you if you return to him.
2 Chronicles 30:9

Blessed is he whose transgressions are forgiven, whose sins are covered. Blessed is the man whose sin the Lord does not count against him and in whose spirit is no deceit. Psalms 32:1-2

Then I acknowledged my sin to you and did not cover up my iniquity. I said, "I will confess my transgressions to the Lord"—and you forgave the guilt of my sin. Selah Psalms 32:5

You are forgiving and good, O Lord, abounding in love to all who call to you. Psalms 86:5

> *The forgiveness of God is the foundation of every bridge from a hopeless past to a courageos present.*
> *- George Adam Smith*

I have swept away your offenses like a cloud, your sins like the morning mist. Return to me, for I have redeemed you. Isaiah 44:22

Who is a God like you, who pardons sin and forgives the transgression of the remnant of his inheritance? You do not stay angry forever but delight to show mercy. You will again have compassion on us; you will tread our sins underfoot and hurl all our iniquities into the depths of the sea. Micah 7:18-19

Forgive us our debts, as we also have forgiven our debtors.
Matthew 6:12

For if you forgive men when they sin against you, your heavenly Father will also forgive you. But if you do not forgive men their sins, your Father will not forgive your sins. Matthew 6:14-15

In him we have redemption through his blood, the forgiveness of sins, in accordance with the riches of God's grace. Ephesians 1:7

For I will forgive their wickedness and will remember their sins no more. Hebrews 8:12

But when this priest had offered for all time one sacrifice for sins, he sat down at the right hand of God. Hebrews 10:12

Then he adds: "Their sins and lawless acts I will remember no more." And where these have been forgiven, there is no longer any sacrifice for sin. Hebrews 10:17-18

If we confess our sins, he is faithful and just and will forgive us our sins and purify us from all unrighteousness. 1 John 1:9

My dear children, I write this to you so that you will not sin. But if anybody does sin, we have one who speaks to the Father in our defense—Jesus Christ, the Righteous One. He is the atoning sacrifice for our sins, and not only for ours but also for the sins of the whole world. 1 John 2:1-2

GOD WILL NOT REMEMBER YOUR SINS

Remember not the sins of my youth and my rebellious ways; according to your love remember me, for you are good, O Lord.
Psalms 25:7

Do not hold against us the sins of the fathers; may your mercy come quickly to meet us, for we are in desperate need. Psalms 79:8

No longer will a man teach his neighbor, or a man his brother, saying, 'Know the Lord,' because they will all know me, from the least of them to the greatest," declares the Lord. "For I will forgive their wickedness and will remember their sins no more."
Jeremiah 31:34

You will again have compassion on us; you will tread our sins underfoot and hurl all our iniquities into the depths of the sea.
Micah 7:19

This is the covenant I will make with them after that time, says the Lord. I will put my laws in their hearts, and I will write them on their minds. Then he adds: "Their sins and lawless acts I will remember no more." Hebrews 10:16-17

GOD WILL BLOT OUT YOUR SINS

Have mercy on me, O God, according to your unfailing love; according to your great compassion blot out my transgressions.
Psalms 51:1

Hide your face from my sins and blot out all my iniquity.
Psalms 51:9

I, even I, am he who blots out your transgressions, for my own sake, and remembers your sins no more. Isaiah 43:25

I have swept away your offenses like a cloud, your sins like the morning mist. Return to me, for I have redeemed you. Isaiah 44:22

Repent, then, and turn to God, so that your sins may be wiped out, that times of refreshing may come from the Lord. Acts 3:19

OVERCOMING GUILT

Brothers, I do not consider myself yet to have taken hold of it. But one thing I do: Forgetting what is behind and straining toward what is ahead. Philippians 3:13

If you return to the Lord, then your brothers and your children will be shown compassion by their captors and will come back to this land, for the Lord your God is gracious and compassionate. He will not turn his face from you if you return to him.
2 Chronicles 30:9

As far as the east is from the west, so far has he removed our transgressions from us. Psalms 103:12

Memory can become a tyrant instead of a treasure chest. From the mistakes of the past, let us learn whatever lessons they teach, then forget them, even as God remembers our sins no more. Let precious memories be benedictions but not bonds. - Vance Havner

Let the wicked forsake his way and the evil man his thoughts. Let him turn to the Lord, and he will have mercy on him, and to our God, for he will freely pardon. Isaiah 55:7

No longer will a man teach his neighbor, or a man his brother, saying, 'Know the Lord,' because they will all know me, from the least of them to the greatest," declares the Lord. "For I will forgive their wickedness and will remember their sins no more."
Jeremiah 31:34

I will cleanse them from all the sin they have committed against me and will forgive all their sins of rebellion against me.
Jeremiah 33:8

For God did not send his Son into the world to condemn the world, but to save the world through him. Whoever believes in him is not condemned, but whoever does not believe stands condemned already because he has not believed in the name of God's one and only Son. John 3:17-18

Therefore, if anyone is in Christ, he is a new creation; the old has gone, the new has come! 2 Corinthians 5:17

For I will forgive their wickedness and will remember their sins no more. Hebrews 8:12

Let us draw near to God with a sincere heart in full assurance of faith, having our hearts sprinkled to cleanse us from a guilty conscience and having our bodies washed with pure water.
Hebrews 10:22

But if we walk in the light, as he is in the light, we have fellowship with one another, and the blood of Jesus, his Son, purifies us from all sin. 1 John 1:7

If we confess our sins, he is faithful and just and will forgive us our sins and purify us from all unrighteousness. 1 John 1:9

I write to you, dear children, because your sins have been forgiven on account of his name. 1 John 2:12

Whenever our hearts condemn us. For God is greater than our hearts, and he knows everything. 1 John 3:20

Sometimes, we want to fly before we walk; we want to be perfect before we start toward perfection. It is not a mark of godliness to be forever condemning oneself in morbid self-accusation.- Vance Havner

OVERCOMING CONDEMNATION

For God did not send his Son into the world to condemn the world, but to save the world through him. John 3:17

I tell you the truth, whoever hears my word and believes him who sent me has eternal life and will not be condemned; he has crossed over from death to life. John 5:24

Therefore, there is now no condemnation for those who are in Christ Jesus, Romans 8:1

Whenever our hearts condemn us. For God is greater than our hearts, and he knows everything. Dear friends, if our hearts do not condemn us, we have confidence before God. 1 John 3:20-21

> *The voice of sin may be loud, but the voice of forgiveness is louder. - D. L. Moody*

YOU ARE SELF-CONDEMNED WHEN YOU

1. REJECT CHRIST

Whoever believes in him is not condemned, but whoever does not believe stands condemned already because he has not believed in the name of God's one and only Son. This is the verdict: Light has come into the world, but men loved darkness instead of light because their deeds were evil. John 3:18-19

2. WILLFULLY SIN

So whatever you believe about these things keep between yourself and God. Blessed is the man who does not condemn himself by what he approves. Romans 14:22

You may be sure that such a man is warped and sinful; he is self-condemned. Titus 3:11

FACING CHALLENGES AND WINNING

FACING FEAR AND WINNING

Do not be afraid, little flock, for your Father has been pleased to give you the kingdom. Luke 12:32

Peace I leave with you; my peace I give you. I do not give to you as the world gives. Do not let your hearts be troubled and do not be afraid. John 14:27

FEAR IS AN evil spirit FROM satan

For you did not receive a spirit that makes you a slave again to fear, but you received the Spirit of sonship. And by him we cry, "Abba, Father." Romans 8:15

For God hath not given us the spirit of fear; but of power, and of love, and of a sound mind. 2 Timothy 1:7 KJV

For God did not give us a spirit of timidity, but a spirit of power, of love and of self-discipline. 2 Timothy 1:7

There is no fear in love. But perfect love drives out fear, because fear has to do with punishment. The one who fears is not made perfect in love. 1 John 4:18

FEAR BRINGS THE PROBLEM TO YOU

What the wicked dreads will overtake him; what the righteous desire will be granted. Proverbs 10:24

Fear of man will prove to be a snare, but whoever trusts in the Lord is kept safe. Proverbs 29:25

What I feared has come upon me; what I dreaded has happened to me. Job 3:25

DON'T FEAR! GOD IS WITH YOU

"Don't be afraid," the prophet answered. "Those who are with us are more than those who are with them." 2 Kings 6:16

For I am the Lord, your God, who takes hold of your right hand and says to you, Do not fear; I will help you. Isaiah 41:13

Even though I walk through the valley of the shadow of death, I will fear no evil, for you are with me; your rod and your staff, they comfort me. Psalms 23:4

The Lord is my light and my salvation—whom shall I fear? The Lord is the stronghold of my life—of whom shall I be afraid?
Psalms 27:1

Though an army besiege me, my heart will not fear; though war break out against me, even then will I be confident. Psalms 27:3

God is our refuge and strength, an ever-present help in trouble.
Psalms 46:1

But whoever listens to me will live in safety and be at ease, without fear of harm. Proverbs 1:33

When you lie down, you will not be afraid; when you lie down, your sleep will be sweet. Have no fear of sudden disaster or of the ruin that overtakes the wicked, for the Lord will be your confidence and will keep your foot from being snared.
Proverbs 3:24-26

On the day the Lord gives you relief from suffering and turmoil and cruel bondage. Isaiah 14:3

When you pass through the waters, I will be with you; and when you pass through the rivers, they will not sweep over you. When you walk through the fire, you will not be burned; the flames will not set you ablaze. Isaiah 43:2

FACING DEATH AND WINNING

Even though I walk through the valley of the shadow of death, I will fear no evil, for you are with me; your rod and your staff, they comfort me. Psalms 23:4

Consider the blameless, observe the upright; there is a future for the man of peace. Psalms 37:37

For this God is our God for ever and ever; he will be our guide even to the end. Psalms 48:14

But God will redeem my life from the grave; he will surely take me to himself. Selah. Psalms 49:15

My flesh and my heart may fail, but God is the strength of my heart and my portion forever. Psalms 73:26

When calamity comes, the wicked are brought down, but even in death the righteous have a refuge. Proverbs 14:32

He will swallow up death forever. The Sovereign Lord will wipe away the tears from all faces; he will remove the disgrace of his people from all the earth. The Lord has spoken. Isaiah 25:8

I will ransom them from the power of the grave; I will redeem them from death. Where, O death, are your plagues? Where, O grave, is your destruction? I will have no compassion. Hosea 13:14

That everyone who believes in him may have eternal life.
John 3:15

I tell you the truth, if anyone keeps my word, he will never see death. John 8:51

Where, O death, is your victory? Where, O death, is your sting? The sting of death is sin, and the power of sin is the law. But thanks be to God! He gives us the victory through our Lord Jesus Christ.
1 Corinthians 15:55-57

Therefore we do not lose heart. Though outwardly we are wasting away, yet inwardly we are being renewed day by day.
2 Corinthians 4:16

Since the children have flesh and blood, he too shared in their humanity so that by his death he might destroy him who holds the power of death—that is, the devil—and free those who all their lives were held in slavery by their fear of death. Hebrews 2:14-15

FACING ENEMIES AND WINNING

For the Lord your God is the one who goes with you to fight for you against your enemies to give you victory. Deuteronomy 20:4

The Lord will grant that the enemies who rise up against you will be defeated before you. They will come at you from one direction but flee from you in seven. Deuteronomy 28:7

"Don't be afraid," the prophet answered. "Those who are with us are more than those who are with them." 2 Kings 6:16

Rather, worship the Lord your God; it is he who will deliver you from the hand of all your enemies." 2 Kings 17:39

In famine he will ransom you from death, and in battle from the stroke of the sword. Job 5:20

Your enemies will be clothed in shame, and the tents of the wicked will be no more. Job 8:22

For in the day of trouble he will keep me safe in his dwelling; he will hide me in the shelter of his tabernacle and set me high upon a rock. Then my head will be exalted above the enemies who surround me; at his tabernacle will I sacrifice with shouts of joy; I will sing and make music to the Lord. Psalms 27:5-6

The Lord helps them and delivers them; he delivers them from the wicked and saves them, because they take refuge in him.
Psalms 37:40

With God we will gain the victory, and he will trample down our enemies. Psalms 60:12

Let those who love the Lord hate evil, for he guards the lives of his faithful ones and delivers them from the hand of the wicked.
Psalms 97:10

His heart is secure, he will have no fear; in the end he will look in triumph on his foes. Psalms 112:8

The Lord is with me; he is my helper. I will look in triumph on my enemies. Psalms 118:7

The scepter of the wicked will not remain over the land allotted to the righteous, for then the righteous might use their hands to do evil. Psalms 125:3

Have no fear of sudden disaster or of the ruin that overtakes the wicked, for the Lord will be your confidence and will keep your foot from being snared. Proverbs 3:25-26

When a man's ways are pleasing to the Lord, he makes even his enemies live at peace with him. Proverbs 16:7

All who rage against you will surely be ashamed and disgraced; those who oppose you will be as nothing and perish. Though you search for your enemies, you will not find them. Those who wage war against you will be as nothing at all. Isaiah 41:11-12

But I will rescue you on that day, declares the Lord; you will not be handed over to those you fear. I will save you; you will not fall by the sword but will escape with your life, because you trust in me, declares the Lord. Jeremiah 39:17-18

Salvation from our enemies and from the hand of all who hate us.
Luke 1:71

To rescue us from the hand of our enemies, and to enable us to serve him without fear. Luke 1:74

HOW TO TREAT YOUR ENEMIES

If your enemy is hungry, give him food to eat; if he is thirsty, give him water to drink. Proverbs 25:21

But I tell you: Love your enemies and pray for those who persecute you. Matthew 5:44

But I tell you who hear me: Love your enemies, do good to those who hate you, bless those who curse you, pray for those who mistreat you. Luke 6:27-28

But love your enemies, do good to them, and lend to them without expecting to get anything back. Then your reward will be great, and you will be sons of the Most High, because he is kind to the ungrateful and wicked. Be merciful, just as your Father is merciful. Luke 6:35-36

411

Bless those who persecute you; bless and do not curse.

Romans 12:14

Love does no harm to its neighbor. Therefore love is the fulfill-ment of the law. Romans 13:10

On the contrary: If your enemy is hungry, feed him; if he is thirsty, give him something to drink. In doing this, you will heap burning coals on his head. Romans 12:20

We work hard with our own hands. When we are cursed, we bless; when we are persecuted, we endure it. 1 Corinthians 4:12

FACING REVENGE AND WINNING

REVENGE IS GOD'S JOB

For we know him who said, "It is mine to avenge; I will repay," and again, "The Lord will judge his people." Hebrews 10:30

It is mine to avenge; I will repay. In due time their foot will slip; their day of disaster is near and their doom rushes upon them.

Deuteronomy 32:35

O Lord, the God who avenges, O God who avenges, shine forth.

Psalms 94:1

Therefore, this is what the Lord says: "See, I will defend your cause and avenge you; I will dry up her sea and make her springs dry.

Jeremiah 51:36

And that in this matter no one should wrong his brother or take advantage of him. The Lord will punish men for all such sins, as we have already told you and warned you. 1 Thessalonians 4:6

DO NOT REJOICE WHEN YOUR ENEMIES SUFFER

He who mocks the poor shows contempt for their Maker; whoever gloats over disaster will not go unpunished. Proverbs 17:5

Do not gloat when your enemy falls; when he stumbles, do not let your heart rejoice. Proverbs 24:17

DO NOT SEEK REVENGE

If a man pays back evil for good, evil will never leave his house.
Proverbs 17:13

And we will be ready to punish every act of disobedience, once your obedience is complete. 2 Corinthians 10:6

He who testifies to these things says, "Yes, I am coming soon." Amen. Come, Lord Jesus. Proverbs 20:22

May the Lord judge between you and me. And may the Lord avenge the wrongs you have done to me, but my hand will not touch you.
1 Samuel 24:12

Do not say, "I'll do to him as he has done to me; I'll pay that man back for what he did." Proverbs 24:29

Do not repay anyone evil for evil. Be careful to do what is right in the eyes of everybody. Romans 12:17

> *Revenge is often like biting a dog because the dog bit you. - Austin O'Malley*

Do not take revenge, my friends, but leave room for God's wrath, for it is written: "It is mine to avenge; I will repay," says the Lord.
Romans 12:19

Do not seek revenge or bear a grudge against one of your people, but love your neighbor as yourself. I am the Lord. Leviticus 19:18

Make sure that nobody pays back wrong for wrong, but always try to be kind to each other and to everyone else. 1 Thessalonians 5:15

FACING PERSECUTION AND WINNING

Blessed are those who are persecuted because of righteousness, for theirs is the kingdom of heaven. Blessed are you when people insult you, persecute you and falsely say all kinds of evil against you because of me. Rejoice and be glad, because great is your reward in heaven, for in the same way they persecuted the prophets who were before you. Matthew 5:10-12

But I tell you: Love your enemies and pray for those who persecute you. Matthew 5:44

When you are living right and doing something for God, you will be criticized by three types of people: those who are jealous, those who are ill-informed, and those who are influenced by or filled with the devil.

Will fail to receive a hundred times as much in this present age (homes, brothers, sisters, mothers, children and fields—and with them, persecutions) and in the age to come, eternal life. Mark 10:30

But before all this, they will lay hands on you and persecute you. They will deliver you to synagogues and prisons, and you will be brought before kings and governors, and all on account of my name.
Luke 21:12

Remember the words I spoke to you: 'No servant is greater than his master.' If they persecuted me, they will persecute you also. If they obeyed my teaching, they will obey yours also. John 15:20

Who shall separate us from the love of Christ? Shall trouble or hardship or persecution or famine or nakedness or danger or sword?
Romans 8:35

Bless those who persecute you; bless and do not curse.
Romans 12:14

We work hard with our own hands. When we are cursed, we bless; when we are persecuted, we endure it. 1 Corinthians 4:12

Persecuted, but not abandoned; struck down, but not destroyed.
2 Corinthians 4:9

That is why, for Christ's sake, I delight in weaknesses, in insults, in hardships, in persecutions, in difficulties. For when I am weak, then I am strong. 2 Corinthians 12:10

At that time the son born in the ordinary way persecuted the son born by the power of the Spirit. It is the same now. Galatians 4:29

Therefore, among God's churches we boast about your perseverance and faith in all the persecutions and trials you are enduring.
2 Thessalonians 1:4

Persecutions, sufferings—what kinds of things happened to me in Antioch, Iconium and Lystra, the persecutions I endured. Yet the Lord rescued me from all of them. 2 Timothy 3:11

In fact, everyone who wants to live a godly life in Christ Jesus will be persecuted. 2 Timothy 3:12

> *We Christians are not called to respond to criticism; we are called to respond to God. - John Mason*

FACING LONELINESS AND WINNING

I am with you and will watch over you wherever you go, and I will bring you back to this land. I will not leave you until I have done what I have promised you. Genesis 28:15

Be strong and courageous. Do not be afraid or terrified because of them, for the Lord your God goes with you; he will never leave you nor forsake you. Deuteronomy 31:6

The Lord is a refuge for the oppressed, a stronghold in times of trouble. Those who know your name will trust in you, for you, Lord, have never forsaken those who seek you. Psalms 9:9-10

I will be glad and rejoice in your love, for you saw my affliction and knew the anguish of my soul. Psalms 31:7

God is our refuge and strength, an ever-present help in trouble.
Psalms 46:1

Cast your cares on the Lord and he will sustain you; he will never let the righteous fall. Psalms 55:22

O people of Zion, who live in Jerusalem, you will weep no more. How gracious he will be when you cry for help! As soon as he hears, he will answer you. Isaiah 30:19

So do not fear, for I am with you; do not be dismayed, for I am your God. I will strengthen you and help you; I will uphold you with my righteous right hand. Isaiah 41:10

Then you will call, and the Lord will answer; you will cry for help, and he will say: Here am I. "If you do away with the yoke of oppression, with the pointing finger and malicious talk. Isaiah 58:9

"Am I only a God nearby," declares the Lord, "and not a God far away? Jeremiah 23:23

The Lord is good, a refuge in times of trouble. He cares for those who trust in him. Nahum 1:7

And teaching them to obey everything I have commanded you. And surely I am with you always, to the very end of the age.
Matthew 28:20

Do not let your hearts be troubled. Trust in God; trust also in me.
John 14:1

I will not leave you as orphans; I will come to you. John 14:18

Who shall separate us from the love of Christ? Shall trouble or hardship or persecution or famine or nakedness or danger or sword? As it is written: "For your sake we face death all day long; we are considered as sheep to be slaughtered." No, in all these things we are more than conquerors through him who loved us. For I am convinced that neither death nor life, neither angels nor demons, neither the present nor the future, nor any powers, neither height nor depth, nor anything else in all creation, will be able to separate us from the love of God that is in Christ Jesus our Lord.
Romans 8:35-39

Keep your lives free from the love of money and be content with what you have, because God has said, "Never will I leave you; never will I forsake you." Hebrews 13:5

Cast all your anxiety on him because he cares for you. 1 Peter 5:7

You, dear children, are from God and have overcome them, because the one who is in you is greater than the one who is in the world. 1 John 4:4

FACING TEMPTATION AND WINNING

And lead us not into temptation, but deliver us from the evil one.
Matthew 6:13

"Watch and pray so that you will not fall into temptation. The spirit is willing, but the body is weak." Matthew 26:41

Watch and pray so that you will not fall into temptation. The spirit is willing, but the body is weak. Mark 14:38

Jesus answered, "It says: 'Do not put the Lord your God to the test.'" When the devil had finished all this tempting, he left him until an opportune time. Luke 4:12-13

On reaching the place, he said to them, "Pray that you will not fall into temptation." Luke 22:40

"Why are you sleeping?" he asked them. "Get up and pray so that you will not fall into temptation." Luke 22:46

No temptation has seized you except what is common to man. And God is faithful; he will not let you be tempted beyond what you can bear. But when you are tempted, he will also provide a way out so that you can stand up under it. 1 Corinthians 10:13

Brothers, if someone is caught in a sin, you who are spiritual should restore him gently. But watch yourself, or you also may be tempted.
Galatians 6:1

For this reason, when I could stand it no longer, I sent to find out about your faith. I was afraid that in some way the tempter might have tempted you and our efforts might have been useless.
1 Thessalonians 3:5

People who want to get rich fall into temptation and a trap and into many foolish and harmful desires that plunge men into ruin and destruction. 1 Timothy 6:9

Because he himself suffered when he was tempted, he is able to help those who are being tempted. Hebrews 2:18

For we do not have a high priest who is unable to sympathize with our weaknesses, but we have one who has been tempted in every way, just as we are—yet was without sin. Hebrews 4:15

Temptations either tests your ability to say no, or it tests your conscience to promptly repent. Avoidance of sin is better than the consequences of sin.

Blessed is the man who perseveres under trial, because when he has stood the test, he will receive the crown of life that God has promised to those who love him. When tempted, no one should say, "God is tempting me." For God cannot be tempted by evil, nor does he tempt anyone; but each one is tempted when, by his own evil desire, he is dragged away and enticed. James 1:12-14

Since you have kept my command to endure patiently, I will also keep you from the hour of trial that is going to come upon the whole world to test those who live on the earth. Revelation 3:10

If you would master temptation, you must
first let Christ master you. - Anonymous

FACING STRESS AND DEPRESSION AND WINNING

Consider it pure joy, my brothers, whenever you face trials of many kinds, because you know that the testing of your faith develops perseverance. Perseverance must finish its work so that you may be mature and complete, not lacking anything. James 1:2-4

From six calamities he will rescue you; in seven no harm will befall you. Job 5:19

The Lord is a refuge for the oppressed, a stronghold in times of trouble. Psalms 9:9

For his anger lasts only a moment, but his favor lasts a lifetime; weeping may remain for a night, but rejoicing comes in the morning. Psalms 30:5

Be strong and take heart, all you who hope in the Lord.
Psalms 31:24

A righteous man may have many troubles, but the Lord delivers him from them all. Psalms 34:19

Not to become easily unsettled or alarmed by some prophecy, report or letter supposed to have come from us, saying that the day of the Lord has already come. 2 Thessalonians 2:2

Therefore let everyone who is godly pray to you while you may be found; surely when the mighty waters rise, they will not reach him.

You are my hiding place; you will protect me from trouble and surround me with songs of deliverance. Selah Psalms 32:6-7

Though he stumble, he will not fall, for the Lord upholds him with his hand. Psalms 37:24

The salvation of the righteous comes from the Lord; he is their stronghold in time of trouble. Psalms 37:39

Though I walk in the midst of trouble, you preserve my life; you stretch out your hand against the anger of my foes, with your right hand you save me. Psalms 138:7

He heals the brokenhearted and binds up their wounds. Psalms 147:3

An evil man is trapped by his sinful talk, but a righteous man escapes trouble. Proverbs 12:13

No harm befalls the righteous, but the wicked have their fill of trouble. Proverbs 12:21

The ransomed of the Lord will return. They will enter Zion with singing; everlasting joy will crown their heads. Gladness and joy will overtake them, and sorrow and sighing will flee away.
Isaiah 51:11

The Lord is good, a refuge in times of trouble. He cares for those who trust in him. Nahum 1:7

Then Jesus told his disciples a parable to show them that they should always pray and not give up. Luke 18:1

Do not let your hearts be troubled. Trust in God; trust also in me.
John 14:1

We should glory in our infirmities but not glorify them.
- Vance Havner

I will not leave you as orphans; I will come to you. John 14:18

And we know that in all things God works for the good of those who love him, who have been called according to his purpose.
Romans 8:28

419

I consider that our present sufferings are not worth comparing with the glory that will be revealed in us. Romans 8:18

For I am convinced that neither death nor life, neither angels nor demons, neither the present nor the future, nor any powers, neither height nor depth, nor anything else in all creation, will be able to separate us from the love of God that is in Christ Jesus our 'Lord.
Romans 8:38-39

No temptation has seized you except what is common to man. And God is faithful; he will not let you be tempted beyond what you can bear. But when you are tempted, he will also provide a way out so that you can stand up under it. 1 Corinthians 10:13

Praise be to the God and Father of our Lord Jesus Christ, the Father of compassion and the God of all comfort, who comforts us in all our troubles, so that we can comfort those in any trouble with the comfort we ourselves have received from God.
2 Corinthians 1:3-4

We are hard pressed on every side, but not crushed; perplexed, but not in despair; persecuted, but not abandoned; struck down, but not destroyed. 2 Corinthians 4:8-9

Therefore, since we are surrounded by such a great cloud of witnesses, let us throw off everything that hinders and the sin that so easily entangles, and let us run with perseverance the race marked out for us. Hebrews 12:1

For in Scripture it says: "See, I lay a stone in Zion, a chosen and precious cornerstone, and the one who trusts in him will never be put to shame." 1 Peter 2:6

Dear friends, do not be surprised at the painful trial you are suffering, as though something strange were happening to you. But rejoice that you participate in the sufferings of Christ, so that you may be overjoyed when his glory is revealed. 1 Peter 4:12-13

A Christian is like a teabag—he's not worth much until he's been through some hot water. - Anonymous

Cast all your anxiety on him because he cares for you. 1 Peter 5:7

He will wipe every tear from their eyes. There will be no more death or mourning or crying or pain, for the old order of things has passed away. Revelation 21:4

All the tribulations of this life are but incidents on the road from Groans to Glory. -Vance Havner

FACING ANXIETY AND WORRY AND WINNING

"Therefore I tell you, do not worry about your life, what you will eat or drink; or about your body, what you will wear. Is not life more important than food, and the body more important than clothes? Look at the birds of the air; they do not sow or reap or store away in barns, and yet your heavenly Father feeds them. Are you not much more valuable than they? Who of you by worrying can add a single hour to his life? "And why do you worry about clothes? See how the lilies of the field grow. They do not labor or spin. Yet I tell you that not even Solomon in all his splendor was dressed like one of these. If that is how God clothes the grass of the field, which is here today and tomorrow is thrown into the fire, will he not much more clothe you, O you of little faith? So do not worry, saying, 'What shall we eat?' or 'What shall we drink?' or 'What shall we wear?' For the pagans run after all these things, and your heavenly Father knows that you need them. But seek first his kingdom and his righteousness, and all these things will be given to you as well. Therefore do not worry about tomorrow, for tomorrow will worry about itself. Each day has enough trouble of its own. Matthew 6:25-34

Do not be anxious about anything, but in everything, by prayer and petition, with thanksgiving, present your requests to God.
Philippians 4:6

Consider it pure joy, my brothers, whenever you face trials of many kinds, because you know that the testing of your faith develops perseverance. James 1:2-3

Cast all your anxiety on him because he cares for you. 1 Peter 5:7

Worry is like a rocking chair. It keeps you going but you don't get any where. - Anonymous

JESUS WILL

JESUS WILL GIVE YOU LOVE

The Lord gives sight to the blind, the Lord lifts up those who are bowed down, the Lord loves the righteous. Psalms 146:8

As a young man marries a maiden, so will your sons marry you; as a bridegroom rejoices over his bride, so will your God rejoice over you. Isaiah 62:5

The Lord appeared to us in the past, saying: "I have loved you with an everlasting love; I have drawn you with loving-kindness.
Jeremiah 31:3

I will heal their waywardness and love them freely, for my anger has turned away from them. Hosea 14:4

For God so loved the world that he gave his one and only Son, that whoever believes in him shall not perish but have eternal life.
John 3:16

No, the Father himself loves you because you have loved me and have believed that I came from God. John 16:27

I have given them the glory that you gave me, that they may be one as we are one: I in them and you in me. May they be brought to complete unity to let the world know that you sent me and have loved them even as you have loved me. John 17:22-23

I have made you known to them, and will continue to make you known in order that the love you have for me may be in them and that I myself may be in them. John 17:26

But God demonstrates his own love for us in this: While we were still sinners, Christ died for us. Romans 5:8

But because of his great love for us, God, who is rich in mercy, made us alive with Christ even when we were dead in transgressions—it is by grace you have been saved. And God raised us up with Christ and seated us with him in the heavenly realms in Christ Jesus, in order that in the coming ages he might show the incomparable riches of his grace, expressed in his kindness to us in Christ Jesus. Ephesians 2:4-7

And to know this love that surpasses knowledge—that you may be filled to the measure of all the fullness of God. Ephesians 3:19

May our Lord Jesus Christ himself and God our Father, who loved us and by his grace gave us eternal encouragement and good hope, encourage your hearts and strengthen you in every good deed and word. 2 Thessalonians 2:16-17

How great is the love the Father has lavished on us, that we should be called children of God! And that is what we are! The reason the world does not know us is that it did not know him. 1 John 3:1

Dear friends, let us love one another, for love comes from God. Everyone who loves has been born of God and knows God. Whoever does not love does not know God, because God is love. This is how God showed his love among us: He sent his one and only Son into the world that we might live through him. This is love: not that we loved God, but that he loved us and sent his Son as an atoning sacrifice for our sins. Dear friends, since God so loved us, we also ought to love one another. 1 John 4:7-11

And so we know and rely on the love God has for us. God is love. Whoever lives in love lives in God, and God in him. 1 John 4:16

We love him, because he first loved us. 1 John 4:19

JESUS WILL GIVE YOU HOPE

To them God has chosen to make known among the Gentiles the glorious riches of this mystery, which is Christ in you, the hope of glory. Colossians 1:27

May our Lord Jesus Christ himself and God our Father, who loved us and by his grace gave us eternal encouragement and good hope.
2 Thessalonians 2:16

May your unfailing love rest upon us, O Lord, even as we put our hope in you. Psalms 33:22

But now, Lord, what do I look for? My hope is in you. Psalms 39:7

Why are you downcast, O my soul? Why so disturbed within me? Put your hope in God, for I will yet praise him, my Savior and my God. Psalms 42:11

For you have been my hope, O Sovereign Lord, my confidence since my youth. Psalms 71:5

But as for me, I will always have hope; I will praise you more and more. Psalms 71:14

That they might set their hope in God, and not forget the works of God, but keep his commandments. Psalms 78:7 KJV

Then they would put their trust in God and would not forget his deeds but would keep his commands. Psalms 78:7

O Israel, put your hope in the Lord, for with the Lord is unfailing love and with him is full redemption. Psalms 130:7

O Israel, put your hope in the Lord both now and forevermore.
Psalms 131:3

Blessed is he whose help is the God of Jacob, whose hope is in the Lord his God. Psalms 146:5

It is good that a man should both hope and quietly wait for the salvation of the Lord. Lamentations 3:26 KJV

The Lord also shall roar out of Zion, and utter his voice from Jerusalem; and the heavens and the earth shall shake: but the Lord will be the hope of his people, and the strength of the children of Israel.
Joel 3:16

There is not enough darkness in all the world to put out the light of one small candle. - Anonymous

The Lord will roar from Zion and thunder from Jerusalem; the earth and the sky will tremble. But the Lord will be a refuge for his people, a stronghold for the people of Israel. Joel 3:16

And I have the same hope in God as these men, that there will be a resurrection of both the righteous and the wicked. Acts 24:15

Through whom we have gained access by faith into this grace in which we now stand. And we rejoice in the hope of the glory of God. Romans 5:2

Therefore, prepare your minds for action; be self-controlled; set your hope fully on the grace to be given you when Jesus Christ is revealed. 1 Peter 1:13

But in your hearts set apart Christ as Lord. Always be prepared to give an answer to everyone who asks you to give the reason for the hope that you have. But do this with gentleness and respect.
1 Peter 3:15

Hope means expectancy when things are otherwise hopeless. - G. K. Chesterton

JESUS WILL GIVE YOU JOY

Nehemiah said, "Go and enjoy choice food and sweet drinks, and send some to those who have nothing prepared. This day is sacred to our Lord. Do not grieve, for the joy of the Lord is your strength."
Nehemiah 8:10

While the morning stars sang together and all the angels shouted for joy? Job 38:7

You have made known to me the path of life; you will fill me with joy in your presence, with eternal pleasures at your right hand.
Psalms 16:11

The joy of the Lord is our strength, and joy comes by remaining in God's presence.

Nehemiah said, "Go and enjoy choice food and sweet drinks, and send some to those who have nothing prepared. This day is sacred to our Lord. Do not grieve, for the joy of the Lord is your strength."
Nehemiah 8:10

For his anger lasts only a moment, but his favor lasts a lifetime; weeping may remain for a night, but rejoicing comes in the morning. Psalms 30:5

May those who delight in my vindication shout for joy and gladness; may they always say, "The Lord be exalted, who delights in the well-being of his servant." Psalms 35:27

Restore to me the joy of your salvation and grant me a willing spirit, to sustain me. Psalms 51:12

Those who sow in tears will reap with songs of joy. Psalms 126:5

Let the saints rejoice in this honor and sing for joy on their beds.
Psalms 149:5

A man finds joy in giving an apt reply—and how good is a timely word! Proverbs 15:23

When justice is done, it brings joy to the righteous but terror to evildoers. Proverbs 21:15

Go, eat your food with gladness, and drink your wine with a joyful heart, for it is now that God favors what you do. Ecclesiastes 9:7

And the ransomed of the Lord will return. They will enter Zion with singing; everlasting joy will crown their heads. Gladness and joy will overtake them, and sorrow and sighing will flee away.
Isaiah 35:10

The ransomed of the Lord will return. They will enter Zion with singing; everlasting joy will crown their heads. Gladness and joy will overtake them, and sorrow and sighing will flee away.
Isaiah 51:11

You will go out in joy and be led forth in peace; the mountains and hills will burst into song before you, and all the trees of the field will clap their hands. Isaiah 55:12

He will be a joy and delight to you, and many will rejoice because of his birth. Luke 1:14

But the angel said to them, Do not be afraid. I bring you good news of great joy that will be for all the people. Luke 2:10

Rejoice in that day and leap for joy, because great is your reward in heaven. For that is how their fathers treated the prophets.
Luke 6:23

In the same way, I tell you, there is rejoicing in the presence of the angels of God over one sinner who repents. Luke 15:10

Then they worshiped him and returned to Jerusalem with great joy.
Luke 24:52

I have told you this so that my joy may be in you and that your joy may be complete. John 15:11

I tell you the truth, you will weep and mourn while the world rejoices. You will grieve, but your grief will turn to joy. John 16:20

A woman giving birth to a child has pain because her time has come; but when her baby is born she forgets the anguish because of her joy that a child is born into the world. So with you: Now is your time of grief, but I will see you again and you will rejoice, and no one will take away your joy. In that day you will no longer ask me anything. I tell you the truth, my Father will give you whatever you ask in my name. Until now you have not asked for anything in my name. Ask and you will receive, and your joy will be complete. John 16:21-24

I am coming to you now, but I say these things while I am still in the world, so that they may have the full measure of my joy within them. John 17:13

You have made known to me the paths of life; you will fill me with joy in your presence. Acts 2:28

And the disciples were filled with joy and with the Holy Spirit.
Acts 13:52

Not only is this so, but we also rejoice in God through our Lord Jesus Christ, through whom we have now received reconciliation.
Romans 5:11

For the kingdom of God is not a matter of eating and drinking, but of righteousness, peace and joy in the Holy Spirit. Romans 14:17

May the God of hope fill you with all joy and peace as you trust in him, so that you may overflow with hope by the power of the Holy Spirit. Romans 15:13

Not that we lord it over your faith, but we work with you for your joy, because it is by faith you stand firm. 2 Corinthians 1:24

You became imitators of us and of the Lord; in spite of severe suffering, you welcomed the message with the joy given by the Holy Spirit. 1 Thessalonians 1:6

Consider it pure joy, my brothers, whenever you face trials of many kinds. James 1:2

We write this to make our joy complete. 1 John 1:4

JESUS WILL GIVE YOU MERCY

Give thanks to the Lord, for he is good; his love endures forever.
1 Chronicles 16:34

Surely goodness and mercy shall follow me all the days of my life: and I will dwell in the house of the Lord for ever. Psalms 23:6 KJV

You are forgiving and good, O Lord, abounding in love to all who call to you. Psalms 86:5

For great is your love toward me; you have delivered me from the depths of the grave. Psalms 86:13

But you, O Lord, are a compassionate and gracious God, slow to anger, abounding in love and faithfulness. Psalms 86:15

The Lord is compassionate and gracious, slow to anger, abounding in love. Psalms 103:8

For as high as the heavens are above the earth, so great is his love for those who fear him. Psalms 103:11

As a father has compassion on his children, so the Lord has compassion on those who fear him. Psalms 103:13

Help me, O Lord my God; save me in accordance with your love.
Psalms 109:26

The Lord is gracious and compassionate, slow to anger and rich in love. Psalms 145:8

He who despises his neighbor sins, but blessed is he who is kind to the needy. Do not those who plot evil go astray? But those who plan what is good find love and faithfulness. Proverbs 14:21-22

He who conceals his sins does not prosper, but whoever confesses and renounces them finds mercy. Proverbs 28:13

For my own name's sake I delay my wrath; for the sake of my praise I hold it back from you, so as not to cut you off. Isaiah 48:9

Let the wicked forsake his way and the evil man his thoughts. Let him turn to the Lord, and he will have mercy on him, and to our God, for he will freely pardon. Isaiah 55:7

Blessed are the merciful, for they will be shown mercy.
Matthew 5:7

As far as the gospel is concerned, they are enemies on your account; but as far as election is concerned, they are loved on account of the patriarchs, for God's gifts and his call are irrevocable. Just as you who were at one time disobedient to God have now received mercy as a result of their disobedience, so they too have now become disobedient in order that they too may now receive mercy as a result of God's mercy to you. For God has bound all men over to disobedience so that he may have mercy on them all.
Romans 11:28-32

But because of his great love for us, God, who is rich in mercy.
Ephesians 2:4

He saved us, not because of righteous things we had done, but because of his mercy. He saved us through the washing of rebirth and renewal by the Holy Spirit. Titus 3:5

Let us then approach the throne of grace with confidence, so that we may receive mercy and find grace to help us in our time of need. Hebrews 4:16

As you know, we consider blessed those who have persevered. You have heard of Job's perseverance and have seen what the Lord fi-

nally brought about. The Lord is full of compassion and mercy.
James 5:11

Praise be to the God and Father of our Lord Jesus Christ! In his great mercy he has given us new birth into a living hope through the resurrection of Jesus Christ from the dead. 1 Peter 1:3

Once you were not a people, but now you are the people of God; once you had not received mercy, but now you have received mercy.
1 Peter 2:10

Mercy, peace and love be yours in abundance. Jude 1:2

JESUS WILL GIVE YOU PEACE

And through him to reconcile to himself all things, whether things on earth or things in heaven, by making peace through his blood, shed on the cross. Colossians 1:20

I will lie down and sleep in peace, for you alone, O Lord, make me dwell in safety. Psalms 4:8

The Lord gives strength to his people; the Lord blesses his people with peace. Psalms 29:11

Consider the blameless, observe the upright; there is a future for the man of peace. Psalms 37:37

He hath delivered my soul in peace from the battle that was against me: for there were many with me. Psalms 55:18 KJV

He ransoms me unharmed from the battle waged against me, even though many oppose me. Psalms 55:18

Lord, you establish peace for us; all that we have accomplished you have done for us. Isaiah 26:12

You will go out in joy and be led forth in peace; the mountains and hills will burst into song before you, and all the trees of the field will clap their hands. Isaiah 55:12

Those who walk uprightly enter into peace; they find rest as they lie in death. Isaiah 57:2

To shine on those living in darkness and in the shadow of death, to guide our feet into the path of peace. Luke 1:79

May the God of hope fill you with all joy and peace as you trust in him, so that you may overflow with hope by the power of the Holy Spirit. Romans 15:13

For God is not a God of disorder but of peace. As in all the congregations of the saints. 1 Corinthians 14:33

Let the peace of Christ rule in your hearts, since as members of one body you were called to peace. And be thankful. Colossians 3:15

Now may the Lord of peace himself give you peace at all times and in every way. The Lord be with all of you. 2 Thessalonians 3:16

> *"There is no peace ....to the wicked." The world offers false peace to dull the senses, deaden the conscience, quiet the nerves, but it cannot give peace.*
> *- Vance Havner*

PEACE THROUGH JESUS CHRIST

But now in Christ Jesus you who once were far away have been brought near through the blood of Christ. For he himself is our peace, who has made the two one and has destroyed the barrier, the dividing wall of hostility, by abolishing in his flesh the law with its commandments and regulations. His purpose was to create in himself one new man out of the two, thus making peace.
Ephesians 2:13-15

Therefore, since we have been justified through faith, we have peace with God through our Lord Jesus Christ. Romans 5:1

Peace I leave with you; my peace I give you. I do not give to you as the world gives. Do not let your hearts be troubled and do not be afraid. John 14:27

"I have told you these things, so that in me you may have peace. In this world you will have trouble. But take heart! I have overcome the world." John 16:33

Again Jesus said, "Peace be with you! As the Father has sent me, I am sending you." John 20:21

We will not have peace without righteousness. We will never get rested until we get right. - Vance Havner

PEACE FROM GOD'S WORD

My son, do not forget my teaching, but keep my commands in your heart, for they will prolong your life many years and bring you prosperity. Proverbs 3:1-2

Great peace have they which love thy law: and nothing shall offend them. Psalms 119:165

All your sons will be taught by the Lord, and great will be your children's peace. Isaiah 54:13

Let us therefore make every effort to do what leads to peace and to mutual edification. Romans 14:19

Peace and mercy to all who follow this rule, even to the Israel of God. Galatians 6:16

Do not be anxious about anything, but in everything, by prayer and petition, with thanksgiving, present your requests to God. And the peace of God, which transcends all understanding, will guard your hearts and your minds in Christ Jesus. Finally, brothers, whatever is true, whatever is noble, whatever is right, whatever is pure, whatever is lovely, whatever is admirable—if anything is excellent or praiseworthy—think about such things. Whatever you have learned or received or heard from me, or seen in me—put it into practice. And the God of peace will be with you. Philippians 4:6-9

Grace and peace be yours in abundance through the knowledge of God and of Jesus our Lord. 2 Peter 1:2

HOW TO HAVE PEACE

When a man's ways are pleasing to the Lord, he makes even his enemies live at peace with him. Proverbs 16:7

The mind of sinful man is death, but the mind controlled by the Spirit is life and peace. Romans 8:6

You will keep in perfect peace him whose mind is steadfast, because he trusts in you. Isaiah 26:3

For the kingdom of God is not a matter of eating and drinking, but of righteousness, peace and joy in the Holy Spirit, because anyone who serves Christ in this way is pleasing to God and approved by men. Let us therefore make every effort to do what leads to peace and to mutual edification. Romans 14:17-19

The fruit of righteousness will be peace; the effect of righteousness will be quietness and confidence forever. Isaiah 32:17

JESUS WILL GIVE YOU COMFORT

I, even I, am he who comforts you. Who are you that you fear mortal men, the sons of men, who are but grass. Isaiah 51:12

To proclaim the year of the Lord's favor and the day of vengeance of our God, to comfort all who mourn. Isaiah 61:2

As a mother comforts her child, so will I comfort you; and you will be comforted over Jerusalem. Isaiah 66:13

Blessed are those who mourn, for they will be comforted.
Matthew 5:4

And I will pray the Father, and he shall give you another Comforter, that he may abide with you for ever. John 14:16 KJV

God does not comfort us to make us comfortable but to make us comforters. - J. H. Jowett

Praise be to the God and Father of our Lord Jesus Christ, the Father of compassion and the God of all comfort, who comforts us in all our troubles, so that we can comfort those in any trouble with the comfort we ourselves have received from God. For just as the sufferings of Christ flow over into our lives, so also through Christ our comfort overflows. 2 Corinthians 1:3-5

I have great confidence in you; I take great pride in you. I am greatly encouraged; in all our troubles my joy knows no bounds.
2 Corinthians 7:4

But God, who comforts the downcast, comforted us by the coming of Titus, and not only by his coming but also by the comfort you had given him. He told us about your longing for me, your deep sorrow, your ardent concern for me, so that my joy was greater than ever. 2 Corinthians 7:6-7

God often comforts us, not always by changing the circumstances of our lives, but by changing our attitude toward them. - S. H. B. Masterman

Carry each other's burdens, and in this way you will fulfill the law of Christ. Galatians 6:2

Encourage your hearts and strengthen you in every good deed and word. 2 Thessalonians 2:17

JESUS WILL GIVE YOU ETERNAL LIFE

For God so loved the world that he gave his one and only Son, that whoever believes in him shall not perish but have eternal life.
John 3:16

But whoever drinks the water I give him will never thirst. Indeed, the water I give him will become in him a spring of water welling up to eternal life. John 4:14

I tell you the truth, whoever hears my word and believes him who sent me has eternal life and will not be condemned; he has crossed over from death to life. John 5:24

Do not work for food that spoils, but for food that endures to eternal life, which the Son of Man will give you. On him God the Father has placed his seal of approval. John 6:27

I tell you the truth, he who believes has everlasting life. John 6:47

"I am the living bread that came down from heaven. If anyone eats of this bread, he will live forever. This bread is my flesh, which I will give for the life of the world." John 6:51

Whoever eats my flesh and drinks my blood has eternal life, and I will raise him up at the last day. John 6:54

My sheep listen to my voice; I know them, and they follow me. I give them eternal life, and they shall never perish; no one can snatch them out of my hand. John 10:27-28

Jesus said to her, "I am the resurrection and the life. He who believes in me will live, even though he dies; and whoever lives and believes in me will never die. Do you believe this?" John 11:25-26

"Then they will go away to eternal punishment, but the righteous to eternal life." Matthew 25:46

For you granted him authority over all people that he might give eternal life to all those you have given him. John 17:2

To those who by persistence in doing good seek glory, honor and immortality, he will give eternal life. Romans 2:7

But now that you have been set free from sin and have become slaves to God, the benefit you reap leads to holiness, and the result is eternal life. For the wages of sin is death, but the gift of God is eternal life in Christ Jesus our Lord. Romans 6:22-23

For our light and momentary troubles are achieving for us an eternal glory that far outweighs them all. So we fix our eyes not on what is seen, but on what is unseen. For what is seen is temporary, but what is unseen is eternal. 2 Corinthians 4:17-18

The one who sows to please his sinful nature, from that nature will reap destruction; the one who sows to please the Spirit, from the Spirit will reap eternal life. Galatians 6:8

A faith and knowledge resting on the hope of eternal life, which God, who does not lie, promised before the beginning of time.
Titus 1:2

So that, having been justified by his grace, we might become heirs having the hope of eternal life. Titus 3:7

And this is what he promised us—even eternal life. 1 John 2:25

And this is the testimony: God has given us eternal life, and this life is in his Son. 1 John 5:11

I write these things to you who believe in the name of the Son of God so that you may know that you have eternal life. 1 John 5:13

We know also that the Son of God has come and has given us understanding, so that we may know him who is true. And we are in him who is true—even in his Son Jesus Christ. He is the true God and eternal life. 1 John 5:20

JESUS WILL DELIVER YOU

From six calamities he will rescue you; in seven no harm will befall you. Job 5:19

The angel of the Lord encamps around those who fear him, and he delivers them. Psalms 34:7

A righteous man may have many troubles, but the Lord delivers him from them all. Psalms 34:19

For the Lord loves the just and will not forsake his faithful ones. They will be protected forever, but the offspring of the wicked will be cut off. Psalms 37:28

Then you will know the truth, and the truth will set you free. John 8:32

For we know that our old self was crucified with him so that the body of sin might be done away with, that we should no longer be slaves to sin. Romans 6:6

For sin shall not be your master, because you are not under law, but under grace. Romans 6:14

No temptation has seized you except what is common to man. And God is faithful; he will not let you be tempted beyond what you can bear. But when you are tempted, he will also provide a way out so that you can stand up under it. 1 Corinthians 10:13

Grace and peace to you from God our Father and the Lord Jesus Christ, who gave himself for our sins to rescue us from the present evil age, according to the will of our God and Father. Galatians 1:3-4

But the Lord is faithful, and he will strengthen and protect you from the evil one. 2 Thessalonians 3:3

Because he himself suffered when he was tempted, he is able to help those who are being tempted. Hebrews 2:18

For the eyes of the Lord are on the righteous and his ears are attentive to their prayer, but the face of the Lord is against those who do evil. Who is going to harm you if you are eager to do good?
1 Peter 3:12-13

If this is so, then the Lord knows how to rescue godly men from trials and to hold the unrighteous for the day of judgment, while continuing their punishment. 2 Peter 2:9

JESUS WILL GIVE YOU PERSEVERANCE

Perseverance - persistence; continued efforts; to stick to a task or purpose, no matter how hard or troublesome.
WEBSTER'S NW DIC.

Do you not know that in a race all the runners run, but only one gets the prize? Run in such a way as to get the prize.
1 Corinthians 9:24

Nevertheless, the righteous will hold to their ways, and those with clean hands will grow stronger. Job 17:9

I am still confident of this: I will see the goodness of the Lord in the land of the living. Wait for the Lord; be strong and take heart and wait for the Lord. Psalms 27:13-14

Whatever your hand finds to do, do it with all your might, for in the grave, where you are going, there is neither working nor planning nor knowledge nor wisdom. Ecclesiastes 9:10

The Lord will fulfill his purpose for me; your love, O Lord, endures forever—do not abandon the works of your hands.
Psalms 138:8

The path of the righteous is like the first gleam of dawn, shining ever brighter till the full light of day. Proverbs 4:18

He gives strength to the weary and increases the power of the weak. Even youths grow tired and weary, and young men stumble and fall; but those who hope in the Lord will renew their strength. They will soar on wings like eagles; they will run and not grow weary, they will walk and not be faint. Isaiah 40:29-31

When God sees someone who doesn't quit, He looks down and says, "There is someone I can use."
- John Mason

Ask and it will be given to you; seek and you will find; knock and the door will be opened to you. Matthew 7:7

Therefore, since we are surrounded by such a great cloud of witnesses, let us throw off everything that hinders and the sin that so easily entangles, and let us run with perseverance the race marked out for us. Hebrews 12:1

Therefore, my dear brothers, stand firm. Let nothing move you. Always give yourselves fully to the work of the Lord, because you know that your labor in the Lord is not in vain. 1 Corinthians 15:58

Let us not become weary in doing good, for at the proper time we will reap a harvest if we do not give up. Galatians 6:9

I press on toward the goal to win the prize for which God has called me heavenward in Christ Jesus. Philippians 3:14

Endure hardship with us like a good soldier of Christ Jesus.
2 Timothy 2:3

Difficulties are stepping stones to success. - Anonymous

But my righteous one will live by faith. And if he shrinks back, I will not be pleased with him. Hebrews 10:38

Whatever you do, work at it with all your heart, as working for the Lord, not for men. Colossians 3:23

And so after waiting patiently, Abraham received what was promised. Hebrews 6:15

I have fought the good fight, I have finished the race, I have kept the faith. Now there is in store for me the crown of righteousness, which the Lord, the righteous Judge, will award to me on that day—and not only to me, but also to all who have longed for his appearing. 2 Timothy 4:7-8

Let us hold unswervingly to the hope we profess, for he who promised is faithful. Hebrews 10:23

So do not throw away your confidence; it will be richly rewarded. You need to persevere so that when you have done the will of God, you will receive what he has promised. Hebrews 10:35-36

Therefore put on the full armor of God, so that when the day of evil comes, you may be able to stand your ground, and after you have done everything, to stand. Stand firm then, with the belt of truth buckled around your waist, with the breastplate of righteousness in place. Ephesians 6:13-14

Therefore, my brothers, you whom I love and long for, my joy and crown, that is how you should stand firm in the Lord, dear friends!
Philippians 4:1

Rooted and built up in him, strengthened in the faith as you were taught, and overflowing with thankfulness. Colossians 2:7

Prove all things; hold fast that which is good.
1 Thessalonians 5:21 KJV

Be on your guard; stand firm in the faith; be men of courage; be strong. 1 Corinthians 16:13

Five times I received from the Jews the forty lashes minus one. Three times I was beaten with rods, once I was stoned, three times I was shipwrecked, I spent a night and a day in the open sea, I have been constantly on the move. I have been in danger from rivers, in danger from bandits, in danger from my own countrymen, in danger from Gentiles; in danger in the city, in danger in the country, in danger at sea; and in danger from false brothers. I have labored and toiled and have often gone without sleep; I have known hunger and thirst and have often gone without food; I have been cold and naked. 2 Corinthians 11:24-27

We are hard pressed on every side, but not crushed; perplexed, but not in despair; persecuted, but not abandoned; struck down, but not destroyed. 2 Corinthians 4:8-9

Therefore we do not lose heart. Though outwardly we are wasting away, yet inwardly we are being renewed day by day. For our light and momentary troubles are achieving for us an eternal glory that far outweighs them all. 2 Corinthians 4:16-17

We want each of you to show this same diligence to the very end, in order to make your hope sure. Hebrews 6:11

ETERNITY

HEAVEN

WHO'S GOING TO HEAVEN AND WHY?

Blessed are they that do his commandments, that they may have right to the tree of life, and may enter in through the gates into the city. Revelation 22:14

Blessed are those who wash their robes, that they may have the right to the tree of life and may go through the gates into the city.
Revelation 22:14

Then they will go away to eternal punishment, but the righteous to eternal life. Matthew 25:46

In reply Jesus declared, "I tell you the truth, no one can see the kingdom of God unless he is born again." "How can a man be born when he is old?" Nicodemus asked. "Surely he cannot enter a second time into his mother's womb to be born!" Jesus answered, "I tell you the truth, no one can enter the kingdom of God unless he is born again." Flesh gives birth to flesh, but the Spirit gives birth to spirit. You should not be surprised at my saying, You Must be born again. John 3:3-7

But whoever drinks the water I give him will never thirst. Indeed, the water I give him will become in him a spring of water welling up to eternal life. John 4:14

I tell you the truth, whoever hears my word and believes him who sent me has eternal life and will not be condemned; he has crossed over from death to life. John 5:24

I tell you the truth, if anyone keeps my word, he will never see death. John 8:51

Jesus said to her, "I am the resurrection and the life. He who believes in me will live, even though he dies; and whoever lives and believes in me will never die. Do you believe this?" John 11:25-26

WHAT IS HEAVEN LIKE?

However, as it is written: "No eye has seen, no ear has heard, no mind has conceived what God has prepared for those who love him." 1 Corinthians 2:9

The Lord has established his throne in heaven, and his kingdom rules over all. Psalms 103:19

Your sun will never set again, and your moon will wane no more; the Lord will be your everlasting light, and your days of sorrow will end. Then will all your people be righteous and they will possess the land forever. They are the shoot I have planted, the work of my hands, for the display of my splendor. Isaiah 60:20-21

In my Father's house are many rooms; if it were not so, I would have told you. I am going there to prepare a place for you. And if I go and prepare a place for you, I will come back and take you to be with me that you also may be where I am. John 14:2-3

Instead, they were longing for a better country—a heavenly one. Therefore God is not ashamed to be called their God, for he has prepared a city for them. Hebrews 11:16

There is only one thing better than going to heaven and that is to take someone with you. - Anonymous

But in keeping with his promise we are looking forward to a new heaven and a new earth, the home of righteousness. 2 Peter 3:13

Therefore, "they are before the throne of God and serve him day and night in his temple; and he who sits on the throne will spread his tent over them. Never again will they hunger; never again will they thirst. The sun will not beat upon them, nor any scorching heat. For the Lamb at the center of the throne will be their shepherd; he will lead them to springs of living water. And God will wipe away every tear from their eyes." Revelation 7:15-17

He who has an ear, let him hear what the Spirit says to the churches. To him who overcomes, I will give the right to eat from the tree of life, which is in the paradise of God. Revelation 2:7

The city does not need the sun or the moon to shine on it, for the glory of God gives it light, and the Lamb is its lamp. The nations will walk by its light, and the kings of the earth will bring their splendor into it. On no day will its gates ever be shut, for there will be no night there. The glory and honor of the nations will be brought into it. Revelation 21:23-26

Then the angel showed me the river of the water of life, as clear as crystal, flowing from the throne of God and of the Lamb down the middle of the great street of the city. On each side of the river stood the tree of life, bearing twelve crops of fruit, yielding its fruit every month. And the leaves of the tree are for the healing of the nations. No longer will there be any curse. The throne of God and of the Lamb will be in the city, and his servants will serve him. They will see his face, and his name will be on their foreheads. There will be no more night. They will not need the light of a lamp or the light of the sun, for the Lord God will give them light. And they will reign for ever and ever. Revelation 22:1-5

BUILDINGS IN HEAVEN

Now we know that if the earthly tent we live in is destroyed, we have a building from God, an eternal house in heaven, not built by human hands. 2 Corinthians 5:1

For he was looking forward to the city with foundations, whose architect and builder is God. Hebrews 11:10

Then I saw a new heaven and a new earth, for the first heaven and the first earth had passed away, and there was no longer any sea. I saw the Holy City, the new Jerusalem, coming down out of heaven from God, prepared as a bride beautifully dressed for her husband.
Revelation 21:1-2

It shone with the glory of God, and its brilliance was like that of a very precious jewel, like a jasper, clear as crystal. It had a great, high wall with twelve gates, and with twelve angels at the gates.

On the gates were written the names of the twelve tribes of Israel. There were three gates on the east, three on the north, three on the south and three on the west. The wall of the city had twelve foundations, and on them were the names of the twelve apostles of the Lamb. The angel who talked with me had a measuring rod of gold to measure the city, its gates and its walls. The city was laid out like a square, as long as it was wide. He measured the city with the rod and found it to be 12,000 stadia in length, and as wide and high as it is long. He measured its wall and it was 144 cubits thick, by man's measurement, which the angel was using. The wall was made of jasper, and the city of pure gold, as pure as glass. The foundations of the city walls were decorated with every kind of precious stone. The first foundation was jasper, the second sapphire, the third chalcedony, the fourth emerald, the fifth sardonyx, the sixth carnelian, the seventh chrysolite, the eighth beryl, the ninth topaz, the tenth chrysoprase, the eleventh jacinth, and the twelfth amethyst. The twelve gates were twelve pearls, each gate made of a single pearl. The great street of the city was of pure gold, like transparent glass. I did not see a temple in the city, because the Lord God Almighty and the Lamb are its temple. Revelation 21:11-22

FELLOWSHIP WITH GOD AND SAINTS IN HEAVEN

And I confer on you a kingdom, just as my Father conferred one on me, so that you may eat and drink at my table in my kingdom and sit on thrones, judging the twelve tribes of Israel. Luke 22:29-30

I say to you that many will come from the east and the west, and will take their places at the feast with Abraham, Isaac and Jacob in the kingdom of heaven. Matthew 8:11

To him who overcomes, I will give the right to sit with me on my throne, just as I overcame and sat down with my Father on his throne. Revelation 3:21

HELL

For we must all appear before the judgment seat of Christ, that each one may receive what is due him for the things done while in the body, whether good or bad. 2 Corinthians 5:10

I am he that liveth, and was dead; and, behold, I am alive for ever-more, Amen; and have the keys of hell and of death.

Revelation 1:18 KJV

I am the Living One; I was dead, and behold I am alive for ever and ever! And I hold the keys of death and Hades. Revelation 1:18

Do not be afraid of those who kill the body but cannot kill the soul. Rather, be afraid of the One who can destroy both soul and body in hell. Matthew 10:28

Death is naked before God; Destruction lies uncovered. Job 26:6

But I tell you that anyone who is angry with his brother will be subject to judgment. Again, anyone who says to his brother, 'Raca,' is answerable to the Sanhedrin. But anyone who says, 'You fool!' will be in danger of the fire of hell. Matthew 5:22

Hell is truth seen too late - duty neglected in its season.
- Tryon Edwards

You snakes! You brood of vipers! How will you escape being con-demned to hell? Matthew 23:33

But whoever blasphemes against the Holy Spirit will never be for-given; he is guilty of an eternal sin. Mark 3:29

WHO IS HELL FOR?

Then he will say to those on his left, 'Depart from me, you who are cursed, into the eternal fire prepared for the devil and his angels.
Matthew 25:41

In their greed these teachers will exploit you with stories they have made up. Their condemnation has long been hanging over them, and their destruction has not been sleeping. For if God did not spare angels when they sinned, but sent them to hell, putting them into gloomy dungeons to be held for judgment. 2 Peter 2:3-4

But the beast was captured, and with him the false prophet who had performed the miraculous signs on his behalf. With these signs he had deluded those who had received the mark of the beast and worshiped his image. The two of them were thrown alive into the fiery lake of burning sulfur. Revelation 19:20

447

And I saw an angel coming down out of heaven, having the key to the Abyss and holding in his hand a great chain. He seized the dragon, that ancient serpent, who is the devil, or Satan, and bound him for a thousand years. He threw him into the Abyss, and locked and sealed it over him, to keep him from deceiving the nations anymore until the thousand years were ended. After that, he must be set free for a short time. Revelation 20:1-3

And the devil, who deceived them, was thrown into the lake of burning sulfur, where the beast and the false prophet had been thrown. They will be tormented day and night for ever and ever.
Revelation 20:10

Then death and Hades were thrown into the lake of fire. The lake of fire is the second death. If anyone's name was not found written in the book of life, he was thrown into the lake of fire.
Revelation 20:14-15

There are no humanists, agnostics or atheists in hell, because every soul in hell believes in Jesus, bows to Jesus, and confess that Jesus is Lord. For some only after damnation awakes does reality break.

WHO'S GOING TO HELL AND WHY?

The wicked return to the grave, all the nations that forget God.
Psalms 9:17

Whoever believes and is baptized will be saved, but whoever does not believe will be condemned. Mark 16:16

Consequently, he who rebels against the authority is rebelling against what God has instituted, and those who do so will bring judgment on themselves. Romans 13:2

For the Lord watches over the way of the righteous, but the way of the wicked will perish. Psalms 1:6

And so that all will be condemned who have not believed the truth but have delighted in wickedness. 2 Thessalonians 2:12

You grant him relief from days of trouble, till a pit is dug for the wicked. Psalms 94:13

Instead, you yourselves cheat and do wrong, and you do this to your brothers. Do you not know that the wicked will not inherit the kingdom of God? Do not be deceived: Neither the sexually immoral nor idolaters nor adulterers nor male prostitutes nor homosexual offenders nor thieves nor the greedy nor drunkards nor slanderers nor swindlers will inherit the kingdom of God.
1 Corinthians 6:8-10

> *Life is too short and hell is too hot to play games with your eternal future.*

And envy; drunkenness, orgies, and the like. I warn you, as I did before, that those who live like this will not inherit the kingdom of God. Galatians 5:21

Thus they bring judgment on themselves, because they have broken their first pledge. 1 Timothy 5:12

HOW SERIOUS IS HELL?

And if your eye causes you to sin, gouge it out and throw it away. It is better for you to enter life with one eye than to have two eyes and be thrown into the fire of hell. Matthew 18:9

If your right eye causes you to sin, gouge it out and throw it away. It is better for you to lose one part of your body than for your whole body to be thrown into hell. And if your right hand causes you to sin, cut it off and throw it away. It is better for you to lose one part of your body than for your whole body to go into hell.
Matthew 5:29-30

If your hand causes you to sin, cut it off. It is better for you to enter life maimed than with two hands to go into hell, where the fire never goes out. And if your foot causes you to sin, cut it off. It is better for you to enter life crippled than to have two feet and be thrown into hell. And if your eye causes you to sin, pluck it out. It is better for you to enter the kingdom of God with one eye than to have two eyes and be thrown into hell, where their worm does not die, and the fire is not quenched. Mark 9:43-48

EXAMPLE OF HELL

At his gate was laid a beggar named Lazarus, covered with sores and longing to eat what fell from the rich man's table. Even the dogs came and licked his sores. "The time came when the beggar died and the angels carried him to Abraham's side. The rich man also died and was buried. In hell, where he was in torment, he looked up and saw Abraham far away, with Lazarus by his side. So he called to him, 'Father Abraham, have pity on me and send Lazarus to dip the tip of his finger in water and cool my tongue, because I am in agony in this fire.' "But Abraham replied, 'Son, remember that in your lifetime you received your good things, while Lazarus received bad things, but now he is comforted here and you are in agony. And besides all this, between us and you a great chasm has been fixed, so that those who want to go from here to you cannot, nor can anyone cross over from there to us.' "He answered, 'Then I beg you, father, send Lazarus to my father's house, for I have five brothers. Let him warn them, so that they will not also come to this place of torment.' "Abraham replied, 'They have Moses and the Prophets; let them listen to them.' "'No, father Abraham,' he said, 'but if someone from the dead goes to them, they will repent.' "He said to him, 'If they do not listen to Moses and the Prophets, they will not be convinced even if someone rises from the dead.' Luke 16:20-31

WHAT IS HELL LIKE?

When he opened the Abyss, smoke rose from it like the smoke from a gigantic furnace. The sun and sky were darkened by the smoke from the Abyss. Revelation 9:2

And the devil, who deceived them, was thrown into the lake of burning sulfur, where the beast and the false prophet had been thrown. They will be tormented day and night for ever and ever.
Revelation 20:10

The sinners in Zion are terrified; trembling grips the godless: "Who of us can dwell with the consuming fire? Who of us can dwell with everlasting burning?" Isaiah 33:14

Where their worm does not die, and the fire is not quenched.

Mark 9:48

DIFFERENT LEVELS OF PUNISHMENT IN HELL

Woe to you, teachers of the law and Pharisees, you hypocrites! You devour widows' houses and for a show make lengthy prayer. Therefore you will be punished more severely. Matthew 23:14

But suppose the servant says to himself, 'My master is taking a long time in coming,' and he then begins to beat the menservants and maidservants and to eat and drink and get drunk. The master of that servant will come on a day when he does not expect him and at an hour he is not aware of. He will cut him to pieces and assign him a place with the unbelievers. "That servant who knows his master's will and does not get ready or does not do what his master wants will be beaten with many blows. But the one who does not know and does things deserving punishment will be beaten with few blows. From everyone who has been given much, much will be demanded; and from the one who has been entrusted with much, much more will be asked. Luke 12:45-48

LOCATION OF HELL

Then I will bring you down with those who go down to the pit, to the people of long ago. I will make you dwell in the earth below, as in ancient ruins, with those who go down to the pit, and you will not return or take your place in the land of the living. I will bring you to a horrible end and you will be no more. You will be sought, but you will never again be found, declares the Sovereign Lord.

Ezekiel 26:20-21

But he knoweth not that the dead are there; and that her guests are in the depths of hell. Proverbs 9:18 KJV

The way of life is above to the wise, that he may depart from hell beneath. Proverbs 15:24 KJV

Therefore hell hath enlarged herself, and opened her mouth without measure: and their glory, and their multitude, and their pomp, and he that rejoiceth, shall descend into it. Isaiah 5:14 KJV

451

Therefore the grave enlarges its appetite and opens its mouth without limit; into it will descend their nobles and masses with all their brawlers and revelers. Isaiah 5:14

Wherefore he saith, When he ascended up on high, he led captivity captive, and gave gifts unto men. Now that he ascended, what is it but that he also descended first into the lower parts of the earth? He that descended is the same also that ascended up far above all heavens, that he might fill all things. Ephesians 4:8-10 KJV

This is why it says: "When he ascended on high, he led captives in his train and gave gifts to men." What does "he ascended" mean except that he also descended to the lower, earthly regions? He who descended is the very one who ascended higher than all the heavens, in order to fill the whole universe. Ephesians 4:8-10

HELL IS A BOTTOMLESS PIT

And the fifth angel sounded, and I saw a star fall from heaven unto the earth: and to him was given the key of the bottomless pit.
Revelation 9:1 KJV

And he opened the bottomless pit; and there arose a smoke out of the pit, as the smoke of a great furnace; and the sun and the air were darkened by reason of the smoke of the pit.
Revelation 9:2 KJV

When he opened the Abyss, smoke rose from it like the smoke from a gigantic furnace. The sun and sky were darkened by the smoke from the Abyss. Revelation 9:2

And they had a king over them, which is the angel of the bottomless pit, whose name in the Hebrew tongue is Abaddon, but in the Greek tongue hath his name Apollyon. Revelation 9:11 KJV

And when they shall have finished their testimony, the beast that ascendeth out of the bottomless pit shall make war against them, and shall overcome them, and kill them. Revelation 11:7 KJV

And I saw an angel come down from heaven, having the key of the bottomless pit and a great chain in his hand. And he laid hold on the dragon, that old serpent, which is the Devil, and Satan, and bound him a thousand years, And cast him into the bottomless pit, and shut him up, and set a seal upon him, that he should deceive the nations no more, till the thousand years should be fulfilled: and after that he must be loosed a little season. Revelation 20:1-3 KJV

And I saw an angel coming down out of heaven, having the key to the Abyss and holding in his hand a great chain. He seized the dragon, that ancient serpent, who is the devil, or Satan, and bound him for a thousand years. He threw him into the Abyss, and locked and sealed it over him, to keep him from deceiving the nations anymore until the thousand years were ended. After that, he must be set free for a short time. Revelation 20:1-3

satan's PAST

All your pomp has been brought down to the grave, along with the noise of your harps; maggots are spread out beneath you and worms cover you. How you have fallen from heaven, O morning star, son of the dawn! You have been cast down to the earth, you who once laid low the nations! You said in your heart, "I will ascend to heaven; I will raise my throne above the stars of God; I will sit enthroned on the mount of assembly, on the utmost heights of the sacred mountain. I will ascend above the tops of the clouds; I will make myself like the Most High." But you are brought down to the grave, to the depths of the pit. Those who see you stare at you, they ponder your fate: "Is this the man who shook the earth and made kingdoms tremble, the man who made the world a desert, who overthrew its cities and would not let his captives go home?" All the kings of the nations lie in state, each in his own tomb. But you are cast out of your tomb like a rejected branch; you are covered with the slain, with those pierced by the sword, those who descend to the stones of the pit. Like a corpse trampled underfoot, you will not join them in burial, for you have destroyed your land and killed your people. The offspring of the wicked will never be mentioned again. Isaiah 14:11-20

And having disarmed the powers and authorities, he made a public spectacle of them, triumphing over them by the cross.

Colossians 2:15

453

He who does what is sinful is of the devil, because the devil has been sinning from the beginning. The reason the Son of God appeared was to destroy the devil's work. 1 John 3:8

> *Whenever satan tries to torment your mind with your past sins and failures, which God has already forgiven, blotted out, and thrown into the depths of the sea, audibly remind satan of his notorious past and flaming eternal future in the lake of fire.*

The ruthless will vanish, the mockers will disappear, and all who have an eye for evil will be cut down. Isaiah 29:20

You belong to your father, the devil, and you want to carry out your father's desire. He was a murderer from the beginning, not holding to the truth, for there is no truth in him. When he lies, he speaks his native language, for he is a liar and the father of lies.
                                                                John 8:44

The thief comes only to steal and kill and destroy; I have come that they may have life, and have it to the full. John 10:10

Be sober, be vigilant; because your adversary the devil, AS a roaring lion, walketh about, seeking whom he MAY devour.
                                                                1 Peter 5:8 KJV

Be self-controlled and alert. Your enemy the devil prowls around like a roaring lion looking for someone to devour. 1 Peter 5:8

He who does what is sinful is of the devil, because the devil has been sinning from the beginning. The reason the Son of God appeared was to destroy the devil's work. 1 John 3:8

For the accuser of our brothers, who accuses them before our God day and night, has been hurled down. Revelation 12:10

And even if our gospel is veiled, it is veiled to those who are perishing. The god of this age has blinded the minds of unbelievers, so that they cannot see the light of the gospel of the glory of Christ, who is the image of God. 2 Corinthians 4:3-4

In which you used to live when you followed the ways of this world and of the ruler of the kingdom of the air, the spirit who is now at work in those who are disobedient. Ephesians 2:2

But he was not strong enough, and they lost their place in heaven.
Revelation 12:8

satan's ETERNAL FUTURE

Then he will say to those on his left, 'Depart from me, you who are cursed, into the eternal fire prepared for the devil and his angels.
Matthew 25:41

Now is the time for judgment on this world; now the prince of this world will be driven out. John 12:31

The God of peace will soon crush Satan under your feet. The grace of our Lord Jesus be with you. Romans 16:20

For if God did not spare angels when they sinned, but sent them to hell, putting them into gloomy dungeons to be held for judgment.
2 Peter 2:4

These men are springs without water and mists driven by a storm. Blackest darkness is reserved for them. 2 Peter 2:17

He who does what is sinful is of the devil, because the devil has been sinning from the beginning. The reason the Son of God appeared was to destroy the devil's work. 1 John 3:8

And the angels who did not keep their positions of authority but abandoned their own home—these he has kept in darkness, bound with everlasting chains for judgment on the great Day. Jude 1:6

And he opened the bottomless pit; and there arose a smoke out of the pit, as the smoke of a great furnace; and the sun and the air were darkened by reason of the smoke of the pit. Revelation 9:2

When he opened the Abyss, smoke rose from it like the smoke from a gigantic furnace. The sun and sky were darkened by the smoke from the Abyss. Revelation 9:2

Therefore rejoice, you heavens and you who dwell in them! But woe to the earth and the sea, because the devil has gone down to you! He is filled with fury, because he knows that his time is short.
Revelation 12:12

A third angel followed them and said in a loud voice: "If anyone worships the beast and his image and receives his mark on the forehead or on the hand, he, too, will drink of the wine of God's fury, which has been poured full strength into the cup of his wrath. He will be tormented with burning sulfur in the presence of the holy angels and of the Lamb. And the smoke of their torment rises for ever and ever. There is no rest day or night for those who worship the beast and his image, or for anyone who receives the mark of his name." Revelation 14:9-11

But the beast was captured, and with him the false prophet who had performed the miraculous signs on his behalf. With these signs he had deluded those who had received the mark of the beast and worshiped his image. The two of them were thrown alive into the fiery lake of burning sulfur. Revelation 19:20

And I saw an angel coming down out of heaven, having the key to the Abyss and holding in his hand a great chain. He seized the dragon, that ancient serpent, who is the devil, or Satan, and bound him for a thousand years. He threw him into the Abyss (bottomless pit), and locked and sealed it over him, to keep him from deceiving the nations anymore until the thousand years were ended. After that, he must be set free for a short time. Revelation 20:1-3

They marched across the breadth of the earth and surrounded the camp of God's people, the city he loves. But fire came down from heaven and devoured them. And the devil, who deceived them, was thrown into the lake of burning sulfur, where the beast and the false prophet had been thrown. They will be tormented day and night for ever and ever. Revelation 20:9-10

Then death and Hades were thrown into the lake of fire. The lake of fire is the second death. If anyone's name was not found written in the book of life, he was thrown into the lake of fire.

Revelation 20:14-15

PART III

Inspiration for the African Diaspora

Articles

LEARNING TO BE LEADERS

by Myles Munroe

Learning to be Leaders

The world is filled with followers, supervisors, and managers but very few leaders. Leadership is like beauty, it's hard to define but you know it when you see it. Time has produced a legacy of distinguished and outstanding individuals who have impacted history and the ongoing development of mankind. These people were both men and women, rich and poor, learned and unlearned, trained and untrained. They came from every race, color, language and culture of the world. Many of them had no ambition to become great or renowned. In fact, most of the individuals who have greatly affected mankind were simple people who were victims of circumstances that demanded the hidden qualities of their character, or they were driven by a personal passionate goal.

Leaders are ordinary people who accept or are placed under extraordinary circumstances that bring forth their latent potential, producing a character that inspires the confidence and trust of others. Our world today is in desperate need of such individuals.

William Shakespeare once wrote, "There is a tide in the affairs of men." In these words, he was expressing his observation of the turning pages of history and their influence upon our lives. It's as if we, as men and nations, are caught in a tide of providential events. There have been eras in the history of our world in which multiple sets of tide-like influences have impacted our civilization and culture at nearly the same time. These historical incidents are known as "crossroads of history." I would suggest that, in the twentieth century, we are at a confluence of historic tides.

In the past two decades, a relatively short span of time within this century, the world has experienced many remarkable changes in the realms of science, technology, medicine, space and hundreds of other so-called advancements in our nations. Strangely, this century has also seen more distressing things than any previous century, devastating wars, monstrous new weapons, countless natural disasters and fatal diseases.

We must agree that our generation lives in a swirling tide of events, dreams, promises, threats and changing ideas about the present and the future. Certainly our century has been the most politically interesting, the bloodiest, the most revolutionary and the most unpredictable of any century in history. This confluence of strange conditions presses this generation to ask anew, "Why am I here? What is the purpose of life? Why are life and reality the way they are?"

The leaders of our time are bewildered when they are called upon to explain the reasons that our world is the way it is, or to suggest a direction for the future. Many in positions of public trust confess that they are just trying to keep the lid on, and others have abandoned even that hope. We need competent leaders.

Added to this bleak environment is the painful reality that over the past few decades there seems to have been a dramatic leadership vacuum developed throughout the world. In every arena there is an absence of quality, effective leadership. In the political, civic, economic, social and spiritual arenas, recent events indicate that previous generations have produced a poor quality of characters who fade in the presence of true leadership and leave our present generation in this same leadership vacuum.

The recent disgrace and fall of many renowned Christian leaders, the exposure of corruption and unethical activities among political leaders, and the covert conspiracies of governments betraying their own people is evidence that this lack of quality leadership is affecting every sphere of our lives.

It is in this environment that we, as stewards of this present age, must face the challenge of identifying, developing, training, releasing and reproducing a generation of leaders who would secure the future for our children and their children.

Tapping Your Potential

"A good leader not only knows where he is going, but he can inspire others to go with him."

In every person, there is potential for leadership. Despite this latent ability lying below the surface, there are very few individuals who realize this power and fewer still who have responded effectively to the call. As a result, our nations, societies and communities are suffering from an astounding leadership vacuum.

Everyone deplores this lack of true leadership throughout the world, and the blame usually lands at the feet of the individual who hasn't made the grade. Greed, timidity and lack of vision are rampant among the current crop of "pseudoleaders."

Where are the genuine leaders? Where are the individuals who are willing to take responsibility for the present situation and conditions in the world? Who is willing to accept the challenge, to face it head on with integrity, character and a commitment to execute righteous judgment for a better world? From America to Australia, from China to Chile and from Canada to the Caribbean, the world is in desperate need of true leaders.

Our communities need positive role models, our children need fathers and our world needs direction. Where are the leaders? Who are they? What makes an individual a leader? Who becomes a leader? When does one become a leader?

This is not the first time that an obvious vacuum of quality, effective leadership has prevailed throughout the world. A quick glance at the historical record will show that during periods when moral, social, economic, spiritual and political chaos gripped nations, the greatest leaders in history surfaced. Even the biblical record reveals God's demand for quality leaders during times of human crisis.

His search for effective leadership is expressed in numerous statements such as the following:

"But now your kingdom will not endure; the Lord has sought out a man after his own heart and appointed him leader of his people.
(1 Samuel 13:14)

"I looked, and there were no people. . ." (Jeremiah 4:25)

"Go up and down the streets of Jerusalem, look around and consider, search through her squares. If you can find but one person who deals honestly and seeks the truth, I will forgive this city."
(Jeremiah 5:1)

"I looked for a man among them who would build up the wall and stand before me in the gap on behalf of the land so I would not have to destroy it, but I found none." (Ezekiel 22:30)

463

These Scriptures reveal that whenever a nation has a lack of quality, legitimate, and just leaders, national deterioration occurs. They also reveal that God's remedy to this type of situation is the discovery and raising up of new, trained leaders committed to justice and righteousness. Quality leadership is the key to a prosperous and peaceful life and nation.

It is obvious that our nations are painfully in need of such leaders. The church is desperately in need of leaders. Our homes are crying out for leadership. Our youth are begging for leaders. God's answer to all our social, moral, and economic problems is qualified, just, and righteous leaders. However, it is impossible for an unrighteous world to produce righteous leaders and an unjust system to produce just characteristics, just as it is impossible for a bitter spring to bring forth sweet water.

The essence of leadership is the exercise of influence for a common cause. For instance, the command given to the Christian church by Christ is, "Go and make disciples of all nations, teaching them the things I have taught you." This is a direct mandate to provide leadership for nations, instructing them to live according to the principles of the kingdom of God.

This commission clearly places the responsibility for producing the quality leaders that this nation and the world needs upon the shoulders of the Christian church, yet it is sad that even the church itself is in need of quality leadership. Perhaps this is because the focus of the church and its theology has been preoccupied with heaven and preparing individuals to leave the planet, thus forsaking the responsibility of producing quality leaders for our nations. Today, the responsibility to meet this need is the challenge of our generation for the sake of the generations to come.

Because you're reading this, you are now responsible to hear the cry in your nation, your city, your community, your church and your family for leaders. You are a candidate for leadership in your generation.

Becoming a leader isn't easy, just as becoming a doctor or poet isn't easy; Anyone who claims otherwise is fooling himself. However, learning to lead is a lot easier than most of us think it is, because each of us possesses the capacity for leadership. In fact, every one of us can point to some leadership experience, whether it was in a classroom, a gang, a Sunday school play, or at home.

Whatever your leadership experience, it's a good place to start. We cannot function without leaders. Our quality of life depends on the quality of our leaders. Since no one else seems to be volunteering, it's up to you. If you've ever had dreams of leadership, now is the time, and this is the place. We need you.

A Word to the Third World

The quality of tomorrow's leaders lies in the character of today's followers.

Today there are over five billion people on planet earth. Over half of these people live in countries and conditions that have been labeled Third World. This term was invented by a French economist who was attempting to describe the various groupings of people throughout the world based on their socioeconomic status. Whether or not this term is valid, it is generally accepted as a description or element of identification for millions of people.

I was born and live in a part of the world that is said to fall within this category. The term is identified as any people who did not benefit from or participate in the industrial revolution. A large majority of these people were not allowed to benefit from the industrial revolution because they were subjugated at the time, being used to fuel the economic base for the revolution. Many of them were reduced to slaves and indentured servants, thus robbing them of their identity, dignity, self-worth, and self-respect.

However, despite the changes in conditions and a greater measure of freedom and independence, many of these peoples are still grappling with their identity and their sense of self-worth. Many of the nations that progressed and developed through the industrial revolution have reinforced (by attitude, policies, and legislation) the notion that these Third World peoples do not possess the potential to develop the skills, intelligence and sophistication necessary to equal that of industrialized states.

465

With this prejudice and misconception in mind, I wish to say to all Third World peoples everywhere--African, Indian, Latin, Oriental and other nationalities--your potential is limitless and cannot be measured by the opinions of others. You possess the ability to achieve, develop, accomplish, produce, create, with all the potential you need to fulfill your purpose in this life.

Zeal Without Skill

Historically, the Third World peoples have always been a hardworking, dedicated, zealous, and highly sensitive people. Many of them are products of oppression and have had instilled in them a sense of timidity, a lack of self-confidence and a spirit of dependency. They fail, in many cases, to realize the capacity of the leadership potential within them.

In most of these Third World countries, the system of colonialism and the process of colonization carried with it the dehumanizing element of fostering dependency and robbing individuals of the essential aspect of creative development. This debilitating system also provided its subjects with basic training for service but not for productivity.

In essence, they were taught how to grow sugar cane, but not how to make sugar; they were taught how to grow cotton but not how to make cloth. The result was a perpetuation of dependency, for even after they were "liberated," or as some call it "emancipated," they were left with the raw material but no ability to transform it into end products.

In effect, they were left with the zeal of freedom without the skill for development. This is the reason why so many of our Third World nations today are still experiencing tremendous hardship and turmoil. The industrialized states that once colonized them have maintained a sense of control and superiority that manifests itself in a sophisticated form of economic colonialism instead of political colonialism.

The Third World nations in effect are led to still look to the industrially developed states for their measure of standard, quality and excellence. This in turn breeds a sense of disrespect and suspicion for their own products and a denial of the great potential that lies dormant in these great people everywhere. This distrust and denial of potential was also transferred to the church world through mission efforts. Many churches throughout the Third World are products of foreign based missions and in most cases were dependent on a "mother" church organization. This dependency factor continued even to the time of national independence, leaving many of these ministries without well trained, confident, competent, and skilled leaders. Even to this day, despite the fact that many of these church organizations have qualified and capable leaders, there is still the notion that the presence of a foreign element is necessary for the maintenance of excellence and quality.

However, there is a fresh wind of responsibility blowing throughout these Third World countries stirring a sense of destiny and purpose in the hearts of these people everywhere. This awakening of the spirit of responsibility is being felt in all arenas, political, social, civic and spiritual. It is therefore imperative that the Third World people look to the inner strength and potential lying deep within them, and with a renewed commitment to the Creator, Jesus Christ, and prepare themselves for the refinement of skills. Ecclesiastes 10:10 states, "If the axe is dull and its edge unsharpened, more strength is needed but skill will bring success."

It is my desire that every man, woman, boy, and girl, in every nation and every race, come to realize the tremendous potential and capacity for greatness that lies dormant within them.

True Leadership is Freedom

No man is truly free until every man is free. This is the essence of life and the goal of leadership. Much of what we call freedom is not freedom at all, but simply permission given by an oppressor to become somebody. This is not freedom. If the source of your liberty is another person or a group, then you are only as free as they allow you to be. Freedom cannot be given by another.

True freedom is a product of truth, not legislation. It comes from the revelation of agitation. Jesus, expressing God's concept of freedom stated, "And you shall know the truth, and the truth shall make you free." In essence, He saw true freedom as a result of understanding the truth about yourself and everyone else. In other words, no one can give you the "right" to be free. Freedom is not something you receive, it is something that happens to you. Free men can never be bound.

> *True leadership sets followers free*
> *to be led by the Holy Spirit.*

The concept of freedom is concealed in the very word "freedom." This word is a grammatical construction of the words "free" and "dominion" and it comes from the concept of having the liberty to dominate. This truth is the very heart of the purpose for man's creation and is expressed in the very foundation of God's intention for mankind. In Genesis 1:26 He declared, "And let them rule over all the earth." This established not only the purpose for man's creation, but also the measure of his fulfillment.

In essence, no man is truly free until he has the liberty to dominate his environment, not other men. This is the heart of true leadership, to inspire men to declare independence from the bondage of other men's opinions and pre-judgements, and to tap the unlimited potential within them to creatively dominate the earth, which is his destiny.

Therefore, any leadership that restricts, denies, inhibits, limits, suppresses, oppresses, obstructs, or frustrates this God-given mandate and capacity, is not leadership at all. True leadership sets followers free to be led by the Holy Spirit, for only him whom the Son sets free is truly free indeed.

"None of us is free until all of us are free."

EMBRACING THE CALL TO GREATNESS

by James Giles

Embracing the Call to Greatness

As a nation and as individuals we are called to embrace the greatness that lies within us as people of African descent. To do so, it is imperative that we understand that the essence of greatness is time-conscious.

Those who understand the call to greatness also understand that every moment spent in making excuses or reinforcing them is time wasted. *Kairos* is the Greek word for a particular point in the continuum of history. Kairos is pushy and insistent. It is similar to pregnancy in that when the time has come for delivery, for the great push, then there is time for nothing else.

History tells us that the African people were the only people who did not come to this country with a vision for religious, social, and political freedom and economic prosperity. They did not come consciously to build "the land of the free and the home of the brave." African people did not come to the shores of America to make a covenant with the land or to carve out of the wilderness a great "civilization." It was the Europeans who had the vision for America, though not all Europeans came to America of their own free will. It was certain Europeans who saw the enormous prospects for prosperity and freedom. Yes, they had the vision but ultimately Africans, and other non-dominant European cultures provided the labor upon which the agricultural and later industrial strength of America was built. A friend pointed out the distinction to be made between poor Irish immigrants who had vision but no opportunity, and Africans who were even denied vision.

These Africans were not allowed to have any major stake in the vision for America; they merely provided the physical labor force. What obviously happens in this scenario is that the people with the vision for the land, in this case the Europeans, end up loving the land and its copious productivity. The people who merely provide the labor force and who have no covenant with the land, nor any serious stake in the vision for the land end up hating the land. These people's lot never changes. They see how the fruit of their labor is drastically improving the quality of life for the vision bearers while they benefit not. Almost ten generations of people of African descent have lived in America without a covenant of land or purpose. The African people never received their twenty acres and a mule promised in the 1860's. However, between 1915-1920 when the black population of the country was half its present number, African-Americans owned fifteen million (15,000,000) acres of land. For approximately twelve million (12,000,000) blacks this constituted more than one acre per person. By 1980, according to studies, twenty-five million blacks owned only six million acres of land in the "good ole" USA. As you can see, with more than twice the population, blacks owned less than half the land that they owned in the early twentieth century.

Every major covenant with God involved land, also called "real estate." A people who possess a land covenant understand their responsibility to work the land, extracting from it its potential yield. No land is barren except that which is under a curse. Land is intended by God to be productive. I have heard Dr. Mensa Otabil say that when a people lose faith in the ability of the land to produce, they themselves become nonproductive. As long as African-Americans see themselves as having no stake in the future of America we will not prosper. I believe God never intended the back to Africa movements to succeed. The African-American presence in America is real and permanent, and God does not will us to remain hanging by a thread, continuing to dangle over poverty, death, and destruction.

Korean businessman Kim Woo Choong tells the story of building Daewoo, the conglomerate of companies he oversees. He and a few others had a vision for Korea when that country was in the throes of poverty. Some twenty-five years ago the average income in Korea was $75. Today that income has risen to approximately $6,000. Chairman Kim talks of a committed group of visionaries who worked from seven or eight in the morning until eleven or twelve midnight over protracted periods of time. They believed in their hearts that what they were doing had to be done for "the country, the company, and for themselves". What vision, to believe that your efforts can lift a country out of poverty and blight. It does no good to sit around lamenting or perpetually analyzing a negative situation.

In less than fifty years the Japanese have rebuilt a country ravaged by the horrors of two atomic bombings. The Jews suffered the Holocaust but never lost faith in themselves as a people or in their ability to produce. Many second generation descendants of Jewish families who experienced the Holocaust have come to America and built large fortunes. Some of these Jews control major segments of the American economy. My point is that these people, though they suffered deep and regrettable atrocities, never lost their faith in themselves and historically, wherever they have found themselves, they have been productive. It is because they never allowed their spirits to die.

The Bible says in Proverbs 18:14 "The spirit of a man will sustain his infirmity; but a wounded spirit who can bear?" Again Proverbs 15:13 says, ". . . by sorrow of the heart the spirit is broken." A people who spend too much time grieving over their circumstances are a people who are not going to be quick in rebuilding. Human pain and suffering is real but so is the nobility of the human spirit inflamed with vision and purpose.

Exodus 6:9 says, "And Moses spake unto the children of Israel: but they harkened not unto Moses for anguish of spirit, and for cruel bondage."

"Anguish" is from the Hebrew word *qotser* (ko-tser) or *qarsar* (kaw-tsar). The word means shortness or impatience of spirit. It also means to dock off or curtail the harvest; to cut down; much discouraged, grieved, loathe, mourn, weep; troubled or vexed. The "spirit" here refers to the mind. Because of their historic circumstances, the people of Israel were unable to hear from God's prophet the word of deliverance. Too often, the past conditions our expectations for the future.

What makes the children of Israel's predicament even more interesting is the fact that they had been praying for God to intervene on their behalf. Finally, when He did they did not believe in the present possibility of what they had prayed for, namely their own deliverance (See Exodus chapters two and three). Ultimately we find that Israel did not calculate the cost of freedom. Freedom for Israel in the mind of God was not merely release from the cruel yoke of Pharaoh. God's plan was that they build Him a new nation

473

built upon the principles of righteousness and justice. Too many people today are exhausting their creative energies wailing and lamenting while the walls of America's inner cities lie in ruins. It is deeply saddening to see communities and individuals wallowing in fatalism concerning their futures. We face a global crisis today, and if any solution is possible it will come from those who still possess the capacity to dream and who can strengthen their wills to work. We are in desperate need of a prophetic word from God for our nation. Politicians play to our need for hope with slogans and vain promises, but the Prophet declares the heartbeat of God Almighty.

What is needed for the rebuilding of America's inner cities is the spirit of Nehemiah and his people. Nehemiah (whose name means Jehovah consoles), upon hearing of the deplorable condition of his countrymen in Judea, took leave of his position in the palace and went to Jerusalem determined to better the living conditions of his brethren. The Bible describes the conditions which faced Nehemiah. In Nehemiah 1:2 and 3, we are told that "Hanani, one of my brethren, came, he and certain men of Judah; and I asked them concerning the Jews that had escaped, which were left of the captivity, and concerning Jerusalem. And they said unto me, The remnant that are left of the captivity there in the province are in great affliction and reproach: the wall of Jerusalem is broken down and the gates thereof are burned with fire."

This is certainly the report on America's inner cities. Nehemiah was told that his people were in "affliction" and "reproach." Affliction is from the Hebrew word *rah* or *raa* (rawah). The word means to spoil literally by breaking into pieces. It means: to be good for nothing; to do mischief; to show self friendly by mistake; to do harm; to be, deal, or do worse. The word also means: bad calamity; exceeding great grief; marked by mischief; ill-favored; displeasure. Reproach is from the word *chelpah* or *charap*h (khawraf) meaning: to expose by pulling or stripping off; to surrender, blaspheme, defy, or upbraid; disgraced or shamed; to defame, rail at, chide, taunt, revile; to suffer.

In major cities all over America there is affliction and reproach. African-Americans in inner cities or ghettos; Native American brothers and sisters on reservations; Mexican and Latino brothers and sisters in barrios; displaced farmers and poor rural whites many of whom have lost hope. This time of crisis demands more than political sloganizing from career politicians. These times require the honesty and courage to confront the real issues and to sacrifice. These are times that require the stubborn persistence of the human will to live in the image of God. No matter in what set of circumstances you may find yourself you may not give up. You do not have the right to convince yourself that your efforts won't matter. We need for you to rebel against inhumanity, injustice, poverty, and self-pity. This is a time when historically oppressed people must come forth helping to shape the conscience of a new America. It's time to stop playing the blame game: understanding that white people are not devils, and that racism and white people are not ultimately to be held responsible for the challenges that many ethnic communities and people of color face.

Black, Native American, Brown, and White, our blood lines mingle. The only Ubermenschen (master or super race) is the human race. White people, will not save America alone, nor should they be asked to. It is negligent, irresponsible, and ungodly for people of color to neglect America when we are most needed. I am not advocating some shallow, pathetic, denial centered patriotism, but a will to live and fulfill the purpose of God to our generation. We do not need the sanction of anyone to begin rebuilding our people and neighborhoods. The essence of greatness calls, beckons, summons. It is the hour of the trailblazer, the pathfinder. We need to cut covenant with the land God has given us. For if we sow curses to the land we will reap nothing more than curses.

I do not need to be reminded of the infamous history of this nation. I have studied it in detail. However, a people looking only backward cannot journey forward. I am also aware that what I am suggesting here is not simplistic but is rather the work of our own and subsequent generations. Many of our parents, grandparents, and great grandparents, though they themselves did not taste the fruits of prosperity, challenged us to live heroically. They challenged us to make a difference. They told us that we had an outstanding debt that it would take our lives to repay. We found out that we owed Jesus Christ, Sojourner Truth, Ida B. Wells, Nat Turner, Frederick Douglass, Thurgood Marshall, Martin Luther King, Rosa

Parks, E.D. Nixon, the local preacher, school teacher, barber, businessman or woman, the editor of the local ethnic newspaper, and a host of others. We were taught that if you chose failure you let down not just yourself but an entire community which held high expectations for you.

To this day I am thankful for every neighbor who prayed for me and who refused to give up on me even when I gave them very little over which to be encouraged. One of the great tragedies of our day is the disappearing sense of neighborhood and community all over America: little cohesion or communal caring, few stories from the elders. A sign of the moral and spiritual decline of our culture is the rampant disrespect for the elders. We need their wisdom, their stories, their perspective and their encouragement. They helped us to know that we have more than simply ourselves to live for.

It saddens me when I visit the homes and offices of many of my African-American ministerial colleagues and find no libraries, no books, journals, magazines, newspapers, interesting software, or other stimulating multimedia hardware. How can a church whose leaders suffer from information-deprivation syndrome have a prophetic word for these times? Prayer is critically important but it is only one dimension of spirituality. I like what William Stringfellow wrote in his wonderful little book *The Politics of Spirituality*:

"There is no biblical spirituality to be found in a vacuum, cut off from the remainder of humanity within the totality of creation. Indeed, biblical spirituality is significantly about the restoration or renewal of these relationships throughout the realm of created life. To put the same differently, biblical spirituality concerns living in the midst of the era of the Fall, wherein all relationships whatsoever have been lost or damaged or diminished or twisted or broken, in a way which is open to transcendence of the fallen state of each and every relationship and in which these relationships are recovered or rendered new. This transfiguration wrought in biblical spirituality includes one's relationship with oneself, in the most self-conscious and radically personal sense, but it simultaneously implicates one concretely in reconciliation with the rest of creation and is thus the most profoundly political reality available to human experience."

476

From a biblical perspective, therefore, the assertion of some species of so-called spirituality which is privatized and nonpolitical or anti-political is, simply, nonsense. Where there is poverty, spirituality strives to eliminate it and bring prosperity. Where there is hopelessness, spirituality labors for hope. Where there is destruction and despair, spirituality exalts vision and faith. Spirituality is about the renewal, the rekindling of the human spirit. It is about transforming ghettos, barrios, reservations, and slums into places of peace and productivity. The social agenda of this or that presidential, congressional, senatorial, gubernatorial, or mayoral candidate is not going to substantially improve conditions in these areas. God never intended that we turn the whole of our destiny over to any one man or "race." As tough, naive, or historically uninformed as it may sound, it is time for some good old personal responsibility. Don't wait for someone to tell you it's all right to make something of your life. Don't wait for America to ask you to make a difference! As one shoe company would say, Just Do It!

Have you read the story of the East St. Louis, Illinois high school football coach Bob Shannon? In the city with the nation's highest murder rate and over fifty percent (50%) unemployment; with no running water for toilets, sinks, or urinals; with tattered uniforms and a playing field full of potholes, Bob Shannon has done the unthinkable. In fourteen years as head coach Shannon has amassed a 144 and 20 record. He has coached his teams to the state championship seven times, winning five of those times. At one stretch Coach Shannon won forty-four (44) straight games. Under conditions which would have forced out a lesser man Coach Shannon exemplifies the essence of greatness though he probably would recoil at the notion.

Coach Shannon is repairing wounded spirits and saving dreams. He is snatching the ghetto out of the souls of many young men and inspiring them to translate their winning football ways to other areas of life. I want you to know today that in spite of your physical surroundings you are an incredible person. The essence of greatness percolates in your bosom. You can triumph over seemingly impossible odds. I know you can! You have an unfathomable amount of untapped potential waiting to be explored.

Throughout the course of history men and women have triumphed over poverty, hopelessness, disease, despair, national crisis, racism, sexism, the small expectations of others, past failure, and a host of other obstacles to do great things. The world has yet to see a black man or woman start a company from nothing and build its net worth to a billion or more dollars employing and educating tens or hundreds of thousands of people in the process. The world has yet to see an automobile designed, manufactured, and marketed by an African-American or Native American. The world has yet to see a five million (5,000,000) square foot shopping mall designed and or built by a Mexican or Latino. This is not at all to suggest that none of these people already have significant accomplishments for which they should be very proud! However, the level of productivity that will remove feelings of inferiority and reproach from scores of people has yet to be fulfilled.

I love young people, and I am committed to raising their consciousness of God, their self-dignity and value, and their aspirations. Once after speaking in one of America's inner cities I was approached by a young African-American girl of fifteen or sixteen years. She was beaming with joy and possessed a luminous smile. She said to me, "All my life I've wanted to be a lawyer but never thought I could; now I know I can!" It almost brought tears to my eyes. Another time, after an engagement in New York, my escort and I were pressing through the crowd of hundreds, mostly adults. As we passed through the thickest part of the crowd there stood a beautiful little girl of about eleven or twelve years. She looked up at me and said, "I just want you to know that you are an excellent role model for black youth and I love you very much." She then placed her arms around my waist and hugged me. Whew! No accolades in the world can top this! Now I certainly do not consider myself an excellent role model for anyone. However, I would like to think that I try very hard and I want to thank these kids for their votes of confidence.

What the world needs is more people builders, more dream builders, more lamplighters. It has been said that both optimists and pessimists contribute to society. Proof? The optimist invents the airplane and the pessimist invents the parachute. Henry Ford once said that the ability to encourage others is one of life's finest assets.

The auto inventor and manufacturer knew the power of encouragement. He had learned of it as a young man. Memorable to him was the time, at the beginning of his career, when he made a drawing of his newly built engine for Thomas A. Edison. Young Henry had endured much criticism and ridicule. Most mechanical experts of that day were convinced that electric carriages would be the popular passenger cars of the future. But attending a dinner one evening at which Edison was present, Ford began explaining his engine to the men nearest him at the table. He noticed that Edison, seated several chairs away, was listening. Finally the great man moved closer and asked the young inventor to make a drawing. When the crude sketch was complete, Edison studied it intently, then suddenly banged his fist on the table. "Young man," he said, "that's the thing! You have it!" Years later, Ford recalled, "The thump of that fist upon the table was worth worlds to me."

LET US STRIVE TO BECOME DREAM BUILDERS AND ENCOURAGERS! Proverbs 25:28 says, "He that hath no rule over his own spirit is like a city that is broken down and without walls." Your spirit is that part of you where God speaks and reveals your purpose and destiny. Proverbs 20:27 says, "The spirit of man is the candle of the Lord, searching all the inward parts of the belly." Do not allow any thing or any person to kill your spirit. The Word of God says we must rule our own spirits. Your life's purpose and destiny lie within your spirit. God has known you from birth. You have gained a strength from adversity and a courage to face future challenges.

I encourage to you allow God to confront you with the challenge of excellence, the essence of greatness. We must lead a people back to God, back to nobility and heroism. We must become as warriors committed to the restoration of a people, a church and a nation. In Jesus' Name the summons has been served!

PRINCIPLES OF GREATNESS

by James Giles

Principles of Greatness

Discovering the presence of blacks in the Bible opens our eyes to one singular fact: we are a people of greatness! That greatness is not just historical, but ever-present. Understanding, and tapping into the principles of greatness will change your life — forever!

Webster's Dictionary defines a principle as "the ultimate source, origin, or cause of something; a natural or original tendency, faculty or endowment; a fundamental truth, law, doctrine, or motivating force, upon which others are based; an essential element, constituent, or quality, especially one that produces a specific effect; the method of a thing's operation."

It is amazing to me that the public schools in this country, generally speaking, do not deal with principles of success or greatness. They teach principles of mediocrity and conformity. They do not teach excellence but tolerate the very minimum standards.

All the time I hear kids griping about too much responsibility. Many of them think home is a hotel with an unlimited food and beverage tab, all the video games they can play, all the latest cassettes or CDs (complimentary of course), and a monthly all expenses paid trip to the mall of their choice.They feel that no reciprocal demands should be placed upon them at all, and in many cases their strongest ally is the school where they spend six or seven hours five days a week. This attitude breeds sloth, cynicism, greed, arrogance, irresponsibility, and ultimately destruction. These are certainly not the values or character traits necessary for success and fulfillment.

The spirit and essence of greatness is born when children are told of their uniqueness and of their special potential. We all have a responsibility to make a contribution to mankind and the sooner we are taught that the better. We should teach children that there are going to be obstacles and that sometimes the road will be so rough that quitting seems to be the only option. We should teach them that there is hatred, racism, and sexism, and that some will doubt your ability because of your race or sex. In spite of this, what is important is that you refuse to doubt your own God-given ability. We should teach that obstacles are inevitable but not necessarily insurmountable! These obstacles may be overcome by understanding the universal laws which govern success and achievement. A random, disorganized mind, will never produce success and fulfillment. The great ones develop and practice habits of spiritual, mental, and physical discipline.

Once, I was listening to a tape by sales and motivation expert Brian Tracy. Mr. Tracy had interviewed several successful people in order to gain an understanding as to what secrets they had discovered and parlayed into success. He tells of asking a famous billionaire, "What are the secrets to success?" The billionaire thought for a moment then responded, "The secret to success is that there are no secrets to success!" In other words, success is no secret, neither is greatness. No one in this world who ever succeeded did so accidentally.

The major barriers to your fulfilling God's purpose for your life are in your own mind.

Principles of Greatness

Success and failure both result from the choices you and I make moment by moment, hour by hour, and day by day. Success is deliberate and so is failure and mediocrity. Become a student of those principles that produced the lives and accomplishments of your heroes. Following is my list of PRINCIPLES OF GREATNESS. My list is not exhaustive so add your own principles.

1. Know Your Intrinsic Value.
2. Know That You Have A Purpose For Being Alive.
3. Discover Your Purpose.
4. Decide To Fulfill Your Purpose.
5. Decide Not To Be Mediocre.
6. Dream Of What You Can Do.
7. Become A Master Of What You Do.
8. Share What You Know!
9. Never Stop Learning And Growing!
10. Think Generationally!

11. Don't Practice Defiance For Its Own Sake, But When Necessary March To The Beat Of Your Own Drummer.

12. Draw From The Power Of The Holy Spirit In You.

13. Make Wise Use Of Your Time.

14. Develop Strong Listening Skills.

15. Read One Non-Fiction Book Each Month Related To Your Area Of Interest!

16. Find Mentors.

17. Practice The Power Of Prayer.

18. Visualize Your Success.

19. Record God's Exploits In And Through You For Posterity. This Journal May Someday Become Your Memoirs!

20. Work Long, Hard, And Smart!

Wisdom is the Principal Thing

I believe the Holy Bible to be the most profound book of practical wisdom ever written. This great book of wisdom has been under attack for centuries. Many African-Americans and other people of color have launched a reactionary attack upon the Bible protesting the white man's use of it as a tool of exploitation. The Bible has been used as such a tool but so have other famous scriptural writings. This does not in any way excuse or atone for the atrocities committed against people of color in the name of God, Jesus, and the Holy Scriptures. What we need to do is study history for the proper perspective so that we can look at the Bible apart from its often ignoble history.

There are also several other excellent works you might want to get for your library, check your local bookstore. When we remove the Bible from its heritage of exploitation then we can begin to see that there is wisdom to be gleaned from its pages. Maybe even more important than the study of history, we need to study and master the universal Godly principles of success found in the pages of the Holy Bible.

The book of Proverbs in the Bible is chock full of jewels of wisdom that will develop in you and me the mindset being discussed here. Whatever you and I achieve in life begins in our minds. The Bible is a spiritual book. By this I do not mean goofy out of this world, out of your mind wanderings. True spirituality is practical and must be understood as such. The Bible will teach us how to develop a mindset that is strong, tough, and resilient. Meditating in the Proverbs will build God's timeless wisdom for every situation into our lives. *It is my personal conviction that one cannot truly know one's purpose apart from knowing God.* God created us and has foreordained our purpose. First Corinthians 2:9-11 says, "But as it is written, Eye hath not seen, nor ear heard, neither have entered into the heart of man, the things which God hath prepared for them that love him. But God hath revealed them unto us by his Spirit: for the Spirit searcheth all things, yea, the deep things of God. For what man knoweth the things of man, save the spirit of man which is in him? even so the things of God knoweth no man, but the Spirit of God."

God reveals His things or thoughts by His Holy Spirit. The Spirit of God says to the Prophet Jeremiah in the book bearing his name: "Before I formed thee in the belly I knew thee; and before thou camest forth out of the womb I sanctified thee, and I ordained thee a prophet unto the nations" (Jeremiah 1:5). Your purpose spiritually identifies you and gives focus to the use of your gifts and talents. You are established and given a tree of life by fulfilling the dream and vision God the Father has placed in your heart.

The essence of greatness entails the pursuit of wisdom. Proverbs 1:7 says, "The fear of the Lord is the beginning of knowledge: but fools despise wisdom and instruction." The Hebrew word for "knowledge" is *daath* (dah-ath). It means wit or cunning. It also means to be diligent, to discern or discover; to be a man of skill; to teach, to understand, to comprehend, to be or make famous. When we begin to "fear" or reverently worship God our purpose is stirred within us. As we continue to worship God as a lifestyle versus a weekly ritual, and apply ourselves to know the mind of God we begin to develop skill. There is a much more in-depth discussion of skill in my book *The God Factor.* In Proverbs 2:2 we are told to turn our ear toward wisdom and apply our heart (mind) to understanding. Wisdom and understanding are indispensable to the discovery of purpose. Proverbs 20:5 says, "The purposes of a man's heart are deep waters, but a man of understanding draws them out" (NIV).

Before you can aspire to greatness in God you must know who you are in God. Understanding draws out your purpose from the depths of your heart. Let me say here that there is a distinction to be made between purpose and vocation, profession, or career. Your purpose may become your career if you choose to call it such. However, you may have attended ten years of college obtaining the highest academic degrees only to find yourself out of the will and purpose of God. Your purpose is who, what, when, where, how, and why God intended you to be. This may or may not have to do with attending college or university. You may need to attend university to hone the skills necessary for the fulfilling of your purpose, but not necessarily. One of the great tragedies of our time is the number of people walking around university campuses without the foggiest idea why they are there. Unfortunately, many people do not realize they are in the wrong place until tens of thousands of dollars later.

You will cheat yourself if you study only the lives of great men and women of one culture or ethnic group. True greatness transcends culture and ethnicity. Though I do not agree with some of his theories, I believe the British physicist Stephen Hawking demonstrates characteristics of the great ones. Dr. Hawking was already in pursuit of his Ph.D. when he discovered that he had amyotrophic lateral sclerosis (ASL); also known as motor neuron or Lou Gehrig's Disease. This disease affects the nerves of the spinal cord and the parts of the brain which produce voluntary motor functions. The degeneration of cells is followed by muscular atrophy and paralysis. The body literally wastes away though the mind is not affected directly. Confined to a wheelchair and only able to converse via a special hi-tech tool, Dr. Hawking completed his Ph.D. and went on to become, in the words of some, Einstein's heir apparent. He also married and had children. Dr. Hawking's life is a testament to the force of the human will when directed by a strong sense of purpose and infused with the courage to overcome obstacles. His life is also a rebuke to those of strong constitution but without vision who constantly complain about their disadvantages.

I also admire the story of Steven Jobs who sold his Volkswagen bus for $1,500 and in his parents' garage pursued his vision of the personal computer. Five or six years later, Jobs — still in his twenties, a college dropout — and his Apple Computer was listed on the Fortune 500. Then there's the story of William Henry (Bill) Gates who left Harvard to start Microsoft. I have read that ninety percent(90%) of the world's software is Microsoft software. A recent national publication listed Gates as the richest man in America.

What was it that drove Jobs and Gates to believe so powerfully in visions that have literally changed the world? Some would suggest all to simplistically that it was megalomania, the greatly-inflated ego. It was more; a peering beyond the veil, if you will. I am not for a moment suggesting that ego had nothing to do with it. All men and women have egos and the great ones seem to some extent driven by theirs. It is quite interesting that the Greek word for "I" is ego (pronounced the same as Eggo, as in waffle). I believe that healthy egos are those with honest assessments of their own abilities but are at the same time able to understand their limitations and fully appreciate the gifts of others.

There are other African-Americans who have built fortunes as well. The stories of John Johnson and A.G. Gaston are only a couple of examples. Both were born in extreme poverty and had to overcome tremendous odds to rise to their respective pinnacles. Mr. Johnson oversees the Johnson Publishing empire and other combined interests said to be worth in the area of a half-billion dollars. Dr. Gaston's business and investment interests are said to be worth around forty million dollars. We are not principally focusing on the money here. I am talking about vision, thrift, and overcoming obstacles to achieve your dreams. Your dreams are packed with the essence of greatness, and these men have paved the way letting you and I know what is possible. The stories of both Mr. Johnson and Dr. Gaston are available in print. Mr. Johnson's is entitled *Succeeding Against The Odds;* Dr. Gaston's is *Green Power.* Go to your favorite bookstore today and get them or have them ordered.

I am concerned that many African-American males do not have a success consciousness developed in them in this country. However, it could be argued fairly persuasively that no group, so to speak, as a whole has a developed success consciousness. But no one would argue though that white youth who aspire to accomplishment have no dearth of role models from which to choose. I suggest that African-Americans who aspire to greatness read the stories of pioneers and great ones of all cultures and ethnicities. I have read literally hundreds of biographies and autobiographies of achievers. In all of their lives there were certain universal principles which went beyond sex, ethnicity, country of origin, and often extreme physical challenges. You read to assimilate and where permissible to duplicate the principles. Also your conversational repertoire is expanding along with your capacity to dream. Remember, though, in order to build your dream, you must wake up, get up, and go to work.

Earlier we talked about the fear of the Lord. Now I want you to look at a positively powerful verse in the Bible. Proverbs 22:4 says, "By humility and the fear of the Lord are riches, and honour, and life." Wow! The word "riches" here means to accumulate; far richer riches. "Honour" is the word *kabod* (kaw-bode) which means weight, splendor, copiousness, glory, and honour. "Life" means: to be fresh, strong, and fully alive; merry, maintenance, running, springing; to revive, to keep alive, to certainly promise life, to preserve alive, to surely be whole. Isn't this incredible? The Bible says that riches, honour, and life accompany the fear of the Lord.

Proverbs 10:22 says, "The blessing of the Lord, it maketh rich, and he addeth no sorrow with it." It is worth our while to study the words in this verse for they are pregnant with revelation. "Blessing" is from the Hebrew word *barak* (baw-rak) which means: to kneel; an act of adoration; to speak well concerning, to give a benediction; to abundantly or all together bless; to congratulate. It also means to be liberal; and prosperity. "Lord" in this verse refers to the covenant name Jehovah. It means: to be or being; to live or have life. The name Jehovah denotes favour, fellowship, and blessing. "Of" literally means from. "Maketh" is a very interesting word. It is from a Hebrew word meaning to appoint, bring, call [a name], charge, commit, determine, to mark out by name; to ordain, preserve, purpose, rehearse, reward, cause to set up on, to steadfastly take and tell.

Do you see what the Word of God is saying? The well spoken benediction of God appoints, charges, commits, ordains you to be rich. Now before that old religious spirit rises up in you, remember all I am doing is studying the Word of God with you! "Rich" is from the Hebrew word *ashar* (aw-shar). It means: to accumulate, to grow rich, to tithe; to surely have the tenth; to surely give the tenth; to wax rich, wealth; far richer riches; ten in combinations.

Understand, dear reader, that God has an inexhaustible supply of all kinds of wealth! Wealth upon which no demand has yet been placed. It would be nothing for Him to make all five billion occupants of this planet billionaires. There is enough wealth on planet Earth for this to happen. Men are not rich or poor by the heavenly roll of the dice. There are several contributing factors to man finding himself in poverty or wealth. Both poverty and wealth become relative terms at some point, but they both include a component not measurable in terms of the size of one's investment portfolio. In Deuteronomy 8:18 the word wealth means resources. "Get" in the same verse (Deuteronomy 8:18) means: to accomplish, bring forth, fulfill, furnish or gather; to indeed be industrious; to labour or maintain; to be upon an industrious journey; to be a warrior or workman. Wealth has to do with the availability and accessibility of critical resources for the accomplishment of meaningful purposes.

Your need for resources will be determined by the personal and corporate visions which God calls you to be part of. Another Hebrew word for wealth is *own* (one) meaning successful effort or journey. Throughout the Bible this kind of wealth always connotes the favour of God and His expectation of a successful journey on your part. In local churches I believe God is trying to give visions to people of color concerning the launching of successful corporations which will be used to help finance the end time harvest. God will have to give us the wealth we need to undertake such ventures.

Now we know that the Bible says riches, honour, and life are with the fear of the Lord. Earlier on we also mentioned wisdom, which the Bible talks a lot about. The entire eighth Proverb deals with "wisdom." Verse eighteen says, "Riches and honour are with me; yea, durable riches and righteousness." You may think the most important word in this verse is riches. Wrong answer! *What about righteousness?* No, wrong answer again. The key word in this verse is "durable," and it pertains to riches. "Durable" means: to grow old; antique; valued or to have value. God says here that wisdom will bring old, antique, valued money. Again, all we are doing is studying the Word of God. The great ones from Abraham to Moses and Joshua did not have a poverty consciousness. You and I will never be able to accomplish the will of God for our generation with a poverty mentality.

My brother and sister, we need to develop a consciousness soaked in the Word of God and pregnant with the expectation of the fulfillment of God's promises. I tell you in the Name of Jesus, God has given us the vision for profitable businesses and for corporate ventures. I am not talking about the historically African-American owned and only marginally profitable businesses, but rather trailblazing innovative ventures. Not that we should abandon service businesses such as barber, or beauty salons and restaurants. These, however, must always be held to the highest standards of excellence and integrity. God is going to give us profitable investment and reinvestment strategies, but first let us look at something very important.

Proverbs 17:16 (NIV) says, "Of what use is money in the hand of a fool, since he has no desire to get wisdom?" We must stop seeing money strictly through consumer eyes. We must begin to develop investment consciousness. We must become familiar with wealth and with what it produces and perpetuates. Consumer crazed persons do not store up investment capital, neither do beggars adequately understand the concept of ownership. Do not think for a moment that Abraham, Moses, or David maintained the wealth God had given them by being ignorant.

You will notice that in the Body of Christ there are certain financial newsletters such as "Pat Robertson's Perspective." This is good, however, we need more people of color, especially in churches, who are knowledgeable about the intricacies of finance. We need a commitment to educate this segment of the Body who may not be so astute in financial matters. I see very little wealth building material written by people of color. Now, I am not talking about "get rich quick" schemes, but sound, long-term investment strategies. God says in His Word that He will not give us money if we do not seek after wisdom! You must understand money, inflation, recession, interest, taxes, corporate structuring, wages, and technology to properly steward that which God is birthing in your hearts. Get wisdom and do not wait until tomorrow. Start today. This is the essence of greatness; wisdom, knowledge, and understanding. Proverbs 18:2 says, "A fool finds no pleasure in understanding but delights in airing his own opinions."

The great ones realize they do not need to reinvent the wheel. They read widely, gaining a broad knowledge base, then they incorporate useful ideas into their own thinking. The great ones eschew plagiarism as lowly and disreputable. When they borrow from the ideas, writings, and lectures of others they are quick to credit the originator of the idea. Those who aspire to greatness seek out profound minds with which to cross pollinate. They want to learn from the best and the brightest in their field.

Ten minutes spent in the presence of a great man or woman would be worth more than ten years spent with a fool or a dilettante. If you repeatedly called the offices of John H. Johnson, of Johnson's publishing empire, or Earl Graves, of *Black Enterprise* Magazine, requesting an appointment and after many attempts were given ten minutes, what would you do? Would you sulk, accusing these men of being arrogant? Would you say, "they have forgotten the little man?" Or would you request permission to record your conversation then develop a list of the ten most probing questions you could think of allowing your interviewee almost a minute to answer each question?

There would be little time to spend in foolish flattery which these men probably do not need and are certainly not impressed with. Before the interview you would carefully arrange the order of the questions from most to least important in case your time expired before getting to all the questions. Then you would rehearse asking them in the clearest, most concise manner possible. All that's left is your grooming; you select the proper clothing, making sure your hair and nails are clean and neatly trimmed and your shoes are immaculately polished. Then you pray, asking God for favor. Now you are ready for one of the most important ten minutes in your life. I hope you see why it is so necessary to spend all this time preparing for just ten minutes. This could be the ten minutes that alter your course, setting you in the direction of destiny.

Of course as soon as you arrive back at your office or home you have your secretary, wife, or someone capable, type a thank you letter. A little wisdom would dictate that you go easy on the verbiage; just get to the point. Have the letter typed on your letterhead or on clean, fresh paper, and fire it off. All that remains is to use what you learned in those ten minutes for the rest of your life.

Earlier, we mentioned that one cheats oneself when one does not read of the accomplishments of another person because of their culture or ethnicity. Another man whose accomplishments I admire is Dr. Robert H. Schuller. Sure to some he is considered controversial, but this is often a badge the great ones wear with honour. This man of God came from the Midwest with his wife, a few hundred dollars, and a great vision of the kind of church God would build in sunny California. To go from small and humble beginnings on the roof of a drive-in theater, to the opulence of the Crystal Cathedral requires tremendous faith and uncommon vision.

I recently left our Sunday morning worship service and drove to the mall to pick up a copy of Schuller's biography *Goliath*. The author of this book, James Penner, is Schuller's son-in-law. This is a profound principle that I will deal with more in a moment. I took the book home and began to skim through, intending to read the introduction and maybe the jacket notes. So much for my plans. By Tuesday afternoon of that same week I had finished all four-hundred and forty (440) pages. I found my faith charged and after reading of some of the trials encountered by Schuller and his family, my appreciation for what God has done in and through him grew enormously. Now, as for Schuller's son-in-law being the author of this book I want you to think about something. Proverbs 13:22 says, "A good man leaveth an inheritance to his children's children: and the wealth of the sinner is laid up for the just."

The inheritance being spoken of here is more than money, though money or wealth is certainly included.

Picture this: several years from now when Dr. Schuller has gone on to be with the Lord, the family gathers for some special time together. There is a roaring fire in the fireplace and all the kids are gathered around with popcorn and cocoa. Out comes the family heirloom edition of *Goliath*, richly bound in leather, pages gilded in gold. From this book is read the deeds, the exploits of God in and through these children's grandparents. The photographs show Grandpa and Grandma with influential, history making people in different locations around the world, and at different periods in their lives. What kind of an impact do you think that is going to have on all the little Schullers? They will be left a legacy of lofty aspirations. They have recorded evidence that dreams and visions are real and can come true. The great ones live their lives generationally. They record God's workings in and through them not for ego gratification but for generational inspiration. Then each succeeding generation has family heroes and champions whose stories are told and retold.

What about you? Are you asking God for a vision, a mission larger than yourself? A dream or vision that will impact lives for generations to come? If not, you're depriving us and you're depriving your children and grandchildren. Now if that isn't enough you are also depriving my children and grandchildren, and I charge you to desist immediately! Maybe your greatness has been tarnished by living in a ghetto, or by repeated personal encounters of racism, sexism, or other types of dehumanization. Hear me when I say, you are greater than the ghetto. Your spirit is stronger than perpetual poverty. You are more visionary than welfare. Hear me when I say that it's too early for you to quit. You are not a failure! You are not defeated! You are inferior to no one!

Did you know that those dreams you have when no one else is around, the ones you're ashamed to share for fear of being called silly or unrealistic, might just be God's way of summoning you to the essence of greatness? Some time back I read of an African-American woman from New York City's ghettos who did the unthinkable. This woman was on welfare and had four or five kids. She became sick and tired of being sick and tired so she decided to do something. Having made up her mind she went through Harvard College, then Harvard Medical School with a perfect 4.0 grade point average. She is now a successful physician and role model. Do you want to know something? All the time this woman was collecting welfare and feeling sad and discouraged she had powerful potential inside her screaming to be released, and so do you. Rise up now and stop feeling sorry for yourself. If you knew how great you are you would repent over every moment you've spent feeling sorry for yourself and get busy making the world a better place!

GOD'S VISITATION

by Mensa Otabil

God's Visitation

Whenever God comes to town He visits the oppressed to set them free. When He visited Moses He said, "Go and tell Pharaoh; Let my people go." The Pharaohic systems of this world must get ready to hear God say again: "Let my people go." Psalm 146:5-7 states, "Happy is he that hath the God of Jacob for his help, whose hope is in the Lord his God: Which made heaven and earth, the sea, and all that therein is: Which keepeth truth forever: Which executeth judgment for the oppressed: which giveth food to the hungry. The Lord looseth the prisoners."

All over the world, there is the feeling that God is once more shaking the nations. Kingdoms are falling and people who had, for years, been bound through misinformation, by oppressive political systems, are experiencing liberty. The mighty pillars of Apartheid are crumbling before our eyes and the prisoners are coming out free. It is as if a divine clock is ticking to signify a new time for the nations of the world. God is visiting the nations of the world and sovereignly overthrowing powers and domains. He is setting the oppressed free by allowing a new wind of truth to blow across the land.

I believe what we are seeing is the beginning of more fundamental and foundational changes. There is a shaking in the land! God is going to visit the black people of this world to bring them out of the state they are in, into their portion. As I travel to the Caribbean, the United States, Europe and Africa, there is a sense of urgency and a feeling of an appointment with destiny among black people. It is a feeling that makes you know that your time has come, and God is bringing to fruition the days of intense intercessions for His justice to prevail.

I keep running into preachers declaring this message of restoration for the black race. It sometimes makes non-black people nervous to hear their black brothers preach this message. As a matter of fact, there is nothing to be nervous about because God is not destroying one race to lift up another. All He is doing is bringing the truth that would destroy the oppressive and discriminatory structures in the church and the world, so as to establish His purposes for the nations.

The church world is going to have some major shakings as the truth of God marches on. It is a shame to know the pillars of Apartheid were built on the teachings of the Dutch Reformed Church. I have actually read a book written by a "Bible-believing" Canadian minister which taught that the black man is what the Bible calls the "beast of the field." This teaching would have been funny if it was not so pathetic and destructive!

Anti-Oppression Serum

Because of the role organized religion has played in the domination of the black race, there is the cry in many quarters for us to go back to our ancestral religions and totally reject the Bible. That is not the way out! When a man is bitten by a snake, it takes an anti-snake bite serum prepared from a snake to bring healing and restoration to that person. I totally believe that if the Bible was misused and misapplied to bind our people, we would need an "anti-oppression serum" prepared from the revealed Truth in God's Word to bring healing, liberty, and restoration to us.

In Numbers 21, the people of Israel suffered a plague of snakes as a result of their murmuring. This killed a lot of people and threatened the survival of the whole nation until the people sought the face of God in forgiveness and asked for a remedy.

"Therefore the people came to Moses, and said, We have sinned, for we have spoken against the LORD, and against thee; pray unto the LORD, that he take away the serpents from us. And Moses prayed for the people. And the LORD said unto Moses, Make thee a fiery serpent, and set it upon a pole: and it shall come to pass, that every one that is bitten, when he looketh upon it, shall live.

And Moses made a serpent of brass, and put it upon a pole, and it came to pass, that if a serpent had bitten any man, when he beheld the serpent of brass, he lived" (Num. 21:7-9).

As we look again into the Word of God, let the truth in His Word about us as a people restore the broken confidence and dignity.

It is only then that you can look at all the negatives committed against you and see that it is only a form which has no effect on you. The Word of God takes the sting from the bite. Anger does not liberate, it makes you a victim instead of a victor! It is only the truth which will set you free. The Word of God is the key to freedom!

Preachers from Africa and of African descent can no longer continue preaching an escapist, pie-in-the-sky message. We cannot continue singing about the "flying away" message, while our people battle the harsh realities of life. I fully believe in heaven and hell, but I also believe that God created man on earth to have dominion and not to be dominated by poverty, ignorance, and fear.

We need to redefine our theology to establish the true liberty of Christ in the lives of our people. They must know the truth!

Take The Veil Off

Second Corinthians 3:12-14 states, "Seeing then that we have such hope, we use great plainness of speech. And not as Moses, which put a veil over his face, that the children of Israel could not steadfastly look to the end of that which is abolished: But their minds were blinded: for until this day remaineth the same veil untaken away in the reading of the old testament; which veil is done away in Christ."

Just as Moses covered his face with a veil, many of us read the Bible with blindfolds on. In my early Christian life, nobody ever taught me that black people played any role in the Bible. It was as if a veil covered my eyes whenever I read the Bible, because I assumed that all the characters in the Bible were white. I used to wonder why my people were deprived and oppressed on every continent that they lived on.

Our treasures were misused and our people abused long before we were born. Our generation just inherited the fruits of colonialism and slavery. There must be an explanation why a whole race could be so dominated.

The African primal religion, which seeks to understand God through His creation, developed a philosophy that explains away the inexplicable, as a manifestation of deity. God, then is not a far removed being in heaven, but lives among men and works through the agency of lesser gods who sometimes inhabit trees, rivers, mountains and even manifest themselves in human apparitions. This has led to the revering and in many instances the worship of the creature instead of the Creator.

It is easy to imagine how the first Africans might have felt on first seeing this individual that had a pale skin, long hair, blue eyes and spoke a different language, with the ability to work "miracles" through his technological advancement. The logical option for those early Africans was to reason out the situation the only way they knew how, and that was spiritual. This human apparition was either a demon or a messenger from the gods. I guess they decided on the latter. For any adventurous explorer in those days, whether he was a trader or a missionary, this situation would be the most heaven-sent opportunity to exploit.

The first missionaries introduced their African converts to their religion and their "God." This deity had long blond hair, a long beard, blue eyes and had a pale complexion. In effect, the image which the missionary presented to the African looked just like the missionary! Whoever tried to portray Jesus Christ as an Anglo-Saxon might have had very noble reasons to help his people identify with Christ.

However, for other racial groupings, cultural imperialism will result if Christ is presented as just an image, especially if the converts do not know Christ on a personal basis. The logic that this situation produces is that if the missionary's race looks just like his "God' then they are in one class and the rest of us in another class.

It is little wonder that in Ghana, we have a saying which literally translated means, "When you see the white man you have seen your God." That is a total blasphemy and an abomination! It is supplanting the image of God with the image of man.

In order to change that concept, black people have advocated that Jesus Christ should be portrayed as a black man. That is swinging from one extreme to another. Their frustration is real but the answer is wrong. Second Corinthians 5:16 has this to say, "Wherefore henceforth know we no man after the flesh: yea, though we have known Christ after the flesh, yet now henceforth know we him no more."

In other words, although Jesus Christ was manifested among men in a physical form, you can only know Him through the Spirit. The physical image of the man Jesus therefore is of no consequence in your knowledge of Him. He is beyond our petty color-barriers; He transcends race.

It tickles me to see people hang in their homes plaques with the inscription, "Christ is the Head of this House..." and then have an image of a Scandinavian-looking man represented who they say is Jesus. If that was Jesus, what about the other picture in the other room that portrays a man that looks German! Let's take the veil off our eyes and really know Him in Spirit and in truth.

A New Nature, Not a Foreign Culture

Because the early missionaries did not understand us, they assumed that everything about us was evil and demonized. Our names were all thought to be demonized, our songs and music forms and even clothing were seen as evil. In their place, we were christened with new European names, put on European clothing and sung musical forms that did not move us. All this the missionaries did, forgetting that some of the celebrations they presented as Christian and some of the music forms which were accepted as church music used to be employed in pagan rituals and sung in the taverns. You see, musically, there is no pagan "B flat," worldly "B flat," and Christian "B flat." B flat is B flat! Music forms are not evil in themselves, it is the musician and the lyrics that may be evil. Instead of introducing us to the new nature in Christ, we were introduced to a new culture from Europe!

Christianity came to us clothed with European cultural norms, so much so that it becomes difficult to separate the wheat from the chaff.

Much of what is seen as Christianity is just chaff! Rituals, ceremonies, celebrations, legalism and ignorance. For most people, Christianity was and still is just an external status symbol because when crisis hits, they regress to the power of the fetish. Just wearing a shirt and a tie and having a nice English name will not drive out demons until you have had a personal encounter with the Lord Jesus, which makes you really know that He is relevant, Yesterday, Today and Forever. The Gospel must be proclaimed in power and simplicity.

Paul said in Romans 1:16, "For I am not ashamed of the Gospel of Christ: for it is the power of God unto salvation. . ." The power of God is in the Gospel and not a picture or symbol.

The Gospel outlines God's plan of salvation that whosoever, black, white, yellow, red, believes will have eternal life. When the Bible talks about eternal life, the reference is not just to a futuristic promise, but to a dynamic relationship with God that literally affects every aspect of life here on earth. The Gospel does not just emphasize the teachings of Jesus, it reveals God's forgiveness through the eternal atonement of the shed blood of Christ. It is God's response to man's universal need for atonement, cleansing and restoration of relationship.

When the Gospel is presented in truth, it focuses your faith not in Jesus the Jew, but in Christ the Son of the Living God. The Gospel exalts the believer with the gift of righteousness. It brings value and honor to the believer. Knowing the story of Christ and His teachings without having a personal relationship with Him, is like knowing all about the sweetness of a pudding but not having experienced its taste. Biblical Christianity is not a cultural introduction but the experience of a new nature. "Therefore, if any man be in Christ, he is a new creature: old things are passed away; behold, all things are become new" (2 Cor. 5:17).

I received Christ as Lord without fully grasping the depth of my experience. My salvation did not radically change my earlier mental programming; I sort of got saved without being converted. Salvation is of the Spirit, but conversion takes place when an individual's mind has been effectively renewed to conform to the Spirit of Christ.

As I grew in the knowledge of Christ, I became more and more acquainted with His truth and consequently started questioning things I had always taken for granted. From then on something inside of me would rise up in rebellion against any suggestion that I was intrinsically inferior to another because of my heritage and the pigmentation of my skin. I took steps to reclaim that which was lost.

I have had people come up to me and ask, "Is Mensa Otabil your full name?"

I would reply "Well my full name is Mensa Anamua Otabil."

"You mean you don't have any Christian name."

"Oh sure I do" I would respond, "Mensa is my Christian name."

"You mean you don't have a name like John, Daniel, Charles...?"

I tell them, "John is the Greek version of a Hebrew name and some of the names you have in mind may be English, French, German or Portuguese."

You see, no name by itself is Christian because Christianity is not about names but a relationship with Christ. It is a Christian person who makes a name Christian, and not the other way around. If I am a Christian, whatever name I bear is Christian!

We also have people who refer to certain places here on earth as "Holy Land." Well, the Bible teaches under the New Testament that wherever two or three are gathered in the name of Jesus Christ they can be assured of God's presence.

Answering the question of the woman of Samaria, Jesus said, "Woman, believe me, the hour cometh, when ye shall neither in this mountain, nor yet at Jerusalem worship the father. . . But the hour cometh, and now is, when the true worshippers shall worship the Father in Spirit and in truth; for the Father seeketh such to worship Him" (John 4:21-23).

With such understanding of what Christianity is about, I have desired to help break the imposed bondage that man's religion has put on my kinsmen according to the flesh.

Later, when I was called into ministry, one of the things the Lord led me to do was to liberate my people from mental slavery through the preaching of the Gospel, and to lift up the image of the black man so as to be a channel of blessing to the nations of the world. The Scriptures opened up to me in a new way and revealed to me things I had never been taught as a Christian. One of the questions that had agitated my mind was whether black people had played any role in the Bible. Did God ever use black people? Are we on God's agenda? I found my answers in the Word of God.

GET READY TO RUN

by Mensa Otabil

Get Ready to Run

In Luke 12:54-56 the Bible states, "And he said also to the people, When ye see a cloud rise out of the west, straightway ye say, There cometh a shower; and so it is. And when ye see the south wind blow, ye say, There will be heat; and it cometh to pass. Ye hypocrites, ye can discern the face of the sky and of the earth; but how is it that ye do not discern this time?"

Jesus rebukes people who are not able to discern the times they are living in and calls them hypocrites. It is hypocritical to know the natural signs but not understand the spiritual signs. It is hypocritical to be able to predict rain and not be able to predict what God is doing. When God works, He never leaves Himself without a witness. He makes His way clear, so that there will be no shadow of doubt as to His plans, purposes, and intentions.

It is important to know the times and seasons of God and to realize when your time has come.

There is nothing more tragic than doing the right thing at the wrong time. Sometimes, we get so used to a phase in our lives that we institutionalize that phase and make it a permanent feature in our lives. In other words, what was comfortable to do yesterday becomes comfortable to do forever. Yesterday was for yesterday, today is for today, and tomorrow will be for tomorrow. The only person who remains eternal and unchangeable is God Almighty. Apart from Him, man changes in line with the changing of the times and seasons.

In 2 Samuel 18:19-32, David had a son named Absalom who had a sister Tamar. This sister was unfortunately raped by one of David's sons who was not of the same mother with Tamar and Absalom. After that incident, Absalom planned to kill his brother. He waited for an opportunity and finally after four years planned a party, invited his brother to be there and killed this brother who had raped his sister. Afterwards, Absalom was banished from Jerusalem.

He later came back and started to plan to take over the throne of David, and temporarily, succeeded. He marshalled his forces against his father David, to fight him and to kill him and in the battle that ensued, Absalom was killed, even though David had given the instruction for him not to be killed. Joab, the chief of the army of David, killed him and when Absalom was killed, it was necessary for the message to be delivered back to David about what had happened at the camp.

This recorded incident gives us an indication of the process by which the message was supposed to be sent back to David.

"Then said Ahimaaz the son of Zadok, Let me now run, and bear the king tidings, how that the LORD hath avenged him of his enemies.

And Joab said unto him, Thou shalt not bear tidings this day, but thou shalt bear tidings another day: but this day thou shalt bear no tidings, because the king's son is dead.

Then said Joab to Cushi, Go tell the king what thou hast seen. And Cushi bowed himself unto Joab, and ran.

Then said Ahimaaz the son of Zadok yet again to Joab, But howsoever, let me, I pray thee, also run after Cushi. And Joab said, Wherefore wilt thou run, my son, seeing that thou hast no tidings ready?

But howsoever, said he, let me run. And he said unto him, Run. Then Ahimaaz ran by the way of the plain and overran Cushi.

And David sat between the two gates: and the watchman went up to the roof over the gate unto the wall, and lifted up his eyes, and looked and behold a man running alone. And the watchman cried, and told the king. And the king said, If he be alone, there is tidings in his mouth. And he came apace, and drew near.

And the watchman saw another man running: and the watchman called unto the porter, and said, Behold another man running alone. And the king said, He also bringeth tidings.

And the watchman said, Me thinketh the running of the foremost is like the running of Ahimaaz the son of Zadok. And the king said, He is a good man, and cometh with good tidings.

And Ahimaaz called, and said unto the king, All is well. And he fell down to the earth upon his face before the king, and said, Blessed be the LORD thy God, which hath delivered up the men that lifted up their hand against my lord the king.

And the king said, Is the young man Absalom safe? And Ahimaaz answered, When Joab sent the king's servant, and me thy servant, I saw a great tumult, but I knew not what it was.

And the king said unto him, Turn aside, and stand here. And he turned aside, and stood still.

And, behold, Cushi came; and Cushi said, Tidings, my lord the king: for the LORD hath avenged thee this day of all them that rose up against thee.

And the king said unto Cushi, Is the young man Absalom safe? And Cushi answered, The enemies of my lord the king, and all that rise against thee to do thee hurt, be as that young man is."

The Scripture is talking about two people: a man called Ahimaaz and another man whom the King James Version calls the "Cushi." The name "Cushi" was not his name but was a description of who he was. He was a Cushite. From our Biblical understanding we know that Cush simply means Ethiopian, and the Cushite refers to the black person or the black individual. Here we see an account of a message to be delivered by a potential of two people — Ahimaaz and Cush. The Bible says that after victory had been won the normal thing to have been done in this situation was for Ahimaaz to send the message because he was the man who had been sending the message all the time.

As a matter of fact, if you read the same 2nd Samuel 15:36 it states: "Behold, they have there with them their two sons, Ahimaaz Zadok's son, and Jonathan Abiathar's son; and by them ye shall send unto me every thing that ye can hear."

In other words, David was giving the instructions that since he was moving out of Jerusalem because of the return of Absalom, any message that was supposed to be sent to him should come through Ahimaaz and another man called Jonathan. So Ahimaaz was the appointed message deliverer to David.

In Chapter 17:17 we read; "Now Jonathan and Ahimaaz stayed by Enrogel; for they might not be seen to come into the city: and a

wench went and told them; and they went and told king David."
Ahimaaz and Jonathan were set between Jerusalem and the place
where David was encamped so if anybody wanted to send a message they told Ahimaaz and then he sent it to David.

He was an already established, experienced messenger. So on
this occasion when the king had won a great victory, the natural
thing was for Ahimaaz to go and deliver the message. Apart from
that, Ahimaaz was also the son of a priest called Zadok and also a
man of experience. He was a very fast runner. He had been used to
that ministry of delivering messages to the king or acting as the
king's messenger. However, on this special occasion the times had
changed and there was the need for a new order of delivering of
messages.

You need to understand that the black people and the Israelites
have always been dwelling together. The children of Keturah
through Abraham, who were black people, had an inheritance
amongst the tribe of Judah. These people have always been dwelling with the Israelites. It is not strange to find black people all
throughout the history of Israel; it was not strange that in the army
of David there was a Cushite, and when it was time to deliver the
message Joab turned to the Cushite and said: "This is your time.
"Ahimaaz is experienced but this is your time to go and deliver the
message."

Ahimaaz insisted three times to go and deliver the message. The
Cushite never asked to deliver the message, he was given the opportunity without asking for it.

The reason why Joab decided not to send Ahimaaz was because
this message had to be borne by a man of maturity. Joab knew the
two occasions that people with such information had been killed
by David. After Saul had died and someone came to report the
news, David killed him. The second time another person came to
report that Ishbosheth had died, David killed him. Thus, whoever
was supposed to carry this new message should know how to carry
this message with a measure of caution. He had to carry the message with such tact, wisdom, and maturity and say it in such a way
that David would not kill him.

At this point in time, Joab saw the experienced Ahimaaz but he knew he could not take the message. "It is not your time. You have been doing it every time but we need somebody who can handle this message better." When they needed somebody to tell the message with better precision they had to call on the Cushite.

Verse 21 states: "Then said Joab to Cushi, Go tell the king what thou hast seen. And Cushi bowed himself unto Joab, and ran." I like that. He did not tell the Cushite go and tell the king what he had heard or what he had been told but what he had seen. "Be the original person. You are going to deliver the message which is original to you. You are not going to tell a message which is a duplication of what you have heard before but you have to take the responsibility of reporting the things that have been shown to you."

I believe that the Spirit of God is calling on the Cushites of this era, that it is time to deliver the message concerning the things that we have seen, that have been taught us personally, uniquely, originally and individually. I believe that the time of duplicating messages which we have read from others is over.

It is time for the Cushite to deliver the message which he himself has tasted of. There was a time when every message we delivered was a message that had been reported to us. We quoted what had been, but the time has come when the Cushite should hear from God himself. The time has come when the Cushite does not have to look up to somebody for credibility. The time has come when the Cushite must tell the message which does not have to be validated by a "white" man.

For most of us, we think something is true because a white man has confirmed it. We do not need the confirmation of any man for our message. The only person who needs to confirm our message is God Almighty!

When I travel to the nations, I do not go to give them what they have given to me. I give them what God has given me.

Let us tell the nations what we have seen. Have you seen anything? Has God shown you anything? Has God taught you anything? Then tell the nations about it!! The Cushite took the message and started running with that message. While he was run-

513

ning, this man who had always been doing the job - Ahimaaz said, "give me the chance." Joab said, "your time is not now you do not have any message and you cannot run without a message," but he said, "whether I have a message or not let me run." Joab said "you are not ready." Ahimaaz replied," whether I am ready or not, I want to run."

When people's times are past, they still want to run. Ahimaaz will run although he has no message. He will still move. He will still use his experience. When Ahimaaz started running the Bible says, he outran the Cushite because he was a fast runner.

He had the technology. He had the infrastructure, so he was faster, although he had no message. The Bible says he ran faster because he ran in the plain. He ran in the cool area.

The Cushite, on the contrary, was running through the hard, rocky areas because he did not know the short cut. He had to go through the long process. He was running through the thorny areas, through the poverty deprivation, malnourished areas but he was running. He was running because he had been sent to run.

The Bible says how lovely are the feet of those who carry the good news. He had lovely feet but he pierced his feet, wounded his feet because he was running in the terrain he was not accustomed to. He was running in a situation that he was not familiar with, but he had to run because he had been given a message. The Bible says Ahimaaz was spotted from afar off. David said "surely if it is Ahimaaz and he is running alone then he must have a message." Men with a message sometimes have to run alone. Men who always need to run in company may lose their message because they need the company of other peoples opinion in order to move. When he arrived David asked:

"What did you see?" He replied: "Well, there is good news for the king. Your enemies have been defeated."

David then asked: "What happened to Absalom?"

Ahimaaz responded: "I did not see anything. When Joab sent me I saw people gather, but I did not see what they were looking at. I just saw them and that is all." He did not have any message. He was not a first hand witness. David said to him: "Stand aside." When you run without a message you will be told to stand aside. No matter how fast you run, brothers and sisters, you have to have something in your mouth.

If you have nothing in your mouth and you run as fast as possible, when you get there and you are asked what message you have, you will start scratching your head. People who run without messages always are sidelined. It does not matter how far you travel, how many times you travel, if you do not have any message you will be told to stand aside. The important thing is not whether you go but what is in your mouth.

It's A New Day!

I am not keen on running unless I have something to say. When you have something to say, the running gives you substance. God is telling Ahimaaz to stand aside because he has run before but this time "he doesn't have a message."

The Lord is telling Ahimaaz, "you do not have any message." Ahimaaz will fight. It is difficult to stand aside because he is used to running. Gone are the days when all of Africa would just sit down and organize one big crusade for one white man to come and turn all our pastors into ushers and counselors; the days when we would pack our Bibles and go to a conference somewhere and listen to a white man lecture us on how to win Africa when he has not been to Africa before, are over! God is saying, stand aside Ahimaaz. You did it yesterday but today, stand aside because there is a new hour, a new day and a new man must deliver the message. This is our time to reach our own.

When your time comes you must know how to run with the message. There is time for everything. There is time for babies to be men and there is time for men to be old men. When you are an old man, your baby takes care of you because he is now the man. Sometime ago, some people came to give us the message of the Gospel; they preached to us. They taught us the ways of God. Now they have also become old men!

515

I believe that God is prophetically speaking to the modern day Cushite not to be intimidated by the fast running of Ahimaaz. God is telling the modern day Cushite, "you may not have the money and all the technology that the people have but I have given you a message. You must know that I have put something inside you that must be told to the nations of the world."

Sometimes when God calls you, it is very easy to look to the people who have been running all along and question God, "But they did it yesterday," when God will be telling you it is your time. When it is your time to tell the message, although you have not run before, you must learn how to run. You may run slowly, make some mistakes, go through thorny places but you have to run. It is time to run and when our time comes to run, there should be no excuse.

We cannot complain that we do not have money because when your time comes to run you do not need to complain, you just exercise your feet. If you do not run, no message will be delivered, because the people you are trusting to run and deliver the message do not have any message.

God is telling black people all over the world that their time has come. The time of servanthood and slavery of the black man has come to an end. For so many years we have been in bondage, but that time has come to an end. The last system that needs to be broken will be broken in South Africa, and when that is done, it will signify the completeness of the time of slavery of black people all over the world and usher in the time for their lifting up, because God has a process of making leaders. He makes leaders by first making them servants.

God does not raise leaders who have never served. He makes you a servant and then you become a leader. Before God chose Israel to be a nation among nations, they had to serve for four hundred years. They had to be servants and then after that God said "I will make you a special people."

We have to discern the times. The clock is ticking, the times are changing. We need to recognize this and we need to bear the responsibility that comes with that understanding, because until we are able to bear the responsibility, our time will pass us by.

I fear to think of our time passing us by; that our suffering has been in vain, that we have suffered so long, like the people of Israel who were in Egypt. They suffered so long in the wilderness and when the time of deliverance came, they died in the wilderness because they did not discern the time. All they needed to do was to change their slave mentality and start to think differently, but they could not because they had been taught to think as slaves.

When it is your time to run you have to run. When it is your time to speak you have to speak. When it is your time to launch out, you have to launch out because that is the only time you have. If you miss it that is the end. It is like buying a rain coat in the rainy season and packing it in your wardrobe. If you fail to wear it in the rainy season you cannot wear it in the hot weather. When it is the rainy season and you have your rain coat, wear it! There is nothing permanent. God's spotlight keeps moving, it stays on you to do what you are supposed to do, then to another, until they do what they are supposed to do and it keeps moving. It will not stay on you forever. It stays on you for a time and for a purpose. When the light is on you and God says now you run and tell my message, you have to run in all the power He has given to you.

We need to understand what the Spirit of God is saying in this hour. When it is your time to run you may arrive late but you will have the word. God is not just interested in how fast you run, He is interested in what message you are running with.

Romans 9:15 & 16 says, "For he saith to Moses, I will have mercy on whom I will have mercy, and I will have compassion on whom I will have compassion. So then it is not of him that willeth, nor of him that runneth, but of God that showeth mercy."

The Bible says the race is not for the swift, it is not for the man who has a church and has all the nice furnishings, the race is not for the person who is bold, but the race is for the person who has received the mercy of God at a point in time. That is why you do not need to be intimidated because you see someone running faster than you, particularly if he had gadgets which caused him to run faster.

517

Businessmen, lawyers, inventors, teachers, your time has come; Young people, your time has come. You may be starting late but you must run with purpose. You are starting late but the important thing is that God has shown mercy on you at this time. You are starting late but you have the favor of God. I believe we have what it takes. I know that we do not have the best of everything. Our neighborhoods are deprived economically because of circumstances within our control which we did not control. We have messed up some good opportunities and we are suffering for it, but I hope we will learn our lessons.

You do not let the past stop you and so put your head between your two legs and start crying that God has not given you anything. You may not have the legs but you have a message.

In these times, I believe God is going to raise giants. I do not know how He is going to do it. It is going to be a miracle. The only way we can do the things we want is through miracles. The day we stop trusting God for miracles we are doomed. We do not move by the economy.

God promises, "I will cause rivers of living water to break forth in the wilderness for you." We do not move because there is a change in government legislation. Our hope is not in a democratic rule. We have to believe in the supernatural and God taking us up by miracles. If God does not carry us we are stuck where we are. It is the miracles of God that will save us, and we have to live in the miraculous. We have to trust God to do beyond what our natural ability can do because we are years behind the world.

When I tell you that God has put his finger on us at this time, it is prophetically right. We need to know our history so we can know our future. We have to move backwards in order to move forwards. When we want to trace black history, we do not trace it in a narrow cultural sense. We have to go backward and see how God has dealt with us in difficult times.

Whenever the world has been in a crisis the black man has always appeared on the scene. After the flood, when the world needed a leader, He called Nimrod the son of Cush. When Moses was taken out of Pharaoh's camp, it took a black man, Jethro to teach him the ways of God. When the people of Israel were going to the promised land it took a black man, Hobab to direct them to the promised land. They have always been around. God has always relied on these black people in times of crises.

When it was a time of crisis and nobody could speak to David, it took a black man to take the message to him. He knew how to take the message. He had the wisdom to tackle the problem. When Jeremiah, the prophet, was put into a dungeon, and Israel was in a crisis, it took an Ethiopian eunuch to set him free.

When it was time for Paul to be sent to the mission field it took black men to lay hands on him and send him out. When Jesus was going to the cross it took a black man to carry the cross.

Even though Nimrod messed up God's plan with selfish ambition, in this new restoration, we must be careful to give God all the glory. Thank God for Jesus. He sets us free, He liberates our mind.

The Liberator is Jesus the Son of the Living God. When you come to Him, He does not just liberate your spirit, He also liberates your mind and your thinking. He redefines your history and puts you on a winning path. We need Jesus to liberate us because He is the connection to our true history!

INVENTIONS BY BLACKS

I wisdom dwell with prudence, and find out knowledge of witty inventions. Proverbs 8:12

INVENTIONS BY BLACKS
1834-1990

Inventor	Invention	Date	Patent
Abrams, W.B.	Hame attachment	Apr. 14, 1891	450,550
Allen, C.W.	Self-leveling table	Nov. 1, 1898	613,436
Allen, J.B.	Clothes line support	Dec. 10, 1895	551,105
Ancker Johnson, Betsy	Signal Generator	Nov. 22, 1966	3,287,659
Ashbourne, A.P.	Process for preparing coconutfor domestic use	June 1, 1875	163,962
Ashbourne, A.P.	Biscuit Cutter	Nov. 30, 1875	170,460
Ashbourne, A.P.	Refining coconut oil	July 27, 1880	230,518
Ashbourne, A.P.	Process of treating coconut	Aug. 21, 1877	194,287
Bailes, William	Ladder scaffold-support	Aug. 5, 1879	218,154
Bailey, L.C.	Combined truss and bandage	Sept. 25, 1883	285,545
Bailey, L.C.	Folding Bed	July 18, 1899	629,286
Bailiff, C.O.	Shampoo headrest	Oct. 11, 1898	612,008
Ballow, W.J.	Combined hat rack and table	Mar. 29, 1898	601,422
Barnes, G.A.E.	Design for sign	Aug. 19, 1889	29,173
Beard, A.J.	Rotary engine	July 5, 1892	478,271
Beard, A.J.	Car-coupler	Nov 23, 1897	594,059
Becket, G.E.	Letter box	Oct. 4, 1892	483,525
Bell, L.	Locomotive smoke stack	May 23, 1871	115,153
Bell, L.	Dough kneader	Dec. 10, 1872	133,823
Benjamin, L.W.	Broom moisteners and bridles	May 16, 1893	497,747
Benjamin, M.E.	Gong & signal chairs for hotels	July 17, 1888	386,286
Binga, M.W.	Street sprinkling apparatus	July 22, 1879	217,843
Blackburn, A.B.	Railway signal	Jan. 10, 1888	376,362
Blackburn, A.B.	Spring Seat for chairs	Apr. 3, 1888	380,420
Blackburn, A.B.	Cash carrier	Oct. 23, 1888	391,577
Blair, Henry	Corn Planter	Oct. 14, 1834	
Blair, Henry	Cotton Planter	Aug. 31, 1836	
Blue, L.	Hand corn shelling device	May 20, 1884	298,937
Bluford, Sr. G.S.	Artillery Ammunition Training Round	Feb. 13, 1951	2,541,025
Booker, L.F.	Design rubber scraping knife	Mar. 28, 1899	30,404
Boone, Sarah	Ironing board	Apr. 26, 1892	473,653
Bowman, H.A.	Making flags	Feb. 23, 1892	469,395
Brooks, C.B.	Punch	Oct. 31, 1899	636,197

Inventor	Invention	Date	Patent
Brooks, C.B.	Street-sweepers	Mar. 17, 1896	556,711
Brooks, C.B.	Street-sweepers	May 12, 1896	560,154
Brooks, Hallstead & Page	Street-sweepers	Apr. 21, 1896	558,719
Brown, Henry	Receptacle for storing & preserving papers	Nov. 2, 1886	352,036
Brown, L.F.	Bridle Bit	Oct. 25, 1892	484,994
Brown, O.E.	Horseshoe	Aug. 23, 1892	481,271
Brown & Latimer	Water closets for railway cars	Feb. 10, 1874	147,363
Bundy, R.	Signal Generator	Jan. 26, 1960	2,922,924
Burr, J.A.	Lawn Mower	May 9, 1899	624,749
Burr, W.F.	Switching device for railways	Oct. 31, 1899	636,197
Burwell, W.	Boot or shoe	Nov. 28, 1899	638,143
Butler, R.A.	Train alarm	June 15, 1897	584,540
Butts, J.W.	Luggage Carrier	Oct. 10, 1899	634,611
Byrd, T.J.	Improvement in holders for reins for horses	Feb. 6, 1872	123,328
Byrd, T.J.	Apparatus for detaching horses from carriages	Mar. 19, 1872	124,790
Byrd, T.J.	Improvement in neck yokes for wagons	Mar. 11, 1872	124,790
Byrd, T.J.	Improvement in car couplings	Dec. 1, 1874	157,370
Campbell, W.S.	Self-setting animal trap	Aug. 30, 1881	246,369
Cagill, B.F.	Invalid cot	July 25, 1899	629,658
Carrington, T.A.	Range	July 25, 1876	180,323
Carter, W.C.	Umbrella stand	Aug. 4, 1885	323,397
Camuthers, Geo. R.	Image Converter for Dect. Electromagnetic, Etc.	Nov. 11, 1969	3,478,216
Carter, J.L. & M. Weiner & R.J. Youmans	Distributed pulse forming network for magnetic modulator	Sept. 16, 1986	4,612,455
Certain, J.M.	Parcel carrier for bicycles	Dec. 26, 1899	639,708
Cherry, M.A.	Velocipede	May 8, 1888	382,351
Cherry, M.A.	Street car fender	Jan. 1, 1895	531,908
Church, T.S.	Carpet beating machine	July 29, 1884	302,237
Clae, O.B.	Trestle	Oct. 9, 1888	390,752
Coates, R.	Overboot for horses	Apr. 19, 1892	473,295
Cook, G.	Automatic fishing device	May 30, 1899	625,829
Coolidge, J.S.	Harness attachment	Nov. 13, 1888	392,908
Cooper, A.R.	Shoemakers jack	Aug. 22, 1899	631,519
Cooper, J.	Shutter and fastening	May 1, 1883	276,563
Cooper, J.	Elevator device	Apr. 2, 1895	536,605

Inventor	Invention	Date	Patent
Cooper, J.	Elevator device	Sept. 21, 1897	590,257
Cornwell, P.W.	Draft regulator	Oct. 2, 1888	390,284
Cornwell, P.W.	Draft regulator	Feb. 7, 1893	491,082
Cralle, A.L.	Ice-cream mold	Feb. 2, 1897	576,395
Creamer, H.	Steam feed water trap	Mar. 17, 1895	313,854
Creamer, H.	Steam trap feeder	Dec. 11, 1888	394,463
Cosgove, W.F.	Automotive stop plug for gas oil pipes	Mar. 17, 1885	313,993
Darkins, J.T.	Ventilation aid (variation)	Feb. 19, 1895	534,322
Davis, I.D.	Tonic	Nov. 2, 1886	351,829
Davis, W.D.	Riding saddles	Oct. 6, 1896	568,939
Davis, W.R. Jr.	Library table	Sept. 24, 1878	208,378
Deitz, W.A.	Shoe	Apr. 30, 1867	64,205
Dickinson, J.H.	Pianola	NA 1899	NA
Dixon Jr. S. & T. R. AuCoin & R.J. Malik	Monolithic planar doped barrier limiter	Mar. 31, 1987	4,654,773
Dixon Jr. S. & R.J.Malik	Monolithic planar doped barrier subharmonic mixer	Jan. 7, 1986	4,563,773
Dorsey, O.	Door Holding device	Dec. 10, 1878	210,764
Dorticus, C.J.	Device for applying coloring liquids to sides of soles or heels of shoe	Mar. 19, 1895	535,820
Dorticus, C.J.	Machine for embossing photo	Apr. 16, 1895	537,442
Dorticus, C.J.	Photographic print wash	Apr. 23, 1875	537,968
Dorticus, C.J.	Hose leak stop	July 18, 1899	629,315
Downing, P.B.	Electric Switch for railroad	June 17, 1890	430,118
Downing, P.B.	Letter Box	Oct. 27, 1891	462,093
Downing, P.B.	Street letter box	Oct. 27, 1891	462,096
Dunnington, J.H.	Horse detachers	Mar. 16, 1897	578,979
Edmonds, T.H.	Separating Screens	July 20, 1897	586,724
Elkins, T.	Dining, ironing table and quilting frame combined	Feb. 22, 1870	100,020
Elkins, T.	Chamber commode	Jan. 9, 1872	122,518
Elkins, T.	Refrigerating apparatus	Nov. 4, 1879	221,222
Evans, J.H.	Convertible settees	Oct. 5, 1897	591,095
Faulkner, H.	Ventilated shoe	Apr. 29, 1890	426,495
Ferrell, F.J.	Steam Trap	Feb. 11, 1890	420,993
Ferrell, F.J.	Apparatus for melting snow	May 27, 1890	428,670
Fisher, D.	Joiners clamp	Apr. 20, 1875	162,281
Fisher, D.C.	Furniture castor	Mar. 14, 1876	174,794
Flemming, F., Jr.	Guitar (variation)	Mar. 3, 1886	338,727

Inventor	Invention	Date	Patent
Forten, J.	Sail Control(described in Mass. Newspaper) 1850		
Goode, Sarah E.	Folding cabinet bed	July 14, 1885	322,177
Gourdine, M.C.	Electogas dynamic mtd. & apparatus	June 10, 1969	3,449,667
Grant, G.F.	Golf tee	Dec. 12, 1899	638,920
Grant, W.	Curtain rod support	Aug. 4, 1896	565,075
Gray, R.H.	Bailing press	Aug. 28, 1894	525,203
Gray, R.H.	Cistern cleaners	Apr. 9, 1895	537,151
Gregory, J.	Motor	Apr. 26, 1887	361,937
Grenon, H.	Razor stropping device	Feb. 18, 1896	554,867
Griffin, F.W.	Pool table attachment	June 13, 1899	626,902
Gunn, S.W.	Boot or shoe (variation)	Jan. 16, 1900	641,642
Haines, J.H.	Portable basin	Sept. 28, 1897	590,833
Hale, Wm.	An improvement in aeroplanes	Apr. 7, 1925	1,563,278
Hall, LLoyd A.	Manuf. stable dry papain composition	March 15, 1949	2,464,200
Hall, Lloyd A.	Asphalt emulsion & Manuf. thereof	Oct. 18, 1932	1,882,834
Hall, Lloyd A.	Sterilizing foodstuff	Feb. 8, 1938	2,107,697
Hall, Lloyd A.	Puncture sealing composition & manuf. thereof	Sept. 5, 1944	2,357,650
Hammonds, J.F.	Apparatus for holding yarn skeins	Dec. 15, 1896	572,985
Harding, F.H.	Extension banquet table	Nov. 22, 1898	614,468
Harper, Solomon	Electric Hair Treatment	Aug. 5, 1930	1,772,002
Harper, Solomon	Thermostatic Control Hair Curlers	Aug. 8, 1953	2,648,757
Harper, S.	Thermostatic Controlled Fur	Aug. 11, 1953	2,711,095
Hawkins, J.	Gridiron	Mar. 26, 1845	3,973
Hawkins, R.	Harness attachment	Oct. 4, 1887	370,943
Headen, M.	Foot power hammer	Oct. 5, 1886	350,363
Hearness, R.	Detachable car fender	July 4, 1899	628,003
Hilyer, A.F.	Water evaporator attachment for hot air registers	Aug. 26, 1890	435,095
Hilyer, A.F.	Registers	Oct. 14, 1890	438,159
Holmes, E.H.	Gage	Nov. 12, 1895	549,513
Hyde, R.N.	Portable weighing scales	Nov. 3, 1896	570,553
Jackson, B.F.	Composition for cleaning and preserving carpets	Nov. 6, 1888	392,205

Inventor	Invention	Date	Patent
Jackson, B.F.	Matnx drying apparatus	May 10, 1898	603,879
Jackson, B.F.	Gas Burner	Apr. 4, 1899	622,482
Jackson, H.A.	Kitchen table (variation)	Oct. 6, 1896	569,135
Jackson, W.H.	Railway switch	Mar. 9, 1897	578,641
Jackson, W.H.	Railway switch	Mar. 16, 1897	593,665
Jackson, W.H.	Automatic locking switch	Aug. 23, 1898	609,436
Johnson, D.	Rotary dining table	Jan. 15, 1888	396,089
Johnson, D.	Lawn mower attachment	Sept. 10, 1889	410,836
Johnson, D.	Grass receivers for lawn mowers	June 10, 1890	429,629
Johnson, I.R.	Bicycle frame	Oct. 10, 1899	634,823
Johnson, P.	Swinging chairs	Nov. 15, 1881	249,530
Johnson, P.	Eye Protector	Nov. 2, 1880	234,039
Johnson, W.	Egg beater	Feb. 5, 1884	292,821
Johnson, W.	Velocipede	June 20, 1899	627,335
Johnson, W.A.	Paint vehicle	Dec. 4, 1888	393,763
Johnson, W.H.	Overcoming dead centers	Feb. 4, 1896	554,223
Johnson, W.H.	Overcoming dead centers	Oct. 11, 1898	612,345
Jones, F.M.	Ticket dispensing machine	June 27, 1939	2,163,754
Jones, F.M.	Air conditioning unit	July 12, 1949	2,475,841
Jones, F.M.	Two-cycle gasoline engine	Nov. 28, 1950	2,523,273
Jones, F.M.	Starter Generator	July 12, 1949	2,475,842
Jones, F.M.	Thermostat and temperature control system	Feb. 23, 1960	2,926,005
Jones & Long	Caps for bottles	Sept. 13, 1898	610,715
Joyce, J.A.	Ore bucket	Apr. 26, 1898	603,143
Julian, Hubert	Airplane safety device	May 24, 1920	1,379,264
Julian, Percy L.	Preparation of Cortisone	Aug. 10, 1910	2,752,339
Julian, P.C. et al.	Recovery of sterols	Oct. 22, 1940	2,718,971
Latimer, L.H.	Lamp Fixture	Aug. 10, 1910	968,787
Latimer, L.H.	Manufacturing carbons	June 17, 1882	252,386
Latimer, L.H.	Apparatus for cooling and disinfecting	Jan. 12, 1886	334,078
Latimer, L.H.	Locking racks for hats, coats, and umbrellas	Mar. 24, 1896	557,076
Latimer & Nichols	Electric Lamp	Sept. 13, 1881	247,097
Latimer & Tregoning	Globe support for electric lamps	Mar. 21, 1882	255,212
Lavalette, W.	Printing press (variation)	Sept. 17, 1878	208,208
Lee, H.	Animal trap	Feb. 12, 1867	61,941
Lee, J.	Kneading machine	Aug. 7, 1894	524,042
Lee, J.	Bread crumbing machine	June 4, 1895	540,553

Inventor	Invention	Date	Patent
Leslie, F.W.	Envelope Seal	Sept. 21, 1897	590,325
Lewis, A.L.	Window cleaner	Sept. 27, 1892	483,359
Lewis, E.R.	Spring Gun	May 3, 1887	362,096
Linden, H.	Piano Truck	Sept. 8, 1891	459,365
Little, E.	Bridle-Bit	Mar. 7, 1887	254,666
Loudin, F.J.	Sash Fastener	Dec. 12, 1892	510,432
Loudin, F.J.	Key fastener	Jan. 9, 1894	512,308
Love, J.L.	Plasterers Hawk	July 9, 1895	542,419
Love, J.L.	Pencil sharpener	Nov. 23, 1897	594,114
Marshall, T.J.	Fire extinguisher (variation)	May 26, 1872	125,063
Marshall, W.	Grain binder	May 11, 1886	341,599
Martin, W.A.	Lock	July 23, 1889	407,738
Martin, W.A.	Lock	Dec. 30, 1890	443,945
Matzeliger, J.E.	Mechanism for distributing tacks	Nov. 26, 1899	415,726
Matzeliger, J.E.	Nailing machine	Feb. 25, 1896	421,954
Matzeliger, J.E.	Tack separating mechanism	Mar. 25, 1890	423,937
Matzeliger, J.E.	Lasting machine	Sept. 22, 1891	459,899
McCoy, E.	Lubricator for steam engines	July 2, 1872	129,843
McCoy, E.	Lubricator for steam engines	Aug. 6, 1872	130,305
McCoy, E.	Steam Lubricator	Jan. 20, 1874	146,697
McCoy, E.	Ironing Table	May 12, 1874	150,876
McCoy, E.	Steam cylinder lubricator	Feb. 1, 1876	173,032
McCoy, E.	Steam cylinder lubricator	July 4, 1876	179,585
McCoy, E.	Law sprinkler design	Sept. 26, 1899	631,549
McCoy, E.	Steam dome	June 16, 1885	320,354
McCoy, E.	Lubricator attachment	Apr. 19, 1887	361,435
McCoy, E.	Lubricator for safety valves	May 24, 1887	363,529
McCoy, E.	Drip cup	Sept. 29, 1891	460,215
McCoy & Hodges	Lubricator	Dec. 24, 1889	418,139
McCree, D.	Portable fire escape	Nov. 11, 1890	440,322
Mendenhall, A.	Holder for driving reins	Nov. 28, 1899	637,811
Miles, A.	Elevator	Oct. 11, 1887	371,207
Mitchell, C.L.	Phoneterism	Jan. 1, 1884	291,071
Mitchell, J.M.	Check row corn planter	Jan. 16, 1900	641,462
Moody, W.U.	Game board design	May 11, 1897	27,046
Morehead, K.	Reel carrier	Oct. 6, 1896	568,916
Murray, G.W.	Combined furrow opener and stalk-knocker	Apr. 10, 1894	517,960
Murray, G.W.	Cultivator and marker	Apr. 10, 1894	517,961
Murray, G.W.	Planter	June 5, 1894	520,887

Inventor	Invention	Date	Patent
Murray, G.W.	Cotton chopper	June 5, 1894	520,888
Murray, G.W.	Fertilizer distributor	June 5, 1894	520,889
Murray, G.W.	Planter	June 5, 1894	520,891
Murray, G.W.	Planter and fertilizer distributor reaper	June 5, 1894	520,892
Murray, W.	Attachment for bicycles	Jan. 27, 1891	445,452
Nance, L.	Game apparatus	Dec. 1, 1891	464,035
Nash, H.H.	Life-preserving stool	Oct. 5, 1875	168,519
Newson, S.	Oil heater or cooker	May 22, 1894	520,188
Nichols & Latimer	Electric lamp (variation)	Sept. 13, 1881	247,097
Nickerson, W.J.	Mandolin & guitar attachment for pianos	June 27, 1899	627,739
O'Conner & Turner	Alarm for boilers	Aug. 25, 1896	566,612
O'Conner & Turner	Steam gauge	Aug. 25, 1896	566,613
O'Conner & Turner	Alarm for coasts containing vessels	Feb. 8, 1898	598,572
Outlaw, J.W.	Alarm for coasts containing vessels	Feb. 8, 1898	598,572
Outlaw, J.W.	Horseshoes	Nov. 15, 1966	3,284,239
Perryman, F.R.	Caterers tray table	Feb. 2, 1892	402,189
Perry, John Jr. & Hunger, H.F.	Biochern Fuel Cell	Nov. 8, 1966	579,242
Peterson, H.	Attachment for lawn mowers	Apr. 30, 1889	402,189
Phelps, W.H.	Apparatus for washing vehicles	Mar. 23, 1897	579,242
Pickering, J.F.	Air Ship	Feb. 20, 1900	643,975
Pickett, H.	Scaffold	June 30, 1874	152,511
Pinn, T.B.	File Folder	Aug. 17, 1880	231,355
Polk, A.J.	Bicycle support	Apr. 14, 1896	558,103
Prather, Al.G.B.	Man powered glider aircraft	Feb. 6, 1973	3,715,011
Pugsley, A.	Blind Stop	July 29, 1890	433,306
Purdy, W.	Device for sharpening edged tools	Oct. 27, 1896	570,337
Purdy, W.	Design for sharpening edged tools	Aug. 16, 1898	609,367
Purdy, W.	Design for sharpening edged tools	Aug. 1, 1899	630,106
Purdy & Peters	Design for spoons	Apr. 23, 1895	24,228
Purdy & Sadgwar	Folding chair	June 11, 1889	405,117
Purvis, W.B.	Bag fastener	Apr. 25, 1882	256,856
Purvis, W.B.	Hand stamp	Feb. 27, 1883	273,149
Purvis, W.B.	Fountain pen	Jan. 7, 1890	419,065
Purvis, W.B.	Electric Railway (variation)	May 1, 1894	519,291
Purvis, W.B.	Magnetic car balancing device	May 21, 1895	539,542
Purvis, W.B.	Electric Railway switch	Aug. 17, 1897	588,176
Queen, W.	Guard for companion ways and hatches	Aug. 18, 1891	458,131

Inventor	Invention	Date	Patent
Ray, E.P.	Chair supporting device	Feb. 21, 1899	620,078
Ray, L.P.	Dust Pan	Aug. 3, 1897	587,607
Reed, J.W.	Dough kneader and roller	Sept. 23, 1884	305,474
Reynolds, H.H.	Window ventilator for railroad cars	Apr. 3, 1883	275,271
Reynolds, H.H.	Safety gate for bridges	Oct. 7, 1890	437,937
Reynolds, R.R.	Nonrefillable bottle	May 2, 1899	624,092
Rhodes, J.B.	Water closets	Dec. 19, 1899	639,290
Richardson, A.C.	Hame fastener	Mar. 14, 1882	255,022
Richardson, A.C.	Churn	Feb. 17, 1891	466,470
Richardson, A.C.	Casket-lowering device	Nov. 13, 1894	529,311
Richardson, A.C.	Insect destroyer	Feb. 28, 1899	620,363
Richardson, A.C.	Bottle	Dec. 12, 1899	638,811
Richardson, W.H.	Cotton Chopper	June 1, 1886	343,140
Richardson, W.H.	Child's carriage	June 18, 1889	405,599
Richardson, W.H.	Child's carriage	June 18, 1889	405,600
Richey, C.V.	Car coupling	June 15, 1897	584,650
Richey, C.V.	Railroad Switch	Aug. 3, 1897	587,657
Richey, C.V.	Railroad Switch	Oct. 26, 1897	592,448
Richey, C.V.	Fire escape bracket	Dec. 28, 1897	596,427
Richey, C.V.	Combined hammock & stretcher	Dec. 13, 1898	615,907
Rickman, A.L.	Overshoe	Feb. 8, 1898	598,816
Ricks, J.	Horseshoe	Mar. 30, 1886	338,781
Ricks, J.	Overshoes for horses	June 6, 1899	626,245
Rillieux, N.	Sugar refiner (evaporating pan)	Dec. 10, 1846	4,879
Robinson, E.R.	Electric Railway trolley	Sept. 19, 1893	505,370
Robinson, E.R.	Casting composite	Nov. 23, 1897	594,386
Robinson, J.H.	Lifesaving guards for locomotive	Mar. 14, 1899	621,143
Robinson, J.H.	Lifesaving guards for street cars	Apr. 25, 1899	623,929
Robinson, J.	Dinner pail	Feb. 1, 1887	356,852
Romain, A.	Passenger register	Apr. 23, 1889	402,035
Ross, A.L.	Runner for stops	Aug. 4, 1896	565,301
Ross, A.L.	Bag closure	June 7, 1898	605,343
Ross, A.L.	Trousers support	Nov. 28, 1993	638,068
Ross, J.	Bailing press	Sept. 5, 1899	632,539
Roster, D.N.	Feather curler	Mar. 10, 1896	556,166
Ruffin, S.	Vessels for liquids and manner of sealing	Nov. 20, 1899	737,603
Russell, L.A.	Guard attachment for beds	Aug. 13, 1895	544,381
Sampson, G.T.	Slep propeller	Feb. 17, 1880	312,388
Sampson, G.T.	Clothes drier	June 7, 1892	476,416

Inventor	Invention	Date	Patent
Scrotton, S.R.	Adjustable window cornice	Feb. 17, 1880	224,732
Scrotton, S.R.	Cornice	Jan. 16, 1883	270,851
Scrotton, S.R.	Pole Tip	Sept. 21, 1886	349,525
Scrotton, S.R.	Curtain rod	Aug. 30, 1892	481,720
Scrotton, S.R.	Supporting bracket	Sept. 12, 1893	505,008
Shanks, S.C.	Sleeping car berth register	July 21, 1897	587,165
Shewcraft, Frank	Letter box	Detroit, Mich.	
Shorter, D.W.	Feed rack	May 17, 1887	363,089
Smith, B. & L.E.B.	Mtd. or preparing nonlaminiating anisotropic Boron Nitride	Oct. 1, 1985	4,544,535
Smith, J.W.	Improvement in games	Apr. 17, 1900	647,887
Smith, J.W.	Lawn sprinkler	May 4, 1897	581,785
Smith, J.W.	Lawn sprinkler	Mar. 22, 1898	601,065
Smith, P.D.	Potato digger	Jan. 21, 1891	445,206
Smith, P.D.	Grain binder	Feb. 23, 1892	469,279
Snow & Johns	Liniment	Oct. 7, 1890	437,728
Spears, H.	Portable shield for infantry	Dec. 27, 1870	110,599
Spikes, R.B.	Combination milk bottle opener and bottle cover	June 29, 1926	1,590,557
Spikes, R.B.	Method & apparatus for obtaining average samples and temperature of tank liquids	Oct. 27, 1931	1,828,753
Spikes, R.B.	Automatic gear shift	Dec. 6, 1932	1,889,814
Spikes, R.B.	Transmission & shifting thereof	Nov. 28, 1933	1,936,996
Spikes, R.B.	Self-locking rack for billiard cues	around 1910	not found
Spikes, R.B.	Automatic shoeshine chair	around 1939	not found
Spikes, R.B.	Multiple barrel machine gun	c1940	not found
Standard, J.	Oil stove	Oct. 29, 1889	413,689
Standard, J.	Refrigerator	July 14, 1891	455,891
Stewart, E.W.	Punching machine	May 3, 1887	362,190
Stewart, E.W.	Machine for forming vehicle seat bars	Mar. 22, 1887	373,698
Stewart, T.W.	Mop	June 13, 1893	499,402
Stewart, T.W.	Station indicator	June 20, 1893	499,895
Stewart & Johnson	Metal bending machine	Dec. 27, 1887	375,512
Sutton, E.H.	Cotton cultivator	Apr. 7, 1878	149,543
Sweeting, J.A.	Device for rolling cigarettes	Nov. 30, 1897	594,501
Sweeting, J.A.	Combined knife and scoop	June 7, 1898	605,209
Taylor, B.H.	Rotary engine	Apr. 23, 1878	202,888
Taylor, B.H.	Slide valve	July 6, 1897	585,798
Temple, L.	Toggle harpoon	1848	

Inventor	Invention	Date	Patent
Thomas, S.E.	Waste trap	Oct. 16, 1883	286,746
Thomas, S.E.	Waste trap for basins, closets, etc.	Oct. 4, 1887	371,107
Thomas, S.E.	Casting	July 31, 1888	386,941
Thomas, S.E.	Pipe connection	Oct. 9, 1888	390,821
Toliver, George	Propeller for vessels	Apr. 28, 1891	451,086
Tregoning & Latimer	Globe supporter for electric lamps	Mar. 21, 1882	255,212
Walker, Peter	Machine for cleaning seed cotton	Feb. 16,1897	577,153
Walker, Peter	Bait holder	Mar. 8, 1898	600,241
Waller, J.N.	Shoemakers cabinet or bench	Feb. 3, 1880	224,253
Washington, Wade	Corn husking machine	Aug. 14, 1883	283,173
Watkins, Isaac	Scrubbing frame	Oct. 7, 1890	437,849
Watts, J.R.	Bracket for miners lamp	Mar. 7, 1893	493,137
West, E.H.	Weather shield	Sept. 5, 1899	632,385
West, J.W.	Wagon	Oct. 18, 1870	108,419
White, D.L.	Extension steps for cars	Jan. 12, 1897	574,969
White, J.T.	Lemon squeezer	Dec. 8, 1896	572,849
Williams, Carter	Canopy frame	Feb. 2, 1892	468,280
Williams, J.P.	Pillow sham holder	Oct. 10, 1899	634,784
Winn, Frank	Direct acting steam engine	Dec. 4, 1888	394,047
Winters, J.R.	Fire escape ladder	May 7, 1878	203,517
Winters, J.R.	Fire escape ladder	Apr. 8, 1879	214,224
Woods, G.T.	Steam boiler furnace	June 3, 1884	299,894
Woods, G.T.	Telephone transmitter (variation)	Dec. 2, 1884	3,088,176
Woods, G.T.	Relay instrument	June 7, 1887	364,619
Woods, G.T.	Polarized relay	July 5, 1887	366,192
Woods, G.T.	Electromechanical brake	Aug. 16, 1887	368,265
Woods, G.T.	Telephone system & apparatus	Oct. 11, 1887	371,241
Woods, G.T.	Electromagnetic brake apparatus	Oct. 18, 1887	371,655
Woods, G.T.	Railway telegraphy	Nov. 15, 1887	373,383
Woods, G.T.	Induction telegraph system	Nov. 29, 1887	373,915
Woods, G.T.	Overhead conducting system for electric railway	May 29, 1888	383,844
Woods, G.T.	Electromotive railway system	June 26, 1888	385,034
Woods, G.T.	Tunnel construction for electric railway	July 17, 1888	386,282
Woods, G.T.	Galvanic battery	Aug. 14, 1888	387,839
Woods, G.T.	Railway telegraphy	Aug. 28, 1888	388,803
Woods, G.T.	Automatic safety cut-out for electric circuits	Jan. 1, 1889	395,533

Inventor	Invention	Date	Patent
Woods, G.T.	Automatic safety cut-out for electric circuits	Oct. 14, 1889	438,590
Woods, G.T.	Electric railway systems	Nov. 10, 1891	463,020
Woods, G.T.	Electric railway conduit	Nov. 21, 1893	509,065
Woods, G.T.	Electric railway supply system	Oct. 31, 1893	507,606
Woods, G.T.	System of electrical distribution	Oct. 13, 1896	569,443
Woods, G.T.	Amusement apparatus	Dec. 19, 1899	639,692
Wormley, James	Lifesaving apparatus	May 24, 1881	242,091

DAILY BIBLE READING PLAN

Bible Reading Plan

Day	Date	Text	Day	Date	Text
1	Jan. 1	Gen. 1-3	49	Feb. 18	Lev. 8-10
2	Jan. 2	Gen. 4:1—6:8	50	Feb. 19	Lev. 11-12
3	Jan. 3	Gen. 6:9—9:29	51	Feb. 20	Lev. 13-14
4	Jan. 4	Gen. 10-11	52	Feb. 21	Lev. 15-17
5	Jan. 5	Gen. 12-14	53	Feb. 22	Lev. 18-20
6	Jan. 6	Gen. 15-17	54	Feb. 23	Lev. 21-23
7	Jan. 7	Gen. 18-19	55	Feb. 24	Lev. 24-25
8	Jan. 8	Gen. 20-22	56	Feb. 25	Lev. 26-27
9	Jan. 9	Gen. 23-24	57	Feb. 26	Num. 1-2
10	Jan. 10	Gen. 25-26	58	Feb. 27	Num. 3-4
11	Jan. 11	Gen. 27-28	59	Feb. 28	Num. 5-6
12	Jan. 12	Gen. 29-30	60	Mar. 1	Num. 7
13	Jan. 13	Gen. 31-32	61	Mar. 2	Num. 8-10
14	Jan. 14	Gen. 33-35	62	Mar. 3	Num. 11-13
15	Jan. 15	Gen. 36-37	63	Mar. 4	Num. 14-15
16	Jan. 16	Gen. 38-40	64	Mar. 5	Num. 16-18
17	Jan. 17	Gen. 41-42	65	Mar. 6	Num. 19-21
18	Jan. 18	Gen. 43-45	66	Mar. 7	Num. 22-24
19	Jan. 19	Gen. 46-47	67	Mar. 8	Num. 25-26
20	Jan. 20	Gen. 48-50	68	Mar. 9	Num. 27-29
21	Jan. 21	Job 1-3	69	Mar. 10	Num. 30-31
22	Jan. 22	Job 4-7	70	Mar. 11	Num. 32-33
23	Jan. 23	Job 8-11	71	Mar. 12	Num. 34-36
24	Jan. 24	Job 12-15	72	Mar. 13	Deut. 1-2
25	Jan. 25	Job 16-19	73	Mar. 14	Deut. 3-4
26	Jan. 26	Job 20-22	74	Mar. 15	Deut. 5-7
27	Jan. 27	Job 23-28	75	Mar. 16	Deut. 8-10
28	Jan. 28	Job 29-31	76	Mar. 17	Deut. 11-13
29	Jan. 29	Job 32-34	77	Mar. 18	Deut. 14-17
30	Jan. 30	Job 35-37	78	Mar. 19	Deut. 18-21
31	Jan. 31	Job 38-42	79	Mar. 20	Deut. 22-25
32	Feb. 1	Ex. 1-4	80	Mar. 21	Deut. 26-28
33	Feb. 2	Ex. 5-8	81	Mar. 22	Deut. 29:1—31:29
34	Feb. 3	Ex. 9-11	82	Mar. 23	Deut. 31:30—34:12
35	Feb. 4	Ex. 12-13	83	Mar. 24	Josh. 1-4
36	Feb. 5	Ex. 14-15	84	Mar. 25	Josh. 5-8
37	Feb. 6	Ex. 16-18	85	Mar. 26	Josh. 9-11
38	Feb. 7	Ex. 19-21	86	Mar. 27	Josh. 12-14
39	Feb. 8	Ex. 22-24	87	Mar. 28	Josh. 15-17
40	Feb. 9	Ex. 25-27	88	Mar. 29	Josh. 18-19
41	Feb. 10	Ex. 28-29	89	Mar. 30	Josh. 20-22
42	Feb. 11	Ex. 30-31	90	Mar. 31	Josh. 23—Judg. 1
43	Feb. 12	Ex. 32-34	91	Apr. 1	Judg. 2-5
44	Feb. 13	Ex. 35-36	92	Apr. 2	Judg. 6-8
45	Feb. 14	Ex. 37-38	93	Apr. 3	Judg. 9
46	Feb. 15	Ex. 39-40	94	Apr. 4	Judg. 10-12
47	Feb. 16	Lev. 1:1—5:13	95	Apr. 5	Judg. 13-16
48	Feb. 17	Lev. 5:14—7:38	96	Apr. 6	Judg. 17-19

Day	Date	Text	Day	Date	Text
97	Apr. 7	Judg. 20-21	131	May 11	Pss. 108-9; 120-21;
98	Apr. 8	Ruth			140; 143-44
99	Apr. 9	1 Sam. 1-3	132	May 12	Pss. 1; 14-15; 36-37; 39
100	Apr. 10	1 Sam. 4-7	133	May 13	Pss. 40; 49-50; 73
101	Apr. 11	1 Sam. 8-10	134	May 14	Pss. 76; 82; 84; 90;
102	Apr. 12	1 Sam. 11-13			92; 112; 115
103	Apr. 13	1 Sam. 14-15	135	May 15	Pss. 8-9; 16; 19; 21;
104	Apr. 14	1 Sam. 16-17			24; 29
105	Apr. 15	1 Sam. 18-19; Ps. 59	136	May 16	Pss. 33; 65-68
106	Apr. 16	1 Sam. 20-21;	137	May 17	Pss. 75; 93-94; 97-100
		Pss. 56; 34	138	May 18	Pss. 103-4; 113-14; 117
107	Apr. 17	1 Sam. 22-23;	139	May 19	Ps. 119:1-88
		1 Chron. 12:8-18;	140	May 20	Ps. 119:89-176
		Pss. 52; 54; 63;142	141	May 21	Pss. 122; 124; 133-36
108	Apr. 18	1 Sam. 24; Ps. 57;	142	May 22	Pss. 138-39;
		1 Sam. 25			145:148; 150
109	Apr. 19	1 Sam. 26-29;	143	May 23	Pss. 4; 12; 20; 25; 32; 38
		1 Chron. 12:1-7, 19-22	144	May 24	Pss. 42; 53; 58; 81;
110	Apr. 20	1 Sam. 30-31;			101; 111; 130-31;
		1 Chron. 10; 2Sam. 1			141; 146
111	Apr. 21	2 Sam. 2-4	145	May 25	Pss. 2; 22; 27
112	Apr. 22	2 Sam. 5:1—6:11;	146	May 26	Pss. 45; 47-48; 87;110
		1 Chron. 11:1-9;	147	May 27	1 Kings 1:1—2:12;
		12:23-40; 13:1—14:17			2 Sam. 23:1-7
113	Apr. 23	2 Sam. 22; Ps. 18	148	May 28	1 Kings 2:13—3:28;
114	Apr. 24	1 Chron. 15-16;			2 Chron. 1:1-13
		2 Sam. 6:12-23; Ps. 96	149	May 29	1 Kings 5-6;
115	Apr. 25	Ps. 105; 2 Sam. 7;			2 Chron. 2-3
		1 Chron. 17	150	May 30	1 Kings 7; 2 Chron. 4
116	Apr. 26	2 Sam. 8-10;	151	May 31	1 Kings 8;
		1 Chron. 18-19; Ps. 60			2 Chron. 5:1—7:10
117	Apr. 27	2 Sam. 11-12;	152	June 1	1 Kings 9:1—10:13;
		1 Chron. 20:1-3; Ps. 51			2 Chron. 7:11—9:12
118	Apr. 28	2 Sam. 13-14	153	June 2	1 Kings 4; 10:14-29;
119	Apr. 29	2 Sam. 15-17			2 Chron. 1:14-17;
120	Apr. 30	Ps. 3; 2 Sam. 18-19			9:13-28; Ps. 72
121	May 1	2 Sam. 20-21; 23:8-23;	154	June 3	Prov. 1-3
		1 Chron. 20:4-8;	155	June 4	Prov. 4-6
		11:10-25	156	June 5	Prov. 7-9
122	May 2	2 Sam. 23:24—24:25;	157	June 6	Prov. 10-12
		1 Chron. 11:26-47;	158	June 7	Prov. 13-15
		21:1-30	159	June 8	Prav. 16-18
123	May 3	1 Chron. 22-24	160	June 9	Prov. 19-21
124	May 4	Ps. 30; 1 Chron. 25-26	161	June 10	Prov. 22-24
125	May 5	1 Chron. 27-29	162	June 11	Prov. 25-27
126	May 6	Pss. 5-7; 10;11;13;17	163	June 12	Prov. 28-29
127	May 7	Pss. 23; 26; 28; 31; 35	164	June 13	Prov. 30-31; Ps. 127
128	May 8	Pss. 41; 43; 46; 55;	165	June 14	Song of Songs
		61; 62; 64	166	June 15	1 Kings 11:1-40;
129	May 9	Pss. 69-71; 77			Eccles. 1-2
130	May 10	Pss. 83; 86; 88; 91; 95	167	June 16	Eccles. 3-7

Day	Date	Text
168	June 17	Eccles. 8-12; 1 Kings 11:41-43; 2 Chron. 9 29-31
169	June 18	1 Kings 12; 2 Chron. 10:1—11:17
170	June 19	1 Kings 13-14; 2 Chron. 11:18—12:16
171	June 20	1 Kings 15:1-24; 2 Chron. 13-16
172	June 21	1 Kings 15:25—16:34; 2 Chron. 17; 1 Kings 17
173	June 22	1 Kings 18-19
174	June 23	1 Kings 20-21
175	June 24	1 Kings 22:1-40; 2 Chron. 18
176	June 25	1 Kings 22:41-53; 2 Kings 1; 2 Chron. 19:1—21:3
177	June 26	2 Kings 2-4
178	June 27	2 Kings 5-7
179	June 28	2 Kings 8-9; 2 Chron. 21:4—22:9
180	June 29	2 Kings 10-11; 2 Chron. 22:10—23:21
181	June 30	Joel
182	July 1	2 Kings 12-13; 2 Chron. 24
183	July 2	2 Kings 14; 2 Chron. 25; Jonah
184	July 3	Hos. 1-7
185	July 4	Hos. 8-14
186	July 5	2 Kings 15:1-7; 2 Chron. 26; Amos 1-4
187	July 6	Amos5-9; 2 Kings 15:8-18
188	July 7	Isa. 1-4
189	July 8	2 Kings 15:19-38; 2 Chron. 27; Isa. 5-6
190	July 9	Micah
191	July 10	2 Kings 16; 2 Chron. 28; Isa. 7-8
192	July 11	Isa. 9-12
193	July 12	Isa. 13-16
194	July 13	Isa. 17-22
195	July 14	Isa. 23-27
196	July 15	Isa. 28-30
197	July 16	Isa. 31-35
198	July 17	2 Kings 18:1-8; 2 Chron. 29-31

Day	Date	Text
199	July 18	2 Kings 17;18:9-37; 2 Chron. 32:1-19; Isa. 36
200	July 19	2 Kings 19; 2 Chron. 32:20-23; Isa. 37
201	July 20	2 Kings 20; 2 Chron. 32:24-33; Isa. 38-39
202	July 21	2 Kings 21:1-18; 2 Chron. 33:1-20; Isa. 40
203	July 22	Isa. 41-43
204	July 23	Isa. 44-47
205	July 24	Isa. 48-51
206	July 25	Isa. 52-57
207	July 26	Isa. 58-62
208	July 27	Isa. 63-66
209	July 28	2 Kings 21:19-26; 2 Chron. 33:21—34:7; Zephaniah
210	July 29	Jer. 1-3
211	July 30	Jer. 4-6
212	July 31	Jer. 7-9
213	Aug. 1	Jer. 10-13
214	Aug. 2	Jer. 14-16
215	Aug. 3	Jer. 17-20
216	Aug. 4	2 Kings 22:1—23:28; 2 Chron. 34:8—35:19
217	Aug. 5	Nahum; 2 Kings 23:29-37; 2 Chron. 35:20—36:5; Jer. 22:10-17
218	Aug. 6	Jer. 26; Habakkuk
219	Aug. 7	Jer. 46-47; 2 Kings 24:1-4, 7; 2 Chron. 36:6-7; Jer. 25, 35
220	Aug. 8	Jer. 36, 45, 48
221	Aug. 9	Jer. 49:1-33; Dan. 1-2
222	Aug. 10	Jer. 22:18-30; 2 Kings 24:5-20; 2 Chron. 36:8-12; Jer. 37:1-2; 52:1-3; 24; 29
223	Aug. 11	Jer. 27-28, 23
224	Aug. 12	Jer. 50-51
225	Aug. 13	Jer. 49:34-39; 34:1-22; Ezek. 1-3
226	Aug. 14	Ezek. 4-7
227	Aug. 15	Ezek. 8-11

Day	Date	Text	Day	Date	Text
228	Aug. 16	Ezek. 12-14	258	Sept. 15	Zech. 9-14
229	Aug. 17	Ezek. 15-17	259	Sept. 16	Esther 1-4
230	Aug. 18	Ezek. 18-20	260	Sept. 17	Esther 5-10
231	Aug. 19	Ezek. 21-23	261	Sept. 18	Ezra 7-8
232	Aug. 20	2 Kings 25:1;	262	Sept. 19	Ezra 9-10
		2 Chron. 36:13-16;	263	Sept. 20	Neh. 1-5
		Jer. 39:1; 52:4;	264	Sept. 21	Neh. 6-7
		Ezek. 24;	265	Sept. 22	Neh. 8-10
		Jer. 21:1—22:9;	266	Sept. 23	Neh. 11-13
		32:1-44	267	Sept. 24	Malachi
233	Aug. 21	Jer. 30-31, 33	268	Sept. 25	1 Chron. 1-2
234	Aug. 22	Ezek. 25; 29:1-16;	269	Sept. 26	1 Chron. 3-5
		30; 31	270	Sept. 27	1 Chron. 6
235	Aug. 23	Ezek. 26-28	271	Sept. 28	1 Chron. 7:1—8:27
236	Aug. 24	Jer. 37:3—39:10;	272	Sept. 29	1 Chron. 8:28—9:44
		52:5-30;	273	Sept. 30	John 1:1-18; Mark 1:1;
		2 Kings 25:2-21;			Luke 1:1-4; 3:23-38;
		2 Chron. 36:17-21			Matt. 1:1-17
237	Aug. 25	2 Kings 25:22;	274	Oct. 1	Luke 1:5-80
		Jer. 39:11—40:6;	275	Oct. 2	Matt. 1:18—2:23;
		Lam. 1-3			Luke 2
238	Aug. 26	Larn. 4-5; Obadiah	276	Oct. 3	Matt. 3:1—4:11;
239	Aug. 27	Jer. 40:7—44:30;			Mark 1:2-13;
		2 Kings 25:23-26			Luke 3:1-23; 4:1-13;
240	Aug. 28	Ezek. 33:21—36:38			John 1:19-34
241	Aug. 29	Ezek. 37-39	277	Oct. 4	John 1:35—3:36
242	Aug. 30	Ezek. 32:1—33:20;	278	Oct. 5	John 4; Matt. 4:12-17;
		Dan. 3			Mark 1:14-15;
243	Aug. 31	Ezek. 40-42			Luke 4:14-30
244	Sept. 1	Ezek. 43-45	279	Oct. 6	Mark 1:16-45;
245	Sept. 2	Ezek. 46-48			Matt. 4:18-25;
246	Sept. 3	Ezek. 29:17-21;			8:2-4,14-17;
		Dan. 4; Jer. 52:31-34;			Luke 4:31—5:16
		2 Kings 25:27-30;	280	Oct. 7	Matt. 9:1-17;
		Ps. 44			Mark 2:1-22;
247	Sept. 4	Pss. 74; 79-80; 89			Luke 5:17-39
248	Sept. 5	Pss. 85; 102; 106;	281	Oct. 8	John 5; Matt. 12:1-21;
		123; 137			Mark 2:23—3:12;
249	Sept. 6	Dan. 7-8; 5			Luke 6:1-11
250	Sept. 7	Dan. 9; 6	282	Oct. 9	Matt. 5; Mark 3:13-19;
251	Sept. 8	2 Chron. 36:22-23;			Luke 6:12-36
		Ezra 1:1—4:5	283	Oct. 10	Matt. 6-7;
252	Sept. 9	Dan. 10-12			Luke 6:37-49
253	Sept. 10	Ezra 4:6—6:13;	284	Oct. 11	Luke 7;
		Haggai			Matt. 8:1, 5-13;
254	Sept. 11	Zech. 1-6			11:2-30
255	Sept. 12	Zech. 7-8;	285	Oct. 12	Matt. 12:22-50;
		Ezra 6:14-22; Ps. 78			Mark 3:20-35;
256	Sept. 13	Pss. 107; 116; 118			Luke 8:1-21
257	Sept. 14	Pss. 125-26; 128-29;	286	Oct. 13	Mark 4:1-34;
		132; 147; 149			Matt. 13:1-53

Day	Date	Text	Day	Date	Text
287	Oct. 14	Mark 4:35—5:43; Matt. 8; 18, 23-34; 9; 18-34; Luke 8;22-56	306	Nov. 2	Matt. 23; Mark 12:38-44; Luke 20:45—21:4
288	Oct. 15	Mark 6;1-30; Matt. 13; 54-58; 9:35—11:1; 14:1-12; Luke 9:1-10	307	Nov. 3	Matt. 24:1-31; Mark 13:1-27; Luke 21:5-27
289	Oct. 16	Matt. 14:13-36; Mark 6:31-56; Luke 9:11-17; John 6:1-21	308	Nov. 4	Matt. 24:32—26:5, 14-16; Mark 13:28—14:2, 10-11; Luke 21:28—22:6
290	Oct. 17	John 6:22—7:1; Matt. 15:1-20; Mark 7:1-23	309	Nov. 5	Matt. 26:17-29; Mark 14:12-25; Luke 22:7-38; John 13
291	Oct. 18	Matt. 15:21—16:20; Mark 7:24—8:30; Luke 9:18-21	310	Nov. 6	John 14-16
			311	Nov. 7	John 17:1—18:1; Matt. 26:30-46; Mark 14:26-42; Luke 22:39-46
292	Oct. 19	Matt. 16:21—17:27; Mark 8:31—9:32; Luke 9:22-45			
293	Oct. 20	Matt. 18; 8:19-22; Mark 9:33-50; Luke 9:46-62; John 7:2-10	312	Nov. 8	Matt. 26:47-75; Mark 14:43-72; Luke 22:47-65; John 18:2-27
294	Oct. 21	John 7:11—8:59	313	Nov. 9	Matt. 27:1-26; Mark 15:1-15; Luke 22:66—23:25; John 18:28—19:16
295	Oct. 22	Luke 10:1—11:36			
296	Oct. 23	Luke 11:37—13:21			
297	Oct. 24	John 9-10			
298	Oct. 25	Luke 13:22—15:32	314	Nov. 10	Matt. 27:27-56; Mark 15:16-41; Luke 23:26-49; John 19:17-30
299	Oct. 26	Luke 16:1—17:10; John 11:1-54			
300	Oct. 27	Luke 17:11—18:17; Matt. 19:1-15; Mark 10:1-16	315	Nov. 11	Matt. 27:57—28:8; Mark 15:42—16:8; Luke 23:50—24:12; John 19:31—20:10
301	Oct. 28	Matt. 19:16—20:28; Mark 10:17-45; Luke 18:18-34	316	Nov. 12	Matt. 28:9-20; Mark 16:9-20; Luke 24:13-53; John 20:11—21:25
302	Oct. 29	Matt. 20:29-34; 26:6-13; Mark 10:46-52; 14:3-9; Luke 18:35—19:28; John 11:55—12:11	317	Nov. 13	Acts 1-2
			318	Nov. 14	Acts 3-5
303	Oct. 30	Matt. 21:1-22; Mark 11:1-26; Luke 19:29-48; John 12:12-50	319	Nov. 15	Acts6:1—8:1
			320	Nov. 16	Acts 82—9:43
			321	Nov. 17	Acts 10-11
			322	Nov. 18	Acts 12-13
304	Oct. 31	Matt. 21:23—22:14; Mark 11:27—12:12; Luke 20:1-19	323	Nov. 19	Acts 14-15
			324	Nov. 20	Gal. 1-3
			325	Nov. 21	Gal. 4-6
305	Nov. 1	Matt. 22:15-46; Mark 12:13-37; Luke 20;20-44	326	Nov. 22	James
			327	Nov. 23	Acts 16:1—18:11
			328	Nov. 24	1 Thessalonians

Day	Date	Text
329	Nov. 25	2 Thessalonians; Acts 18:12—19:22
330	Nov. 26	1 Cor. 1-4
331	Nov. 27	1 Cor. 5-8
332	Nov. 28	1 Cor. 9-11
333	Nov. 29	1 Cor. 12-14
334	Nov. 30	1 Cor. 15-16
335	Dec. 1	Acts 19:23—20:1; 2 Cor. 1-4
336	Dec. 2	2 Cor. 5-9
337	Dec. 3	2 Cor. 10-13
338	Dec. 4	Rom. 1-3
339	Dec. 5	Rom. 4-6
340	Dec. 6	Rom. 7-8
341	Dec. 7	Rom. 9-11
342	Dec. 8	Rom. 12-15
343	Dec. 9	Rom. 16; Acts 20:2—21:16
344	Dec. 10	Acts 21:17—23:35
345	Dec. 11	Acts 24-26
346	Dec. 12	Acts 27-28
347	Dec. 13	Eph. 1-3
348	Dec. 14	Eph. 4-6
349	Dec. 15	Colossians
350	Dec. 16	Philippians
351	Dec. 17	Philemon; 1 Tim. 1-3
352	Dec. 18	1 Tim. 4-6; Titus
353	Dec. 19	2 Timothy
354	Dec. 20	1 Peter
355	Dec. 21	Jude; 2 Peter
356	Dec. 22	Heb. 1:1—5:10
357	Dec. 23	Heb. 5:11—9:28
358	Dec. 24	Heb. 10-11
359	Dec. 25	Heb. 12-13; 2 John; 3John
360	Dec. 26	1 John
361	Dec. 27	Rev. 1-3
362	Dec. 28	Rev. 4-9
363	Dec. 29	Rev. 10-14
364	Dec. 30	Rev. 15-18
365	Dec. 31	Rev. 19-22

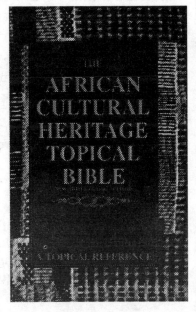

OTHER BOOKS FROM
Pneuma Life Publishing

The Flaming Sword
by Tai Ikomi
Scripture memorization and meditation bring tremendous spiritual power, however many Christians find it to be an uphill task. Committing Scriptures to memory will transform the mediocre Christian to a spiritual giant. This book will help you to become addicted to the powerful practice of scripture memorization and help you obtain the victory that you desire in every area of your life. The Flaming Sword is your pathway to spiritual growth and a more intimate relationship with God.

Opening the Front Door of Your Church
by Dr. Leonard Lovett
A creative approach for small to medium churches who want to develop a more effective ministry. Did you know that 75% of churches in the United States have 150 attendance? Opening the Front Door of your Church is an insightful and creative approach to church development and expansion, especially for churches within the urban environment.

This is My Story
by Candi Staton
This is My Story is a touching Autobiography about a gifted young child who rose from obscurity and poverty to stardom and wealth. With million-selling albums and a top-charting music career, came a life of heart-brokenness, loneliness and despair. This book will make you both cry and laugh as you witness one woman's search for success and love.

Another Look at Sex
by Charles Phillips
This book is undoubtedly a head turner and eye opener that will cause you to take another close look at sex. In this book, Charles Phillips openly addresses this seldom discussed subject and giver life-changing advice on sex to married couples and singles. If you have questions about sex, this is the book for you.

Four Laws of Productivity
by Dr. Mensa Otabil
Success has no favorites. But it does have associates. Success will come to anyone who will pay the price to receive its benefits. *Four Laws of Productivity* will give you four powerful keys that will help you achieve your life's goals. *Four Laws of Productivity* by Dr. Mensa Otabil will show you how to: Discover God's gift in you, develop your gift, perfect your gift, and utilized your gift to its maximum potential. The principles revealed in this timely book will radically change your life.

Single Life
by Earl D. Johnson
The book gives a fresh light on practical issues such as coping with sexual desires, loneliness and preparation for future mate. Written in a lively style, the author admonishes the singles to seek first the Kingdom of God and rest assured in God's promise to supply their needs.... including a life partner!

Strategies for Saving the Next Generation
by Dave Burrows
This book will teach you how to start and effectively operate a vibrant youth ministry. This book is filled with practical tips and insight gained over a number of years working with young people from the street to the parks to the church. Dave Burrows offers the reader vital information that will produce results if carefully considered and adapted. Excellent for Pastors and Youth Pastor as well as youth workers and those involved with youth ministry.

The Church A Mystery Revealed
by Turnel Nelson
In this book, Pastor Turnel Nelson addresses and outlines some of the fundamental measures that need to be taken in order to revitalize the Church for 21st century evangelism and discipleship.

The Call of God
by Jefferson Edwards
The Call of God will help you to: • Have clarity from God as to what ministry involves • Be able to identify and affirm the call in your life • See what stage you are in your call from God

• Remove confusion in relation to the processing of a call or the making of the person • Understand the development of the anointing to fulfill your call.

Leadership in the New Testament Church
by Earl D. Johnson
Leadership in the New Testament Church offers practical and applicable insight into the role of leadership in the present day church. In this book, the author explains the qualities that leaders must have, explores the interpersonal relationships between the leader and his staff, the leaders' influence in the church and society and how to handle conflicts that arise among leaders.

Becoming A Leader
by Myles Munroe
Becoming A Leader uncovers the secrets of dynamic leadership that will show you how to be a leader in your family, school, community, church and job.
Where ever you are or whatever you do in life this book can help you inevitably become a leader. Remember it is never too late to become a leader. As in every tree there is a forest, so in every follower there is a leader.

Becoming A Leader Workbook
by Myles Munroe
Now you can activate your leadership potential through the **Becoming A Leader Workbook**. This workbook has been designed to take you step by step through the leadership principles taught in Becoming A Leader. As you participate in the work studies in this workbook you will see the true leader inside you develop and grow into maturity. "Knowledge **with action produces results.**"

Mobilizing Human Resources
by Richard Pinder
Pastor Pinder gives an in-depth look at how to organize, motivate and deploy members of the body of Christ in a manner that produces maximum effect for your ministry. This book will assist you in organizing and motivating your 'troops' for effective and efficient ministry. It will also help the individual believer in recognizing their place in the body, using their God given abilities and talents to maximum effect.

The Minister's Topical Bible
by Derwin Stewart
The Minister's Topical Bible covers every aspect of the ministry providing quick and easy access to scriptures in a variety of ministry related topics. This handy reference tool can be effectively used in leadership training, counseling, teaching, sermon preparation and personal study.

The Believer's Topical Bible
by Derwin Stewart
The Believer's Topical Bible covers every aspect of a Christian's relationship with God and man, providing biblical answers and solutions for all challenges. It is a quick, convenient, and thorough reference Bible that has been designed for use in personal devotions, and group bible studies. Over 3500 verses that are systematically organized under 240 topics, and is the largest devotional-topical Bible available in NIV and KJV.

The Layman's Guide to Counseling
by Susan Wallace
The increasing need for counseling has caused today's Christian leaders to become more sensitive to raise up lay-counselors to share this burden with them. Jesus' command is to *"set the captives free."* The Layman's guide to Counseling shows you how.

All books available at your Local Book store or by contacting:

Pneuma Life Publishing
**P.O. Box 10612,
Bakersfield, CA 93389-0612**

1-800-727-3218

1-805-324-1741